*Bill Plummer*

# A Series of Their Own

છ૰૰ૡ૰ઝ૰ૡ

### The History of the
### Women's College World Series

છ૰૰ૡ૰ઝ૰ૡ

## Bill Plummer III and Larry C. Floyd

Turnkey Communications Inc.
Oklahoma City, Oklahoma

Turnkey Communications Inc.
P. O. Box 721625
Oklahoma City, Oklahoma 73172

The publisher of this book can bring the authors to your event to speak, for a book signing or for an interview. For more information or to book an event, contact Turnkey Communications by email at:

info@seriesoftheirown.com
or by phone at: (405) 373-3467

Cover design and printing by Transcript Press (Norman, Okla.)

This edition printed in 2013.

1  3  5  7  9  10  8  6  4  2

Library of Congress Control Number: 2013939216

ISBN 978-0-9893007-0-4

For more information about the writing of this book, the authors or to order autographed copies by the authors online:
**www.SeriesofTheirOwn.com**

Dedicated to Connie Claussen, who labored so knowledgeably and diligently in the early years of the Women's College World Series, and to Marita Hynes, who was given the responsibilities of directing an already successful national championship and expanded it into a showcase event. But foremost, this book is dedicated to the women college athletes who before the late 1970s laced up worn-out athletic shoes, wore mismatched uniforms, and competed on shoddy playing fields, and to the selfless coaches who nurtured these young players. These athletes and their mentors pursued their chosen sport with little or no funding, and without the support and recognition given freely to their male counterparts. And they did it for the purest of reasons—the childlike love of their sport and the joyous excitement of athletic competition.

# Acknowledgments
❧✦❧✦

T his book was possible only with the assistance of numerous people, and the authors are indebted to those who added to the narrative with their personal files, comments and encouragement. Connie Claussen's lovingly saved programs, news clippings and photos from the first decade of the women's series were invaluable for the narration of the event's first decade. Laurie Cannon of the NCAA patiently provided much of the less readily available information on tournament play in more recent years. Debra Copp of the University of Oklahoma gave access to the obscure tournament information from the three AIAW national championships from 1980-82 in Norman, Okla. Reba Sims, former coach of Southwest Missouri State, sent photos and information from several of the early tournaments. Former J. F. Kennedy College players Catherine Buell and Beth Richards also helped with information on the early years. Mary Higgins, former Creighton University softball coach and women's series tournament director, provided information and news clippings from the years Creighton University served as host for the tournament.

Numerous staff from various universities helped with photos and information from records at their respective schools, including: Meredith Collier and Will Edwards (Texas A&M), Jeremy Strachan (Creighton University), James Ybiernas (University of California at Los Angeles) and staff from the University of Arizona.

Oklahoma City councilman Pete White, former Oklahoma City All Sports Association president Glenn Boyer, and current All Sports Association executive director Tim Brassfield helped with the history of the tournament's relocation to Oklahoma City and its subsequent growth.

The authors received support and guidance from their "softball gurus," who read some or all of the early manuscript of the book. These former college softball coaches and current softball administrators included: Connie Claussen, Marie Tuite, Marita Hynes, Cindy Bristow, Margie Wright, Sandy Fischer, Judi Garman and Lacy Lee Baker.

Oklahoma residents Darl DeVault and Marcia Bond helped with compilation of the indexes and proofreading.

# Foreword
꽈ꇰꙿꙿꇰꙿ

I was a player in the early days of the Women's College World Series in the 1970s and later coached in a number of these events. So *A Series of Their Own: The History of the Women's College World Series* chronicles much of my own world as an athlete and a mentor of young softball players. I am honored and humbled to write this foreword and naturally take a personal interest and pride in this book.

This is the only comprehensive book written about the history of the Women's College World Series. It is a must-read if you were, or still are, involved in college softball or its national championship. It is also a must-read for young softball athletes to better understand where this event got its roots. College softball and this national championship will continue to flourish if the players who aspire to play in this event will follow the lead and spirit of so many who came before.

Those who played, coached and participated in college softball and in this national championship since the late 1960s will also identify with much of this exciting narrative. What a journey this has been for those of us who lived this dramatic growth in the Women's College World Series. This book is a compelling, historical look at this journey and the growth of college softball, which before the Women's College World Series, was little more than women's teams getting together for a little outdoor recreation on "play days." With this championship, college softball had a framework and foundation from which to develop.

The athletes and coaches played the major role in the development of college softball. Their love of playing and coaching the sport is evident throughout this book. In the early years of college softball, they played their game without the needed support that would later come. In the end, these athletes and coaches persevered to get "a series of their own" and left a legacy for future players.

As well as documenting the growth and development of this national championship, the authors have made a point to include many of the individual names, deeds and words of the players and coaches who have participated. This book is a personal tribute to them and to college softball. Read, remember, enjoy— and keep this spirit and tradition alive.

**Margie Wright**
**(twenty-seven years as head coach at Fresno State
University and the NCAA's winningest Div. I softball coach)**

# Contents

# Introduction
‿❧‿❧‿❧

*"It's just the thrill of that one moment when you were the best team in the United States. It's exciting to have everybody playing their best at that point and winning with your teammates. I never thought being a national champion would follow my life the way it has. I still have people say they heard I played softball and was a national champion, and I will say, 'Yes, ... I was.'"*
**– statement by Diane Spoelstra in her 2012 induction profile for the Michigan State University Athletics Hall of Fame**

T he above statement powerfully affirms how participation and achievement in competitive athletics can shape lives and promote self-esteem. Diane Spoelstra, a "first-generation daughter" of Title IX, was indeed fortunate to have had the opportunity in 1976 to play on a team that won a women's collegiate national championship in softball. Those opportunities for women athletes were not always available, of course. Quality athletic competition and organized tournaments for college women were quite limited before the doors began to open in the 1970s, owing largely to changing social attitudes and implementation of Title IX legislation. Narrating when these competitive opportunities became available to college softball players and documenting the growth of college softball's national championship lie at the heart of *A Series of Their Own: The History of the Women's College World Series*.

The narrative follows college softball's national championship at the highest level, which from 1980 forward included only Division I schools. The size of this project precluded information on the Division II and Division III national softball championships, but these competitions are also a part of college softball's continued growth and success.

This book provides promoters and scholars of women's athletics a historical view of the growth of the Women's College World Series within the context of the social and legislative changes that so dramatically affected the growth of women's sports and college softball in the last quarter of the twentieth century. The positive aspects of participation in play at this national championship event can be heard in the voices of some of these competitors, like that of former student-athlete Diane Spoelstra's above. The related achievements in the lives of many of the participants are noted in "Life After the WCWS..." following each of the tournament narratives.

For coaches and softball players, the pages ahead chronicle the participants and their experiences in the thrilling crucible of athletic competition. Those who study the sport can learn from the successes and failures of players and teams from forty-three years of national championship competition. The voices of softball players and coaches are captured in these narratives as they describe their feelings of exhilaration or despair in their competitive trials. Following the action during the tournaments also provides insight into some of the coaching tactics and strategies during these competitions. Reviewing the players' accomplishments provides role models and inspiration to aspiring softball stars of the future.

Finally, this book serves as a permanent and comprehensive record of the players, coaches, teams and organizers who pioneered the early days of the Women's College World Series and of those that have participated since the maturation of this exciting annual event. The names of all the teams and many of the players and coaches can be found on these pages and in the book's index and appendices. Both the teams and the competitors who are a part of softball's national championships from 1969 to 2012 now have a written narrative of their achievements and participation. If these players' children, relatives or friends ask them if they were truly among those elite athletes who competed in college softball's national championship, they can point to their name or their team in this book and reply: "Yes, ... I was."

# One
## (1969-1972)
### ৡৢৡৢ

# After 'Play Days' and Punch and Cookies

Before the increased funding that followed Title IX, which was not significant until well after 1972, women's college softball in the 1960s was a far cry from the well organized, highly competitive game played today. Mary Littlewood, Arizona State University softball coach from 1966-1989, recalled the early days of college softball when the teams set "play days" for their competition. "We'd invite a junior college over, all the kids would wear their own white shirts and shorts, and afterward we'd buy punch and cookies for everybody," Littlewood said. "It wasn't very organized. We just felt like the girls should have the opportunity to do something competitively. That's the way it was back then."

The emphasis was on the social aspect of the day—not the competition. "For some reason it was thought that women either weren't capable of competing with a high level of skill, or they had no interest in doing so," Littlewood said. Those who thought so were wrong, the former college coach contended. During the era before well-established women's intercollegiate athletics, female softball players all over the country were slugging the ball, sliding into home, and berating umpires with one thought in mind—beating the other Amateur Softball Association (ASA) team. Established in 1933, the ASA is a nonprofit affiliation of state and local softball associations that was named the governing body for U.S. softball by the U.S. Olympic Committee in 1978. Until the late 1990s, the ASA had a solid women's fastpitch program separate from college and university programs. Before the late 1960s, this program filled the void for aspiring female athletes who wanted to compete in fast-pitch softball. Without scholarships or full-time coaches, college softball had not been developed to any significant degree.

Women's college softball took a big step forward in the late 1960s, however, and the "play days" would soon be a quaint memory. Softball coach Don "Pappy" Joe of John F. Kennedy College in Wahoo, Neb., believed his Patriettes fastpitch team to be the best college team in the nation. Joe had formed the team in 1967, and the Patriettes had been quite successful their first two years. The team had compiled an overall record of eighty-two wins and seventeen losses, while winning two Nebraska state championships. Joe wanted to test his team's mettle against other college softball teams in the country. The only way to do this would be on the field of competition in a kind of college "world series" format. But no such championship tournament for women's college softball existed at that time.

To rectify this, Joe contacted Nebraska ASA Commissioner O.W. "Bill" Smith and suggested that Omaha sponsor a "women's college world series" to determine the best women's college fastpitch team. Omaha was no stranger to college world series, having served as host for the men's baseball College World Series since 1950. Baseball's College World Series had been started in 1947 in Kalamazoo, Mich., and had moved to Omaha three years later where it had blossomed into a premier men's intercollegiate sports event. So Smith, who didn't have the facilities or the funds for a women's championship, contacted Metro Omaha softball commissioner Carl Kelley in late summer 1968 to discuss the idea. A meeting was held at Kelley's home shortly thereafter, attended by Kelley, his wife, Bill Smith, coach Don Joe, and Omaha Softball Association secretary Kay Werner.

Initial planning for the proposed event began. Kelley believed the group needed someone to contact the various colleges and organize the tournament under college rules and regulations. Fortunately for the future of what would become the Women's College World Series, Kelley contacted Connie Claussen, then chair of the Women's Physical Education Department at the University of Nebraska at Omaha and coach of the school's softball team. Kelley asked her to join the group, and Claussen's efforts as a kind of guiding genius would prove invaluable in the direction and development of the tournament in its first decade. A second meeting was subsequently held with the above participants, plus the athletic directors of Creighton University and the University of Nebraska at Omaha. Kelley and Claussen were named tournament co-directors for the event, which was planned for spring 1969. Some of the games would be played in Fremont, Neb., and the balance in Omaha.

Smith eventually contacted ASA officials in Oklahoma City to obtain their blessings for a "women's college world series" similar to the men's College World Series. ASA officials asked Smith to prepare a formal presentation for the ASA board of directors. To supplement his efforts, Smith formed a committee that included Joe Darrell Anderson, a member of the Fremont Parks and Recreation Department; Carl Kelley, Omaha ASA commissioner; and Hardley "Hap" Fruites, Fremont Tribune sports editor. Smith held a planning meeting at his home in November 1968, and it was agreed that he would make the formal presentation to the ASA board of directors at their home office in Oklahoma City.

At the Oklahoma City meeting, the board agreed that a definite need for such a women's tournament existed. It was pointed out that with the growth of women's athletics, it would be in ASA's best interest to take the lead in the development of this event. The ASA board offered Smith support in the development of plans for a women's college softball national championship, with the event sanctioned by the ASA and the Division of Girls' and Women's Sports (DGWS). It also was decided to allow a player to compete for her school under the ASA rules and to transfer to another ASA for summer competition. Smith thereafter named a steering committee for the inaugural Women's College World Series scheduled for May 1969. The members included those from Smith's initial committee, plus Kay Werner and Connie Claussen, who was national chair of the newly formed softball committee of the DGWS in addition to her duties at the University of Nebraska at Omaha.

The event was originally scheduled over the Memorial Day weekend of 1969, but some of the participating colleges requested the date be moved to May 16-18. Smith even received a telegram from the distant Far Eastern University in Manila, Republic of the Philippines, requesting their team's entry into the event. Fremont did not have a true softball facility for the games, so some were played at the city's Moller Field, the American Legion baseball field. The other games were scheduled in Omaha at Boyd Field. Smith, Kelly and Claussen all served officially as the tournament directors, and they dedicated the souvenir program to the first Women's College World Series, which had a field of nine teams.

Connie Claussen in 2012: "It's amazing what has happened to women's athletics."

"Our only desire is to get this type of a tournament for college women started — then follow through and watch it grow," they wrote in a dedication letter in the first tournament program. And grow it would in the years to follow.

Smith, who passed away in 2012 at age eighty-six, admitted to being surprised at what later transpired. "I don't think any of us ever envisioned the program growing to the size and importance it is now," he said. "We did have a dream that — just maybe — it could be an event that would be held in Omaha as a women's version of the NCAA men's College World Series. But back then we knew that was a long way off." Claussen also did not foresee women's college softball and the Women's College World Series becoming as popular as it has. "But I hoped it would," she said. "It's amazing what has happened to women's athletics."

Even before the days of social media, the Internet and ESPN, the Women's College World Series managed to survive and later to thrive. Its participants and supporters certainly now perceive it as more than just a "women's version" of baseball's College World Series. But in 1969 and in its first few years, the women's championship in Omaha needed careful nurturing. It would have been easy for the early organizers to call it quits after a couple of years. Women's intercollegiate sports should be grateful for the perseverance of visionaries like Bill Smith, Carl Kelley, Don Joe, Connie Claussen, Darrell Anderson, Kay Werner and a handful of others who believed in both this event and the importance of women's athletic competition. Owing much to their efforts in the late 1960s, the Women's College World Series has become a premier women's sports spectacular.

And all Don Joe had wanted was a chance to showcase the skills of his JFK women's fastpitch softball team. Fortunately for women's fastpitch softball, Joe and his girls got that opportunity in May 1969.

## 1969: John F. Kennedy's First of Three Titles

Having coached the John F. Kennedy College women's softball team since 1967, Don Joe knew what he had—a solid softball squad. But he wondered how they would fare against other teams. He definitely had prepared them, coaching them through several seasons of forty-to-sixty games. Reflecting on her former coach, former JFK star catcher Cathy Buell said: "He was one of a kind. He never raised his voice. He told us what it would take to win, and we did it. He was ahead of his time." Joe had the gift of gab, was an outstanding recruiter, and could motivate players. Events would show that he had done a masterful job in preparing the JFK Patriettes for the initial Women's College World Series, May 16-18 in Omaha and Fremont, Neb.

Much of JFK's preparation included two- and three-hour practice sessions, totaling about 20 hours per week of drills and competition. In a newspaper interview before the 1969 series, the Patriette girls told a reporter that their heavy involvement with softball caused some problems in arranging times for college studies, dates and other extra-curricular activities. "Be sure to include none of us are on softball scholarships," one of the team members exhorted the reporter.

The event was originally supposed to be ten teams playing a double-elimination format. And this first "women's world series" in Omaha started out to be truly international. Far Eastern University of Manila planned to attend. Mechanical problems with their airplane, however, forced the heart-broken Filipino girls to land in Tokyo and then return home. With nine teams ready to play, the series got off to a soggy start. Rain canceled the opening night's games on Friday at the tournament sites in Omaha and nearby Fremont. Because of the wet conditions,

As seen on the program cover above, the first Women's College World Series was sanctioned by the Division of Girls' and Women's Sports and the Amateur Softball Association.

these opening games were moved to noon Saturday. Games in Fremont were played on a diamond in the outfield grass at Moller Field. Volunteers spent all morning attempting to get Omaha's Boyd Field suitable for play. Chemical absorbent and sawdust were spread on the field, and after considerable raking first-round games began. Competition continued at both sites despite a damp and chilly Saturday.

Playing with workmanlike precision, the Patriettes had little difficulty with each team they faced. Joe's team swept through the field undefeated, beating Illinois State 2-0 in the championship game. Before blanking the Illinois team in the finals, JFK had defeated them 3-2 in eight innings the previous day on Cindy Thompson's RBI single that scored Lois Stuflick. The Illinois State Red Birds had fought back through the losers bracket to gain the championship round, defeating Kearney State 12-1, St. Petersburg (Fla.) Junior College 2-0, Colorado State 4-0, and Southwest Missouri, 5-0.

Just how impressive was JFK College? In five games they outscored the opposition 39-4 and out-hit them, 46-17. Patriettes pitcher Judy Lloyd limited Illinois State to one hit in the finals and won four of the team's five games. Kay Sharr won the other game. Lloyd's outstanding performance earned her the most outstanding player designation. She even batted a respectable .333. Her teammates Sharr and catcher Cathy Buell were the leading hitters with averages of .500 (9-for-18) and .471 (8-for-17), respectively.

Each member of the top four teams received a trophy. Organizers Bill Smith, Carl Kelley and tournament director Connie Claussen, who also coached the University of Nebraska at Omaha team in the series, received awards for their administration of the event. Despite Illinois State's runner-up finish, Red Bird coach Carmen Imel was named the event's most outstanding coach. Each of her players also received an award, and players named to the all-tournament team received special awards. Illinois State and JFK shared top honors on the all-tournament team, each placing four players. Players named all-tournament included Illinois State's Marilyn Mosier, Tudy Schmied, Dot Melvin and Karen Roppa; JFK's Cathy Buell, Kay Sharr, Judy Lloyd and Cindy Thompson; Southwest Missouri's Mary Shaffer and Dayna Aust; Colorado State's Gaylynn Ecton and Kay McDaniel; and St. Petersburg Junior College's Betty McGee and Diane Davidson.

Tournament officials were encouraged by the enthusiasm and good sportsmanship displayed by the participants. The officials received many favorable comments from the managers and players, and several teams indicated they would enter the next series in 1970 when all games would be held in Omaha. The event was also a financial success, garnering a modest profit from income of $642.50 and expenses of $606.03. But the tournament was followed by a surprise. Joe, who had coached the Patriettes for three years, announced he was stepping down. Patriette assistant coach Ken Christensen would now coach the JFK team. Joe had received his opportunity to show how well his John F. Kennedy Patriettes played softball. His girls had proved that they played superbly.

## 1969 Final Standings

| | |
|---|---|
| John F. Kennedy College (Wahoo, Neb.) | 5-0 |
| Illinois State University (Normal) | 4-2 |
| Southwest Missouri State College (Springfield) | 2-2 |
| Colorado State College (Greeley, Colo.) | 2-2 |
| St. Petersburg Junior College (St. Petersburg, Fla.) | 1-2 |
| Black Hills State College (Spearfish, S.D.) | 1-2 |
| Kearney State College (Kearney, Neb.) | 1-2 |
| Creighton University (Omaha, Neb.) | 0-2 |
| University of Nebraska (Omaha) | 0-2 |

## Life After the WCWS…

**Don Joe** later moved to Canon City, Colo., where he served as manager of the chamber of commerce and coached the Canon City Royals. In 1974 he returned to coach JFK College and in 1977 was inducted into the Nebraska ASA Hall of Fame. Joe died in 1989. After graduation from JFK in 1970 with a degree in health and physical education, **Judy Lloyd** remained in Nebraska, teaching and coaching in elementary schools and high schools before retiring in 2006. After graduation from JFK College, **Cathy Buell** moved to Atlanta and played for the famed Lorelei

1969 John F. Kennedy Patriettes national championship team. Top row from left: Ken Christensen, Sandy Messerich, Adrienne Perrino, Karen Hughes, Cindy Thompson, Kay Sharr and Don Joe. Center row from left: Charlene Thompson, Ginny Nelson, Judy Lloyd, Linda Manning and Sandy Konrad. Bottom row from left: Karen Peitz, Cathy Buell, Jeanne Schliffke, Lois Stuflick and Beth Richards. *(Photo courtesy of Connie Claussen)*

Ladies of Atlanta, one of the nation's premier fastpitch teams at the time. In 1979 Buell was inducted into the Nebraska ASA Hall of Fame. She earned a master's degree in exercise physiology from Georgia State University in 1980 and retired from a lengthy teaching career in 2002. **Connie Claussen** was still involved in athletics in 2013, although she retired from the University of Nebraska at Omaha as associate athletic director in 1998 after thirty-five years with the school. Claussen also coached during her career at Omaha, compiling a nine-year softball record of 98-59 and winning the 1975 national championship. She is a member of the National Fast Pitch Coaches Association Hall of Fame.

## 1970: JFK Holds Off Southwest Missouri State

New John F. Kennedy College head coach Ken Christensen knew that repeating as Women's College World Series champion would not be easy. Teams were getting better. But the former semi-pro baseball player had prepared the Patriettes and had faith in them as a solid team. Christensen and his predecessor, Don Joe, had different coaching styles. Joe had been a master motivator who "sold" the Patriettes on what it took to win. An amiable coach, Christensen stressed solid softball fundamentals.

Defending champion JFK was seeded No. 1, while Illinois State, runner-up in 1969, was seeded No. 2. The remaining teams would draw for places. Christensen was unfamiliar with most of the teams entered, but he expected the caliber of softball to be even stronger than the previous year. The second series increased to seventeen teams from six states and was held May 15-17, with all games at the new George W. Dill Softball Center in Omaha's Benson Park. The event continued to be sanctioned by the Division of Girls' and Women's Sports (DGWS) and the Amateur Softball Association. It was sponsored by the Omaha Amateur Softball Association, the Nebraska Amateur Softball Association, and the University of Nebraska at Omaha's Women's Physical Education Department.

Undefeated in the inaugural series, JFK extended its series streak to nine in a row after winning its first four games in the second championship. The Patriettes had first beat Upper Iowa 2-0, as Kay Camp hurled a one-hitter and had two hits, as did her catcher Cathy Buell. The defending champs then blanked Western Illinois 10-0 with a six-run first inning keying the win, as Lindy Albertson limited the opposition to one infield hit. The Patriettes next pounded Southwest Missouri State College with twelve hits, winning 4-1 with pitchers Beth Richards and Kay Camp combining for the win. They then cruised past the University of Nebraska at Omaha by a score of 4-1, with ten hits while Camp limited UNO to just five. It was the first loss for UNO after having won its first three games.

Even with this impressive four-win start, Christensen knew that the bats could go cold and the team could still have a bad game. But he wasn't expecting it in the next game with Southwest Missouri State on Sunday night. JFK collected only four hits off Southwest Missouri's Debbie Bellman in a 2-0 loss. Bellman had nearly been pulled during the game by coach Reba Sims, who worried that her pitcher was growing tired. "When I met her on the field, she had tears in her eyes and did not want to come out," Sims recalled years later. "She assured me she could do it, and I changed my mind and left her in. ... That really took some guts for her to be able to do that, and she was a freshman." JFK pitcher Beth Richards took the loss, although she allowed only four hits. Richards wasn't surprised that Southwest Missouri State had beaten her team. "We had played them a lot during the summer, and they were a very, very good team," she said.

The loss forced the defending champs to play the if-necessary game for the series title. In this final game, Southwest Missouri scored twice in the second inning to take an early 2-0 lead. But the Patriettes tallied four runs in the third, as Lindy Albertson tripled, Richards singled, Cindy Thompson doubled, and Teri Johnston tripled. JFK took the lead for good. The Patriettes increased their lead to 7-3 in the fourth on singles by Buell, Richards, Thompson and Johnston. Southwest Missouri scored one run in the fifth and two more in the sixth, with the title game concluding 7-6 and near midnight.

As a team JFK batted .269 (58-for-156) with Thompson's .500 batting average (10-for-20) leading the way. Trailing her were: Camp (.471), Sandra Messerich (.471, 7-for-18), Karen Peitz (.444, 8-for-18), Teri Johnston (.400, 8-for-20), Buell (.368, 7-for-19) and Albertson (.333, 3-for-9).

**Nebraska-Omaha catcher Marlene Donahue played effectively in the 1970 women's series with her fractured left ankle in a cast.** *(Photo courtesy of Connie Claussen)*

Southwest Missouri finished the series with a 6-2 record. The University of Nebraska at Omaha finished third, with 1969 runner-up Illinois State fourth. Mary Shaffer, Southwest Missouri's slugging outfielder, was the winner of the top hitter award and her eight hits included a double, a triple and two homers. JFK's Camp was named the most valuable player after she posted a 4-0 pitching record with a .471 batting average (7-for-18). She played third base when not in the circle. The outstanding manager award went to Sims of Southwest Missouri State. She didn't expect to be named to the honor. "I was surprised," Sims said many years later. "It was really a nice thing to do, and I had no inkling I would win it."

Trophies were presented to the twelve-player all-tournament team.

## 1970 Final Standings

| | |
|---|---|
| John F. Kennedy College (Wahoo, Neb.) | 5-1 |
| Southwest Missouri State College (Springfield) | 6-2 |
| University of Nebraska (Omaha) | 4-2 |
| Illinois State University (Normal) | 3-2 |
| Western Illinois University (Macomb) | 3-2 |
| Luther College (Decorah, Iowa) | 4-2 |
| Kearney State College (Kearney, Neb.) | 2-2 |
| University of Minnesota (Duluth) | 2-2 |
| Midland Lutheran College (Fremont, Neb.) | 1-2 |
| University of Northern Colorado (Greeley) | 1-2 |
| Southern Illinois University (Carbondale) | 1-2 |
| Midwestern College (Dennison, Iowa) | 1-2 |
| Minot State College (Minot, N.D.) | 0-2 |
| Wayne State College (Wayne, Neb.) | 0-2 |
| Concordia Teachers College (Seward, Neb.) | 0-2 |
| University of Nebraska (Lincoln) | 0-2 |
| Upper Iowa University (Fayette) | 0-2 |

Those players included: JFK's Thompson, Johnston and Camp; Southwest Missouri's Sue Schuble and Shaffer; University of Nebraska at Omaha's Deanna Grindle and Barb Filipowicz; Illinois State's Jan Smith and Tudy Schmied; Luther's Cheri Kolander; University of Minnesota at Duluth's Marcia LaRock; and Kearney State's Sally Studnicka.

Although there wasn't a "most courageous award" presented, University of Nebraska at Omaha catcher Marlene Donahue would have been the hands-down winner. She talked coach Connie Claussen out of benching her after she fractured her ankle. She continued play in a cast at her regular position behind the plate. Donahue collected five hits and drove in the go-ahead run in two of the games, and according to the Omaha World-Herald "was the talk of tourney fans." For her courageous play, she would be listed the following year in the 1971 souvenir program as the "People's Choice" player for the 1970 series.

## Life After the WCWS...

**Ken Christensen** coached JFK three more years after the 1970 championship. He compiled a record of 300 wins against only 99 losses, winning the Nebraska state championship three times, the Women's College World Series twice, and the Mid-Central Regional once. He stayed active as a coach in youth sports until his death by a heart attack in 1987. **Beth Richards** graduated from JFK in 1973, then played softball with the Canon City (Colo.) Royals, coached by her former coach Don Joe. She taught school for three years in Iowa before starting a furniture-stripping business and beginning work for the U.S. Postal System in Omaha, Neb. Richards retired from the postal system in 2009. **Reba Sims**, who won the tournament's outstanding manager in her first year of coaching softball at Southwest Missouri State College, coached softball for another season and then coached basketball for ten years. She spent forty-three years at Southwest Missouri State before retiring in May 2012. Also an accomplished umpire, she officiated in the women's series three times, twice when it was held in Norman, Okla., and in 1982 when it returned to Omaha with the NCAA as sponsor. She is the only person to have both managed and umpired in college softball's national championship.

## 1971: Patriettes Three-peat

The year 1971 was memorable for many of the student-athletes gathering for the Women's College World Series in Omaha, as many of these young softball players would soon be eligible to vote for the first time in local, state and federal elections. The 26th Amendment to the Constitution was being ratified by the states that spring, lowering the legal voting age to eighteen. It was also a memorable year for the Omaha series, with a record twenty-eight schools and universities from eleven states competing May 14-16 at the George W. Dill Softball Center.

John F. Kennedy College coach Ken Christensen keenly anticipated this tournament because his solid JFK team had prevailed in the previous two championships and was knocking on the door to claim a third consecutive title. Still, he was concerned with the number of teams that year and the increasing competition from the talented teams that stemmed from the growing interest in women's college fast pitch. But he also knew that the JFK team was determined and poised.

Drawing early attention in the tournament play was University of Nebraska at Omaha's leading pitcher Deanna Grindle. The UNO junior had gained fame outside of softball as an Amateur Athletic Union All-American in basketball and was a four-time national free-throw champion. Grindle helped her team to a good start with a 9-1 win over Concordia College on the opening day's competition. But the Iowa native said that her preferred sport was basketball.

JFK catcher Cathy Buell recalled that she had felt confident of success that year, owing largely to teammate Georgia Gomez, whom Buell remembered as "one heck of a pitcher." Indeed she was. Gomez compiled a 42-18 record in 1971 and came up big when it counted the most—in the national championship. She fanned seven batters (finishing the year with 291 strikeouts in 393 innings) and allowed only a pair of hits in the national title game, as JFK turned back Iowa State 4-0 to finish the series at 7-1. After having been upset 7-6 by Iowa State on Saturday night, JFK fought back from the loser's bracket with five wins in a row to claim its third consecutive national title.

In the championship game grudge-match, Gomez survived Iowa State's only threat in the fifth inning on singles by Sue Siever and Diane DeWitt, and a walk to Joyce Howard that loaded the bases. But Gomez forced a pop-up by infielder Sherry Meinecke for the third out to end the threat. Gomez had ensured the if-necessary game by defeating Iowa State 6-0, the Cyclonettes' first loss in the double-elimination event. Gomez went five innings and allowed one hit, with Beth Richards finishing up. Earlier that afternoon, Gomez had hurled three innings to preserve a 5-3 win over Arizona State, and Richards had dominated Nebraska 16-2 and Southwest Missouri 3-0.

Iowa State had proved to be more than a worthy foe for JFK and had advanced to the championship round by defeating Southwest Missouri 12-9. Southwest Missouri finished third, and ASU finished fourth in the twenty-eight-team field.

Combined with Gomez's monster 1971 season, Richards finished for JFK at 18-4 with Kathy Bull (21-4), Lindy Albertson (9-1) and Marilyn Schultz (1-0) contributing to the 92-27 season. Seven players batted .300 or higher, with Charlene Thompson on top with a .335 average. Following her were Albertson (.328), Betty Alig (.325), Schultz (.321), Cathy Buell (.311), Karen Peitz (.307) and Marianne DeShazer (.301). Thompson also led the team in RBIs (84) and home runs (18). Besides first-place in the championship, the Patriettes won two invitationals, fin-

ished second in another, and took third in the ASA Mid-Central Regional. The JFK team did not know it at the time, but 1971 would be the high point of their short reign in the Women's College World Series.

JFK and Iowa State each had three players named to the series all-star team. Players selected were: JFK's Gomez, Teri Johnston (a repeat selection) and Charlene Thompson; Iowa State's Julie Wykle, Val Haraldson, and Kathy Proeschoeldt; Arizona State's Judy Hoke and Ginger Kurtz; Southwest Missouri's Jan Trotter and Carole Myers; Kansas State Teachers College's Donna Stone; and Illinois State's Jan Smith.

Pat Noe of Iowa State was named the outstanding manager. A physical education instructor at ISU, Noe had started the softball program that season with no funding from the school. "But they told me if I could give it the time to go ahead and start the team," she said. The ISU team raised

**Pat Noe of Iowa State was named outstanding manager at the 1971 tournament. She started the school's softball program without funding.**

## 1971 Final Standings

| | |
|---|---|
| John F. Kennedy College (Wahoo, Neb.) | 7-1 |
| Iowa State University (Ames) | 5-2 |
| Southwest Missouri State College (Springfield) | 3-2 |
| Arizona State University (Tempe) | 5-2 |
| University of Nebraska (Lincoln) | 5-2 |
| Kansas State Teachers College (Emporia) | 2-2 |
| Southern Illinois University (Carbondale) | 3-2 |
| Illinois State University (Normal) | 3-2 |
| Eastern Illinois University (Charleston) | 3-2 |
| Parsons College (Fairfield, Iowa) | 2-2 |
| Luther College (Decorah, Iowa) | 3-2 |
| University of Northern Colorado (Greeley) | 3-2 |
| Wartburg College (Waverly, Iowa) | 2-2 |
| Central Missouri State College (Warrensburg) | 1-2 |
| Minot State College (Minot, N.D.) | 1-2 |
| Concordia Teachers College (Seward, Neb.) | 1-2 |
| Wisconsin State University (Eau Claire) | 1-2 |
| Kearney State College (Kearney, Neb.) | 1-2 |
| Upper Iowa University (Fayette) | 1-2 |
| University of Minnesota (Duluth) | 0-2 |
| University of Nebraska (Omaha) | 1-2 |
| South Dakota State University (Brookings) | 1-2 |
| Wayne State College (Wayne, Neb.) | 1-2 |
| University of South Dakota (Vermillion) | 0-2 |
| Midland Lutheran College (Fremont, Neb.) | 0-2 |
| Southwest Baptist College (Bolivar, Mo.) | 0-2 |
| Buena Vista College (Storm Lake, Iowa) | 0-2 |
| Simpson College (Indianola, Iowa) | 0-2 |

money for travel and uniforms with bake sales and other projects. ASU pitcher Paula Miller won the most valuable player award for her pitching. She hurled a pair of one-hitters and a two-hitter, while pitching all seven games in three days. In addition, she smacked eight hits to finish with a .320 batting average. Miller's team finished fourth that year.

If it had not been for Arizona State coach Mary Littlewood, Miller's Sun Devils might never have competed in the event. That spring Littlewood had read about the new Women's College World Series and wanted to find out how her team matched up. But she did not have the money for the trip, considering her pre-Title IX budget at Arizona State for three sports—volleyball, basketball and softball—was all of $500.

"We raised enough money for the plane fare through bake sales, car washes, et cetera," Littlewood said. "We stayed in a house owned by a school principal, who was also a friend of the family of one of our players, and we paid for our own food. We took eleven players and me, stayed in the basement of the house, slept in sleeping bags on the floor—except I got the one bed—and took showers at the school. What an experience!" Once the ASU girls had shared the thrill of competition at the women's series, there was no turning back. Every year thereafter, going to the tournament was their goal.

## Life After the WCWS…

**Georgia Gomez** left JFK College after 1973 and played softball for the Atlanta-based Lorelei Ladies and the Orlando (Fla.) Suns. In 2013 she was a patient advocate for the Winnebago Indian Health Services in Winnebago, Neb., and mother of a ten-year-old daughter, Jaciah Earth. She was also coaching a 12-under girls softball team. **Mary Littlewood** went on to lead the ASU Sun Devils to the national title in 1972 and 1973. Besides the two national titles, Littlewood coached her team to four fourth-place finishes in the women's series (1971, 1976, 1977 and 1982). She led the Sun Devils to three conference titles, and in 1986 was named Pacific West Conference co-coach of the year. She compiled a coaching record of 468-202-1 (.699 winning percentage) in her nineteen years at ASU. In 1998, she authored *The Path to the Gold: An Historical Look at Women's Fastpitch in the United States*. Softball and basketball star **Deanna Grindle** went on to a long teaching and coaching career at Benson High School in Omaha, Neb.

# 1972: Arizona State Bests Japanese Team

After winning a third consecutive Women's College World Series in 1971, John F. Kennedy College had no chance to win a fourth consecutive national title against the sixteen teams gathered May 18-21 in Omaha at the George W. Dill Softball Center. The women's series was assured of a new champion even before play began. JFK College had apparently provided financial assistance to women athletes, thus making it ineligible for the tournament. This was the ruling by the Nebraska Women's Intercollegiate Council on Sports (NWICS), which was following the rules of the Division of Girls' and Women's Sports (DGWS), one of the tournament's sanctioning bodies.

"The DGWS feels a girl should go to college primarily to get an education," said Carl Kelley, Metro Omaha Amateur Softball Association commissioner at the time, "and not just participate in athletics." JFK had previously been suspected of giving athletic scholarships, Kelley said, but it never could be proved. Despite these suspicions, the school had been allowed to compete in the first three series. "They even admitted in a story in the World-Herald that they gave scholarships to their women basketball players," the Omaha commissioner said. Tournament director

and DGWS advocate Connie Claussen said at the time that the event's sanctioning body "does not believe in athletic scholarships or recruiting girls specifically
for athletics. We think a student should be a student first and then, if she has time,
she can compete in intercollegiate athletics." Claussen received a number of nasty
letters from JFK boosters for supporting this position.

Nebraska ASA state commissioner Bill Smith said that Ken Christensen, the
new coach of JFK, blamed jealousy as the motive for the action taken against his
school by the DGWS. Christensen, who called the ruling "foul," was obviously
miffed by the decision handed down. "We are accused of offering scholarships to
softball players," the JFK coach said. "They have nothing to base their decision on.
We feel we certainly got a raw deal. We meet all their requirements. We were very
careful to do so."

When asked if JFK gave scholarships to softball players, Christensen said, "We
have some on basketball scholarships. We provided them with a list of students on
basketball scholarships." None of the basketball players on scholarship were on the
softball team, he added. Christensen did not think that scholarships were the real
issue. He said that he believed jealousy of the school's physical education graduates
and personal dislike for him were behind the team's disqualification. The coach
also called the NWICS ruling "dishonest and underhanded" and said JFK would
not return to play in the women's series. "We feel it is to our advantage not to be
associated with that group of people. We can live without it."

After handing down its ruling, NWICS officials went one step further and approved a clause to its constitution in a meeting on April 23, 1972, that said a school
"will not be a member of the Council as long as it gives scholarships in any girls'
sports." The clause passed unanimously, according to council president June Beck-
er. In addition to JFK's disqualification, the field of teams was limited to sixteen
state-tournament winners, the number approved by a vote of the coaches at the
1971 tournament. If the sixteen-team bracket could not be filled by state tournament winners, the additional teams would be named by the area DGWS director.

The festering issue of women's athletic scholarships aside, the fourth annual
tournament truly took on a "world series" flavor in 1972, when the University of
Tokyo was recommended to compete with the state champions in the tournament.
The crowds attending the games gushed over the Japanese girls and treated them
as the darlings of the tournament. The Japanese team was led by ace hurler Yruiko
Tagashira, who had a sweet tooth for American vanilla ice cream. Her coaches
promised her all the ice cream she could eat if she continued to win games. The
hard-pitching right-hander came through in the first round with a 4-0 shutout of
Central Missouri.

The Tokyo University squad proved formidable to its other opponents. Only
Arizona State University, which finished fourth the year before, could stay with
the Japanese girls. The two teams remained undefeated on their collision course
in the series. When the two teams met on Saturday, Tagashira was cruising with
a two-hitter and a 1-0 lead in the sixth when the ASU Sun Devils erupted for four

straight singles. The ASU rally gave them a narrow 2-1 win and moved them within one victory of the championship title.

Western Illinois stayed alive through Saturday with a 2-1 win over Illinois State. Western Illinois won the game despite ISU's Margie Wright throwing a no-hitter. Errors plagued Illinois State, and Western Illinois cashed in on them. The Western Illinois squad advanced to play the Japanese, with the winner to face ASU for the title.

The Japanese team eliminated Western Illinois on Sunday morning to secure a rematch with ASU. Western Illinois pitcher Sandy Fischer has vivid and fond memories of the game. "We lost, but it was one of my greatest memories having pitched against them," Fischer said in 2012. "I really came away from that game with great respect for their talent and work ethic." The Japanese used a "bat-knob, drop bunt" several times against the Western Illinois team, and Fischer recalled feeling a bit intimidated by their speed and their "hustle." Still, the game left a positive impression on the young hurler. "I wore it like a badge of honor to have pitched against an international team."

In the Japanese team's first game against ASU, the tireless Tagashira prevailed, notching a 1-0 win against pitcher Paula Miller. The two pitchers continued to battle each other in 90-degree heat in the final game. Both teams were well matched, as only one run had separated them earlier in their first two games. Miller and Tagashira both showed their mettle throughout the eighteen innings of play in the two teams' final two games to decide the series championship.

Miller, who compiled a 4-1 series record, had one of her team's five consecutive singles in a three-run eleventh inning to secure the 8-5 win in the final game. Arizona State had taken an early 4-1 lead with four runs in the first two innings on an RBI triple and a three-run, inside-the-park home run by Ginger Kurtz. Tokyo then scored once in the bottom of the second and eventually evened the score with two in the fifth and another in the seventh. Each team scored a run in the eighth inning before the Sun Devils broke out in the eleventh inning for its fifth win in six games. Both pitchers said they did not immediately realize that the game had gone into extra innings.

"All I thought of was pitching," said Miller. "I couldn't think of anything else." Following the game, losing pitcher Tagashira graciously came across the field to congratulate Miller with a broken-English "nice pitch."

Tokyo finished 5-2, and its play in the 1972 tournament marked the first and the last time a team from outside the United States played in the women's series. Western Illinois finished third at 5-2 and Illinois State fourth at 4-2. As a bonus to her solid pitching, Miller finished with the fourth highest batting average, .471 (8-for-17), with Jean Holzkamp of South Dakota State leading all hitters with a .500 batting average (7-for-14). Besides Miller, other top hitters for ASU were Marilyn Rau .429 (6-for-14) and Lynn Mooney .400 (10-for-25). ASU led all teams with a team batting average of .295. Named the event's outstanding manager was Valerie Lindbloom of Western Illinois University.

## 1972 Final Standings

| | |
|---|---|
| Arizona State University (Tempe) | 5-1 |
| University of Tokyo-Nihon (Japan) | 5-2 |
| Western Illinois University (Macomb) | 5-2 |
| Illinois State University (Normal) | 4-2 |
| University of Northern Colorado (Greeley) | 2-2 |
| South Dakota State University (Brookings) | 2-2 |
| Wayne State College (Wayne, Neb.) | 2-2 |
| Central Missouri State College (Warrensburg) | 2-2 |
| Keene State College (Keene, N.H.) | 1-2 |
| University of Nebraska (Omaha) | 1-2 |
| Luther College (Decorah, Iowa) | 1-2 |
| Southwest Missouri State University (Springfield) | 1-2 |
| University of South Carolina (Columbia) | 0-2 |
| Minot State College (Minot, N.D.) | 0-2 |
| Kansas State Teachers College (Emporia) | 0-2 |
| Purdue University (West Lafayette, Ind.) | 0-2 |

## Life After the WCWS...

ASU's **Marilyn Rau** was named an ASA All-American 11 times during her playing career (1960-1986) and was a member of the 1979 USA Pan American Team, which won the gold medal in the Pan American Games in San Juan Puerto Rico. In 1979, she led the Sun City (Ariz.) Saints to the ASA national title and was named the tournament's most valuable player. Rau was elected to the ASU and ASA National Softball Halls of Fame in 1991. In 2000, she was elected to the Arizona Softball Foundation Hall of Fame. She is one of only five catchers named to the ASA National Softball Hall of Fame. **Jean Holzkamp** returned to her hometown of Brookings, S.D., following college, where she became the mother of twin daughters and a respected franchise owner of several 7-Eleven stores. She died of cancer in 2010. **Valerie Lindbloom** went on to a distinguished career as a professor of kinesiology at Western Illinois University, where she taught until 1996. Her specialty was adaptive physical education and athletic training. She died in 2008.

# *Two*

## (1973-1979)
ِو‌‌ِ‌‌‌‌‌‌‌‌‌‌‌‌‌‌‌‌

# Title IX and AIAW Championships

*No person in the United States shall, on the basis of sex, be excluded
from participation in, be denied the benefits of, or be subjected to
discrimination under any educational program or activity receiving
Federal financial assistance.*

— Title IX provision of Education Amendments of 1972 legislation

AS THE WOMEN'S COLLEGE WORLD SERIES entered only its fifth
year of existence in 1973, heady changes for women's intercollegiate sports
were already in the wind. Some of these impending changes were not wide-
ly reported nor well understood. Nonetheless, they would dramatically increase the
quality of competition at the softball championship and the stature of this event
before the decade's end.

A milestone in the administration of women's college sports had occurred in
1971 when the Division of Girls' and Women's Sports (DGWS) formed the Association of Intercollegiate Athletics for Women (AIAW). The DGWS, which had
sanctioned the women's college softball championship since its beginning in 1969,
began development of an organizational framework to govern intercollegiate athletics for women, including national championships, as far back as 1966. The for-
mation of the AIAW was the end result of these efforts. The AIAW was formed by a
women's group, to be run by women, and to operate on behalf of women athletes.
Although established as an organization independent of the DGWS, the AIAW obviously shared the same philosophy for women's college sports as its parent group.
(In 1976 the DGWS changed to its current name, the National Association for
Girls and Women in Sport.)

The promotion of better athletic opportunities for college women lay at the
core of these two closely affiliated groups' shared philosophy. The AIAW was to focus on elite-level competition among the association's affiliate college institutions,
including the annual national championships for various women's college sports.

The two groups also shared both a belief in the importance of limited athletic recruiting and a focus on women sports participants as students before athletes. So, at least in the AIAW's first couple of years, their affiliate schools were banned from offering athletic scholarships. In 1977 the AIAW officially began co-sanctioning the Women's College World Series with the Amateur Softball Association. By then, the AIAW was sponsoring or co-sponsoring more than two-dozen intercollegiate national championships. The AIAW would competently nurture the women's series through a rapidly changing intercollegiate sports landscape in the late 1970s and early 1980s.

The year 1972 brought another event that would have a resounding and lasting impact on women's intercollegiate athletics—and by default on the Women's College World Series. This change would result from the new Education Amendments legislation signed into law by President Richard Nixon the month after the 1972 women's series in Omaha. This new law contained a provision originally written as "Title X," but which had become "Title IX" when another part of the larger bill was dropped. The Title IX provision banned sex discrimination in schools, and its original focus was on eliminating discrimination against women applying for graduate schools or for teaching opportunities at colleges and universities.

The DGWS and AIAW wholeheartedly supported the Title IX provision of the Education Amendments legislation as it passed through the lengthy and sometimes frustrating process of lawmaking. The provision had been added into the larger U.S. House bill by Oregon Representative Edith Starrett Green, a former schoolteacher and education advocate since the 1930s. The House passed the bill with the Title IX provision in 1971, but it then made its way to the Senate for consideration. Indiana Senator Birch Bayh sponsored the Title IX provision in the Senate version of the Education Amendments bill, and little attention was given to the potential impact of this provision on women's intercollegiate athletics. The Senate passed the bill in May 1972.

The Title IX legislation would have little formal effect on women's college sports or the Women's College World Series until later in the decade. Officials with the Department of Health, Education and Welfare (HEW) first had to write the regulations for the implementation of Title IX, an undertaking of several years. With new scrutiny during this period, the provision's impact on athletics suddenly became apparent and moved to the forefront of intercollegiate sports controversy. Opposition from some corners became strong and vocal. As University of Iowa women's athletic director at the time, Christine Grant, succinctly described it: "All hell broke loose." Athletic directors for men's sports programs readily envisioned how their budgets could get squeezed and decried the new law's implications. The National Collegiate Athletic Association (NCAA), which governed only men's sports at the time, set aside $1 million to minimize the effects of Title IX on men's college athletics.

In response to the outcry from some quarters, Texas Senator John Tower in 1974 passed an amendment in the Senate excluding football and other revenue-producing sports from Title IX coverage. Some women's groups fought back hard, realizing that an important principal was at stake: if women lost this battle, the field would be open to other "exceptions" to full equality. The AIAW hired lawyer Margot Polivy and began a full-court press of lobbying and letter writing. Their efforts were rewarded when a congressional joint conference committee eliminated the Tower Amendment just months after it had passed. "The women in AIAW were very committed to what they were doing," Grant later said. "I'm not just talking about the leadership. I'm talking about the average member."

In July 1975, the HEW regulations became final. The wording for full compliance with Title IX left little room for recalcitrant college athletic directors: "A school must provide equal athletic opportunity for both sexes." In measuring a school's provision of equal opportunity, a number of factors would be considered, including "facilities, equipment, supplies, game and practice schedules, travel and per diem allowances, coaching, academic tutoring" and more. Schools would have three years to comply.

The momentous legislation of 1972 and its potential for the growth of women's college sports was a prime topic of discussion at the Women's College World Series as early as the 1973 event. Some of the players and coaches wondered if colleges might soon start recruiting softball players. Wayne State softball player Ann Fulkerson presciently speculated that softball might even someday be accepted in the Olympic Games.

Women's athletic scholarships did become widespread just a few years after the 1973 softball championship. Basketball star Anne Meyers received a full-ride scholarship from the University of California at Los Angeles in 1974—the first in the nation given to a female athlete. The high level of athletic talent stemming from financial assistance to women athletes and the overall increased support of women's college softball became apparent at the Omaha tournament in the late 1970s. The last championship events of the decade were marked by athletic star power from a number of surging college softball programs.

Female coaches also benefitted by the mid-1970s when many colleges and universities began new women's teams, almost exclusively coached by females at the time. Women physical-education graduate students in 1975 suddenly began getting offers to coach these startup programs. Before the late 1970s, women's softball coaches had taught a full load of classes in addition to their coaching duties. But the times they were a changin'. Judi Garman took a full-time softball coaching position in 1979 with California State University at Fullerton—the first such opportunity for a softball coach in the nation. Garman and other women softball coaches had long wondered if the day would ever come when they could coach without a full teaching load. "Many of us felt it would never be in our lifetime," she later recalled.

But as the teams gathered in Omaha for the 1973 softball championship—almost a year after Title IX was signed—all these momentous changes still lay ahead. Perhaps the controversy-marred tournament banning John F. Kennedy College in

1972 had been a harbinger of the big changes ahead for women's college athletics. The DGWS and its offshoot organization, AIAW, would brook no women's athletic scholarships from its affiliates—at least not in 1972. That would no longer be the policy just one year later after a group of Florida-based athletes and coaches filed a lawsuit contesting this ban. In March 1973, DGWS and AIAW announced that they would allow affiliates to provide financial aid to female athletes within certain guidelines.

Yes, the times were indeed a changin' in 1973. And women's intercollegiate sports and the Women's College World Series would benefit immensely from these changes throughout the decade and beyond.

## 1973: Arizona State Repeats Despite Wright's Epic Day

Just two months prior to the 1973 Women's College World Series, the recently formed Association of Intercollegiate Athletics for Women (AIAW) announced that it would no longer prohibit its affiliates from offering athletic scholarships. So discussion at the tournament was heard about the recruitment of softball players and of someday adding the sport to the Olympics. And with participation in the sport growing and the level of competition improving, the discussion of fastpitch softball's bright future pervaded the tournament before play began May 17-20. "I think it might be put in the Olympics," said softball player Ann Fulkerson of Wayne State. "I think softball should be represented. It's gaining in popularity all over."

Although Fulkerson and her teammate, Sherri Harpoole, could not conceive of women softball players being recruited by colleges, their coach G. I. Willoughby could. "Well, it just might get to that," the Wayne State coach said. "I'm afraid it might get to recruiting, but I don't want it to—then it's winning at any cost." What the players and coaches discussed in the early 1970s would eventually happen, of course, as athletic scholarships for softball players became pervasive in the 1980s, and the sport would be accepted into the Olympics in 1991, making its debut in 1996. But that was a long way from 1973.

Sixteen teams from thirteen states competed in the 1973 championship, including newcomers Weber State, Michigan State, Utah and Michigan. Most of the teams had won state championships, so a total of thirteen states from across the country were represented. The AIAW began recognition of the women's series as the official national championship for college softball in 1973, and the women's athletics association would become a co-sponsor of the event a few years later. And it was evident right from the start of the 1973 tournament that the teams and athletes were getting better. The games went down to the wire as the athletes went all-out for a chance to win a national collegiate championship. As the field narrowed to reigning champion Arizona State and Illinois State, these two teams battled tooth and nail to decide the 1973 national title.

Arizona State had shoved Illinois State into the losers bracket on Saturday with a 9-2 beat-down. So the ISU Redbirds were forced to dispatch Southwest Missouri in Sunday's first game, with the pitching of Margie Wright securing the 5-0 shutout. The determined Wright then handed the Sun Devils their first loss (4-0) Sunday afternoon, allowing only three hits. Her teammates provided her with lots of help, pounding out ten hits to square things with ASU at one game all. Coni Staff and Bev Barnes went 3-for-3 for the Redbirds, who needed to beat the Sun Devils again that day to claim the title. Series veteran Arizona State had no intention of going down easy—if at all.

The two teams battled in a marathon struggle to determine the national champion. The title game went back and forth as Illinois State scored an unearned run in the top of the first and added another run in the third on a pair of errors. ASU countered with a score on a wild pitch in the third and then took the lead on consecutive singles by Lynn Mooney, pitcher Paula Miller, Betty Barr and Roxanne Motrenec. Despite giving up these hits, Wright stayed in the game for the Redbirds. The Illinois State lineup provided support for their pitcher in the sixth inning with a single, a walk, a hit batter, and another walk that tied the game at 3-3.

The score stayed locked at 3-all for inning after inning as the Sunday duel ground on. After nine scoreless innings, ASU finally scored in the 16th when Judy Hoke singled in Jean Killingsworth for the deciding run. Killingsworth had advanced after a walk and an error. Miller was credited with the 4-3 ASU victory, giving the Sun Devils a second consecutive championship title. The indefatigable Wright had compiled a 2-1 record that Sunday, hurling thirty innings in a heroic effort that had narrowly failed to carry her team to victory. "Being second was difficult to handle when we were so close," Wright said years later, "but the fight and strategy that we went into those games with was second to none."

Ironically, for hurling too many innings on that legendary day in May 1973, a three-woman Illinois sports commission suspended Wright from pitching in her upcoming senior year. Her Illinois State softball team was also punished with a ban from post-season play in 1974. Looking back at the incident nearly forty years later, Wright thinks the Illinois commission's punitive ruling may have been a reaction to the recently passed Title IX legislation and the state group's perceived loss of control of women athletes. "Anyway, I survived and so did Title IX," she said in 2013. "So their decision hurt my teammates and a returning team that finished second by one run in the Women's College World Series. What a waste."

Before the sixteen-inning win for the series title, ASU had defeated Western Illinois 4-2, Northern Colorado 9-1, Illinois State 9-2, and Kansas 1-0. ASU finished the year 16-4. Illinois State, meanwhile, had defeated Iowa State 2-1, Wayne State 10-0, Southwest Missouri State 5-1 and 5-0, and ASU 4-0. Cheryl Birkhead (.407) and Beverly Barnes (.400) were the leading hitters for the ISU Redbirds. In all, 30 games were played in the 1973 series, including three extra inning contests: the marathon championship game, Kansas beating University of Nebraska-Omaha 4-3 in nine innings, and Southwest Missouri state edging Western Illinois 3-2 in ten.

Western Illinois pitcher Sandy Fischer saw her team's hopes crushed by the loss to Southwest Missouri on Saturday, but she remembers Wright's heroics on the tournament's final day. "Margie and I are the same age, so we battled our whole college careers and beyond on the mound," Fischer recalled in 2012. "Little did I know at the time that Margie and I would play against each other in the pro league in the late 1970s and coach against each other for over twenty-three years in the college ranks."

Individual trophies were presented to the champions and the runner-up team members. Team trophies were given to the top four teams: ASU, Illinois State, Southwest Missouri and Western Illinois. Kris Meyer of the University of Northern Iowa led the event in batting with a .417 average.

## 1973 Final Standings

| | |
|---|---|
| Arizona State University (Tempe) | 5-1 |
| Illinois State University (Normal) | 5-2 |
| Southwest Missouri State University (Springfield) | 4-2 |
| Western Illinois University (Macomb) | 4-2 |
| University of Northern Colorado (Greeley) | 3-2 |
| University of Kansas (Lawrence) | 2-2 |
| University of Northern Iowa (Cedar Falls) | 2-2 |
| University of Nebraska (Omaha) | 2-2 |
| South Dakota State University (Brookings) | 1-2 |
| Weber State College (Ogden, Utah) | 1-2 |
| Michigan State University (E. Lansing) | 1-2 |
| Wayne State College (Wayne, Neb.) | 1-2 |
| Iowa State University (Ames) | 0-2 |
| Ball State University (Muncie, Ind.) | 0-2 |
| University of South Carolina (Columbia) | 0-2 |
| North Dakota State University (Fargo) | 0-2 |

## Life after the WCWS…

Although falling short in the 1973 title game, **Margie Wright** would go on to pitch for the St. Louis Hummers professional softball team, and eventually to twenty-seven seasons as head coach of the Fresno State University softball program. A quarter century after her disappointment in 1973, she directed the Bulldogs to a national title in 1998 and guided the program to the national tournament ten times. In her ten appearances, she owned a 26-19 women's series ledger that included the championship, three national runner-up finishes, three third-place showings, and three fifth-place finishes. She was the first NCAA Division I softball coach and twenty-fourth overall in NCAA Division I history, regardless of sport, to amass 1,000 Division I career victories, and the first to tally 1,400 fastpitch wins. She owns an impressive mark of 1,294-450-1 (.742) at Frenso State, a thirty-three-year career record of 1,457-542-3 (.728), and is the NCAA's winningest softball coach. On the international stage, Wright led the USA National Team to a gold medal as the head coach at the 1998 ISF World Championship. Wright has been inducted into fourteen halls of fame, including the Women's Sports Foundation International, the National Fastpitch Coaches Association, the Illinois State University's Athletic Hall of Fame, and the ASA National Softball Hall of Fame (2013). A published author and noted sports celebrity, she retired from Fresno in 2012. "I have learned how to teach others about the values of life through a sport," the softball legend said of her career. Western Illinois pitcher **Sandy Fischer** went on to play in the Women's Professional Softball League from 1976-79. She notched 900 victories in her twenty three seasons as head coach at Oklahoma State University (1978-2001). Her Cowgirls competed in the women's series six times, finishing second at the AIAW-sanctioned event in 1982. After nine Big 8 Conference titles, she left OSU and coached for the Professional Fastpitch Extreme Tour. She later worked with Oregon State's Kirk Walker to develop the Tee Stacker softball-training product and founded Gametime Training Tools. The Illinois native was inducted into the National Fastpitch Coaches Association Hall of Fame (2008) and the Western Illinois University Hall of Fame (1990). After having starred at Arizona State University, **Paula Miller-Noel** was eventually named head softball coach at University of Arizona and compiled a record of 110-96 from 1981-85 during the school's affiliation with the Western Collegiate Athletic Association. Miller also was a member of the Sun City (Ariz.) Saints and the 1979 USA Pan American team, which won the gold medal in softball's debut in the Pan American Games. In 2005, she was inducted into the Arizona Softball Foundation Hall of Fame.

## 1974: Southwest Missouri State Wins National Title

Worrying about the competition was only half the battle for the teams in the sixth annual Women's College World Series, which was held May 16-19, partially at Dill Softball Center in Omaha and partially on artificial turf at the University of Nebraska at Omaha. The other half of the battle for the teams representing eighteen different states was whether it would ever stop raining long enough to determine the national champion.

Eighteen teams—all state champions—entered the 1974 series, with the University of Arizona seeded first, followed by Eastern Illinois, Southwest Missouri State and Northern Colorado. Arizona State, champion the past two years, had been defeated by archrival Arizona in the state tournament; thus a new titleholder was assured for 1974. The Wildcat team's win over the previous champion allowed them to make their debut in the tournament as the top seed. Two of the eighteen schools that year were two-year schools: Golden West College and Nassau Community College. A junior college division would be started for these smaller schools in the 1975 tournament. Series officials said they were also working to schedule area tournaments across the country in the future, much like the men's College World Series. These area tournaments were planned to encourage more teams to compete for berths in the championship. The national championship was sanctioned by the Association of Intercollegiate Athletics for Women and the Amateur Softball Association.

The rainy conditions throughout the tournament forced teams to be ready to play at a moment's notice, knowing they might play only a few innings or a complete game—if lucky. Mother Nature took its own course, and unfortunately struck early. Rain fell the morning of the first day of competition on Thursday. This delayed the opening round of games for two hours. During this delay, players of opposing teams—wearing uniforms ranging from staid navy blues and maroons to the bright yellow of North Dakota State and the Kelly green of California's Golden West College—mingled with each other and with spectators. It was an opportunity for some opposing players to make lifelong friends.

The all clear was finally sounded and players took the field at 7:45 p.m. Thursday evening. Still, only two of the three fields were deemed playable. Despite the conditions, all eight scheduled games were played, although the last contest between Wayne State College and Michigan State tested the dedication of their fans. It didn't finish until 2 a.m. Friday, with Wayne State's 4-3 win in eight innings on winning pitcher Mary Gerken's RBI single. Gerken's hit scored Cheryl Finke in the bottom of the inning. Finke had reached base on a fielder's choice and moved

The rain-soaked fields at Dill Softball Complex forced tournament play onto the University of Nebraska at Omaha's artificial-turf football field, where Southwest Missouri State defeated the University of Northern Colorado in the 1974 national championship.

into scoring position on another fielder's choice before the game-winning hit.

The favored Arizona Wildcats were impressive in their opening game, routing West Georgia 16-0, while the other seeded teams also easily won their openers. Eastern Illinois shutout South Carolina 10-0, Southwest Missouri clobbered Massachusetts 11-1, and Northern Colorado disposed of Weber State 7-2.

Unseeded teams sometimes surprised top seeds, as was the case on Friday when Wayne State upset top-seeded Arizona 2-0 behind Gerken's four-hitter, which included twelve strikeouts. Both of the Wayne State runs were unearned, with Carol North and Jan Nyquist scoring on a two-out error in the top of the first inning. The three other seeded teams, however, managed to remain unbeaten. Southwest Missouri edged Luther College 1-0 on Cindy Henderson's two-hitter with fifteen strikeouts; Eastern Illinois shut out Indiana State 9-0; and Northern Colorado nipped the University of Kansas 1-0.

Intermittent showers Friday and Saturday forced tournament officials to move from the Dill Softball Complex to the University of Nebraska at Omaha's artificial-turf football field. On Saturday two of the seeded teams met, with Southwest Missouri handing Eastern Illinois its first loss 9-8. Southwest Missouri then defeated Wayne State 8-5 to remain unbeaten. Wayne State earlier had handed Northern Colorado its first loss in the highest scoring game of the event, 23-7, before a crowd of about 600 people. With the weather still unpredictable, the losers bracket games on Saturday were reduced to five innings. Top-seed Arizona was eliminated late Saturday by Kansas 8-1.

After its loss to Southwest Missouri State on Saturday, Wayne State was eliminated on Sunday by Northern Colorado 9-8 in eight innings on the UNO artificial turf. A shower Sunday morning canceled plans to move the already rain-soaked event to south Omaha's Churchich Field for the final two games. Wayne State, which finished third, had an 8-4 lead going into the bottom of the fifth inning against Northern Colorado, but couldn't maintain it. Northern Colorado tied the game with three runs in the fifth and one in the sixth, thus setting the stage for first baseman Fran Sixkiller's game-winning line drive in the bottom of the eighth inning. Sixkiller drilled it the width of the football field down the right field line with two runners on. She had slugged a two-run home run in the third inning.

The win advanced Northern Colorado to the championship game against Southwest Missouri State. Both of these women's series veterans were making their sixth consecutive trip to Omaha. It would be Northern Colorado's fifth game in two days, and the fatigue from these games showed. Southwest Missouri jumped out to an early 14-2 lead, scoring eight runs in the first inning, adding three in the second, and three more in the fourth. Northern Colorado closed the game to its final 14-7 score with two runs in the top of the sixth and seventh innings, and one in the eighth. By then unbeaten Southwest Missouri could coast, and starting pitcher Cindy Henderson was moved to first base. Henderson, who had fanned a tourney-high fifteen batters in the 1-0 win over Luther College on Friday, fanned only three in the championship game. But with her 11-0 lead after two innings, she said that she just "let the fielders do the work."

Henderson also had a pair of hits, while teammates Glenda Bond and Janet Cutbirth tallied three hits in five trips to the plate. Karen Bethurem, Mary Doyen and Robbie Johnson also had two hits apiece for the winners. In all, Southwest Missouri pounded out fifteen hits—all singles—in the championship game. Cutbirth was the leading hitter for the winners with a .444 average (8-for-18). Leading hitter in the series was Gail Gault of the University of Arizona with a sizzling .615 average (8-for-13).

Winning coach Mary Kay Hunter was asked if she had thought her team could win the tournament, and she replied: "We were counting on it." But Hunter admitted she had been worried about switching from Dill Field to the artificial turf. But her team had adjusted well—with a little help. "We were really fortunate that the California team (Golden West College) let us borrow their rubber spikes," Hunter said. "All we had were metal cleats and tennis shoes."

## Life After The WCWS...

In April 2004, **Janet Cutbirth** was one of the former Southwest Missouri team members to attend a tailgate party in Springfield, Mo., celebrating the thirtieth anniversary of Southwest Missouri's national title. Southwest Missouri played a doubleheader against Illinois State that day, with the members of the 1974 championship team introduced between games. Also attending was head coach **Mary Kay Hunter**, who compiled a record of 227-111 (.672 winning percentage) during her

**Southwest Missouri State University played frequently in the women's series in its early years in Omaha. The school's efforts were rewarded with a national championship in 1974.** *(Photo courtesy of Reba Sims)*

# 1974 Final Standings

| | |
|---|---|
| Southwest Missouri State University (Springfield) | 5-0 |
| University of Northern Colorado (Greeley) | 5-2 |
| Wayne State College (Wayne, Neb.) | 3-2 |
| University of Kansas (Lawrence) | 5-2 |
| Eastern Illinois University (Charleston) | 2-2 |
| Indiana State University (Terre Haute) | 3-2 |
| University of Arizona (Tucson) | 2-2 |
| Luther College (Decorah, Iowa) | 3-2 |
| Michigan State University (E. Lansing) | 2-2 |
| South Dakota State University (Brookings) | 2-2 |
| University of Massachusetts (Amherst) | 1-2 |
| Weber State College (Ogden, Utah) | 1-2 |
| West Georgia College (Carrollton) | 0-2 |
| University of South Carolina (Columbia) | 0-2 |
| Golden West College (Huntington Beach, Calif.) | 0-2 |
| North Dakota State University (Fargo) | 0-2 |
| Winona State College (Winona, Minn.) | 0-2 |
| Nassau Community College (E. Garden City, N.Y.) | 0-2 |

softball-coaching career at Southwest Missouri. **Glenda Bond** came to Southwest Missouri from Neosho, Mo., and was a basketball guard and softball shortstop-third baseman in a two-sport college career from 1973 to 1976. Teaming with Southwest Missouri standout Cindy Henderson, Bond played on the 1973-1974 basketball squad that posted a 21-7 record for coach Reba Sims, won an AIAW state championship, and took third-place at the AIAW regional tournament in Lawrence, Kans. In 2001, Bond was inducted into the Missouri State Athletics Hall of Fame. **Karen Bethurem** was a volleyball, basketball and softball standout for Southwest Missouri from 1970 to 1974 and played in four women's series. She was inducted into the Missouri State Athletics Hall of Fame in 1985. The tournament's leading batter, **Gail Gault** of Arizona, went on to a career as an educator, retiring as principal of La Cima Middle School in Tucson. Gault was still playing softball in fall 2012 as a member of the Wildcat alumni team that played the varsity squad at Hillenbrand Stadium in Tucson.

# 1975: UNO Wins Title for Tournament Director

Just as the year before, rain would be a major contention for the teams at the seventh annual Women's College World Series, May 15-18 at the Dill Softball Complex in Omaha. Mother Nature had struck an even harder blow before the teams gathered when a tornado in the first week of May smacked the bleachers at the Dill Softball Complex. For the 1975 series, many fans had to bring folding chairs to ensure a place to sit to watch the competition. "Most of the bleachers were destroyed by the tornado," warned Carl Kelley, Metro Omaha ASA commissioner, as the tournament got underway, "and there hasn't been time to replace them. So if you don't want to stand, you'd better bring a chair."

The tornado that hit Omaha was part of a two-day outbreak that struck the Midwest and the southern United States in early May. South Dakota, Iowa, Texas and Mississippi were struck by several tornadoes. In total, thirty-six tornadoes touched down across six states. The outbreak killed three people while injuring hundreds more. Fortunately, the tornadoes were long gone when the twenty-three teams arrived for the 1975 series, with eighteen in the four-year college division and five in the junior-college division. This was the first junior-college division championship at the series. One of these junior colleges, Golden West College of Huntington

Beach, Calif., had made its initial appearance in the 1974 tournament with the four-year schools.

The University of Oklahoma made its debut at the championship event, with a women's athletic program picking up steam — typical of many universities across the country in 1975. The Sooner squad was coached by the school's women's athletic director, thirty-one-year-old Amy Dahl, who also coached the Sooner women's basketball and volleyball teams. "We have a good, growing athletic program for women at Oklahoma," Dahl said. "The university has really been trying to help us." Women's athletics at Oklahoma was run with a $41,000 budget in 1975, she added.

It was anyone's guess which team would win that year as the defending champion, Southwest Missouri State University, had not qualified following elimination in the state tournament by Northwest Missouri State. Twelve

**Tournament director Connie Claussen takes a ride after her UNO Maverettes win the 1975 title.**

games were played on opening day, drawing a crowd of about

800. The University of Nebraska at Omaha opened with an impressive five-inning win over Northern State College of Aberdeen, S.D. UNO went up 18-0, scoring nine runs in the first inning and nine more in the fifth inning. The Omaha team continued its unbeaten ways, slipping past Oregon College of Education 1-0 behind the pitching of Julie Wolfe. The single run for UNO came in the sixth inning when Judy Melius singled and then scored on Connie Wichman's double. UNO was one of four unbeaten teams after the first two days of play.

By Saturday, the Omaha squad emerged as the only undefeated team, winning a couple of close games—Western Illinois 4-2 in 11 innings and Northern Iowa 1-0. Julie Wolfe continued as the mainstay of the pitching staff and collected the two wins. She worked five innings of relief to get the win over Western Illinois, which was decided by Melius's triple down the first base line in the eleventh inning. Wolfe helped her own cause against Northern Iowa by driving in Mickey Gehringer in the top of the fourth inning. Gehringer had reached base on an error and was then sacrificed to second before scoring on Wolfe's single, one of only two hits by the resourceful UNO girls. Northern Iowa collected five hits off Wolfe, but failed to capitalize on any of them.

The win advanced UNO to the championship round on Sunday, needing only one win to capture the title. The day before, Northern Iowa had defeated third-place finisher Michigan State 7-3 to advance to the championship round. And Northern Iowa proved to be more than a worthy foe, swamping UNO 11-1 in the first game to force the if-necessary game. It was the first loss for the Maverettes.

Although with six freshman starters and one of the youngest teams in the event, the Maverettes gathered themselves after the loss to play the deciding game. The youthful players kept their poise, even after Northern Iowa had taken an early 1-0 lead in the first inning. UNO bounced back and scored two runs in the bottom of the inning on three fielding errors and a double by Connie Wichman. The Maverettes tallied four runs in the second inning on three singles and two Northern Iowa errors. Error-plagued Northern Iowa closed the game to its final margin with a three-run rally in the seventh, but UNO pitcher Pat Linson prevailed for the win. Linson also batted .333 in the series. Kathy Drickey was the leading hitter for UNO, sporting a .455 average (5-for-11), followed by Melius .385 (5-for-13) and Gehringer .348 (8-for-23).

UNO finished the year 17-7 and came together at the right time to win the national title after a previous best of third in the 1970 championship. Going into the women's series, some had counted on the talented UNO squad to win the national title. One of them was UNO head coach Connie Claussen, who garnered her first title after five previous efforts. "I expected to win, even after we lost that first game," said Claussen. "I knew we had the ball club."

Claussen was forced to juggle her lineup when starting shortstop Drickey was struck in the eye by a pitched ball on Saturday, but the coach said it caused few problems. She had faith in her players and their ability to adapt to different positions. "The biggest asset our team had was that I could put players in different

## 1975 Final Standings

| | |
|---|---|
| University of Nebraska (Omaha) | 5-1 |
| University of Northern Iowa (Cedar Falls) | 5-2 |
| Michigan State University (E. Lansing) | 5-2 |
| University of Northern Colorado (Greeley) | 4-2 |
| University of Kansas (Lawrence) | 2-2 |
| Western Illinois University (Macomb) | 2-2 |
| Oregon College of Education (Monmouth) | 3-2 |
| University of Arizona (Tucson) | 2-2 |
| Weber State College (Ogden, Utah) | 1-2 |
| Northwest Missouri State University (Maryville) | 1-2 |
| Ball State University (Muncie, Ind.) | 1-2 |
| Ohio University (Athens) | 2-2 |
| Texas Woman's University (Denton) | 1-2 |
| North Dakota State University (Fargo) | 0-2 |
| East Stroudsburg State College (E. Stroudsburg, Pa.) | 1-2 |
| Northern State College (Aberdeen, S.D.) | 0-2 |
| University of Oklahoma (Norman) | 0-2 |
| Mankato State (Mankato, Minn.) | 0-2 |

positions," said Claussen, who had finally won a national championship from the tournament that owed a big part of its existence to her efforts and guidance as tournament director.

The only graduating starter for UNO was pitcher-third baseman Julie Wolfe, who pitched three wins in the 1975 series. The UNO players were honored by their school that year in September at Ross's Steak House in Omaha. Weber State's Chris Thornock led the four-year college players with an astounding .900 batting average (9-for-10).

In the title game for the new junior-college tournament, favorite Golden West College (Calif.) routed Northeastern Colorado, 22-0, with the game ended by the ten-run mercy rule after five innings. Melannie Kyler hurled a perfect game for Golden West, striking out eleven of the fifteen batters she faced.

## Life After the WCWS...

**Dianne Baker** was a member of the 1975 Texas Woman's University team and went on to a seventeen-year career in coaching from 1978-1995 at Stephen F. Austin State University in Nacogdoches, Texas. She won 764 games and led the Ladyjacks to a national title in 1986. She also served as assistant athletic director during that time. In 2009 she was inducted into the Stephen F. Austin Sports Hall of Fame and the NFCA Hall of Fame in 1998. In 2012, she was working as the national promotions manager for Schutt Sports. Weber State's stellar hitter **Chris Thornock**, who also played basketball and volleyball for the school, was inducted into the Weber State Athletics Hall of Fame in 1997.

## 1976: Growing Talent Pool Attracts Scouts to Series

As the nation prepared for its bi-centennial birthday party the summer of 1976, the Women's College World Series celebrated its eighth annual gathering in Omaha for the four days of the national championship, May 13-16. An indication of the series's growing talent pool was the presence of Raybestos Brakettes manager Ralph Raymond, who was scouting for new players for his storied women's fastpitch softball team. Raymond's Brakettes team had lost most of its players to the new women's professional league started by softball legend Joan Joyce, tennis star Billie Jean King, and pro golfer Jane Blaylock. "That second baseman (Kathy Strahan) from Michigan State is a pretty good little player," said Raymond as he scouted the players. He would later coach Strahan when she played for the Brakettes from 1977-1981.

Most of the nineteen teams at the series had won state championships to qualify for the tournament. The University of Nebraska at Omaha (UNO) was the defending champion and returned six of the nine starters from 1975. Missing was shortstop Kathy Drickey who suffered a fractured ankle while sliding in a game against University of Nebraska at Lincoln before the series. Probably the oldest player in the tournament was thirty-eight-year-old UNO pitcher Marlene McCauley. UNO head coach Connie Claussen, who continued her double duty as tournament director, was optimistic about her team's chances of repeating. "What we have this year that we didn't last year is more depth," said Claussen. "We're more flexible than we were a year ago."

Rain prior to the start of the event forced schedule revisions on the first day of play at Dill Softball Center, but it did not stop UNO opening up in an impressive manner. The Maverettes beat Mayville (North Dakota) State College 10-0 in five innings on a one-hitter by Pat Linson, who had hurled the championship game the year earlier against Northern Iowa. UNO, which was top-seeded in the 1976 tournament, had seven hits and took advantage of six Mayville errors. Linson fanned seven and allowed only a single by Connie Larson in the third inning. Pat Dennis had three singles for UNO, driving in three runs.

The opening round of games also featured a no-hitter by Lynn Kuchinskas who hurled East Stroudsburg (Pennsylvania) State, past South Carolina, 10-0, compelling the "mercy rule" in the fifth inning. Kuchinskas fanned ten and issued only one walk in her impressive opener. Arizona State pitcher Margaret Anne Rebenar also raised eyebrows the opening night with the Sun Devils' 2-0 win over Northern Iowa. But it was not just her pitching that drew the attention. Rebenar knocked two home runs for ASU, the only scores in the game.

McCauley proved invaluable for UNO, hurling two complete-game wins on Friday, beating Tarkio (Missouri) College 3-1 and second-seeded Northern Colorado 3-2. Other impressive pitchers in the opening days of play were Northern Colorado's Phyllis Schachterle, who no-hit Illinois State 5-1, and University of Texas at Arlington hurler Sarah Tidwell, who no-hit Kansas in a 2-0 win. While UNO remained undefeated, so did Michigan State, beating Minnesota 2-1, Kansas 6-5, and Arizona State 2-0.

The rain returned Saturday with the three scheduled games moved to the artificial turf on Al Caniglia Field at the University of Nebraska at Omaha's football stadium. The Arizona State-Tarkio game was suspended on Saturday with Tarkio leading 1-0. ASU eventually won 5-4 the next morning.

The final games of the tournament began on Sunday with UNO suffering its first defeat to Michigan State 1-0 on a four-hitter by Gloria Becksford. Michigan State scored the game's only run in the sixth inning on a single by Diane Spoelstra and a triple by Nancy Green. Spoelstra went on to become the leading hitter in the series with a .467 (7-for-15) batting average. UNO then lost to Northern Colorado 3-2, avenging an earlier 3-2 loss to the Maverettes. Pitcher Phyllis Schachterle, who came on in the second inning, got the win for Northern Colorado. McCauley hurled UNO's last two games and finished the tournament 2-2.

Northern Colorado earlier had eliminated Arizona State 13-3 with Venus Jennings hitting a grand slam in the bottom of the fifth. So Northern Colorado and unbeaten Michigan State squared off to decide the champion.

1976 Michigan State national softball championship team. Front row from left: Dee Roberts, Pam Berlinski, Gayle Barrons, Cathy Payne, Nancy Lyons, Nancy Green and Ann Nolan. Middle row from left: Gwen White, Gloria Becksford, Susan Lawson, Ann Anderson, Laury Ward, Kathy Strahan, bat girl Connie Krambeck. Back row from left: Jan Lawrence, L. Lefesque, Diane Spoelstra, Linda Haglund, coach Diane Ulibarri, Carmen King, Pat Lawson and Carol Hutchins. *(Photo courtesy of Connie Claussen)*

# 1976 Final Standings

| | |
|---|---|
| Michigan State University (E. Lansing) | 5-0 |
| University of Northern Colorado (Greeley) | 5-2 |
| University of Nebraska (Omaha) | 3-2 |
| Arizona State University (Tempe) | 3-2 |
| Tarkio College (Tarkio, Mo.) | 3-2 |
| University of Northern Iowa (Cedar Falls) | 3-2 |
| Illinois State University (Normal) | 2-2 |
| University of Texas (Arlington) | 2-2 |
| University of Kansas (Lawrence) | 1-2 |
| East Stroudsburg State College (E. Stroudsburg, Pa.) | 2-2 |
| Indiana State University (Terre Haute) | 1-2 |
| California State University (Sacramento) | 2-2 |
| University of Utah (Salt Lake City) | 1-2 |
| University of South Carolina (Columbia) | 1-2 |
| University of Minnesota (Minneapolis) | 1-2 |
| University of Oregon (Eugene) | 1-2 |
| Northwestern Oklahoma State University (Alva) | 0-2 |
| Northern State College (Aberdeen, S.D.) | 0-2 |
| Mayville State College (Mayville, N.D.) | 0-2 |

The title game was scoreless until the sixth inning when Michigan State outfielder Susan Lawson opened the inning with a single and scored one out later when shortstop Carol Hutchins reached base on an error. Center fielder Nancy Green flew out, but first baseman Gayle Barrons and left fielder Laury Ward followed with consecutive run-scoring singles. Winning pitcher Becksford fanned two batters in the 3-0 Michigan win, while Schachterle struck out five and allowed seven hits. Becksford limited her opponents to three singles as she won her fifth game of the tournament.

Michigan State ended the tourney with three consecutive shutouts. UNO's Claussen was surprised that the Spartans could accomplish this with the wet conditions. The artificial turf was slipping, but MSU still played well under the circumstances. The games could not be postponed owing to financial limitations. "Most women's programs don't have the money to wait," said Claussen at the time. "If money was no problem we would have waited until the diamonds dried."

Team trophies were presented to the top four teams and members of the top two teams received individual trophies.

## Life After the WCWS...

Michigan State's **Carol Hutchins** eventually went into coaching softball and developed the University of Michigan into one of the nation's finest programs.

Hutchins started her twenty-ninth year in 2013 after leading the Wolverines to the national championship tournament nine of the previous seventeen years. In 2005 Michigan became only the second program east of the Mississippi to claim the women's series title. In 2003, she was chosen as the recipient of the Nell Jackson Award, considered the highest honor the Michigan State Varsity "S" Club can award to alumna for professional accomplishments and community service. She was also inducted into the Greater Lansing Athletic Hall of Fame in July 2000. **Kathy Strahan** batted .400 (10-for-25) in the 1975 championship for third-place Michigan State and in 1976 played for the MSU team that won the title. Strahan completed her twentieth season of coaching in 2012 at Sacramento (Calif.) State University, with a record of 554-513-2. Her overall twenty-nine-year coaching record in 2012 stood at 801-758-3 (.514 winning percentage). Before being named head coach at Sacramento State, she coached at California State-Dominguez Hills and San Jose (Calif.) State. As a player she starred as a shortstop for the Raybestos Brakettes from 1977-1981 and was a member of the 1979 USA team when softball made its debut in the Pan American Games. She was inducted into the Michigan ASA Hall of Fame (1994) and the Lansing Sports Hall of Fame (2001). **Diane Spoelstra** is one of only two female student-athletes at Michigan State to play in three sports (basketball, softball, volleyball) and went on to become an operations production manager at Kellogg's in Grand Rapids, Mich. Spoelstra was a "first-generation daughter" of Title IX: "I was a junior in high school when Title IX happened, and we were just starting to play other teams in girls' sports and actually have a league," she said long after her competitive years ended. "I never thought being a national champion would follow my life the way it has. I still have people say they heard I played softball and was a national champion." She was inducted into the Michigan State Athletics Hall of Fame in 2012.

## 1977: Northern Iowa Wins First AIAW-Sponsored Series

The Women's College World Series reached a milestone in 1977 when the Association for Intercollegiate Athletics for Women (AIAW) became a co-sponsor of the series with the Amateur Softball Association, which had its national office in Oklahoma City. The AIAW had previously recognized the Omaha event as the official national championship for intercollegiate softball in years past but had not been an official sponsor. Judith Holland, then president of the AIAW, gave special thanks to tournament director Connie Claussen and other local organizers who had brought the championship along since 1969. "Their organizational efforts make these playoffs worthy of the title 'World Series,'" Holland wrote in a letter printed in the tournament program. So the official tournament name on the program was now the "AIAW/ASA Women's College World Series."

Organized in 1971, the AIAW was at the time the national governing body for women's intercollegiate athletics, and softball was one of eighteen national championships in twelve sports conducted by the group for colleges of various sizes. In 1977, AIAW had a membership of 871 colleges and universities. The tournament's affiliation with the AIAW also helped to improve the overall quality of teams competing in the women's series, said Connie Claussen, tournament director and head softball coach at the University of Nebraska at Omaha. "The procedure used by the AIAW for determining who will play in the World Series weeds out the weaker teams and assures a quality field," she said. With the AIAW overseeing the regional tournaments to determine women's series qualifiers, the field was narrowed to no more than sixteen teams.

As tournament co-host with the Omaha Softball Association, University of Nebraska at Omaha automatically qualified for the tournament. Although it was not welcome news to locals, women's series officials in Omaha were told by the AIAW that the tournament would be rotated throughout the country after 1979 to add to the event's exposure and prestige.

In addition to the new AIAW involvement, an aggressive public relations campaign was conducted to publicize the national championship in 1977. The results were evident the opening night of the ninth consecutive national tournament on May 25 with an estimated 1,500 in attendance. Scheduled to end Memorial Day weekend, play was to run from Wednesday through Saturday, May 28, at Omaha's Dill Softball Center. A "rain day" had been included in the schedule, a precaution taken after the rain-soaked tournament the year before.

Players from the sixteen teams were treated on opening day to a breakfast at a local Holiday Inn with a speech by women's fastpitch legend Joan Joyce. One of the top female athletes in America since her former years with the amateur Raybestos Brakettes of Stratford, Conn., Joyce inspired the young athletes with her talk prior to play that day. A player for the Connecticut Falcons of the Women's Professional Softball League in the mid-1970s, Joyce also served as the league's president in her last years as a softball player in the late 1970s.

The first day of competition was highlighted by outstanding pitching performances by Melannie Kyler of Arizona State and Northern Iowa's Pat Stockman. Kyler, who had pitched superbly for the 1975 and 1976 junior-college series champ Golden West, hurled her second game Thursday, less than twenty-four hours after beating Cal State-Sacramento 2-1 in nine innings. She paralyzed Southwest Missouri hitters in a one-hit, 2-0 win. She lost her bid for a no-hitter in the fifth inning when Jan Nelson singled with one out. Cindy Sharpe tripled home ASU's first run in the fifth and later scored on an infield error.

Stockman, meanwhile, ran her perfect record to 17-0 on Thursday with a 4-0 shutout of Kansas on a four-hitter. Northern Iowa had begun its play in the tournament with a 3-0 win over Southern Illinois on a three-hitter by Michelle Thomas and was one of four teams undefeated after the first two rounds, including defending champion Michigan State, Arizona State and Arizona. Arizona had opened with a 4-3 win over Texas-Arlington, although not without some anxious moments. The Wildcats trailed 3-1 until they scored three runs in the bottom of the seventh inning. The runs were all unearned and came on a single and two errors on the same play. With runners on first and second, Bertha Lozano's single bounced through the right fielder for two runs and a bad relay throw to home ultimately brought in the deciding run. "Something like this should never happen," said a disappointed Texas-Arlington coach Butch McBroom, who also coached the school's baseball team.

Arizona forged to 2-0 by defeating host University of Nebraska at Omaha 7-4, despite being out-hit by the Mavericks twelve to ten. UNO couldn't bring enough runners home, stranding eleven. Carla Fitzpatrick took the loss for UNO and gave up three hits to Arizona catcher Gail Davenport, who had a three-run triple in the second inning and also contributed a double. Kathy Drickey had four of UNO's dozen hits and was the hottest hitter in the tournament at that point (7-for-8).

Defending champ Michigan State opened with a 6-2 win over West Chester State on a four-hitter by Nancy Lyons, then edged Northern Colorado 5-4 in eight innings with Lyons scoring the deciding run. She had singled, then came all the way around to score when a sacrifice bunt was thrown wildly into right field. Lyons replaced starting pitcher Laurel Hills in the fifth.

Mother Nature cooperated until the afternoon session of the second day of the tournament, when dark clouds began to roll in. Rain postponed some of the Thursday evening session, but not before eight games were completed. Because of the rainy weather, tournament officials resorted to using a helicopter to dry the fields on Friday while the grounds crew did their best to get the fields ready to play. But the weather wouldn't cooperate, halting play until the next day. Finally on Saturday, tournament officials got a break—sunshine and good weather. It appeared play would go on as scheduled, and fans and players kept their fingers crossed.

Three games were played in the winners bracket on Saturday, with Arizona and Northern Iowa the only unbeaten teams by afternoon. Michigan State and Arizona State survived losers bracket games. The evening session Saturday was jeopardized when an isolated thunderstorm dumped more rain on the fields. Fortunately the rains moved out without forcing another postponement. In the winners bracket games, Arizona shut out archrival ASU by a score of 1-0. Northern Iowa remained undefeated, next beating Michigan State 7-3 and Arizona 1-0 in eight innings. Sophomore hurler Michelle Thomas got her second tournament win on a five-hitter against MSU in the afternoon before Stockman one-hit Arizona at night for her second win. Stockman's victory was her eighteenth in her undefeated season.

Tonja Adreon went the distance for Arizona in collecting her third series win, hurling a no-hitter against the Sun Devils. The win over the Wildcats' archrival was special for Adreon, 13-6 on the season. "We'd played them seven times before this game and beat them only once," she said after her win. "All eight of the games between us had been decided by one run." Arizona coach Ginny Parrish called the win against ASU a "great victory" for Adreon. "She's had a tough year," said Parrish. "She's been bothered all season by tendonitis in her pitching arm. But today she was really on." Melannie Kyler allowed only four hits in the 1-0 loss to Northern

Iowa, but one of them was an eighth-inning triple by Kris McCartney, who later scored on a single by Kathy Santi. Attendance for the two Saturday sessions totaled more than 3,500, with more than 2,000 for the evening session. Many sat on the hillside after the bleachers were filled.

The final round on Sunday saw ideal weather for Michigan State's elimination of Arizona State 3-2, with the Sun Devils finishing fourth. Arizona then edged the Spartans 2-1 in the third-place game, and Northern Colorado topped the University of Nebraska at Omaha 3-0 in the fifth-place game. The Mavs finished 3-3 in the tournament and completed the season 21-15.

With the field down to two teams, Arizona would need to beat undefeated Northern Iowa twice to win the title. Wildcat ace Adreon stifled the Panther offense in the first game and allowed only a single to right field by Kris McCartney in the eighth inning. It was Northern Iowa's only base runner. Arizona scored an unearned run in the ninth inning to seal the 1-0 win, handing Stockman her only loss of the season. Stockman had cruised along with a two-hitter entering the ninth inning. Then Wildcat catcher Gail Davenport led off with a single and advanced one out later on a ground ball. UNI second baseman Janeen Benson bobbled a grounder, allowing Davenport to score.

But Stockman showed her mettle in the second and deciding game as she hurled a two-hit shutout, 7-0, before a crowd of 1,300. Both of the hits Stockman allowed came in the third inning and only one other runner reached base for the

**Northern Iowa became the only Iowa school to win college softball's national championship. The UNO Panthers were led by pitcher Pat Stockman, who faced the Arizona Wildcat's Tonja Adreon in the deciding game. Adreon later said the strong showing of Arizona in the 1977 tournament paved the way for the school's outstanding record two decades later. *(Photo courtesy of Connie Claussen)***

Wildcats. The first Iowa school to win the women's series, UNI scored six runs on five singles, an error, two wild pitches and a passed ball in the fifth inning against Adreon, who gave up nine hits in her third game pitched that day. UNI scored its other run in the fourth inning. The final game was Adreon's fifth in two days, with fatigue seemingly playing a role in her sub-par performance. "I think she tired down a little bit," winning pitcher Stockman said graciously. Stockman was philosophic about her loss earlier: "That's the way the ball bounces." The Iowan finished the tournament 3-1 and fanned thirty-two batters in thirty-one innings, allowing ten hits while walking only two.

Despite the loss, Wildcat pitcher Adreon, who turned pro the week after the series, retained extraordinary recollections from the 1977 tournament. "That world series in Omaha will always be my best and number one memory, and playing pro comes in second," she said in 2011. "The only thing that was disappointing about this wonderful part of my life is that when I returned home, someone stole my runner-up trophy, which meant everything to me and symbolized that game against ASU. So I have nothing to show for my best athletic moment in my life."

Gayle Barrons of Michigan State emerged as the tournament's leading hitter with a .450 average (9-for-20), with Venus Jennings of the University of Northern Colorado second at .428 (9-for-21). Drickey of UNO, who started like a house afire with seven hits in her first eight at-bats, cooled off and finished at .409 (9-for-22), fifth best in the series.

Tournament officials were delighted with the 5,251 paid attendance over the five-day series, a new record. They were also pleased that the tournament was completed on a softball field rather than a football field, as was the case the year before.

## 1977 Final Standings

| | |
|---|---|
| University of Northern Iowa (Cedar Falls) | 5-1 |
| University of Arizona (Tucson) | 5-2 |
| Michigan State University (E. Lansing) | 4-2 |
| University of Northern Colorado (Greeley) | 4-2 |
| University of Nebraska (Omaha) | 3-3 |
| Arizona State University (Tempe) | 3-2 |
| University of Kansas (Lawrence) | 2-2 |
| Southwest Missouri State University (Springfield) | 2-2 |
| University of Texas (Arlington) | 1-2 |
| California State University (Sacramento) | 1-2 |
| Oklahoma State University (Stillwater) | 1-2 |
| Oregon State University (Corvallis) | 1-2 |
| Southern Illinois University (Carbondale) | 0-2 |
| West Chester State College (West Chester, Pa.) | 0-2 |
| Springfield College (Massachusetts) | 0-2 |
| Western Illinois University (Macomb) | 0-2 |

Tournament director Claussen was encouraged, calling the 1977 series "the best one ever in Omaha. Teams are certainly getting better and the fans are getting hooked on the Women's College World Series." Claussen said she hoped Omaha leaders would work together to keep the tournament. She was heartened by the tournament committee's $3,000 contribution for promotional purposes and by the Omaha Junior League's providing a hospitality room for the teams.

## Life After the WCWS...

Northern Iowa's **Pat Stockman** was drafted by the Buffalo Breski of the Women's Professional League and played from 1977-1979. In 1988 she was inducted into the UNI Athletic Hall of Fame. After her days at UNI, **Michelle Thomas** played for the renowned Sun City (Ariz.) Saints and earned ASA All-American honors four times, pitching for the Saints in the 1983 U.S. Olympic Festival in Indianapolis. Later in her career, Thomas coached softball at the University of Oklahoma (1985-1993). Arizona's **Tonja Adreon** turned pro following the 1977 season, pitching for the St. Louis Hummers of the Women's Professional League. The Wildcat pitcher said in 2011 she believed the 1977 showing by the Arizona team paved the way for the later years of success by the stellar Arizona softball program.

# 1978: UCLA Bruins Make Spectacular Debut

The tenth anniversary Women's College World Series in 1978 built on the competitive, well-attended tournament in Omaha the year before. And the tenth national tournament would provide the star power and large crowds to top even the previous year's event. Weather again forced scheduling adjustments but did little to dampen the fierce competition or the fan turnout, as the field of sixteen teams competed at Dill Softball Center with play scheduled for May 25-28. The field included teams familiar to tournament fans, but several debutants added intrigue to the 1978 event: Texas Woman's University, University of California at Los Angeles (bringing a glittering 26-3 record), Cal Poly Pomona, Portland State University, and the University of Minnesota.

Except for host team University of Nebraska at Omaha (UNO), with new coach Gail Lehrmann, the sixteen teams earned their berths through state and regional playoffs under the auspices of the Association for Intercollegiate Athletics for Women (AIAW). The AIAW and the Amateur Softball Association sponsored the event for the second year in a row.

With nearly a third of the field from large schools making their debut in Omaha, few could confidently predict the tournament winner. It was easier to forecast some of the tournament's pitching stars. Arizona State's Melannie Kyler (18-0) and Kathy Arendsen of Texas Woman's University (51-13) received much of the early attention by the media. "I never really had a chance to travel this much before,"

Arendsen told a local reporter. "I'm enjoying it." Local UNO pitching star Marlene McCauley, playing in her final series at the age of forty, was also spotlighted. Somewhat overlooked by the press early on were two UCLA pitchers, Jan Jeffers and Lisa Richardson. The two Bruin hurlers, however, would receive due attention by the time the series ended.

First-round winners included UCLA, Southwest Missouri State, ASU, Utah State, Southern Illinois, Minnesota, UNO and the University of Northern Colorado. The good weather continued the second day, with Massachusetts, South Carolina, Stephen F. Austin and Illinois eliminated after their second losses. UCLA and Minnesota each won their second and third games on Friday and were the only two unblemished teams after Friday's play. UCLA shut out Southwest Missouri 1-0 and Utah State 7-0 on Friday, while Minnesota beat Southern Illinois University 6-2 and University of Northern Colorado 4-1. UCLA scored a run in the bottom of seventh with two outs to defeat the determined Southwest Missouri State team, with Bruin senior Lisa Richardson going the distance to get the win for the Bruins. Minnesota's Vicki Swanson, meanwhile, then upped her record to 2-0 in the Southern Illinois victory, with Mary Owen's three-run home run highlighting a six-run fourth inning.

Minnesota and UCLA continued to keep pace with each other, as UNO, Portland State, Arizona State and Oregon State were eliminated Friday night. UCLA continued its string of shutouts, making Utah State its third in a row (7-0), while Minnesota turned back the University of Northern Colorado 4-1. UCLA's Jan Jeffers increased her record to 2-0 against Utah State with Gail Edson driving in four runs on a pair of singles. Swanson collected her third win of the tournament for Minnesota, allowing two hits. Shelly Medernach continued to swing a hot bat and scored two runs.

In a battle of unbeatens, UCLA and Minnesota faced off Saturday after morning showers forced the series to relocate to Omaha's Seymour Smith Field for a single, five-game session. UCLA prevailed 3-0 in the eleven-inning battle. The Bruins scored on a home run by Cindy Oeh and a two-run triple by Kathy Maurice. Richardson collected the win for UCLA, with Brooks Swanson taking the loss for Minnesota. In other action Saturday, Cal Poly Pomona eliminated top-seeded Southwest Missouri 1-0 when Sarah Strube scored from second on winning pitcher Barb Reinalda's infield grounder and a dropped throw to first base. It was Reinalda's second straight shutout and third win overall in the tournament. Late Saturday, Texas Woman's University (TWU) shutout Utah State 3-0, and Northern Colorado eliminated Cal Poly 4-3, scoring the winning run in the seventh. Lou Piel notched the win for Northern Colorado, series runner-up in 1974 and 1976.

On Sunday the weather presented the biggest challenge yet for the already soggy Dill Field after another morning shower. But by late afternoon the grounds crew had the field in good shape, setting the stage for the losers bracket showdown between Northern Colorado and Texas Woman's University. Arendsen, ace of the TWU staff, was tagged for seven runs—all unearned—in a 7-3 loss, with six of the runs coming in the second inning. Piel (4-0) got the win for Colorado with Arendsen finishing 4-2 in the tournament, fanning ten Bears to record sixty-seven strikeouts in forty-four innings with a 0.14 ERA. She hurled every game for fourth-place TWU and ended the season 55-15.

Minnesota was scheduled to play Northern Colorado next, but more rain and a tornado warning again halted play. Though Monday's forecast left little room for optimism, the resolute ground crew again prepared the field for play. Northern Colorado, which had lost earlier to Minnesota, gained revenge with a 3-1 win, as Piel collected her fifth win on a three-hitter. Minnesota finished third in its distinguished inaugural appearance in the event.

With an overflow crowd of 3,000 on hand, Northern Colorado had the tall order of beating the Bruins twice Monday afternoon to capture its first title. Northern Colorado started Brooks Swanson in the circle, who had lost earlier pitching against the Bruins. She lasted only two and two-thirds innings, as UCLA took an early 2-0 lead in the third inning. Bruin hitters Jeffers and center fielder Sue Enquist walked, and Jan Wright singled to load the bases. Gail Edson drove in Jeffers and Enquist, and Swanson was replaced by Piel. But the Bruin win appeared inevitable, with UCLA's third and final run coming in the bottom of the fifth. Enquist

**UCLA players, from left, third baseman Marcia Pontoni, pitcher Jan Jeffers and catcher Jan Wright celebrate after the last out against Northern Colorado in the final game. UCLA went undefeated in their first appearance in the women's series, and 1978 would be the first of many national championships to come for the mighty Bruin teams from Los Angeles. *(Reprinted with permission from the Omaha World-Herald)***

singled, advanced to second on a bunt by Wright, and scored on a single by Kathy Maurice.

UCLA made history in its women's series debut, winning its fifth straight game via shutout and holding its tournament opposition scoreless through thirty-nine innings. Coach Sharron Backus said after the game that she worried about her team's lack of experience. "With only three seniors on the team," she said, "we felt as though we were behind the others experience-wise." The win presaged UCLA's unparalleled success in the tournament for decades to come. The Bruins' two stellar pitchers, Jeffers and Richardson, allowed only fourteen hits between them. Jeffers hurled the final game, giving up only three hits. She finished the year with a 15-3 record, and Richardson stayed perfect at 16-0. Overlooked by local media as the tournament began, the pair's sterling performance was noted shortly after the women's series in Sports Illustrated magazine's Faces in the Crowd feature.

In the title game, following the win and a ride around the field on her players' shoulders, Backus said that "the momentum gained in the regionals was UCLA's edge. That momentum carried us throughout the tourney." UCLA seniors Enquist, Richardson, and Lisa Rubarth had provided enough experience to win the championship. And it was the second women's sports title won by a UCLA team that season. Earlier the Bruin basketball team had won the AIAW title March 25 in Los Angeles. "It's going to be very hard to replace Sue, though," Backus said of her center fielder. "She was the team leader." Enquist proved to be not only the Bruins' leader, but also the leading hitter in the series with a .421 batting average (8-for-19). She scored seven of her team's eighteen runs.

Northern Colorado finished runner-up for the third time. Despite the UCLA dominance, the 1978 national tournament was perhaps the most competitive in the event's history. The thirty games played included fourteen shutouts and twelve one-run games. Five of the thirty games went extra innings. Tournament officials estimated the final attendance almost double from 1977, with 10,000 fans watching top-flight women's softball.

The last day of the tournament, the AIAW announced ten nominations and three alternates from players in the women's series to try out for the U.S. team that would compete in the 1979 Pan American softball games. Softball made its debut at this international competition that year, with play underway in early July in San Juan, Puerto Rico.

## Life After the WCWS...

After graduation, UCLA's **Sue Enquist** played summer ball for the renowned Raybestos Brakettes and went on to become a member of four ASA national championship teams and three ASA All-American teams. She was a member of the 1979 USA Pan American team. Enquist eventually joined her coach Sharron Backus at UCLA and served nine seasons as her assistant before being named head coach. She was involved with eleven national championships at UCLA either as a play-

## 1978 Final Standings

| | |
|---|---|
| University of California (Los Angeles) | 5-0 |
| University of Northern Colorado (Greeley) | 5-2 |
| University of Minnesota (Minneapolis) | 3-2 |
| Texas Woman's University (Denton) | 4-2 |
| California Polytechnic Pomona | 3-2 |
| Utah State University (Logan) | 2-2 |
| Southern Illinois University (Carbondale) | 2-2 |
| Southwest Missouri State University (Springfield) | 2-2 |
| Arizona State University (Tempe) | 1-2 |
| Oregon State University (Corvallis) | 1-2 |
| Portland State University (Oregon) | 1-2 |
| University of Nebraska (Omaha) | 1-2 |
| Illinois State University (Normal) | 0-2 |
| University of Massachusetts (Amherst) | 0-2 |
| Stephen F. Austin University (Nacogdoches, Texas) | 0-2 |
| University of South Carolina (Columbia) | 0-2 |

er or a coach. She is UCLA softball's first athletic scholarship, All-American and hall of fame inductee. In 2006, Enquist concluded a storied twenty-seven-year career as an assistant or head coach of the UCLA Bruins. She is the first person in NCAA softball history to win a championship as a head coach and a player. Hailed as a "coaching legend" by ESPN, Enquist's tenure produced fifteen Olympians over four quadrennials (1996-2008). In 2013, she owned BRUWIN Enterprises, a corporate-educational consulting company. Texas Woman's University pitcher **Kathy Arendsen** also played for the Brakettes and compiled a record of 337-26 as a member of nine ASA national championship teams. She also later coached and was inducted into the ASA National Softball Hall of Fame in 1996. Arendsen was working as a financial advisor in 2013 in Oregon. **Barb Reinalda** also played summer softball for the Brakettes and ended up as the team's all-time winning pitcher (441-31) over a nineteen-year career. She was inducted into the ASA National Softball Hall of Fame in 1999. She was named associate head coach at Yale following the 2012 season and began her fifteenth season with the Ivy League school in 2013.

# 1979: Arendsen's Heroic Pitching Carries TWU to Title

The eleventh consecutive Women's College World Series in Omaha was loaded with similar star power as the year before when UCLA had blown away the field, holding opponents scoreless in five games to take the 1978 title. The Bruins were back, but so were numerous other talented teams, including top-seeded Cal Poly Pomona. Cal Poly had beaten UCLA in the regional tournament and came to Omaha with a sparkling 40-2-2 record. Second-seeded University of Northern Colorado made its eleventh consecutive appearance in Omaha and was the only team to have played in every national championship. The UNC Bears had taken the runner-up spot three times in the past and ached for a championship trophy for their years of effort.

The weather would prove uncharacteristically favorable as the sixteen teams representing eight regions from across the country gathered for the May 24-27 tournament at Dill Softball Center. The Association of Intercollegiate Athletics for Women (AIAW) sponsored a breakfast for the players the first day of the tournament, and the event's guest speaker was Donna Lopiano, AIAW commissioner for large-college championships. Despite the continuing success of the series and

the large crowds at the previous year's competition, the AIAW determined on May 22 that the tournament would move to Norman, Okla., in 1980, with the University of Oklahoma as host school. The women's athletic association required future tournament hosts to be Division I schools, and the University of Nebraska at Omaha (UNO), which had been host since the first series in 1969, had registered as a Division II school because of its limited scholarships.

The first page of the 1979 tournament program clearly illustrated both the growth of women's college athletics and the championship tournament. A letter from President Jimmy Carter on White House stationery adorned the opening page of the program, welcoming players to the event and extolling the popularity of women's softball. "The growth of women's softball in college is just another indication of the need to make sure that competitive athletics meets the needs of women as well as men," Carter stated in the letter.

**Texas Woman's University pitcher Kathy Arendsen pitched twenty-one innings and struck out thirty-one on the last day of the 1979 tournament, hurling her team to a national championship against UCLA in the final game. *(Reprinted with permission from the Omaha World-Herald)***

UNO coach Gail Lehrmann expected top-seeded Cal Poly Pomona to play well and unseat the defending champion Bruins. "I see Cal Poly finishing first with TWU (Texas Woman's University) finishing second," said the second-year UNO coach. It didn't take long for Lehrmann and her Lady Mavs to feel Cal Poly's strength. UNO was thumped by Cal Poly in one of the eight first-round games on Thursday, losing 6-0 before a turnout of 1,900 fans. UNO had threatened in the first inning by loading the bases on a pair of singles and a walk with one out, but Cal Poly showed its character and experience in big games. Veteran right-hander Barb Reinalda struck out UNO's losing pitcher Carla Fitzpatrick for the second out and retired Margaret Gehringer on a ground out to retire the side. This win ran her season record to 20-0.

In other opening games, defending champion UCLA extended its perfect record in the series by shutting out Texas A&M 5-0 behind Jan Jeffers who hurled a two-hitter. As a freshman, Jeffers had three of UCLA's five wins in the national tournament a year earlier. UCLA iced the game with four runs in the sixth inning. Northern Colorado had the most difficulty of the opening-game winners, needing eleven innings to handle newcomer Rutgers (24-0 coming to Omaha) 3-2 behind winning pitcher Lou Piel. Third-seeded Kansas blanked Arizona 2-0 behind the pitching and batting of Shelley Sinclair. Other first-round winners were Arizona State, Texas Woman's University, Western Illinois and Indiana University.

Friday's second-round action drew an estimated 3,600 fans, who certainly got more than their money's worth when TWU and Arizona State squared off. It took eighteen innings to decide the winner, with TWU scoring the game's only run on sophomore outfielder Pam Brown's RBI single that brought in Val List from second base. TWU used two pitchers, with Kathy Van Wyk hurling the first six innings and Kathy Arendsen finishing up the win. Still, losing pitcher Lucy Casarez was a model of determination and guts, pitching the entire game and fanning twelve batters.

UCLA, meanwhile, continued its unbeaten ways, downing Kansas 2-0 and Northern Colorado 2-0. The two wins raised the UCLA series record over two tournaments to 8-0 and its opponents' scoreless-inning streak to sixty. Karen Andrews hurled the win against Kansas with Bruin left fielder Gail Edson scoring a run and going 2-for-4. Shelley Sinclair was the loser for Kansas. Against Northern Colorado, Jeffers notched her second win of the series and gave Piel her first loss. The loss to UCLA was hard for the Bears. Northern Colorado had been one of the series' most consistent teams, never finishing below fifth-place in eleven consecutive years. Yet, UNC coach Jane Jensen knew that only winning the tournament outright would give her program the recognition it deserved. "The players want to win more than anything," Jensen said.

With only one loss, Northern Colorado continued play. Eliminated on Friday were Emporia State, Chapman College, Arizona, Arizona State, Rutgers, UNO, Kansas and South Carolina. This left half of the field of sixteen still in pursuit of the title. Four more teams were eliminated when play resumed Saturday morning in the losers' bracket, with Western Illinois, Oregon State University, Texas A&M

and Indiana University all sent home.

Both undefeated, UCLA and Cal Poly faced off Saturday night in a game to remember. The game between the two outstanding California teams was a bitterly fought rematch of the regional when Cal Poly beat the Bruins twice. With two out in the top of the third inning, UCLA center fielder Lucy Innuso reached base on an error and scored on a single by left fielder Gail Edson. "Gail has been our offensive punch throughout the tournament and the season," said UCLA coach Sharron Backus after the game. "She has the power and the timing that really counts." Edson also showed her outstanding defensive skills with a diving catch in the seventh inning. Edson's RBI was the game's only run, extending the Bruins' overall series record to 9-0 and their opponents' scoreless-inning streak to sixty-seven. The winning run was the first scored against Cal Poly in the tournament. Pitcher Karen Andrews collected her second win of the tourney, striking out five. Cal Poly's Reinalda suffered her first loss in twenty-three games, even though she gave up only a pair of hits.

That same evening, Texas Woman's University eliminated Northern Colorado 1-0, shoving the long-suffering Bears into fourth place. The only run TWU need-ed came in the sixth inning when Leslie Phillips reached first on an error and was sacrificed to second by Pam Brown. Phillips went to third as Sue Redding got aboard on an error. Phillips scored when catcher Willie Rucker sent a single up the middle. Winning pitcher Kathy Arendsen boldly stated after the win: "We're going to take this series. We'll get our hitting together and surprise everyone." Earlier Sat-urday, Arendsen had come on in relief in the fifth inning and eliminated Indiana University 2-1 in eleven innings.

With three teams left in the field as Sunday morning dawned, undefeated UCLA could watch TWU and top-seeded Cal Poly Pomona fight for the right to play the Bruins for the title. TWU, which had lost earlier to Cal Poly 1-0 on Friday night, revenged this loss with a 2-0 win. So Cal Poly finished third with the charg-ing Arendsen besting Reinalda with a no-hitter, including fifteen strikeouts and one walk. Still, TWU needed to beat the unbeaten Bruins twice to capture the title. UCLA's Backus said Saturday that the tournament was the strongest that she had ever seen. "A dropped ball here or a mistake there can make the difference in who wins," the veteran coach predicted.

Backus was proved prescient by the results of the two final games played Sun-day before the 2,300 fans. In the first match-up, TWU's Sue Redding bunted past UCLA pitcher Jan Jeffers for an infield double in the third inning, pushing the ball through a hole between first and second base. But a single by TWU catcher Willie Rucker failed to score Redding as she stumbled at third. Missy Mapes then hit to the third baseman, who mishandled the ball as Redding broke for home. The run was ruled earned because of what probably would have been a close play at the plate. It was the first run scored against the Bruins in eleven games and seventy-six innings over the last two series. UCLA's first—and only—threat of the first game came in the last of the fifth inning. With two out, Sue Sherman beat out a per-

## 1979 Final Standings

| | |
|---|---|
| Texas Woman's University (Denton) | 7-1 |
| University of California (Los Angeles) | 4-2 |
| California Polytechnic Pomona | 3-2 |
| University of Northern Colorado (Greeley) | 3-2 |
| Indiana University (Bloomington) | 3-2 |
| Texas A&M University (College Station) | 3-2 |
| Oregon State University (Corvallis) | 2-2 |
| Western Illinois University (Macomb) | 2-2 |
| Arizona State University (Tempe) | 1-2 |
| Rutgers University (New Brunswick, N.J.) | 1-2 |
| University of Kansas (Lawrence) | 1-2 |
| University of Nebraska (Omaha) | 1-2 |
| Chapman College (Orange, Calif.) | 0-2 |
| Emporia State University (Kansas) | 0-2 |
| University of Arizona (Tucson) | 0-2 |
| University of South Carolina (Columbia) | 0-2 |

fect bunt, designated hitter Frankie Butler singled, and Collins walked to load the bases. But Innuso grounded out to end the inning. TWU took the first game 1-0. Arendsen allowed three hits, walked two and struck out nine. The Pioneers had seven hits with catcher Rucker 3-for-3 against loser Jeffers.

TWU's Redding also played a part in the second and deciding game when she singled to third with none out in the first inning. UCLA third baseman Pontoni overthrew Kathy Maurice at first, and Redding tried for third base on the overthrow. Maurice's return throw to Pontoni was in time, but Redding's hard slide knocked the ball loose. The swift left fielder jumped to her feet and sprinted for home. She was ruled safe as she crossed the plate standing up. Pontoni was charged with two errors on the play. After the first inning, the Bruins contained the Pioneer hitters but had trouble putting together a rally of their own against the hard-throwing Arendsen. A small threat was doused in the sixth when UCLA failed to advance pinch hitter Cindy Oeh past second with one out. The Bruins' best chance to score came in the seventh when right fielder Nedra Jerry tripled to lead off. But with one out, Pontoni's grounder had Jerry hung up between third and home, and she was nailed at the plate. Pontoni advanced to third during the rundown, but Arendsen fanned Sherman for the third and final out—and the satisfying 1-0 title victory.

Said Arendsen after pitching the three games that day: "It was work. I was in a lot of pressure situations that really taught me something about myself." Arendsen hurled twenty-one innings on the final day, allowing five hits while striking out thirty-one batters. She was swarmed by her teammates following the final game. The fans watching Arendsen's three-game performance were thrilled by the quality of the fiercely contested games.

Pioneers head coach Donna Terry wasn't able to share the championship with her team that year. She was traveling across China as a member of the Connecticut Falcons women's pro fastpitch team. "We dedicated the games to Miss Terry and we won them for Miss Terry," said Arendsen, who was named one of ten softball nominees from the tournament for the 1979 Broderick Award, an annual honor to the nation's outstanding female collegiate athlete. Following her remarkable year at TWU, Arendsen transferred to California State University at Chico.

Although UNO finished only 1-2 in the tournament, the Lady Mavs had the leading hitter in the event with Sue Reinders at .545 (6-for-11). Susan Bachman of Western Illinois batted .417 (5-for-12) to finish behind Reinders.

The 2,300 well-entertained fans who attended the final two sessions on Sunday increased the overall attendance for the 1979 series to 11,250 over four days. The 1980 tournaments for Divisions I and II would be held in different locations because of the AIAW restructuring. So the championship would leave Omaha for the first time. Division I play was planned in Norman, Okla., and the Division II tournament was scheduled in Sacramento, Calif.

## Life After the WCWS...

ASU's **Suzie Gaw** batted .308 in the 1979 championship and went on to become a star for the renowned Sun City (Ariz.) Saints. She earned ASA All-American honors eleven times and was a member of four USA Pan American teams. She was inducted into the ASA National Softball Hall of Fame in 2001 a year after induction into the Arizona Softball Foundation Hall of Fame. Gaw is a retired firefighter from the Phoenix Fire Department. Northern Colorado's **Mary Lou Piel** was named Colorado Sportswomen of the Year in 1980 after compiling an 18-2 record with 155 strikeouts and an ERA of 0.52. Her career record was 48-7 with an ERA of 0.05. Piel coached the University of South Carolina softball team from 1983-1986 and compiled a record of 100-58-3. The absent TWU Pioneer coach **Donna Terry** played for the Connecticut Falcons of the Women's Professional Softball Association as part of the pitching rotation with the renowned Joan Joyce. She was playing with the first U.S. softball team to tour China when her Pioneers won the back-to-back games against UCLA to win the 1979 title. When TWU softball was dropped in 1981, Terry went to Puerto Rico to coach the national team. Afterward, she enjoyed a successful career at the University of California (Berkeley) from 1983-87 (165-91-1), including two conference titles and a third place finish at the 1986 series. Terry died in 1988 in Little Rock, Ark., from complications due to hepatitis. A softball stadium is named after her in Guaynabo, Puerto Rico.

# *Three*
## (1980-1982)
### ༞ঞ༞ঞ༞

# A Championship in Transition

B Y THE LATE 1970s, women's collegiate athletics was expanding exponen-
tially, and college softball programs were a big part of this growth. Both Title
IX and the increasing acceptance of women's sports at all levels in society
were fueling this boom. Athletic scholarships and recruitment of players had become a part of women's college programs, even as the Association of Intercollegiate
Athletics for Women (AIAW) worked to avoid some of the excesses they perceived
in men's college sports. Although UCLA had not even funded a varsity softball
team until a few years earlier, the school's women's athletic budget had shot up
to $540,000 for the 1978-1979 season, with $5,500 set aside for recruitment. The
somewhat conservative AIAW had its work cut out in the oversight of this brave
new world of women's college sports.

In response to this expansion, the AIAW had announced early in 1979 that
their member schools would be restructured in the 1979-1980 season from large
and small divisions to three new competitive divisions. This restructuring created
Division I, II, and III, and each would have their own national championship for
various sports. The member school's division would be determined by the number of full athletic scholarships allowed by the college for various women's sports
teams. Division I schools would be allowed a maximum of thirteen full scholarships per sport, Division II a maximum of 6.5, and Division III a maximum of only
1.3. The University of Nebraska at Omaha, which had staged the tournament since
it began in 1969, declared for Division II for the 1979-1980 season. The Division
I Women's College World Series host school was required to be Division I, so this
brought a major change to the national championship tournament. It was moved
to Norman, Okla., in 1980 with Division I school University of Oklahoma as host.

Omaha's loss of the tournament was understandably a bitter pill to swallow
for tournament director Connie Claussen, who had played the integral role in
the founding and development of the event since the beginning. Her fledgling
tournament started ten years earlier and was drawing attendance of some 10,000
in 1978, double from the year before. Things were looking up—then suddenly the

women's series was moved. Ironically, Claussen had been a member of the AIAW selection committee that had voted on the tournament's travel to Norman at an evening meeting in Omaha just days before the 1979 championship began. So the longtime tournament director could take consolation only in the tournament that was soon to start and the hope of its future return. "I'm disappointed that the tournament will leave Omaha after this year," she said at the time. "If people want to see the best women's softball in the country, this weekend will be the last chance to see it in Omaha for at least two years."

Adding to the injury to Nebraskans—many of them hard-core Cornhusker football fans—was the event's relocation to Norman, Okla., with the University of Oklahoma as host. Many Nebraskans looked askance at most things associated with the Oklahoma Sooners. The 1970s had witnessed one of the bitterest of rivalries between the two school's football teams. So in 1979, Nebraskans were forced to accept the dreaded Sooners' spiriting away of this premier women's softball event that Omaha had nurtured from infancy.

The tournament's move from Omaha and the selection of Norman for the new site initially appeared puzzling at several levels. Despite the usual soggy spring weather, the 1978 tournament had gone well, with good attendance, excellent media coverage, and a profit of more than $9,000. AIAW officials had expressed satisfaction with the administration of the event, and a motion by officials was expected to keep the women's series in Omaha. But even after the high note of the 1978 championship, director Connie Claussen had expressed some concerns over Omaha's unwillingness or inability to back the event financially. "We have so many volunteers who have been working the Women's College World Series for literally nothing," Claussen said in 1978. "We can't continue this way." Perhaps the town just did not have its heart in supporting both a men and women's "world series." Yet, the local organizing committee for the men's College World Series had contributed several thousand dollars for the women's event each year since 1975.

Reports had circulated for some time prior to the announced move to Norman that AIAW plans called for the tournament's relocation in 1980 to the West Coast, fertile ground for college softball and generally fair weather for outdoor competition. AIAW past president and Californian Judith Holland had visited Omaha for the 1978 tournament. "I'm very happy with everything and everyone connected with the series," she said at the time. "I'm impressed." But Holland also said that the contract between AIAW and the championship's local organizers would expire after the 1979 event. Then, as a matter of AIAW policy, the event would be rotated to a different host school, she added.

Omaha's Creighton University had declared Division I in 1979, so the school could have served as host school with no change in the tournament's location. But Creighton was too late with their bid for the 1980 women's series, according to Donna Lopiano, AIAW coordinator for large-school tournaments. The lack of bids by Division I schools to host the women's series stemmed more from confusion than a lack of interest, she told an Omaha World-Herald reporter at the 1979 tournament. "I think most of the schools figured that UNO would put in a bid as a continuing host for Division I," Lopiano said. "After UNO declared Division II, the only bid we were holding was from Oklahoma."

So the AIAW made the decision to relocate the championship to Norman, and that was that. As the governing body of nearly 1,000 college and university member institutions and nearly 100,000 female student athletes in 1980, the AIAW fully intended to ensure quality competition between these disparate member schools. The tournament's move to Norman was all a part of these intentions.

The AIAW in 1979 had established a separate legal identity from its parent organization, the National Association for Girls and Women in Sport, and had tripled its active membership in less than a decade since its founding in 1971. By 1981 it boasted of its position as the nation's largest governing body for intercollegiate athletics. It offered thirty-nine national championships in seventeen different sports—all for female student-athletes. With its restructuring from large and small divisions into the three new divisions with the 1979-1980 season, it offered eleven national championships in each of the three divisions and six national championships open to all member schools.

The AIAW had championed the successful drive in the 1970s to ensure equal opportunity for female student-athletes through Title IX of the 1972 Education Amendments. The association's overriding theme had been to demonstrate that "student-oriented, educationally based athletics" could be "high caliber, high visibility." The group had continually expressed a desire to work to assure "athletes' rights and freedom from exploitation firmly rooted" in a "long-standing philosophy of first concern for the student-athlete." And the AIAW expressed a hope that their organization might "serve as the model for all intercollegiate athletic organizations." This last statement was probably directed at their counterpart in men's college sports, the National Collegiate Athletic Association. Officials in the women's organization had long expressed their desire to avoid what they perceived as excesses in recruiting and rivalry in men's college sports.

A member of the AIAW softball committee, University of Oklahoma softball coach Marita Hynes led her school's efforts to serve as an accommodating host for the tournament. In fall 1979 she reserved the Ramada Inn in Norman to lodge the field of sixteen teams for the 1980 event. The Division I national softball championship would be held each May from 1980 through 1982 with Hynes as tournament director. Although the tournament would leave Norman after just three years, a fortunate connection for the future of the women's series had been made. Hynes's experience and competence in the tournament's administration would be remembered years afterward. And she would later play the leading role in establishing the tournament in a more permanent, thriving location in the early 1990s.

But in 1980, tournament play would be on the diamonds at Norman's Reaves Park, not far south of OU's Memorial Stadium, site of many of the school's storied football battles in past decades. The bitter struggles between men's football teams at Memorial Stadium would starkly contrast with the friendly softball contests between women's teams at Reaves Park—in a sense underscoring the philosophical difference between the AIAW and the NCAA. Following the title game of the 1980 Women's College World Series, the new national champions would gather in the middle of the diamond at Reaves Park after vanquishing their rival—but not to gloat or taunt. The student-athletes of Utah State University assembled to give a cheer for their defeated, second-place opponents.

The innocence of that gracious scene of sportsmanship in May 1980 would soon be another quaint memory—much like the "play days" and "punch and cookies" of women's college softball in the early 1960s. More dramatic changes in women's college sports and the Women's College World Series were already underway by 1981. The softball tournament in 1982 at Reaves Park would be the sport's final national championship sanctioned by the AIAW. Rising quickly and successfully in the 1970s, this idealistic body that was run by women administrators and for women student-athletes would crumble in the early 1980s even more rapidly than it had risen. In some ways the AIAW became a victim of its own success. The organization's efforts to gain approval of and resources from Title IX had accomplished amazing growth, and this foretold of even greater potential for the funding and expansion of women's college sports.

Nervously eyeing this emerging rival sports group in the early 1980s, the NCAA determined to incorporate the fruits of the AIAW's labors from the 1970s into their own organization in the 1980s. The money, media contacts and administrative support that the NCAA offered to women's college sports proved irresistible to most schools. In 1982 many colleges opted to compete in the NCAA's new women's national championships instead of the AIAW's established events.

But some schools chose to stay with the AIAW's national championship tournaments until the last were concluded. AIAW's final softball championship was in May 1982 at Reaves Park in Norman, Okla.

## 1980: Utah State Wins First AIAW Div. I Tournament

For the first time since its beginning in 1969, the Women's College World Series would be held outside Omaha. Play was scheduled May 22-25 and would finish up on Memorial Day weekend at Norman's Reaves Park with the University of Oklahoma as the host school. The 1980 AIAW Division II national championship was played at the same time in Sacramento, Calif., with California State University at Sacramento as host school for the eleven teams competing for that title.

Although local media referred to the 1980 tournament in Norman as the "Women's College World Series," the AIAW seemed to be attempting to rebrand the title of the women's series since the group at the time sanctioned two college softball national championships. So the 1980 competition was officially named the "AIAW Division I National Softball Championship." Earlier reports on the tournament in Oklahoma City's Daily Oklahoman newspaper reported on the "Women's

College World Series," but the publication's final article reported the champions as having "won the Division I AIAW National Softball Championship."

Oklahoma was a veteran of series play in Omaha and as host in 1980 received an automatic berth in the double-elimination event. Sooner softball coach and tournament director Marita Hynes had her hands full. Another Oklahoma team, coach Sandy Fischer's Oklahoma State Cowgirls, received an at-large berth in the tournament. The Cowgirls had also experienced the excitement of the series in Omaha, as had the team's young coach. Fischer was a veteran of several national championship tournaments from her pitching days at Western Illinois University in the early 1970s. The OU Sooners and OSU Cowgirls joined a field of fourteen other of the AIAW's new Division I teams, including: Western Michigan, Cal Poly Pomona, New Mexico, Texas A&M, Southwest Missouri State, California State (Fullerton), Creighton, Western Illinois, Oregon, Massachusetts, Utah State, University of California (Berkeley), South Carolina and Indiana University.

Cal State-Fullerton had almost miraculously arrived in Norman for the tournament. The Titans softball program was in its first year and badly underfunded. Coach Judi Garman had no assistant, and the team did not even have a home field. Nonetheless, the scrappy Titans had finished second in their competitive regional tournament, assuring them a berth in the national tournament. But when they returned home from regional play, they were initially told that no funding was available to pay their way to the championship in Norman. But somehow the money was found, and the upstart Titans arrived with game faces on. Garman had previously coached Golden West's team to the women's series junior college title in Omaha in 1975. "Our girls were pinching themselves on the plane," Garman said after the Titans arrived in Norman. "They think it's a miracle we're here."

The two Oklahoma teams opened play the afternoon of May 22, with Oklahoma's Hynes doing double duty as coach of the Sooners and tournament director. Oklahoma fell to Western Illinois 1-0, while Oklahoma State squeaked by Western Michigan 5-4. Although Texas A&M was the tournament favorite, Aggie coach Bill Galloway downplayed his team's chances. "We're overrated," said Galloway. "I would say that we're one of the best teams in the tournament, but there's just so much balance throughout the country." Defending champion Texas Woman's University was not in the tournament. TWU had been ineffective in the regional tournament without its top pitcher, who was injured in an auto accident days before play began. And Kathy Arendsen, the team's dominating pitcher the year before, had transferred to California State College at Chico.

The Aggies, who entered the tournament 67-14, which included their fall season, beat a veteran Southwest Missouri team 1-0, scoring the game's only run in the top of the first inning. A&M left-handed pitcher Lori Stoll limited the opposition to four hits in collecting her thirty-third win of the season against five losses. Also winning first-round games were Cal Poly Pomona, Indiana University, Cal State-Fullerton, Western Illinois, Oregon and Utah State, which surprised second-seeded Cal-Berkeley 4-1.

Top-seeded Texas A&M was upset by Indiana University 1-0 on Friday in a winners bracket game. Staying undefeated in their second games were: OSU, beating Cal Poly 1-0; Western Illinois, blanking Cal State-Fullerton 2-0; and Utah State, shutting out Oregon 5-0. Also on Friday host Oklahoma was eliminated by Creighton 3-0 as seven other teams—South Carolina, Massachusetts, New Mexico, Creighton, second-seeded Cal-Berkeley, Southwest Missouri State, and Cal-Fullerton—also dropped from the original field of sixteen following their second loss.

On Saturday, Western Michigan eliminated OSU 1-0 in ten innings, with pitcher Bonni Kinne holding the Cowgirls to three hits. Indiana turned back Utah State 3-2 to remain the only unbeaten team. Both Texas A&M and Western Michigan played three games on Saturday. A&M eliminated Cal Poly 3-2 in eleven innings, Western Illinois 2-0, and Western Michigan 1-0. After beating OSU, Western Michigan eliminated Oregon 1-0 before its own elimination by A&M.

After Saturday's play, only Indiana, Utah State and Texas A&M remained in the tournament. A crowd of 1,500 gathered in the hot Oklahoma sun for the final games on Sunday. In a battle of the Aggies, the Utah State Aggies eliminated top-seeded Texas A&M 1-0 in the first game Sunday morning. So Utah State, which had lost to Indiana by one run the day before, needed to beat the undefeated Hoosiers twice for the title.

In the first Aggie-Hoosier contest, the game was scoreless into the bottom of

**1980 Utah State University Aggies. Standing from left: Janet Leising, Mary Lou Ramm, Heather Borg, Deb Panfil, Margaret Earner, Julie Hacking and Deb Allen. Kneeling from left: Janene Bankson, Robin Petrini, Cindy Krueger, Karen Caywood, Yolanda Arvizu and Kerry Himmelspach. Coach Kelly Phipps not pictured. (Photo courtesy of the University of Oklahoma Athletic Dept.)**

the seventh inning when the Aggies' Janet Lacey led off with a triple to right center. Hoosier pitcher Donna Michalek then intentionally walked Robin Petrini and Janese Bankson to load the bases, setting up a force-out at home. Lacey was beaten with the throw to home when pitcher Mary Lou Ramm grounded out to third. But the next batter, Margaret Earner, drove in Petrini with a bouncing line drive for the Utah State 1-0 win.

In the second game, Indiana took a 1-0 lead with a run in the top of the second when Sue Lilley scored Diane Stephenson, who had reached base on an error. But in the bottom half of the same inning, Utah State struck back when Bankson led off with a double and Ramm walked. Bankson was thrown out at third on a ball hit by Earner, but Michalek delivered a wild pitch moving Ramm to third and Earner to second. Petrini then hit a ball that ricocheted off the third baseman's glove and rolled deep into the outfield, allowing both runners to cross the plate. The scoring ended there, and the Utah State University Aggies didn't need their last at-bats for the 2-1 championship victory. Ramm had pitched all seven Aggie wins in the tournament.

Utah State was coached by twenty-two-year-old Kelly Phipps, who had played shortstop for Kansas in the women's series the year before. Phipps was the youngest coach to win the national championship, a distinction that she will probably hold forever. "I always felt we had a good chance in this tournament, "said Phipps, who inherited the program at Utah State when coach John Horan resigned and turned over the team to her just as the season began. Reflecting on that championship season years later, Phipps said she gave a lot of credit to Horan, who had really "beat the bushes in recruiting and had some good kids." The 1980 Aggie squad had only thirteen players, seven of whom were freshmen. "The really neat thing about this group of players was they were just there to play," Phipps said. "They were interested in getting an education and playing ball."

Utah State pitcher Ramm was named most valuable player of the series. The Aggies went 6-1 during the tournament and finished the season with a 35-16 record, a school record for wins at the time. Ramm and second baseman Yolanda Arvizu were nationally recognized players, while catcher Janet Leising led the team in batting with a .303 average. Rounding out the rest of the Utah State team were: Heather Borg, Deb Panfil, Margaret Earner, Julie Hacking, Deb Allen, Janene Bankston, Robin Petrini, Cindy Krueger, Karen Caywood and Kerry Himmelspach.

Named to the all-tournament team were: Utah State's Mary Lou Ramm; Cal-Berkeley's Shari Fisher and Pam Reinoehl; Cal Poly's Kim Bowles; Western Michigan's Linda Berndt, Patti Rendine, and Bonni Kinne; Western Illinois's Dot Richardson and Pat Stoffel; Indiana's Linda Spagnolo and Donna Michalek; Oklahoma State's Jan Drummond; and Texas A&M's Lori Stoll.

The University of Oklahoma would again serve as host for the tournament the next year in Norman, and tournament director Marita Hynes began planning for the 1981 series as soon as the 1980 tournament ended.

## 1980 Final Standings

| | |
|---|---|
| Utah State University (Logan) | 6-1 |
| Indiana University (Bloomington) | 4-2 |
| Texas A&M University (College Station) | 5-2 |
| Western Michigan University (Kalamazoo) | 4-2 |
| Western Illinois University (Macomb) | 2-2 |
| Oklahoma State University (Stillwater) | 2-2 |
| California Polytechnic Pomona | 2-2 |
| University of Oregon (Eugene) | 2-2 |
| Southwest Missouri State University (Springfield) | 1-2 |
| University of California (Berkeley) | 1-2 |
| California State University (Fullerton) | 1-2 |
| Creighton University (Omaha, Neb.) | 1-2 |
| University of South Carolina (Columbia) | 0-2 |
| University of New Mexico (Albuquerque) | 0-2 |
| University of Oklahoma (Norman) | 0-2 |
| University of Massachusetts (Amherst) | 0-2 |

## Life After the WCWS...

Coach **Kelly Phipps** left Utah State a year later to take over the Iowa State softball program in 1982. In 2013 she was an owner of an alternative health care clinic and information technology director for a company outside Wichita, Kan. In 2011 she and the other members of the 1980 and 1981 Utah State national championship softball teams were inducted into the Utah State Hall of Fame. Aggie pitcher **Mary Lou Ramm** went on to play ASA women's Major fastpitch and was inducted as an individual into the Utah State Athletic Hall of Fame in 1993. She is the school's all-time leader in wins (78) and shutouts (44) and ranked second in career strikeouts (589). In 2013 Ramm was teaching special education and coaching softball at San Diego Mesa College. Western Michigan's **Bonni Kinne** finished her softball career in 1984 as the school's all-time leader in career wins (69) and shutouts (48). She later coached softball for the University of Wisconsin (Eau Claire) and was inducted into the Greater Lansing Area Sports Hall of Fame in 1999.

# 1981: Utah State Aggies Repeat in Norman

The Women's College World Series made its second appearance in Norman, Okla., returning to the college town in 1981 with the University of Oklahoma again serving as host. The Association of Intercollegiate Athletics for Women (AIAW) continued sponsorship of the event, with an official title in 1981 of "AIAW College Softball World Series." So the "World Series" was back in the tournament's name, but not the "Women's." Local media were somewhat inconsistent, but seemed to eventually settle on the title of "AIAW College Softball World Series."

The day before the tournament began, the AIAW announced that the University of Oklahoma would host the event again in 1982. The now-rival National Collegiate Athletic Association (NCAA) had earlier announced that it would sanction national championships in twelve Division I women's intercollegiate sports in 1982, including softball. With this in mind, the AIAW had set May 1, 1981, as the deadline for Division I schools to declare championship intentions for the 1981-1982 season. A majority of the Division I schools chose a dual membership for one or more sports. Oklahoma submitted a host bid for both the AIAW and NCAA's 1982 tournaments.

Perhaps stemming from these distractions, AIAW appeared disorganized in their final selection of the sixteen teams for the 1981 women's series. After Region IX decided not to send representatives to the 1981 tournament, the AIAW softball committee voted to invite Indiana University and Arizona State University. After defending champion Utah State protested this decision, the AIAW national organization revoked the invitations to Indiana and ASU, instead giving tournament berths to Utah State and Oklahoma State.

Creighton University's team had come to Norman for the tournament, and its sports information director Kirk Hendrix commented to a local newspaper reporter about the escalating AIAW-NCAA rivalry. With the NCAA softball championship scheduled for Omaha in 1982, Creighton had already been selected to serve as host school. Hendrix made clear he had already chosen sides. "We see the NCAA getting involved in the growth of women's sports, and we see the need to have a full-time athletic staff and a full-time commitment to college athletics. The AIAW doesn't have that."

Changes and organizational rivalries aside, the sixteen teams gathered for the Memorial Day weekend, double-elimination tournament with play scheduled to run from Thursday, May 21, through Sunday, May 24, in Norman's Reaves Park. For the second year in a row, the New Mexico Lobos came into the series as the top seed, following their Region V tournament win over defending national champion Utah State. The Lobos hoped to improve on their under-achieving 0-2 campaign the year before. Despite their loss in the regional tournament and initial snub by the AIAW softball committee, the Utah State Aggies had ultimately received an at-large invitation and returned with a new coach, Lloydene Searle. Searle replaced Kelly Phipps, who had guided her players to the 1980 title in her first year at the helm and moved on to coach at Iowa State.

As the top seed, the Lobos drew the University of Oklahoma (46-37), which received an automatic berth as host team. Since the Sooner team had not earned their invitation on the field of competition, they were paired with the formidable-appearing Lobos, who had won their last ten games in a row, with six of them as shutouts. "Our pitching and defense have carried us throughout the season, but now our hitting is picking up," said New Mexico coach Susan Craig. "But I think that there are two things more important, intensity and emotion. It's hard to get that kind of excitement until you get into regional and national tournament time."

But Oklahoma coach Marita Hynes liked her team's chances. She blamed fatigue for her team's earlier poor performances in the Big Eight and regional tournament, as Hynes had loaded the Sooners' schedule to play as many games as possible. The Sooners justified their presence in the event by stunning the top-seeded Lobos 1-0. Oklahoma won the game in rare fashion—without getting a hit and taking advantage of three walks and a wild pitch in the sixth inning by Lobo hurler Tippy Borrego.

In another key game in the first round, Utah State and Texas A&M continued their "battle of the Aggies" from the 1980 tournament, where Utah State had eliminated the Aggies from College Station 1-0 in the semi-final game. With A&M (74-10 entering the series) considered by some as the team to beat in this event, the two Aggies were scoreless for three innings before Texas A&M tallied a run in the top of the fourth on an RBI single by Mary Lou Youngblood. But Utah State (29-13 coming to the tournament) came back to score twice in the bottom of the inning and send Texas A&M to the losers' bracket with the 2-1 loss. Kerry Himmelspach's two-run double scored the tying and deciding runs for winning pitcher Mary Lou Ramm. Himmelspach's hit deflected off the glove of Texas A&M second baseman Patti Holthaus, allowing Ramm to score. "There was nothing Patti could do," said Texas A&M coach Bill Galloway. "She didn't have much of a choice but to try and get it. It was a hard hit ball."

In other first round games, Cal State-Fullerton went eight innings to top New Mexico State 7-6; Western Michigan ended Creighton's twenty-game win streak 2-0; 1978 series champ UCLA topped South Carolina 3-0; and Oklahoma State handed Michigan State a 5-1 defeat on a three-hitter by Tina Schell.

On Friday, OSU lost to the Missouri Tigers 5-1, but the Cowgirls then eliminated top-seeded New Mexico 5-2 that night after the Lobos had beaten Illinois State 1-0 Friday morning. So the top-seeded Lobos limped home frustrated at 1-2, only one more win than in their 1980 appearance. In other losers bracket games, Texas A&M came back from its first-round loss to oust Western Michigan 1-0 in eleven innings, keeping the Aggies' championship hopes alive. A&M pitcher Lori Stoll and Western Michigan ace Bonni Kinne went all-out before the Aggies finally scored. UCLA eliminated Creighton 2-1. Utah State sent UCLA to the losers bracket 1-0 early on Friday with winning hurler Ramm hitting a solo home run in the bottom of the sixth. Two of Friday's games were postponed until Saturday morning because of a tornado watch, with Cal State-Berkeley to play a never-say-die Cal State-Fullerton team and Utah State to face Missouri.

On Saturday, OSU was eliminated by UCLA in a shutout, with the Bruins also shutting out Texas A&M and Cal State-Berkeley to earn a spot in the losers bracket final against Cal State-Fullerton. The die-hard Cal State-Fullerton team saw their three-game win streak, all in extra innings, ended by defending champ Utah State, after the Aggies had handed Missouri its first loss 4-2. So Cal-Fullerton dropped into the losers bracket. Undefeated Utah State coach Lloydene Searle said after her team's win over the Titans: "I'm very pleased with the team's performance tonight. Everyone played great and performed well in pressure situations." Asked whether she would prefer to play UCLA or Cal-Fullerton on Sunday, Searle said confidently: "It doesn't really matter. We've beaten both of them, so we're going to be ready."

Texas A&M on Saturday eliminated Michigan State 3-2 and Missouri 1-0 before losing to UCLA 1-0. So the stage was set for Sunday's play, with UCLA to square off with Cal State-Fullerton for the right to play the undefeated Utah State Aggies for the title.

The two California teams clashed on Sunday morning, with the Titans scoring four runs in the third inning to take the lead for good over UCLA. The Bruins scored in the final inning to make things tight, but ultimately succumbed to the Titans 5-4. The Cal-Fullerton team had played throughout the women's series with grit, determination and guts. They next needed to win the first of the championship title games, forcing the if-necessary game. They did easily, whacking Utah State 6-1—the Aggies' first loss of the tournament.

The final game proved as hard-fought as the Titan's pathway through the tournament. After falling behind Utah State 1-0 on Kerry Himmelspach's RBI double in the second inning, the Titans took the lead in the fourth inning when first baseman Sue Lewis hit Ramm's first pitch over the center-field fence for a two-run home run. Pam Edde was already on base after hitting a single with one out. The home run was Lewis' third of the tournament, and she ended with an impressive .636 batting average (14-for-22), tops in the tournament.

The one-run lead didn't last long, however, as Utah State scored two unearned runs in the bottom of the fourth inning. The Aggies loaded the bases with one out when Robin Petrini hit a roller back to Edde on the mound. Edde threw home to get Himmelspach and an attempt was made to double off Petrini at first. But Lewis bobbled the throw, and two runs scored as she threw wildly to home in an attempt to catch the runner coming from second. Titan coach Judi Garman filed a protest, arguing that Petrini interfered with Lewis on the play. The protest committee met for twenty-three minutes but disallowed the protest. As a disappointed Garman walked away from the officials, a fan asked her if she had won her argument. "Yes and no," Garman replied. The Titan coach believed she had proved her case but the decision still went against her.

The Aggies took their 3-2 lead and added an insurance run in the fifth inning. As it did throughout the tournament, Fullerton gamely fought back and came within a run in the top of the seventh. But the battling Titans finally ran out of innings. Utah State ended the Titans' hopes with a double play by Arvizu to end the inning and the game. So the game's final score: Aggies 4, Titans 3. Utah State repeated as national champions. Ramm had gone the distance for the Aggies, fanning five and allowing four hits as she won her fifth game of the tournament. Terry Keasling had started for the Titans with Edde, the losing hurler, replacing her in the fourth inning.

# 1981 Final Standings

| | |
|---|---|
| Utah State University (Logan) | 5-1 |
| California State University (Fullerton) | 5-2 |
| University of California (Los Angeles) | 5-2 |
| Texas A&M University (College Station) | 4-2 |
| University of Missouri (Columbia) | 2-2 |
| University of California (Berkeley) | 2-2 |
| Michigan State University (E. Lansing) | 2-2 |
| Oklahoma State University (Stillwater) | 2-2 |
| University of Oklahoma (Norman) | 1-2 |
| Creighton University (Omaha, Neb.) | 1-2 |
| University of New Mexico (Albuquerque) | 1-2 |
| Western Michigan University (Kalamazoo) | 1-2 |
| University of South Carolina (Columbia) | 0-2 |
| New Mexico State University (Las Cruces) | 0-2 |
| Rutgers University (New Brunswick, N.J.) | 0-2 |
| Illinois State University (Normal) | 0-2 |

Utah State joined Arizona State and John F. Kennedy College as the only teams to win back-to-back national softball titles. But this was not an easy year for rookie coach Searle and the Aggies, who finished the season 34-12. Searle, a former Aggie athlete from North Ogden, Utah, had been hired to take over the defending national champions at her alma mater. "It was a very tough year," Searle said. "We started the season by losing a number of games by one run. Everybody was out to beat the defending champions and would play their best game against you. It was not a cake walk."

Searle had eight new faces on a fourteen-player roster. The biggest challenge had been getting back to the championship series. "Once we got that at-large bid, you could feel we belonged there, that we were going to play our best," Searle said years later. "They really believed they could do it again. And we went and did it."

## Life After the WCWS...

Utah State's **Lloydene Searle** coached at Utah State for seventeen years. She left with a 505-369-2 record and guided the Aggies to four national tournament appearances, while also winning the first High Country Athletic Conference and first Big West Conference championships. In 2013 she was coaching at Indiana Tech in Fort Wayne, Ind. "I was born and raised, my heart was an Aggie," Searle said. "I am forever grateful to have had that opportunity at Utah State." Cal State-Fullerton's **Sue Lewis** was a four-year (1981-84) hitting star from softball's pitching-dominant era, which was before the mound was moved back and the ball enlivened. She was a three-time ASA All-American (1981-82 and 1984) and had a career batting average of .354 with twenty-five home runs and 138 RBIs in an era when many teams hit less than twenty home runs per year. In Titan career rankings as of 2013, she remained first in singles (257), doubles (53), and triples (20); and second in slugging percentage (.585), walks (89) and runs (149). In 2011 she was inducted into the Cal State-Fullerton Athletic Hall of Fame.

## 1982: A&M Wins Their First—and AIAW's Last

As the twelve teams gathered for the fourteenth Women's College World Series, scheduled for May 20-23 at Reaves Park in Norman, dark clouds hung over the AIAW's national championship—literally and figuratively. Heavy rains had caused flooding throughout central Oklahoma, and the start of the tournament appeared in jeopardy right up until the first game on Thursday afternoon. But the series had weathered soggy conditions many times before. The even darker clouds over the tournament, however, would prove fatal for all future AIAW national softball championships.

Most of softball's national powers had opted to play in the first NCAA Women's College World Series in Omaha, which would begin the week following the AIAW tournament in Norman. With their 77-8 season record, Texas A&M could have been a contender in Omaha—maybe even the top seed—against perennial softball powers like UCLA and Fresno State. The Aggies had been invited to the NCAA's first national tournament, but chose not to go. A&M coach Bob Brock had high respect for the eleven-year-old AIAW, even as the NCAA began to overshadow it. Out of a sense of loyalty to the AIAW, Brock said, his school chose the 1982 Norman championship over the NCAA's first in Omaha.

Only one college softball team in 1982 had a chance to win both national championships—the Oklahoma State Cowgirls, who had an at-large berth in both events. Coach Sandy Fischer's team had swept two games from Cal-Poly Pomona to qualify in the competition between the final eight teams at the NCAA tournament. But the ambitious Cowgirls chose to play in both Norman and Omaha. California State-Berkeley coach Bonnie Johnson, competing in Norman with her Golden Bears, admired the Cowgirls' spirit. "Never again will there be a chance to go to two national championships and win both," she said. "That would be a true national champion."

"Different coaches would say different things," Fischer said at the time. "Some would say this is too much. If we were still in school, I would agree." But the Cowgirls had been finished with semester exams for two weeks. They were ready for a different kind of test, and it started the afternoon of May 20 against Western Illinois. They handled the Illinois team roughly with a 7-0 thrashing, then dispatched No. 2-seed Utah by a score of 2-0 later that evening. Another team advancing in the winners bracket on the first day's play was the surprising newcomer, the U.S. International University Gulls. They opened with a win over Ohio State, then scored a stunning 1-0 upset in eight innings over top-seeded Texas A&M that evening. Gull freshman pitcher Jenny Stallard hurled a perfect game against the suddenly reeling Aggies. Fourth-seeded Michigan stayed in the winners bracket with a 4-1 win over Rhode Island, and third-seeded Cal-Berkeley advanced with a 5-0 win over Central Michigan.

OSU continued to clean up, sending Berkeley to the losers bracket on Friday after the Cowgirls scored the game's only runs when three base runners crossed home plate in the third inning after a bad throw to first by the Golden Bear third baseman. On Saturday, the Cowgirls sent Michigan to the losers bracket with a 2-1 loss. So Fischer's OSU crew finished play Saturday at 4-0 in the tournament, the only undefeated team after the dust—or mud—settled that night. The Cowgirls seemed to be playing like they were in a hurry to catch a bus to another tournament—which they were.

Meanwhile, desperate Texas A&M had been battling out of the deep hole they had been pushed into with their opening-game loss. On Friday the Aggies eliminated Southwest Missouri 2-0, then did the same to Western Illinois 1-0. The charging A&M team knocked off Cal-Berkeley 5-0 Saturday morning and eliminated Central Michigan 2-0 later that same day. On Sunday morning, the rejuvenated Aggies squared off with Michigan for the right to meet the Cowgirls in the title game. A&M got hot in the fifth inning, scoring a run and then adding four more on a grand slam by Josie Carter. Shan McDonald pitched the 5-0 win for the Aggies. A&M, now 5-1, was scheduled to play the unbeaten Cowgirls for the title at 5:30 Sunday afternoon, but rainy weather that had threatened play since the first day

**Coach Bob Brock and his 1982 Aggies were one of the top-ranked teams in the nation in 1982 and passed on the opportunity to play that year in the first NCAA national softball championship in Omaha. They opted to play at the final AIAW national softball championship at Reaves Park in Norman, which they won. The Aggies edged out the Oklahoma State Cowgirls, who left the next day for Omaha to play in their second national championship tournament in the same week. *(Photo courtesy of the Texas A&M Athletic Dept.)***

## 1982 Final Standings

| | |
|---|---|
| Texas A&M University (College Station) | 7-1 |
| Oklahoma State University (Stillwater) | 4-2 |
| University of Michigan (Ann Arbor) | 2-2 |
| Central Michigan University (Mount Pleasant) | 4-2 |
| U.S. International University (San Diego, Calif.) | 2-2 |
| University of California (Berkeley) | 1-2 |
| University of Rhode Island (Kingston) | 1-2 |
| Western Illinois University (Macomb) | 1-2 |
| University of Oklahoma (Norman) | 1-2 |
| University of Utah (Salt Lake City) | 0-2 |
| Southwest Missouri State University (Springfield) | 0-2 |
| Ohio State University (Columbus) | 0-2 |

finally brought the proceedings to a halt.

The rains on Sunday continued on Monday, and the OSU-A&M title match was postponed for the second straight day. Contingency plans were made to play on the OU football team's artificial turf at Owen Field in Memorial Stadium on Tuesday. Sandy Fischer had expected to be with her team on a bus headed to Omaha at 7 a.m. Tuesday, but instead she was looking over the wet fields at Reaves Park and worrying about having to play on Owen Field. "They did this one time (played on an artificial surface) when the tournament was held in Omaha and it was terrible," she said. "The winner of today's game will be which team can play the crazy bounce." Tournament director Marita Hynes announced that if the conditions were too wet to play on Tuesday, OSU would be declared the winner of the national championship, as A&M was coming out of the losers bracket.

Crews had the field at Reaves Park in good enough shape for play by 1:30 p.m., however, and the two teams began the contest. A&M needed to win twice, while OSU could take the championship with one win—then hightail it to Omaha. In the first game, the Aggies jumped out to a lead early and added on in the seventh for the 4-1 win. Still, OSU had another chance to win and get out of town. And that looked likely going into the seventh inning of play of the second game with OSU ahead 3-2. But the Aggies got help with a double from Mary Lou Youngblood, then more help from an error by Cowgirl right fielder Paula Smith to tie it up. The Aggies scored two more in the top of the eighth on a double by Shannon Murray. OSU came up empty in their last two at-bats in the 5-3 Aggie win.

So A&M made it seven straight to take the final AIAW national softball championship. It made for a bitter dose for the Cowgirls. Nancy Teehee played on that OSU team and remembered taking the final loss to A&M plenty hard—despite the Cowgirls' taking home the runner-up trophy. "We had a team that was mentally tough and fought hard," she said. "We were used to winning and did not accept losing very well." Teehee and her teammates hustled back north the eighty-five miles to Stillwater to do their laundry and catch a 7 a.m. bus to Omaha the next morning.

Texas A&M won the final AIAW national softball championship. Bob Brock and his Aggies took their first national-title trophy back to College Station. They had developed a taste for more.

AIAW officials announced at the tournament's end the organization's first and last Division I All-American softball team. Any player from a member institution was eligible for the team regardless of which championship her institution played. The nine players selected were: Oklahoma State's Kim Fabian (C), and Pam Harper (1B); Cal-State Fullerton's Kathy Van Wyk (P), and Sue Lewis (OF); Utah State's Yolanda Arvizu (2B); Central Michigan's Cathy Heator (3B) and Linda Pagett (P); Utah's Cindy Lyon (SS); Western Illinois's Pat Stoffel (OF); Texas A&M's Karen Guerrero (OF) and Lori Stoll (at-large); UCLA's Dot Richardson (at-large); and Cal-Berkeley's Shari Fisher (at-large).

## Life After the WCWS...

Pitcher **Linda Pagett** of Central Michigan had a career record of 50-15 from 1979-1982. She fanned 486 batters in 459.2 innings, and had thirty-three shutouts and five no-hitters. Pagett was named an AIAW All-American for her 1982 season and was named the Mid-American Conference's Female Athlete of the Decade for the 1980s. In 1993 she was inducted into the Central Michigan University Hall of Fame. **Pat Stoffel's** .430 batting average ranks second in Western Illinois University history for a single season. She was a Broderick Award nominee her junior and senior years. In 1999 she was inducted into the Western Illinois University Hall of Fame.

# *Four*

(1982-1987)

৵৵৵৵

# Back to Omaha With the NCAA

T HE RETURN OF THE WOMEN'S COLLEGE WORLD SERIES to Omaha in late May 1982 would not have seemed extraordinary if not for the completion of the AIAW Division I national softball championship only the week before in Norman, Okla. Local tournament organizers in Omaha had talked about the possibility of the event's return from the time AIAW officials announced in 1978 that it would be moved to Norman, Okla., in 1980. But few at that time could have imagined the tumultuous events in women's collegiate sports that would take place between the departure of the championship series and its return just three years later.

Just six months after the 1979 tournament in Omaha ended, the Department of Health, Education and Welfare (HEW) issued its final policy interpretations of Title IX. "The law of the land in relation to girls' and women's athletics is stronger than anyone could have hoped for in their wildest dreams," AIAW president Carole Mushier exulted at the time. Soon after this speech, however, some AIAW officials' joy turned to anger—and deep concern. After an NCAA special committee reported that it would be possible for the governing body of men's college sports to financially and administratively accommodate women's sports, officials at the organization floated proposals to start NCAA-sanctioned women's national championships at small and medium-sized schools. Five championship events for Division II and III schools were considered for initiation in the 1981-1982 academic year. Officials at AIAW strenuously opposed these proposals as an infringement, but at the NCAA national meeting in January 1980 in New Orleans, the proposals passed. Most AIAW officials understood that the very survival of their organization was at stake.

Throughout 1980 these proposals were intensely debated, as both the AIAW and the NCAA argued their respective positions in correspondence with university officials. The NCAA's leadership maintained that Title IX requirements for equality in men and women's sports could be better achieved through unitary administration of athletics at member schools. The predominantly male organization proposed the inclusion of hundreds of women into the administration of the NCAA to help with the oversight of women's programs, including approximately 225 women to serve on NCAA committees. Finally, the NCAA argued, schools would not be forced to enter their women's teams in NCAA events. They could choose for themselves. If they chose NCAA championships, perhaps it was because they would receive something the AIAW did not provide.

The AIAW argued that the NCAA's plans were unwarranted and could prove chaotic. Women's intercollegiate athletics were already well served by the AIAW, with thirty-five championships in seventeen different sports. Confusion could result from schools' choosing to participate in both organizations' championships, with different rules for these competitions. But the women's group's most heartfelt arguments against NCAA involvement in women's collegiate sports concerned philosophical differences. The AIAW prided itself in being an advocacy group both for and of female coaches and administrators, and with the best interests of student-athletes in mind. It strove for equality with—but separation from—men's college sports programs.

AIAW and NCAA officials clearly understood that many schools could be wooed with payment of expenses related to women's championships—a benefit the AIAW could not afford. But this was exactly the benefit the NCAA soon offered schools to participate in their events. The NCAA's annual operating budget at this time exceeded $20 million; the AIAW's budget was under $1 million. And unlike the NCAA, which brought in millions annually from television contracts for its major tournaments, the AIAW had barely begun negotiations for these kinds of agreements. The primary source of revenue for the women's organization came from the membership dues of its affiliated schools.

Supporters and opponents of the proposals to incorporate women's sports into the NCAA were primed for debate at the NCAA national meeting in January 1981. But in addition to the previous proposals for NCAA national championships in Division II and III women's sports, new proposals were made at the national meeting to initiate nine NCAA women's championships in Division I and to set aside seats for women on NCAA committees. After rancorous debate, all these proposals passed. The NCAA would begin offering women's championships in all divisions for the 1981-1982 academic year.

Not all women from the AIAW were opposed to NCAA involvement in women's sports. Former AIAW president Judith Holland saw it as inevitable and was not convinced that the AIAW would be destroyed. She became one of the women who helped to design the new NCAA women's championships. Creighton University softball coach and women's athletic director Mary Higgins was another. Just two months after the NCAA national meeting concluded, she was named the head of the NCAA's national women's softball committee. "The NCAA has tremendous resources available in terms of sponsoring championships and providing full-time staff members," Higgins said a few months after being named the chair of the NCAA softball committee. She was especially gratified that the NCAA would pay expenses for teams competing in national tournaments—expenses that the AIAW had no funds to cover.

University of Nebraska at Omaha's women's athletic director Connie Claussen, who had directed the Women's College World Series in its first decade, joined Higgins in the NCAA at this same time as sub-chair on the Division II national softball committee. Claussen said that she was upbeat about the NCAA's involvement in national championships for women. "When it comes to championship travel, I've always had mixed emotions when we qualified for tournaments," she said. "I had to wonder where am I going to get $5,000 or $10,000 to fly somewhere. With the NCAA picking up the expenses, it's going to be much more exciting when we qualify." Claussen said that she was also impressed with the quick response from NCAA staff when she called their national office for information. "The AIAW doesn't have the finances to hire the people in the national office to answer those questions," she said.

In addition to financial help with team expenses and administrative support, the NCAA offered something else that Higgins and Creighton University were interested in at the time—the return of softball's Division I national championship to Omaha. In November 1981, the NCAA announced that Creighton would serve as host school for the "NCAA Division I College Softball World Series" in late May 1982. The event would be at Seymour Smith Softball Complex, not at Dill Softball Center where the tournament had been held throughout the 1970s. Higgins would head the local organizing committee along with several officials with the Omaha City Parks and Recreation Department. Renovations were planned at the complex for the championship's return in 1982.

Meanwhile, many colleges could read the handwriting on the wall and began switching their memberships for women's athletics to the NCAA. By June 1981, the AIAW had lost 20 percent of their membership, and some who renewed said they would opt to play in NCAA championships in the upcoming academic year. The cream of the AIAW Division I schools had been lured away. Events worsened for AIAW when ESPN and NBC television networks announced that they were opting out or limiting planned coverage of AIAW championship events. Finally— and fatally for the AIAW—the NCAA earmarked some $3 million to subsidize their women's championship events in 1982, more than three times the AIAW's entire annual operating budget.

AIAW officials took legal action, first with an injunction to stop the NCAA and then with an anti-trust suit. Both actions failed, and the AIAW closed its doors. AIAW president Donna Lopiano said in 1982 that she believed the women's athletic group was a victim of its own success. "Without money, without position, from scratch," she recounted, "we (AIAW) became too powerful, too threatening for the status quo in intercollegiate athletics to allow us to continue to do our thing." And, perhaps, the AIAW's "separate but equal" model was incongruous with the HEW regulation's requirement of "equal athletic opportunity for both sexes." The very concept of "separate but equal" had been in disfavor with U.S. courts since the 1950s. Still, the women administrators of the AIAW had done a great service for women's college athletic programs in the 1970s and should be remembered for their pioneering efforts.

As chagrined as many AIAW officials and some of their members were at the time, their concerns about women's college sports being forced to the back of the bus were soon assuaged. Too much had happened by the early 1980s in society's acceptance of women's competitive athletics. Women's teams would continue to expand and improve in the 1980s—even under the governance of the former "men only" NCAA. A gender revolution was quietly—and sometimes loudly—taking place in sports. Just five years before the national softball championship returned to Omaha, less than 10 percent of high school girls participated in competitive sports; by 1982 their participation had jumped to 35 percent. And by the academic year 1981-1982, 10,000 young women at more than 700 colleges and universities received athletic grants. The number ten years earlier: zero. This revolution continued throughout the 1980s in a variety of women's college sports, softball included.

Growing national interest in college softball was highlighted a year after the women's series returned to Omaha in a May 1983 Sports Illustrated magazine feature. The article showcased UCLA pitchers Tracy Compton and Debbie Doom and their expected domination of upcoming competition in the "championship at the NCAA finals" in Omaha. Throughout the 1980s, the times kept changing for the better in women's college sports—and for the Women's College World Series.

## 1982: UCLA Wins First NCAA Championship

Just two days after the final AIAW national championship for softball ended, the NCAA held its first softball championship in Omaha, the AIAW's previous site for the tournament from 1969-1979. The year would be double the fun—or perhaps heartbreak—for Oklahoma State University. Coach Sandy Fischer's Cowgirls would spend a wild fortnight preparing for, driving to, and playing in both the AIAW and NCAA tournaments. The OSU team had joined eleven other teams for play at the AIAW championship on May 20 at Reaves Park in Norman, including top-seeded Texas A&M and second-seeded University of Utah. The Cowgirls had just missed the AIAW national championship title in a final-game heartbreaker to Texas A&M on May 25.

"We were devastated," Fischer recalled years later. "Then we took our bus back to Stillwater, and a day later we were back on the bus headed to Omaha for the NCAA's first softball championship. It was a crazy short turnaround time." The OSU Cowgirls have the distinction of being one of the few—if not the only—Division I schools to play in two national championships for the same sport in the same week!

The NCAA's first Women's College World Series began Thursday, May 27, at Omaha's Seymour Smith Softball Complex. The NCAA had invited eight teams to the double-elimination championship following play at five regional tournaments. Omaha's Creighton University served as the host school, and Creighton softball coach Mary Higgins directed the tournament.

The sanctioning of the championship by the NCAA wasn't the only difference in 1982. Softball appeared to be well on its way to acceptance as a part of the college sports scene, whether in Norman, Okla., or Omaha, Neb. This was evident from the crowds making their way to Seymour Smith Park on opening night. Police turned cars away when lots filled, and people parked two and three deep along Harrison Street. Even the temporary outfield bleachers were filled with the crowd massing more than an hour before the Creighton-Nebraska game. "I wasn't expecting a crowd (3,430) like this for opening night," said Cindy Smith, assistant director of women's championships for the NCAA. "Now, I'd anticipate crowds similar to this for the rest of the World Series, particularly after seeing these games tonight."

Three of the four opening games went extra innings. Two of these included Arizona State versus top-seeded Cal State-Fullerton and second-seeded UCLA against the haggard, but game, Oklahoma State Cowgirls. Arizona State ended Titan pitcher Kathy Van Wyk's chances of an undefeated season, winning 2-0 in nine innings. "It hurts," said Van Wyk, who entered the tournament 33-0. "I didn't plan on going undefeated. (But) it's better to lose now at the beginning of nationals." UCLA then went thirteen innings against Oklahoma State, with the Bruins squeaking by 2-1 on Barb Young's RBI single to left field. The Cowgirls had a 1-0 lead with a run in the second before UCLA tied the score at 1-1 in the seventh. The UCLA run in the seventh came with two outs and after the throw to first was dropped by the Oklahoma State first baseman.

The two evening games matched two local teams, Creighton and the University of Nebraska, and women's series debutant Fresno State matched with Western Michigan. The Huskers, who had not played in the women's series since 1971, were extended to eight innings before edging Creighton 3-2 on junior Deanne Carr's RBI single, scoring Andrea Casella, who had singled with two out. Western Michigan ace hurler Bonni Kinne allowed four hits in keeping alive her unbeaten season (17-0) while welcoming newcomer Fresno State with a 5-0 loss and concluding the opening round.

Four games were scheduled on Friday, two each in the losers and winners brackets, but Mother Nature prevailed and rain prevented play. The games were moved to Saturday, making for a long day with pitchers holding the upper hand. Only one of the losing teams scored a run, Creighton in its 4-1 loss in eight innings to Cal State-Fullerton. In the other losers bracket game, Fresno State ended Oklahoma State's crazy post-season by a 1-0 score in fourteen innings. "To this day many players on that team are very close and lifetime friends," Fischer said thirty years later. "In the end and in spite of the heartbreak, it was a great year."

Besides Oklahoma State and Creighton's elimination Saturday, Nebraska and Western Michigan lost twice, leaving four teams in contention for the championship on Sunday. Western Michigan lost to UCLA by the closest of margins, 1-0, and to Cal State Fullerton in eight innings with the same score, while Nebraska lost 2-0 to Arizona State and 1-0 to Fresno State. Nebraska and Western Michigan each finished 1-2. No-hitters were hurled against Western Michigan in both games, with Kinne taking these losses to finish the season 17-2. She lost to UCLA's Debbie Doom and Tracy Compton. Compton hurled until the fourth inning when she left with a pulled muscle in her pitching shoulder. Doom struck out seven to finish the game. Cal State-Fullerton pinch-hitter Terry Keasling had the game-winning RBI in the second game—a single to center field in the eighth inning.

Sunday's play matched Fresno State against Arizona State and undefeated UCLA against archrival Cal State-Fullerton. The tournament was scheduled to end Sunday, but heavy morning rain forced officials to revise the schedule with a doubleheader Sunday night. UCLA had extra motivation—the Titans had won the last eleven games between the two teams over the past two years.

UCLA coach Sharron Backus selected Doom for pitching duties, and the tall hurler came through again, pitching a six-hit shutout in the 1-0 win in ten innings. Backus was nearly beside herself following the victory. "It's just beyond words what I feel right now," she said. "It's like we had a monkey on our back. It wasn't that they were dominating us or anything else. We couldn't get that run across to win." The only run that UCLA needed came in the bottom of the tenth inning. Barbara Young had gotten on base with her third hit of the game off losing hurler Pam Edde, when catcher Barbara Booth hit a single to right field. The ball skidded past Fullerton right fielder Julie Anderson, who was charged with an error, with Young coming all the way around to score. After Anderson's throw back to the infield, she

**The 1982 UCLA Bruins, coached by Sharron Backus at upper left, won the first NCAA national softball championship in Omaha with a perfect 5-0 record. With outstanding pitching by Debbie Doom, front row center, the Bruins made no fielding errors in their five games. *(Photo courtesy of the UCLA Athletic Dept.)***

slumped to her hands and knees on the soggy grass. She stayed motionless for several moments, while UCLA began a jubilant celebration on the infield. "It's a hard way to lose," said Fullerton coach Judi Garman. "Like somebody said, the odds had to swing around some time."

Fresno State gained redemption after its opening loss, winning three straight games and eliminating Arizona State 4-1. "We felt embarrassed," said Fresno State coach Donna Pickel. "We felt we had a lot to prove." The Bulldogs made it happen with aggressive hitting. Eight players got hits against ASU. After loading the bases in the first inning and not scoring, the Bulldogs tallied four runs in the fourth on five singles, a walk and an ASU error. ASU scored only on a home run in the seventh inning by Shawn Ritchey, the first of the tournament in 1982. Wende Ward got the win, allowing five hits with Casarez taking the loss. The game advanced the precocious Bulldogs to the championship round on Monday, needing to beat the undefeated veteran Bruins twice for the title.

The opposing coaches stayed with the pitchers that got them to the championship round, Doom and Ward. A crowd of 1,570 watched as they engaged in a pitching duel with no runs scored through seven innings. "I knew it was just a matter of time before my teammates were going to give me a run," said Doom. "I had to make sure the other team didn't get the run first." Her Bruin teammates did their part in the eighth when Ward, who had allowed only a single by Gina Vecchione in the fourth, walked Stacy Winsberg and Karen Owens. UCLA's Backus was not going to let something happen; she was going to make something happen. She ordered a double steal. "I felt it was time to create something," she said after the game. "Fortunately I saw their shortstop over a step or two and we had good wheels on second. I said, 'What the heck. If they throw her out, we've still got a runner in scoring position on second base.'"

Both runners advanced safely. Winsberg then scored from third on Debbie Hauer's sacrifice fly. Fresno right fielder Kim Muratore was charging Hauer's fly ball and had a chance to nail Winsberg at home—but her throw was off. The Bruins added an insurance run in the eighth, scoring after an error on a ball hit by Vecchione. Ward fanned eight and Doom sat down twelve in her 2-0 win, finishing the tournament with sixty-three strikeouts in forty-one innings over the four days. "I can't say I didn't get tired," said Doom, whose knee bothered her that day. "It's bound to happen when you pitch that much in a short period of time."

UCLA finished the year 33-7-2, allowing only eighteen runs all season and no runs in the last forty-three innings of the tournament. They made no errors in the five games, for a sparkling fielding percentage of 1.000. Doom finished 11-2 and was named to the all-tournament team along with her teammates, Booth, Young, Vecchione and shortstop Dottie Richardson, who had transferred to UCLA in 1981 from Western Illinois. Joining the Bruin players on the all-tournament team were Cal State-Fullerton's Janet Lloyd, Pam Newton and Jan Pierini; and Fresno State's Kim Muratore. Despite the rain, the 1982 tournament drew 14,433. The first NCAA Women's College World Series was history.

## 1982 Women's College World Series Bracket
Omaha, Neb. • May 27-31

## 1982 Final Standings

| | |
|---|---|
| University of California (Los Angeles) | 5-0 |
| California State University (Fresno) | 3-2 |
| California State University (Fullerton) | 2-2 |
| Arizona State University (Tempe) | 2-2 |
| University of Nebraska (Lincoln) | 1-2 |
| Western Michigan University (Kalamazoo) | 1-2 |
| Oklahoma State University (Stillwater) | 0-2 |
| Creighton University (Omaha, Neb.) | 0-2 |

## Life After the WCWS...

Cal State Fullerton's **Kathy Van Wyk** enjoying a phenomenal 1982 season with a 35-1 mark and a 0.18 ERA. The victories remain a single-season record at Cal State Fullerton, and her .972 winning percentage was an NCAA Division I record (thirty or more decisions) until 2001 when Jennie Finch of Arizona went 32-0. Her ERA is eighth-best in Division I history and her thirty-three-game winning streak remains a record. Van Wyk was coaching at San Diego State University in 2013.

# 1983: Texas A&M Wins Its First NCAA Title

As the sponsor for the only national collegiate softball championship in 1983, the National Collegiate Athletic Association had clear title to the year's Women's College World Series, held again in Omaha. The Association of Intercollegiate Athletics for Women had held its last national softball championship the year before in Norman, Okla. The AIAW had passed the championship's torch to the larger, better-funded NCAA, but not before the rapidly declining women's group had guided the women's series through a decade of steady growth.

The benefits of the NCAA's money and media-contacts had been evident in the publicity and record attendance in the previous year's tournament in Omaha. The 1982 event's large-school softball programs and exciting, well-played games—including eight that went extra innings—left the fans and teams wanting more. Along with all the new hoopla came more national media attention on women's college softball, including articles in Sports Illustrated and People magazines. Much of the media attention in 1983 was focused on last year's winner, the University of California (Los Angeles). The Bruins had swept through the tournament undefeated, playing flawless defense. Although UCLA coach Sharron Backus appreciated the media coverage, she asked that her players be left alone on game days. "In one respect it's nice to have the notoriety," the veteran coach said, "but we've got some young kids who've never had much attention."

Play began Wednesday, May 25, at Seymour Smith Park, with the eight teams in the double-elimination tournament scheduled to finish play on Sunday, May 29. The tournament kicked off with two night games on Wednesday—Cal State Fullerton versus Indiana University followed by South Carolina against Texas A&M. In the opening contest, the Titans fell behind in the bottom of the first inning when Indiana's Terry DeLuca drove home Sue O'Callaghan and then scored on a double by Linda Thaler to give Indiana an early 2-0 lead. Falling behind wasn't anything that surprised Cal State coach Judi Garman: "We have a thing at our school called the Titan Coronary and tonight you saw evidence of why." Cal State Fullerton closed the gap when Elise King drove in JoAnn Ferrieri in the third inning, tied the score on Lisa Baker's RBI single in the fourth, and won the game 3-2 when O'Callaghan bobbled winning pitcher Susan LeFebvre's grounder to short in the seventh, allowing King to score.

In the late game Wednesday, South Carolina's Chris Diemer singled off A&M's Lori Stoll to start the sixth inning, and pinch runner Melissa Coulter moved to second on a sacrifice bunt by Lindi James. Sonya Smith hit a grounder up the middle and took second when no one covered the base. Stoll then threw a wild pitch and Coulter crossed the plate to score. Aggie star Stoll's next pitch was also wild, scoring Smith from third. That's all the scoring South Carolina needed for the 2-0 win. Stoll (26-7 coming to Omaha) allowed four hits and threw three wild pitches—two of them costly. Winning pitcher Darlene Lowery (21-2 coming in) gave up three hits and struck out four. Lowery drew praise from South Carolina coach Lou Piel, a former player in the women's series. "She handled the pressure well," Piel said. "There's nothing she can't do."

With 1,800 in attendance for the second day's play, UCLA took on Missouri and Louisiana Tech played University of the Pacific. UCLA right-hander Tracy Compton, who saw limited action in the 1982 tournament because of a shoulder injury, started against the Tigers and held them to one hit—a single in the fifth inning by Donna Sanitate. "That hit was stupid on my part," said Compton. "I messed up on a pitch." Losing pitcher was Teresa Wilson, who allowed six hits and held the Bruins off until the bottom of the seventh inning when Stacy Winsberg scored after Sheila Cornell's sharp grounder was misplayed by third baseman Sanitate. UCLA prevailed 1-0. Missouri coach Joyce Compton (no relation to Tracy), did not castigate Sanitate for the error. "Kids are human," she said, "and if they weren't it would take a lot of fun out of the game."

With both teams making their national championship debut, Louisiana Tech scored runs in the second and fifth innings in the second Thursday game to blank Pacific 2-0. Stacey Johnson allowed Pacific one hit in getting her twentieth win of the season against five losses. Johnson would face a sterner test the next day, when Tech faced defending champion UCLA in the winners bracket.

The two losers-bracket games led off on Friday, with Texas A&M battling Indiana at 1 p.m. The Aggies scored on an error in the bottom of the first inning against the Hoosiers to take the early lead. Then in the third, it appeared that the Hoosiers would tie the game when Sue O'Callaghan pounded a two-hopper to the right-field fence, scoring pinch runner Lori Sisti from first. But before the next pitch, A&M appealed, claiming that Sisti missed second on her way around the bases. The appeal was upheld and the run was negated, with O'Callaghan credited with a single. Indiana did not threaten again against the hard-throwing Stoll, who fanned eight and allowed only the two third-inning hits in the 1-0 win.

In the second losers-bracket game, Pacific scored the game's only run in the twelfth inning while playing Missouri when shortstop Barby Suttman hit a looping, dying drive just fair into left field for a double. Her sister, Becky, sacrificed, moving Barby to third. She scored moments later when Kari Johnson poked a single into right center. Teresa Wilson was the losing hurler for Missouri, striking out six. Shelley Mahoney fanned ten for the 1-0 win.

The first winners-bracket game on Friday featured Cal State Fullerton facing South Carolina at 6 p.m. Titan pitcher Susan LeFebvre frustrated her opposition, allowing only one hit in the game. Cal State scored runs in the first and fourth innings for the 2-0 win and to remain unbeaten.

The final evening game matched unbeatens, UCLA and Louisiana Tech. Debbie Doom fanned fifteen and gave up only four hits, with UCLA scoring all its runs in a huge, eight-run fourth inning. Shortstop Dot Richardson paced the UCLA offense with three hits in four at-bats and drove in a pair of runs, as did her teammate Stacy Winsberg. Stacey Johnson was the losing pitcher with Tami Cyr finishing up. Louisiana Tech made three errors in the 8-0 lop-sided contest, and only one of the eight runs by UCLA was earned.

Following its impressive win over Louisiana Tech, the UCLA team went to dinner late Friday, with a number of players ordering milk shakes. "I recall mine didn't taste all that great," remembered shortstop Richardson in her book, *Living The Dream*. "The next morning I woke up early," she wrote. "I didn't feel very well. I rushed to the bathroom and got sick." She soon heard that eight of the nine UCLA starters had symptoms of food poisoning. The sickened players took the small trash cans from their rooms to the game and developed a routine to handle emergencies. "If somebody got sick," Richardson said, "there would be one person to hold the hair back, one person would have a cold towel to compress on the back of the neck, one person would be holding the bucket. It was disgusting, but we had a national tournament game to play."

With the tournament down to six teams after Friday's play, two more were eliminated on Saturday. South Carolina's Darlene Lowery hurled a four-hitter as her teammates took advantage of two Pacific errors. South Carolina scored both its runs in the bottom of the fifth on RBI singles by Amy Lyons and Chris Diemer. After the two runs, Pacific closed the game to its final 2-1 margin with a run in the top of the sixth on Karen Hough's groundout that scored Kari Johnson. Shelley Mahoney was the losing pitcher for Pacific.

The second Saturday elimination occurred in the A&M-Louisiana Tech game. The Aggies started Shan McDonald instead of their ace, Lori Stoll, and McDonald responded with a three-hitter and eliminated Louisiana Tech 2-0. Stacey Johnson took the loss for Tech, striking out eight batters and allowing five hits. One of the hits was a two-run triple by Patti Holthaus in the top of the third inning, scoring Carrie Austgen and Cindy Cooper—the only runs A&M would need to stay alive in the losers bracket.

The sickened players of UCLA tried their best in the first winners-bracket game against Cal State Fullerton, but the food poisoning had taken its toll. After Cal State Fullerton took a four-run lead, coach Backus took out Compton, Sue Eskerski, and Richardson, sending them back to the hotel to see a doctor. The players were prescribed medicine and bed rest. While convalescing, Richardson got a call from UCLA assistant coach Sue Enquist inquiring on her condition. The shortstop learned that UCLA had lost to Cal State 6-1, the Bruins' first loss in the double-elimination tournament. So Richardson and the other two queasy players went to the field Saturday evening to face South Carolina in a do-or-die elimination game. Texas A&M would be facing Cal State Fullerton in the other game.

The fans got their money's worth in the UCLA-South Carolina game. The game was scoreless until the sixteenth as Darlene Lowery and Doom kept the opposing hitters from crossing home plate. Then in the top of the sixteenth, UCLA's Mary Ricks got aboard on an error and advanced to second when Priscilla Rouse's sacrifice bunt was mishandled by the Gamecock catcher. Rouse eventually scored on Stacy Winsberg's sacrifice fly to give UCLA a 1-0 lead. South Carolina, however, came right back and tied the game in the bottom of the inning on Cindy Long's double down the left field line, scoring Pat Dufficy, who had singled between third and shortstop. UCLA got the deciding run in the top of the seventeenth when Ricks squeeze-bunted home Sheila Cornell and Doom retired South Carolina in order in the bottom half of the inning. Cornell had singled to open the inning, advanced to second on a wild pitch, and went to third on Shelly Aquilar's single down the right field line. Doom fanned fifteen batters and gave up five hits while winning her eighteenth game of the season. Lowery allowed six hits and finished the year 23-4. So the Bruins took the 2-1 win after three and one-half hours of play.

In the last game on Saturday and needing a win to stay alive, A&M faced undefeated Cal State Fullerton. The only run of the game came in the bottom of the fourth when A&M's third baseman Cindy Cooper got aboard on a throwing error by pitcher JoAnn Ferrieri, then was sacrificed to second and scored on Iva Jackson's single to center field. Stoll and Ferrieri each fanned nine batters and allowed three hits. So A&M stayed alive with the 1-0 win. It was the Aggies' fourth consecutive win following their opening-game loss.

On Sunday, A&M next faced UCLA, with the winner facing Cal State Fullerton for the championship. A&M coach Bob Brock stayed with his ace, Stoll, who fanned eleven batters and walked two. A&M's Iva Jackson drove in the game's only run in the top of the fourteenth, bringing across Holthaus, who had tripled down the right field line with one out. The Bruins were held to five hits in the game and settled for third place. Doom was the UCLA loser, allowing seven hits and a 3-for-5 performance by A&M's Jackson. Doom fanned seventeen batters and walked three, concluding her season 18-5.

With four wins in a row, the Aggies needed to beat the once-beaten Titans to claim their first NCAA national championship. Again, Brock didn't change his pitcher. Stoll had gotten the team to the finals and her pitching in the final game would determine the NCAA champion for 1983. Stoll hurled well, allowing five hits and no runs as the Aggies scored twice in the top of the twelfth to win their first NCAA national title. The two runs the Aggies needed to win came when Cooper singled to right field and advanced to third when the ball got by right fielder Vera Bahr. Holthaus then singled off LeFebvre's leg, but Cooper—for some reason—held up at third. Iva Jackson was intentionally walked to load the bases. The Titans hoped to get a ground ball to turn a double play. They got the ground ball from Josie Carter, but second baseman Pam Newton bobbled it and then threw wildly home. Cooper and Holthaus scored the two unearned runs for the 2-0 final score. Stoll finished the year 30-7 with losing pitcher LeFebvre ending at 26-5.

Reflecting on the 1983 WCWS years later, A&M coach Brock said his team had felt good about their chances even after their first-game loss. Stoll gave the A&M players the confidence to battle through the losers bracket. "They were all pulling for her," Brock said. "They told her to just pitch and they would take care of everything else." And they did. After the opening loss, Stoll ended up just short of forty-two scoreless innings in an epic performance for the Aggies.

The championship game drew a crowd of 2,400. The overall attendance at the

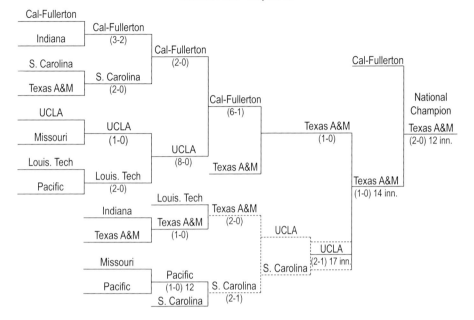

**1983 Women's College World Series Bracket**
Omaha, Neb. • May 25-29

## 1983 Final Standings

Texas A&M University (College Station)     5-1
California State University (Fullerton)     3-2
University of California (Los Angeles)     3-2
University of South Carolina (Columbia)     2-2
Louisiana Tech University (Ruston)     1-2
University of the Pacific (Stockton, Calif.)     1-2
University of Missouri (Columbia)     0-2
Indiana University (Bloomington)     0-2

event was 13,300. Stoll was one of four Aggies named to the all-tournament team. The others were Holthaus (2B), Cooper (3B) and Jackson (OF). Elise King (OF) and Bahr (at large) were chosen from Cal State Fullerton, while UCLA placed Cornell (1B), Richardson (SS) and Ricks (OF). Long (at large) of South Carolina completed the all-tournament squad. Vera Bahr of Cal-Fullerton batted .455 to lead all hitters.

## Life After the WCWS...

UCLA's **Dot Richardson** went on to an outstanding career, capped by leading the United States to gold medals in the 1996 and 2004 Olympics. Richardson hit the game-winning home run in the 3-1 win over China in the gold medal game in 1996. She was a fifteen-time ASA All-American and is a member of the ASA National Softball Hall of Fame. A licensed orthopedic surgeon in Florida, Richardson serves as medical director for the USA Triathlon National Training Center, a part of South Lake Hospital in Clermont. Texas A&M's **Lori Stoll** ended up with the most wins in A&M history (162-24, 0.34 ERA). In 1988, she was inducted into the Texas A&M University Athletic Hall of Fame. UCLA's **Sheila Cornell** was an NCAA All-American (1984) and played on various women's fastpitch teams. She twice was a member of the U.S. Olympic team (1996 and 2000) and is a member of the ASA National Softball Hall of Fame (2006), the ISF Softball Hall of Fame (2007), and the UCLA Sports Hall of Fame (1998).

## 1984: UCLA Wins Title on Mang's Home Run

The UCLA team swaggered into Omaha as the top seed in the 1984 national championship. Their dynamic pitching duo of Debbie Doom and Tracy Compton combined for thirty-nine wins against only five losses during regular season play before the women's series. But a strong Texas A&M team also came to town as defending champions. A year earlier, the Aggies had fought back from an opening loss to sweep their final six games and take home the title. Much of their success the year before, however, stemmed from the outstanding pitching performances of Lori Stoll, who completed her sterling collegiate career with that championship game. The Aggies and the Bruins would keep a perfect record against every team they faced at the 1984 tournament—except each other.

The fierce and thrilling competition at the 1984 women's series was complemented with improvements at the host facility, Seymour Smith Softball Complex. A $21,000 scoreboard had been added, courtesy of the Omaha Softball Association and the local Men's College World Series Committee. "I think it's a tremendous feature of the park," said tournament co-director Mary Higgins of host school Creighton. "It dresses up the facility and creates a big-time atmosphere." In addition to the new scoreboard, teams would now play on a smaller field, with the fences down the left-field and right-field lines moved from 210 feet to 190 feet. "The fence bellies out to 220 in center field because we don't want to eliminate the possibility of an extra-base hit," said Higgins. "We wanted to generate a little more possibility of a home run, not make it routine." In the 1983 tournament, first baseman Sheila Cornell of UCLA was the only player to hit a home run over the fence.

The event was assured of another good fan turnout with advance ticket sales of more than 14,500, well ahead of 1983 pre-tournament sales. Fans would be entertained by another strong field of eight teams, including—besides UCLA and A&M—Utah State, Cal Poly Pomona, Adelphi, Northwestern, Fresno State and local-favorite Nebraska. The opening games on Wednesday, May 23, saw UCLA facing Utah State and Northwestern against Adelphi in the second game.

Utah State had split a doubleheader against UCLA earlier in the year and was optimistic facing the Bruins. But the Aggies lost 6-0 as UCLA's Debbie Doom raised her pitching record to 21-2-1. Utah State loaded the bases against Doom in the second inning, but couldn't capitalize. She settled down and pitched a three-hitter with nine strikeouts. UCLA second baseman Jennifer Simm had the game's big blow—a grand slam in the sixth inning after UCLA had scored twice in the fifth. A junior college transfer from Fullerton College, Simm was overwhelmed and couldn't believe she had hit a grand slam—the first in NCAA softball championship history. "I'm just a base hitter," Simm said. "I don't hit big hits like that. I'm still asking people to pinch me." Simm's home run came off losing pitcher Kristie Skoglund, who allowed six hits.

In the second game before a crowd of 1,300, Northwestern had some anxious moments against Adelphi, although Wildcat hurler Lisa Ishikawa struck out seventeen. Ishikawa had set an NCAA record during the regular season with 414 strikeouts. The game was scoreless until the seventh inning when Northwestern's Lisa Koser scored on a fielder's choice. That's when Adelphi made the game exciting, when Terri Tucker, who had singled to open the inning, tried to steal home as Wildcat catcher Meg Hall was handing the ball to Ishikawa outside the pitching circle. But Ishikawa's throw to the plate was in time for the out, and she fanned the last two batters for the 1-0 win. "It got kind of scary," said Ishikawa (31-5 coming to Omaha). "Especially when the runner on first is the winning run. I was just praying that they wouldn't start hitting the ball then."

In the first game on Thursday, defending champion Texas A&M, which was shutout in its opener the year before, won 1-0 against Cal Poly Pomona in a game that started at 6:35 p.m. but was delayed by rain in the bottom of the twenty-third inning and did not end until Friday evening, which included six hours and 13 minutes of play over the two days. The game was decided in the twenty-fifth inning when Josie Carter doubled, then moved to third on a sacrifice by Cindy Cooper. Iva Jackson then walked. A&M pitcher Shawn Andaya, the next batter, hit a slow grounder to second. Years later Andaya reflected on the hit. "The second baseman actually stopped it, but she couldn't make a play on either myself or the girl going home. ... I think as soon as I hit the ball she (Carter) took off." Andaya pitched all twenty-five innings, striking out fifteen and allowing eleven hits. The twenty-five-inning marathon remains the longest game in women's series history.

In another Thursday game continued on Friday, local favorite Nebraska faced Fresno State with 2,600 in attendance. The game was carried over from Thursday because of the A&M-Cal Poly marathon. Twice Fresno State loaded the bases against Nebraska hurler Mori Emmons but could not capitalize. The Huskers scored two runs on an error in the sixth inning, which was all they needed for the win. Emmons appeared to get stronger as the game continued, but in the sixth she gave up a double to Nusheen Zaregar. Nebraska coach Wayne Daigle pulled her and replaced her with Sandy Wolterman, who earned a save in the 2-0 win.

Also on Friday, Adelphi eliminated Utah State 1-0 behind a perfect game pitched by Julie Bolduc (21-2 coming to Omaha). Bolduc's gem was aided by two spectacular outfield catches, one by center fielder Regina Dooley in the fourth and another in the seventh inning by right fielder Bella Totino. "I put the ball over the plate and they do the rest," said Bolduc, who hurled fifty-nine pitches and fanned two batters.

In the first game Saturday afternoon, Fresno State scored on a wild pitch in the twelfth to eliminate Cal Poly Pomona 1-0 with 564 in attendance. Next on Saturday, UCLA needed a home run in the bottom of the ninth by Tricia Mang to defeat Northwestern. The win by UCLA advanced them to play the winner of the Texas A&M-Nebraska game, which was the next contest on Saturday evening.

Nebraska and A&M had played four times in 1984, and each time A&M had won. Nebraska did not help its cause by making five errors, including two in the fourth inning when A&M scored three of their runs. The Aggies made it five in a row with the 5-2 win. "Five errors is too many to give up in a game against the defending champions," said Nebraska coach Daigle. "But we never quit and we won't tomorrow." The two night games drew a crowd of 3,385.

On Sunday, Nebraska stayed alive with a 2-1 win that eliminated Adelphi, but the tournament was postponed after that game because of rain. Earlier Sunday, Northwestern had eliminated Fresno State, 3-0 in eight innings. Nebraska was now set to play the loser of the upcoming Texas A&M-UCLA matchup, both teams with unblemished records.

Play continued on Monday, with Texas A&M and UCLA up first. The game remained scoreless until the eighth inning. Then the Aggies' Judy Trussell singled off first baseman Sheila Cor-

UCLA's Sheila Cornell greets Trish Mang, right, with a Bruin bear hug after Mang's championship winning home run against Texas A&M. Dejected Aggie catcher Gay McNutt looks away in the background. *(Reprinted with permission from the Omaha World-Herald)*

nell's glove, bringing in Patti Holthaus and Josie Carter. The runs were only the second and third earned runs Doom had allowed during the season. Andaya was winning hurler for A&M. Texas A&M defeated the mighty Bruins 2-0 and would now face Northwestern later Monday.

In the second game on Monday, Jennifer Simm again came through for UCLA, driving in the winning run in the eighth against Nebraska's Emmons, who finished 24-5, allowing seven hits with three strikeouts. The Huskers twice had runners on base in the second and fifth innings against Tracy Compton but didn't score. Compton allowed six hits, including three in the second when the Huskers loaded the bases. Doom relieved Compton in the fifth and held Nebraska to one hit while striking out five the remainder of the game. Still, UCLA coach Sharron Backus was displeased because UCLA had failed to take control of the game early. "We didn't play poorly, but we didn't go out and really take charge and take it," said Backus. "It was so close. A base hit ball or a live drive and you're out."

In the Texas A&M-Northwestern game late Monday, Aggie Cindy Foster singled in the bottom of the eleventh to end Ishikawa's bid for a perfect game. This was A&M's third extra-inning game of the tournament. The Aggies won the game in the thirteenth, loading the bases before Holthaus singled to right to score Trussell and the game's only run. Ishikawa fanned eighteen, finishing the year 33-7.

With the win, Texas A&M advanced to face UCLA on Tuesday with the Bruins needing two wins to claim the title, after losing to A&M the day earlier. Most softball followers expected it would be Debbie Doom against Shawn Andaya, and they were correct. And Doom got the best of Andaya and the Aggies, winning 1-0 on Trish Mang's single scoring Mary Ricks with the game's only run in the sixth inning. The Bruins got six hits off Andaya. Doom allowed only two hits and fanned five in forcing another game to determine the 1984 national champion.

In the if-necessary game it was again Doom, but the Aggies hurled Yvette Lopez, who was relieved by Andaya in the third inning. Andaya finished the game, going ten innings, giving up five hits and one earned run. She fanned three and walked one to conclude the year 33-9. The only run of the game came in the bottom of the thirteenth inning on a dramatic home run by UCLA's hot-hitting Mang, who had driven in the winning run in the previous game. Reflecting on that home run years later, Andaya said: "When I think of Trish Mang's homer, ouch—that still hurts today. ... I threw a flat rise ball to a big girl who was their number four hitter. That was stupid." Doom won again 1-0, allowing five hits and striking out fifteen batters. She finished the year 24-3.

It was Mang's second hit of the game and second home run of the tournament—and one that gave the Bruins their third women's series title. She finished with a .391 batting average, third best in the tournament behind Nebraska hitters Ann Schroeder (.455) and Peg Richardson (.500). Mang was named all-tournament as DH and was joined by teammates Doom, Leslie Rover (SS) and Jennifer Simm (2B). Completing the team were A&M's Andaya (P), Josie Carter (OF) and Gay McNutt (C); Adelphi's Regina Dooley (OF); Northwestern's Lisa Ishikawa (P); and

## 1984 Women's College World Series Bracket
### Omaha, Neb. • May 23-29

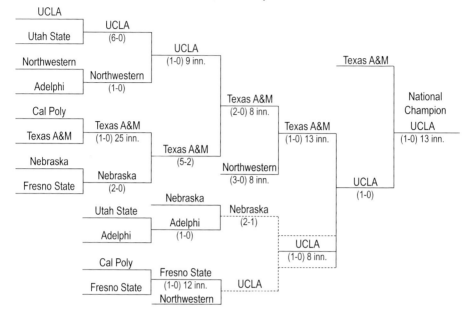

## 1984 Final Standings

| | |
|---|---|
| University of California (Los Angeles) | 5-1 |
| Texas A&M University (College Station) | 4-2 |
| University of Nebraska (Lincoln) | 2-2 |
| Northwestern University (Evanston, Ill.) | 2-2 |
| California State University (Fresno) | 1-2 |
| Adelphi University (Long Island, N.Y.) | 1-2 |
| California Polytechnic Pomona | 0-2 |
| Utah State University (Logan) | 0-2 |

Nebraska's Denice Feldhaus (1B), Peg Richardson (OF) and Ann Schroeder (3B).

## Life After the WCWS...

As of 2013, former Aggie coach **Bob Brock** was the head softball coach at Sam Houston State, his alma mater. His career coaching record in 2013 included 1,010 wins, 607 losses and one tie. In 2006, he was inducted into the Texas A&M Athletic Hall of Fame. UCLA's **Trish Mang** was a first-team NCAA All-American in 1984. She later transferred to San Diego State University and was inducted into the San Diego State Aztec Hall of Fame in 1988.

# 1985: Bruins Beat Local Favorite Nebraska

The six extra-inning games in the 1984 women's series, including the twenty-five-inning marathon between Texas A&M and Cal Poly Pomona, resulted in the NCAA's adoption of a "tiebreaker rule" for subsequent championship tournaments. This new rule called for a runner to be placed on second base as each team went to bat in extra innings of play. The rule was adopted to speed up the game and generate offense, said Mary Higgins, women's athletic director of host school Creighton University and co-director of the tournament with the school's sports information director, Ron Paradis. "It increases the possibility of scoring very quickly," said Higgins. "It puts tremendous pressure on the pitcher and defense." Cal Poly Pomona coach Carol Spanks, however, was one opposed to the new rule. "I detest it with a passion," she said. "I'm sorry it's being used in championship play."

The new rule's effect on the 1985 Women's College World Series would be determined over May 22-26 with a field of eight teams in Omaha, including defending champion UCLA, Cal Poly Pomona, top-ranked California State (Fullerton), Adelphi (the only unranked team), Utah, Nebraska, Northwestern and Louisiana Tech. Play began Wednesday night with a doubleheader: Cal State Fullerton against Adelphi and UCLA opposing Utah. In Thursday's games, Cal Poly Pomona would face Northwestern, and Nebraska would oppose Louisiana Tech, which had upset No. 2-ranked A&M in the regionals.

In the first game on Wednesday evening at Seymour Smith Softball Complex, Cal State Fullerton and Adelphi were scoreless after seven innings, so the tiebreaker rule quickly made its debut in the tournament. Leslie King of Cal State was placed at second base to start the eighth inning. Lisa Baker sacrificed her to third before JoAnn Ferrieri scored her with a single through the gap in left field. Cal State pitcher Debbie Mygind, a native of Auckland, New Zealand, retired twenty-three straight batters to get the 1-0 win after escaping a one-out, bases-loaded jam in the first inning. Mygind baffled the Panther batters, striking out eleven with her change-up and rise ball.

UCLA had played through an up-and-down regular season. Coach Sharron Backus expected a tough game from Utah in the Wednesday evening nightcap, and the Bruins got it. UCLA managed a game-winning run on a strange play in the fifth inning when Lisa Hankerd blooped a single to center field. Chris Olivie scored easily from third when center fielder Pipi Hollingsworth threw home with nobody covering the plate. Catcher Jean Mills had vacated home to back up third base. "We take a run if we can buy it at Sears on sale," Backus said following the game. UCLA pitcher Tracy Compton got the 1-0 win, allowing only a single in the third inning by Pati Rivas.

While pitching dominated the opening games on Wednesday, hitting held the spotlight in the remaining games on Thursday. Cal Poly trailed 3-2 against Northwestern before scoring four runs on four hits in the sixth inning. Cal Poly pitcher Rhonda Wheatley hurled a three-hitter and had one of four hits in the sixth inning—a two-run home run over left center for the final two runs. Lisa Ishikawa took the 6-3 loss for the Wildcats, hurling just over five innings, with Cathy Tawse finishing up.

In Thursday's second game, designated hitter Ginger Cannon had only one hit for Nebraska against Louisiana Tech, but it was a three-run triple with the bases loaded in the first inning. Nebraska's Lori Sippel hurled a no-hitter, walking three and striking out eleven. The Huskers scored four times in the first and twice in the third for the 6-0 win.

In the first game in the losers bracket Friday, Adelphi scored in the sixth inning against Utah when Regina Dooley came home on Mary Wallace's sacrifice fly. Losing pitcher was Teri Richardson in relief of Michelle Townsend. Adelphi pitcher Julie Bolduc allowed just two hits and three base runners while eliminating Utah 1-0. Utah was the first team ousted from the tournament.

The tiebreaker rule was used again in the second losers-bracket game when Louisiana Tech faced Northwestern. Northwestern scored in the eighth inning when Lisa Bruss squeeze-bunted home Amy Kekeisen, who had been placed at second base, then was sacrificed to third by Sue Koopman. It was all Northwestern needed to eliminate Tech 1-0. Northwestern's Lisa Ishikawa and losing pitcher Stacey Johnson each allowed three hits. "The tie-breaker rule is exciting, but it's not the way the game should be played," said Northwestern coach Sharon Drysdale.

Cal State Fullerton faced UCLA in the first winners-bracket game Friday evening. The Titans scored two runs on an RBI single by Lisa Baker in the third inning and a solo homer by Robin Goodin in the sixth inning. It was Goodin's first career home run. UCLA left fielder Stacy Winsberg crashed into the fence trying to catch the ball, and medical personnel rushed to her aid. She ultimately left the game under her own power. Mygind hurled a two-hitter for Cal State in the 2-0 shutout, striking out seven as the Titans beat Debbie Doom for the second time in the 1985 season.

In the Friday nightcap, Nebraska pitcher Mori Emmons allowed only a single into shallow center field by Cal Poly center fielder Shar Bilyeu in the third inning. Emmons' battery mate Lisa Busby had two of the five Husker hits off Cal Poly hurler Rhonda Wheatley. In the third inning, Nebraska scored twice with Stacy Sunny's two-run single the decisive hit. So Nebraska, behind the one-hit pitching of Emmons, blanked Cal Poly Pomona 2-0.

With Utah and Louisiana Tech eliminated, six teams remained in the hunt for the national championship as play advanced to Saturday. Cal State Fullerton and Nebraska were thriving in the winners bracket, and Cal Poly, Adelphi, UCLA and Northwestern were alive in the losers bracket. The Bruins and Northwestern started the competition on Saturday. UCLA's Lisa Hankerd walked to open in the bottom of the seventh and scored the only run of the game when Lisa Ishikawa threw a wild pitch. Tracy Compton fanned sixteen batters for UCLA, allowing only one hit. Ishikawa took the loss, also giving up only one hit in the 1-0 elimination game.

Cal Poly Pomona eliminated Adelphi in the next Saturday game with Margaret Ziegler scoring in the bottom of the eighth inning. Cal Poly hurler Wheatley allowed three hits as her team took advantage of a decision by the Adelphi coach Kathryn Raub that backfired. Ziegler started the eighth inning at second base for Cal Poly, and Raub elected to intentionally walk Kathy Powell—the No. 9 hitter. The runners moved up on a groundout and Shar Bilyeu walked. This loaded the bases for Kandi Burke, who pounded a single up the middle to score the game-winner. "We felt we handled her (Burke) all game," said Raub. "That's the way we play that situation, and it has worked all year." Julie Bolduc was the losing hurler for Adelphi.

Nebraska fans had supported their Huskers with strong turnouts of around 3,000 at their team's games. Husker fans were hoping their team could come through with an upset in the next game on Saturday against the top-ranked Titans. Lori Sippel, a freshman, was scheduled to pitch for the Huskers. She had lost to the Titans on an early-season trip to California and was motivated to avenge the loss. The only hit the freshman allowed was a one-out home run in the sixth inning by Cal State left fielder Terri Oberg. Sippel's one-hitter gave the delighted Husker fans a 5-1 victory over the top seed. Susan LeFebvre and Debbie Mygind threw for the Titans, allowing three runs in the third and a pair in the top of the seventh.

While undefeated Nebraska advanced to the championship game with the win, three teams with one loss each were left to play for the right to meet the Huskers for the title: Cal Poly Pomona, UCLA and Cal State Fullerton. After the afternoon loss to Nebraska earlier Saturday, Cal State Fullerton next faced Cal Poly Pomona. Titan JoAnn Ferrieri drove in a run with a double in the first inning, but Cal Poly came back to knot the game after seven innings. With the tiebreaker rule in play for the fourth time in the tournament, the Titan's Ferrieri singled to drive in Cal State's second run of the game. Susan LeFebvre ended the game in dramatic fashion by striking out Cal Poly's Alison Stowell with the bases loaded in the bottom of the eighth. LeFebvre pitched in relief of starter Debbie Mygind. Rhonda Wheatley took the 2-1 loss for Cal Poly.

In the final game Saturday night, UCLA's Debbie Doom faced Husker pitcher Donna Deardorff, who was relieved by Mori Emmons. The Bruins struck for three runs in the third inning following an error by Husker Denise Eckert that brought in the first and a two-run single by Chris Olivie that closed out the scoring. Nebraska's best threat against Doom came in the sixth when the Huskers had runners at first and third, but Ginger Cannon popped out to first and Lori Richins struck out to end the threat. So UCLA handed Nebraska its first loss, 3-0, with Doom striking out ten and hurling a three-hitter.

With the win, UCLA advanced to play Cal State Fullerton early Sunday afternoon before a crowd of 3,200. It was a game that most softball followers thought would go down to the last inning—and it did. UCLA went with Tracy Compton in the circle while the Titans started Susan LeFebvre. Both were on their game, and not until the last inning would the first and only run be scored. LeFebvre hurled the first three and one-third innings before Debbie Mygind came on to finish up and allowed the only run. In the bottom of the seventh, UCLA shortstop Leslie Rover singled past shortstop, then was sacrificed by Jennifer Simm to second base. First baseman Gina Holstrom then laced a single between third and short and Chris Olivie followed with a single to left field, scoring Rover. UCLA collected six hits off the two Titan pitchers with Rover going two-for-three. Compton allowed only three hits in getting the 1-0 win (her twentieth of 1985) against four losses.

With UCLA and Nebraska each tagged with a loss and facing off in the title game, it was do or die for both. The Bruins sought their third title in four years and Nebraska went after its first. Looking ahead, Husker coach Wayne Daigle had saved his best pitcher, Sippel, for last. Sippel and Doom squared off, and after eight innings the two pitchers had held their opponents to one run each. The Huskers time and again threatened Doom, but all they had been able to score was an un-earned run in the fourth inning.

The tiebreaker rule put the Bruin's Leslie Rover at second base to start the ninth. Jennifer Simm's sacrifice moved Rover to third before Sippel walked the next two batters to set up a double-play situation. But catcher Janet Pinneau crossed up the Nebraska strategy when she smacked a single to right field to score the game-winning run. "I thought I was due when I went to the plate," said Pinneau after the 2-1 Bruin win. She had started the game with no hits in six previous at-bats, then was hitless in her first two at-bats in the championship game before delivering the game-winner against Sippel.

Nebraska stranded twelve runners against Doom, who hurled her third championship game in her four-year college career. She allowed six hits, fanned ten and walked four. Nebraska made no errors, but Doom held on. "It didn't seem like I gave up a lot of real shots toward the end," said Doom. "They were dinking hits." Sippel allowed seven hits, fanned nine, and walked three. The Bruins had won two consecutive national championships.

Named to the all-tournament team were Sippel (P) and Husker teammates Lisa Busby (C), Stacy Sunny (OF), Lori Richins (2B) and Ginger Cannon (1B). Joining them were Alison Stowell (OF) of Cal Poly Pomona, Regina Dooley (OF) of Adelphi, JoAnn Ferrieri (3B) of Cal State Fullerton, and UCLA's Doom (P), Compton (P), Leslie Rover (SS) and utility player Chris Olivie. Ferrieri was the leading hitter (.438).

## Life After the WCWS...

UCLA's **Debbie Doom** pitched the Bruins to three national titles and a third-place during her career, compiling a record of 13-4 in national championship play. She also starred for the Sun City (Ariz.) Saints and was named an ASA All-American eight times. She is the only pitcher in NCAA history to pitch in and win three NCAA College World Series championships. She was a first-team NCAA All-American in 1984, the first year the NCAA so recognized softball players. In 2006, Doom was named to the NCAA Div. I Softball 25th Anniversary Team. Cal

## 1985 Women's College World Series Bracket
Omaha, Neb. • May 22-26

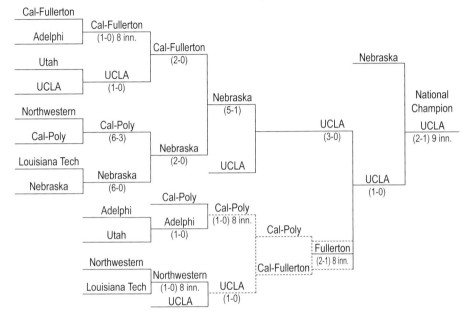

## 1985 Final Standings

| | |
|---|---|
| University of California (Los Angeles) | 5-1 |
| University of Nebraska (Lincoln)* | 3-2 |
| California State University (Fullerton) | 3-2 |
| California Polytechnic Pomona | 2-2 |
| Adelphi University (Long Island, N.Y.) | 1-2 |
| Northwestern University (Evanston, Ill.) | 1-2 |
| Louisiana Tech University (Ruston) | 0-2 |
| University of Utah (Salt Lake City) | 0-2 |

*In October 1986, the NCAA announced that the second-place finish by the 1985 Nebraska softball team would be vacated and the team would have to return its trophy because of participation by two ineligible student-athletes in 1985 championship play.*

Poly Pomona's **Rhonda Wheatley** went on to compile a pitching record of 139-60, fifth best in NCAA history, and was a two-time, first-team NCAA All American (1984-85). She was a member of the 1987 USA Pan American team. She held the NCAA record for most career innings pitched, 1,414.2. Her daughter, Courtney, later played for the University of Washington. Northwestern's **Lisa Ishikawa** was a two-time, first-team NCAA All-American (1984-85). She is the school's career leader in strikeouts (1,200) and shutouts (54). She was working as a senior business analyst for Motorola in 2013. UCLA's **Tracy Compton** holds the NCAA career record for ERA (0.15). In 2013 Compton was teaching at Righetti High School (Santa Maria, Calif.) and coaching the school's golf team.

## 1986: Cal State-Fullerton Finally Takes It All

The University of California at Los Angeles had dominated the Women's College World Series in the early 1980s, winning three titles and compiling a record of 18-4. So most were surprised when the field of eight teams was announced for the 1986 national championship and UCLA was not among them. The Bruins had lost in the regional, leaving the door open for another team. "This is fixin' to be one of the most exciting tournaments we've ever had," said coach Bob Brock of fifth-ranked Texas A&M. "This is the year of the upset." Louisiana Tech coach Bill Galloway agreed: "In the eight or nine years I've been involved in national tournaments, this is by far the most balanced field."

The year marked the fifth tournament under the aegis of the NCAA, and play would begin on Wednesday, May 21, at the familiar Seymour Smith Softball Complex. Besides Texas A&M and Louisiana Tech, the other competitors were: Creighton University, Northwestern, Cal State Fullerton, Indiana, University of California (Berkeley) and California State (Long Beach). Seven of the eight teams had made it to the tournament before; Cal-Long Beach was making its debut.

First-round action began at 6:30 p.m. Wednesday with Cal-Berkeley and Northwestern squaring off. The Golden Bears' center fielder Evelyn Fernandez played some outstanding defense to hold off Northwestern in the early innings, as the Wildcats stranded six runners in the first three innings. Fernandez made a belly-flopping catch with the bases loaded and two out in the first inning to end a threat and prevented a score in the top of the third with a bullet to home. Lisa Martinez allowed six hits but no runs going against her former Lincoln High School (Stockton, Calif.) teammate, Northwestern hurler Lisa Ishikawa. Ishikawa allowed five hits and a pair of runs in the 2-0 Wildcat loss.

In the second game, Sandy Winchester of Cal-Long Beach entered the game with a fourteen-game winning streak and yearned to make the Cal State Fullerton Titans her fifteenth in a row. Winchester was up to the task, but so was Fullerton pitcher Connie Clark. The two hurled zeroes through eight innings before the Titans finally broke through for the only run of the game on Rina Foster's RBI single up the middle with one out in the top of the ninth, scoring Alani Silva. Clark fanned six batters and gave up four hits as Winchester struck out three and allowed seven hits. Fullerton leadoff hitter Chenita Rogers had three hits in four at-bats in the hard-fought 1-0 Titan win.

A determined Creighton team faced Texas A&M in the second day of first-round play on Thursday evening before a crowd of more than 2,000. Creighton had received a berth to the tournament after Nebraska had been forced to forfeit a best-of-three regional between the two teams. The NCAA had disqualified the Huskers for using two ineligible players. The Lady Jays had not played in eleven days but had defeated the Aggies 3-1 in an invitational tournament earlier in the year. They knew they had a good chance.

The Aggies hurled their ace, Shawn Andaya (21-7 coming to Omaha), while Mary Higgins's Lady Jays countered with senior starter Kandy Foust. The game was still scoreless through nine innings when runner Mary Schwind was placed at second for the Aggies in the top of the tenth. (Rule changed to tenth inning in 1986; previously it had been the eighth inning.) After a pop out, Zina Ochoa and Judy Trussell singled to load the bases for the Aggies. Higgins then replaced starter Foust with April Trupp, who had beaten A&M in an invitational tournament earlier in the year. But Trupp's control was off and she walked pinch-hitter Julie Carpenter on four pitches to force in Schwind for the game's only run. The Aggies totaled seven hits in their 1-0 win, but Brock expressed disappointment in his offense. Still, the Aggie coach gave credit to Creighton: "Creighton fought us toe-to-toe. I knew they would be ready."

The second game Thursday matched a pair of NCAA All-Americans, Indiana's Amy Unterbrink and Louisiana Tech's Stacey Johnson. The two hurlers held the opposition scoreless before the Hoosiers grabbed a run in the top of the tenth with the help of the tiebreaker. With Unterbrink at second, designated hitter Stacey Hodge bunted her to third before catcher Mary Haslinger drove her home with a single up the middle. Unterbrink allowed two hits to collect her thirty-second win of the season while Johnson took the loss—her eighth of the year against thirty-five wins. She allowed eight hits by eight different players.

The first two games in the second round on Friday were elimination games, with Cal-Long Beach pitcher Sandy Winchester opposing Northwestern's Ishikawa in the opening game. The game was knotted until the bottom of the tenth inning when Liz Mason drove in the game's only run with a single. In the top of the inning, Northwestern had loaded the bases with no outs, but Winchester struck out Lisa Bruss and Martha Oyog before Julie Greenberg hit a liner toward center field. Outfielder Cissy Rothfuss made a diving catch to end the threat. Ishikawa took the loss, and Northwestern was the first team out of the tournament.

In the second elimination game Friday afternoon, Creighton battled Louisiana Tech and the Lady Jays were determined. They fell behind early 3-0 before scoring three runs in the bottom of the fifth inning to tie the game at 3-3. After that, Creighton encountered frustration, failing to score after loading the bases in the tenth, eleventh and twelfth innings. Double plays by Louisiana Tech in the eleventh and twelfth prevented Creighton from scoring. But in the thirteenth, Creighton's Joey Schope came to bat with one out and runners at second and third, just after Tech left fielder Maria Peralta threw out Ellen Castro at home. Schope, who was hitting .154, ended the Jays' frustration by lining a single off the glove of losing pitcher Stacey Johnson to drive in the winning run and keep the Lady Jays' hopes alive with the 4-3 win. Senior Kandy Foust hurled the win for Creighton in relief of starter April Trupp.

In the battle of the two California schools in the first winners-bracket game, the top-ranked Titans played better against the Golden Bears than in their opening game against Long Beach, Fullerton coach Judi Garman said after the game. "Tonight we were hitting the ball hard all of the time and our defense was just so relaxed," she said. "I hope we're on a roll now." Fullerton starter Susan LeFebvre allowed only one hit, losing her no-hitter in the last inning on a single by Lisa Martinez. The Titans collected seven hits off of two Cal-Berkeley pitchers, Erin Cassidy and Kim Moe, scoring once in the third and twice in the fourth for the 3-0 win.

In the final winners-bracket game of the evening, Texas A&M and Indiana started their respective aces, Andaya and Amy Unterbrink. Andaya allowed only two hits and fanned twelve, while Unterbrink was also effective—until the seventh inning when the Aggies collected seven hits and six runs. These included shortstop Liz Mizera's two-run double. The Aggies finished with nine hits off Unterbrink. Third baseman Cindy Cooper led the Aggie offense in the 6-0 win with three hits in four trips to the plate and one RBI.

Saturday morning, Cal-Berkeley faced a determined Creighton University team with Kim Moe on the mound for the Golden Bears. Kandy Foust relieved

**Cal-Fullerton coach Judi Garman started the school's program from scratch seven years before winning the national championship in 1986. She took the position at Cal-Fullerton as the first full-time softball coach in the nation.** *(Photo courtesy of Judi Garman)*

April Trupp in the eighth inning after California's leadoff hitter Roni Deutch singled up the middle. With the bases loaded soon afterward, Stephanie Hinds walked and scored the game's only run. It was not the way the Lady Jays wanted to lose. "I don't know if I would feel any better if it had been a single to left center," said coach Mary Higgins. "You certainly wish you had a chance to field the ball, but that's the breaks." Moe got the win for the Golden Bears, allowing only three hits as Creighton dropped from the tournament.

In the next elimination game, Indiana coach Gayle Blevins started freshman Roxie Rafik against Long Beach. She was worried about pitcher Amy Unterbrink's ability to come back from Friday's 1-0 loss to Texas A&M. "I felt she was a little bit down and maybe a little too hard on herself in warm-ups," said Blevins. Rafik hurled two innings before Unterbrink came on to finish the game, giving up three hits in eight innings. Long Beach never scored while the Hoosiers tallied twice in the tenth inning on RBI singles by Jenny McDaniel and Kim McKeon against losing hurler Sandy Winchester.

Unbeatens Cal State Fullerton and Texas A&M faced each other in the winners bracket at 4 p.m. Saturday, with Connie Clark hurling for the Titans against Aggie ace Shawn Andaya. It was a game to remember. Clark allowed only two base runners in pitching her second no-hitter of the season. The only base runners she allowed were Carrie Heightley in the first inning on an error and Tory Parks on a walk in the seventh inning. Clark, who fanned seven, was surprised by her no-hitter. "I didn't know it until someone told me after the game was over," she said. Fullerton scored the only run it would need in the third inning when speedster Chenita Rogers (3-for-4) hit a bouncer back to the pitcher to drive in Michelle Gromacki from third. Fullerton scored two more insurance runs in the fifth for the 3-0 win.

With its first loss, the Aggies then played Cal-Berkeley in an elimination game Saturday evening. Andaya pitched again, although she admitted she was a little tired. Andaya collected her third win of the tournament and dodged a bullet in the top of the tenth inning when Berkeley's Caryn Williams, who was on third, broke for home after Andaya hurled a wild pitch. But Aggie catcher Carrie Heightley recovered the ball and threw to Andaya in time to tag Williams for the out. In the bottom of the tenth inning, the Aggies scored the game's lone run on a one-out single by Andaya, scoring Cindy Cooper. Andaya allowed five hits, as did losing hurler Lisa Martinez.

Indiana University then faced Cal State Fullerton in the final game Saturday night. Susan LeFebvre hurled for the Titans against Amy Unterbrink. Indiana surprised the Titans and scored a run in the first, but Cal-Fullerton came back quickly with a score in the second to tie the game. It remained that way as LeFebvre and Unterbrink battled pitch for pitch. Then the Titans scored a pair of runs in the eighth inning, with Alani Silva and JoAnn Ferrieri each driving in a run. LeFebvre allowed only two hits, while Unterbrink allowed six in the 3-1 elimination of the Hoosiers.

## 1986 Women's College World Series Bracket
### Omaha, Neb. • May 21-25

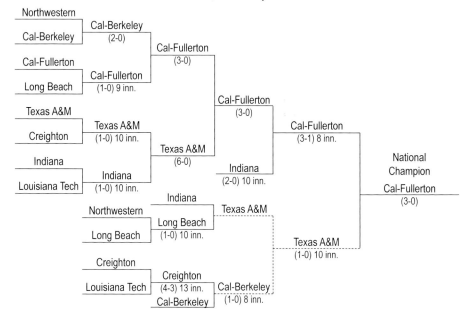

## 1986 Final Standings

| | |
|---|---|
| California State University (Fullerton) | 5-0 |
| Texas A&M University (College Station) | 3-2 |
| Indiana University (Bloomington) | 2-2 |
| University of California (Berkeley) | 2-2 |
| California State University (Long Beach) | 1-2 |
| Creighton University (Omaha, Neb.) | 1-2 |
| Louisiana Tech University (Ruston) | 0-2 |
| Northwestern University (Evanston, Ill.) | 0-2 |

The 4-0 Titans would now play Texas A&M on Sunday, needing only one game to win their first Women's College World Series. Players from the two teams had developed friendships when the two teams had met during the regular season. Saturday night before the championship game, the two teams and their families shared dinner and swapped stories in a reserved banquet room.

Garman went with Clark and Brock with Andaya (3-0 in the tournament). It was a pitcher's duel before the Titans broke through in the fifth inning on Rina Foster's triple for the first hit of the game. Foster scored on Robin Goodin's bouncer to Judy Trussell, who threw home late. Fullerton added a run in the sixth on Terri

Oberg's double and JoAnn Ferrieri's single to the fence. Fullerton players ran onto the field after Ferrieri limped to first for a single, suffering from a knee injury incurred in the regionals. "It's what we've waited for all these years," said Ferrieri, who had finished her last game for Cal-Fullerton. "We felt the best we've ever felt out there." Garman was elated with the championship but just as impressed with Ferrieri's grit. "JoAnn's hit, when she knocked in that run, was the most moving experience in this whole thing," the Fullerton coach said following the 3-0 win.

Clark did not allow an Aggie hit until the sixth inning. She finished with a one-hitter, fanning eight batters and walking none. The Aggies hit only two balls out of the infield. Andaya gave up five hits.

National champion Cal State-Fullerton placed four players on the all-tournament team including Connie Clark (P) Chenita Rogers (OF), Rina Foster (OF) and Robin Goodin (1B). Other players selected were: Sue Trubovitz (C) of Long Beach State; Judy Trussell (2B) of Texas A&M; Liz Mizera (SS) of Texas A&M; Roni Deutch (3B) of Cal-Berkeley; Tammy Connor (OF) of Indiana; Shawn Andaya (P) of Texas A&M; Cindy Cooper (at-large) of Texas A&M; and Joey Schope (at-large) of Creighton.

## Life After the WCWS...

Texas A&M's **Liz Mizera** was a member of the 1987 Aggie national championship team as well as the NCAA's All Decade Team of the 1980s. Mizera was honored by the Philadelphia Sports Writers' Association as the most courageous athlete of 1987 after she defeated cancer. She also was a member of the USA Pan American team in 1987. Mizera was a two-time, first-team NCAA All-American (1987-88) and was inducted into the Texas A&M Athletic Hall of Fame in 1997. Cal State Fullerton's **Susan LeFebvre** won the Broderick Award as the nation's top softball player in 1986. LeFebvre posted a 31-6 pitching record in 1986 and was named a first-team NCAA All-American (1986). She had a career record of 100-21 as a Titan. As of 2013, LeFebvre was a software engineer at Pacific Life. Creighton University's **Mary Higgins** coached the Creighton Blue Jays softball team for seventeen years (1977-1993), compiling a record of 564-298 before moving into administrative positions, including assistant athletic director. She was the Women's College World Series tournament director from 1982 to 1987. In 2013 she was the associate director of Creighton's Ratio Studiorum Program and also the assistant vice president for student retention.

# 1987: Aggies Win Their Third National Title

After adoption of the tiebreaker rule for use in women's intercollegiate softball in 1985, the NCAA made another change in 1987, increasing the distance from the pitcher's mound to home plate from 40 to 43 feet. Coaches complained that softball had become too much of a pitchers' game. While some expected the rule to be tougher on pitchers, others like coach Margie Wright, in her second year at Fresno State, were not so sure. "I don't know that the rule has made it tougher on pitchers," she said. "I think defenses have to be stronger because the ball is put in play more often." And more changes lay ahead for the Women's College World Series. Omaha, which had served as the site for softball's top-level intercollegiate national championship for all but two years since 1969, would see the tournament move westward after the 1987 event. The NCAA national softball committee had recommended in February that the tournament be played in California near the new host school, University of California at Berkeley.

Whether the new rule change would allow more offense to be generated in the 1987 tournament from May 20-24 would be determined by the impressive eight-team field, which included four-time champion UCLA facing Arizona State in the opening game Wednesday evening, followed by the University of Nebraska against Fresno State. The remaining four teams would play their first-round games on Thursday, with defending champion Cal State Fullerton facing Florida State at 6 p.m. followed by Texas A&M against Central Michigan.

In the tournament opener, UCLA and Arizona State battled through six scoreless innings with Bruin sophomore hurler Samantha Ford opposing ASU's Donna Stewart. Ford pitched the first eight innings, allowing two hits, before being replaced by freshman Lisa Longaker in the top of the ninth. With two outs in the bottom of the eighth and Bruin runner Monica Tourville on first, Shauna Wattenberg came to the plate as rain began to fall. She hit the ball over the head of ASU center fielder Kathy Escarcega, who had trouble with the wet ball. Tourville scored all the way from first. Stewart took the loss, allowing eight hits. UCLA's Janice Parks was three-for-four to lead all hitters.

In the second game Wednesday evening, Nebraska pitched Donna Deardorff against Fresno State, which had not faced her before. Fresno started Lori Romeiro-Gardner, who hurled the first three innings before being replaced by Melanie Parrent in the fourth. By the fourth, Nebraska had a 1-0 lead after scoring a run in the bottom of the first on Ruth Chatwin's run-scoring single that brought across Margie Ogrodowicz. In the fourth, however, rain suspended play around 10 p.m. The game picked up at 3 p.m. Thursday with Deardorff allowing no hits through the first six innings. But in the seventh, Fresno's Gena Strang tagged up from third and crossed home when Lori Richins hit a sacrifice fly to right field. But Deardorff appealed to the third-base umpire, saying Strang left early. The umpire called her out. Fresno coach Margie Wright saw it differently—but the call stood. Nebraska took the 1-0 win.

Thursday evening the remaining four teams were in action with defending champion Cal State Fullerton facing Florida State, making its first appearance in the championship. Seminole pitcher Julie Larsen held Fullerton scoreless through three innings before the Titans tallied twice in the top of the fourth with two outs. Freshman Missy Coombes singled home Kristine Glomboske for the game's first run with Lisa Baker scoring on a passed ball for the second. The third and final Titan run came in the fifth inning on an RBI single by Chenita Rogers scoring Alani Silva, who had singled, and was sacrificed to second before coming home on Rogers' single to center. Connie Clark fanned six batters to collect her thirty-second win in the 3-0 game.

In the last contest Thursday, Texas A&M pitcher Shawn Andaya limited Central Michigan to only three hits while her teammates collected eight off two Central Michigan hurlers. A&M scored once in the first and twice in the third to beat Central Michigan for the third time in the season. A&M shortstop Liz Mizera accounted for all of the scoring in the 3-0 win, with an RBI single in the first and a two-run double in the third.

Friday's competition started with a pair of losers-bracket games, Arizona State facing Fresno State followed by Central Michigan versus Florida State. Fresno's Gena Strang, who was involved in the controversial call in her last game, came back strong against the Sun Devils in the elimination game. She hit a grounder in the first inning that was misplayed by the first baseman, allowing Jill Rolen to score and then capped the 3-0 win with a two-run home run in the bottom of the sixth inning. It was the first home run of the tournament. Melanie Parrent allowed only two hits to get her twenty-fourth win of the season.

In the other losers-bracket game, Central Michigan pitcher Karen Wongstrom collected her 18th win of the season by hurling a one-hitter against the Seminoles. The only hit she allowed was a bunt single by Lori Crouse in the fourth inning. Crouse was the only Florida State player to reach base. The only run scored or needed by Central Michigan came with two out in the third inning when Kelly VanderMolen doubled deep to right field and scored on Kris Tipmore's single to center. The Seminoles headed home after their 1-0 loss.

UCLA proved Nebraska's nemesis again in the first winners-bracket game, two years after Debbie Doom beat the Huskers twice in the 1985 tournament. Friday evening Lisa Longaker stepped into the spotlight and fanned thirteen batters. Her performance impressed Nebraska interim coach Ron Wolforth. "She's going to shut out 95 percent of the college teams the way she threw today," said Wolforth, seeing the end of his team's seventeen-game win streak. Longaker allowed only one hit in recording her thirteenth shutout of the season by a 3-0 score. Losing pitcher Lori Sippel, who had beaten the Bruins 3-1 earlier in the season, allowed eight hits. Shauna Wattenberg led UCLA with two hits and a sacrifice. Wattenberg scored the first UCLA run on an obstruction call against Nebraska shortstop Jane Kremer in the fifth inning. An error by first baseman Katy Wolda scored the final two UCLA runs in the seventh inning.

The Texas A&M-Cal State Fullerton game was a rematch from the year before—Connie Clark against Shawn Andaya. The pitchers were on and each team went scoreless for ten innings. In the eleventh, however, Aggie Zina Ochoa was placed on second base with the tiebreaker rule and advanced to third on a fielder's choice by Erin Newkirk. She then scored on Carrie Heightley's single. But Fullerton countered with a run in the bottom of the inning to tie at 1-1 on freshman Missy Coombes' infield single. Andaya, who scattered seven hits and fanned thirteen batters, scored the winning run in the thirteenth when she walked and came home on Newkirk's single up the middle. "What a win," A&M coach Bob Brock said. "I'm a lot more relaxed now. We knew going in it was going to be a one-run game." Andaya's teammates sang "Happy Birthday" as she answered questions in the postgame interview on her twenty-second birthday. Clark allowed four hits and struck out eleven in the 2-1 Titan loss.

Saturday's four games included two losers-bracket games, with Central Michigan facing Nebraska to start things off. Central Michigan's Beth Bull scored on a throwing error by Nebraska catcher Katy Wolda in the top of the second inning, but Nebraska responded with a two-run single up the middle by Lori Richins in the bottom of the third. The scoring ended there. Sippel allowed just four hits in her 2-1 elimination of Central Michigan. It was her twentieth win of the year.

Judi Garman, Cal State Fullerton head coach, was not happy in the second Saturday game as the Titans trailed Fresno State 1-0 in the fifth inning, following catcher Shelly Stokes' RBI single. "I was about ready to give up in the sixth," Garman said afterward. "I figured if we didn't score in the sixth, I didn't think we

**Hustling Texas A&M pitcher Shawn Andaya (shown above tagging out Berkeley's Caryn Williams at home plate in the 1986 national tournament) had lost twice in women's series title games before hurling her Aggies to the 1987 national championship in her final college softball game. *(Reprinted with permission from the Omaha World-Herald)***

had a shot." In the seventh, the Titans' Alani Silva singled to center and catcher Michelle Gromacki reached first on an error by first baseman Gena Strang. An attempt to sacrifice a runner failed. Garman then had Cathi Hall pinch-hit. Hall, a 6-foot-1 junior from Redding, Calif., doubled off the top of the right-field fence, scoring Gromacki from second to tie the game. Chenita Rogers then hit a sacrifice fly to bring across the winning run. Connie Clark allowed two hits in collecting her thirty-third win as she eliminated Fresno State 2-1.

UCLA coach Sharron Backus was concerned that her Bruins wouldn't be up for the winners-bracket game against A&M Saturday afternoon. "I thought we would come out a little flat today," said Backus after the game. "How many times can you keep getting up, getting up and getting up?" At least once more, as the Bruins collected eight hits off Shawn Andaya, who had nine strikeouts. UCLA hurler Lisa Longaker allowed five hits and fanned six. The Bruins got the game's only run in the first inning as Sandra Arledge scored on Gina Holstrom's game-winning single.

The Cal State Fullerton-UCLA game Saturday evening figured to be a "tooth and nail" battle. And it was, with the Bruins using Samantha Ford and Lisa Longaker against the Titans' Connie Clark. Clark ended her season with a four-hitter, but still lost 1-0. Ford allowed only three hits through five innings to get the win. The game's only run came on a miscommunication in the fourth inning when Karen Walker's single dropped between shortstop Charis Monroe and center fielder Rina Foster. "Other than that break, it was a tooth and nail battle," said Backus. Fullerton finished 2-2 in the tournament.

In the nightcap Saturday, Texas A&M senior Shawn Andaya bounced back from her loss against UCLA earlier. She allowed a single by the Husker's Margie Ogrodowicz in the first, a double in the second by Ruth Chatwin and a single by Lori Richins in the seventh. But she retired fifteen in a row during one stretch. "It was kind of do or die, so I had to go for it," said Andaya afterward. "This is my last year, and my goal is to win the national championship." Aggie second baseman Julie Smith had four of her team's nine hits off Donna Deardorff. Smith had been hitless in two previous games. Deardorff held the Aggies for five innings before they scored twice each in the fifth and sixth innings. The runs in the fifth came on an error and Ericka Erickson's sacrifice fly. Judy Trussell's two-run double accounted for the runs in the sixth inning. With their 4-0 loss, the Huskers finished the year 41-11 and 2-2 in the tournament, tied for third with Cal-Fullerton.

On championship Sunday, the Aggies' backs were against the wall, needing two wins to capture the title. And, of course, Andaya was expected to pitch both games, the first championship game and the if-necessary game. It was the third time Andaya had pitched her team to the finals without a title, and the senior knew it was then or never. Before the game A&M coach Bob Brock talked to his team about its finishing second in its last two trips to the championship: "I told the girls that I didn't know if they had thought about it, but I was awful tired of being No. 2." Andaya hurled the first game against UCLA's Lisa Longaker, who had beaten her the last time they met. The game was scoreless through the first five innings. Then

## 1987 Women's College World Series Bracket

Omaha, Neb. • May 20-24

## 1987 Final Standings

| | |
|---|---|
| Texas A&M University (College Station) | 5-1 |
| University of California (Los Angeles) | 4-2 |
| California State University (Fullerton) | 2-2 |
| University of Nebraska (Lincoln) | 2-2 |
| California State University (Fresno) | 1-2 |
| Central Michigan University (Mount Pleasant) | 1-2 |
| Arizona State University (Tempe) | 0-2 |
| Florida State University (Tallahassee) | 0-2 |

in the top of the sixth, the Aggies finally got a run on catcher Carrie Heightley's two-out double. Andaya, meanwhile, put down the Bruins in order and ended with a perfect game, throwing forty-eight strikes in sixty pitches. She fanned six in her second perfect game of the season. Longaker took the loss, allowing five hits.

In the second game, Andaya again got the call while the Bruins hurled Michelle Phillips. Andaya drove in the first run as A&M opened the bottom of the first with three singles. Samantha Ford replaced Phillips in the first inning and finished the game. The Aggies also scored a run in the fourth and two in the fifth. Andaya threw twelve innings of perfect ball over the two games before Janice Parks doubled home Sandra Arledge, who had singled with one out in the top of the sixth inning.

During her perfect game earlier, Andaya had pulled a leg muscle running to first base, but she talked Brock into letting her bat in the second game. She grounded out in the fifth inning to score Julie Smith. "What an effort by Shawn," Brock said after the 4-1 Aggie win. "What can you say? I'm just glad she got it all before her career was over." Judy Trussell scored the other run in the fifth on a wild pitch. Smith finished the tournament with a record-tying nine hits. The Aggies collected nine hits off the two UCLA pitchers.

A&M's Smith, Andaya and shortstop Liz Mizera were named to the all-tournament team. Joining them were Gena Strang (1B) of Fresno State; Kris Tipmore (C) of Central Michigan; Cal State Fullerton's Chenita Rogers (OF); UCLA's Longaker (P), Janice Parks (3B); Lisa Hankerd (at-large); Sandra Arledge (OF); Karen Walker (OF) and Shauna Wattenberg (at-large). Rogers led all hitters with a .467 batting average.

The 1987 Women's College World Series marked another milestone in the event's history. After this tournament, the championship would not return to Omaha—the site of its birth nearly two decades earlier.

## Life After the WCWS...

Texas A&M's **Shawn Andaya** compiled a 114-28 record and in 2006 was named to the NCAA Div. I Softball 25th Anniversary Team. She was a first-team NCAA All-American in 1987. In 2011, Andaya was the first softball player elected to the Texas Sports Hall of Fame. She currently is employed by St. Joseph Foundation of San Antonio as director of major gifts, raising money for a six-county region. In 2013, she and her husband (former A&M basketball player Al Pulliam) had two children. Cal State Fullerton's **Chenita Rogers** was twice named to the all-tournament team at the women's series and was a two-time, first-team NCAA All-American (1986-87). She was one of two Fullerton nominees for the NCAA 25th Anniversary Team and a member of the NCAA All-Decade team for the 1980s. In 2013, she was raising a family and serving as director of sports, recreation and fitness at Emmanuel Community Church in Conyers, Ga. Cal State-Fullerton's **Connie Clark** was named winner of the Broderick Award as softball's top player for 1987. She continued her softball career after college with some of the nation's top ASA amateur teams. She is a member of the Arizona Softball Foundation Hall of Fame, the National Junior College Hall of Fame, the Cal State Fullerton Hall of Fame and the Central Arizona Junior College Hall of Fame. In 1995, Clark was named softball coach at the University of Texas and through 2012 had compiled a coaching record of 645-283-3.

# Five

(1988-1989)

## Cool Reception in the Hotbed of Softball

IN FEBRUARY 1987, Creighton University women's athletic director Mary Higgins told the Omaha World-Herald that the NCAA national softball committee, which she chaired, had recommended that the NCAA executive committee accept the bid by the University of California at Berkeley to serve as host school for the 1988 national softball championship. Before making this recommendation, Higgins's softball committee had reviewed bids by Cal-Berkeley, her own Creighton University, and the University of Oklahoma—host school for the final AIAW national championship in 1982. Tournament director for the championship since its return to Omaha as an NCAA event in 1982, Higgins said that the NCAA had been happy with Omaha but wanted to move it around to give other areas of the country an opportunity. "And money was a factor," she said. "Berkeley submitted a very lucrative bid."

The weather had also been a factor in the move. Coaches had been unhappy with the questionable weather, according to Oklahoma softball coach Marita Hynes. It had frequently been wet in late spring in Omaha, and sometimes cold.

Higgins tried to look on the bright side. As much as she had enjoyed the excitement of the tournament, her duties had been demanding as women's athletic director at Creighton, coach of the softball team, and a national tournament director. "In terms of amount of work that goes into it, it might not be all bad to take a break for a couple of years," she said. So Creighton University and Omaha apparently planned to bid again for this national championship.

The tournament's move to California held promise. The area around Cal-Berkeley was a hotbed of fastpitch softball. Twin Creeks Sports Complex in Sunnyvale, Calif., would be the site of the competition. Constructed in 1985, the sixty-acre complex had quickly established itself as a premier location for softball leagues and tournaments in Silicon Valley. Sunnyvale was situated between San Jose and Palo Alto in Santa Clara County.

In the six years dating back from 1988, twenty high school girls in Santa Clara County had received full or partial softball scholarships from colleges across the country. One of these was Camille Spitaleri—a senior at nearby Homestead High School in 1988. Spitaleri had recently accepted a scholarship to the University of Kansas. She had committed while starting to high school to earn a college scholarship through softball. Hers was becoming a familiar story for talented high school softball players nationwide. Nearly 300 colleges across the U.S. were offering softball scholarships by 1988.

Marie Tuite, Cal-Berkeley's assistant director of women's athletics, was selected to serve as tournament director for the women's series in Sunnyvale. Tuite recalled that the softball community hoped that the acceptance of the Cal-Berkeley bid would position the tournament in an exciting environment for softball fans, especially with the heavy concentration of strong softball programs in California. So the NCAA hoped the move to Sunnyvale would improve attendance.

It did not. Attendance of around 9,000 in each of the two years of the tournament in Sunnyvale—the heart of softball country—was about what it had been in Omaha in 1987. And it was far from the record 16,000 in Omaha in 1985. Some of the attendees at the tournament in 1989 complained about the cool weather. So the move to Sunnyvale proved temporary. The NCAA soon began reviewing bids for the 1990 championship, and the event would move again after two years in Sunnyvale.

Tuite did not recall the exact explanation for the tournament's move after 1989, but she remembered the tremendous amount of effort that she and other Cal-Berkeley staff put into it. "Even though the attendance was not great," she said recently, "it was a good experience for the teams involved." One not-so-good experience Tuite remembered from the tournament was the death of a spectator, who had just pulled up in a van loaded with kids and had a fatal heart attack right in front of her. "I've been involved in a ton of championships and have often talked about being prepared for something tragic," she said. "To this day it shakes me up."

A deputy director in the San Jose State athletic department in 2013, Tuite said that in the 1980s getting good attendance at women's championships was difficult. "During the late 1980s we were searching for the best home," she said, "and it really wasn't until ESPN grabbed onto the Women's College World Series that the attendance figures have skyrocketed. Which is just awesome!"

But that would not come until a few years later. The tournament in Sunnyvale would feature talented teams and exciting play, but without television coverage or noteworthy attendance figures.

## 1988: An All-California Final in Sunnyvale

With the Women's College World Series moving from Omaha to the heart of fastpitch softball country at Twin Creeks Softball Complex in Sunnyvale, Calif., the question loomed whether it would draw comparable or better attendance than in Omaha. Tournament officials soon found the answer as play began for the field

of eight teams on Wednesday, May 25, in this city just northwest of San Jose, Calif. Marie Tuite, Cal-Berkeley's assistant director of women's athletics, served as
tournament director. It would be only the second time college softball's national
championship had been held outside Omaha. It would also be the most prestigious
event held at Twin Creeks, which had been constructed just three years earlier.

The 1988 field included three teams from California: UCLA, Fresno State and
Cal Poly Pomona. Rounding out the field were: Arizona, Northern Illinois, Nebraska, Adelphi, and defending champion Texas A&M. Action began the evening
of the 25th with UCLA versus Northern Illinois, and Fresno State facing defending
champion Texas A&M. On Thursday evening Adelphi would oppose Arizona and
Cal Poly Pomona faced Nebraska.

UCLA coach Sharron Backus had been worried whether her top-seeded Bruins
would be ready for Northern Illinois after playing an emotionally draining regional against Cal State-Fullerton, beating them twice to earn the tournament berth.
UCLA did not hit well, getting only four hits off losing pitcher Beth Schrader.
UCLA right fielder Shanna Flynn had three of those four hits, all singles, including one up the middle in the top of the first inning. With Janice Parks at bat,
Schrader threw a wild pitch that allowed Flynn to slide home from third in the first
inning. It proved to be the game's only run as UCLA pitcher Lisa Longaker shut
out Northern Illinois on three hits, striking out six and walking two. The sophomore pitcher kept the Huskies off stride with a rise ball. Backus could not ask more
from Flynn, who two and a half weeks earlier had undergone an appendectomy.

In the second game, Fresno State and defending national champion Texas
A&M battled through a scoreless four innings before the Bulldogs got to Aggie
hurler Julie Carpenter and scored three runs. One came on a solo home run by
Carie Dever with two out in the fifth inning, and two more followed in the sixth inning on RBI singles by Gina LoPiccolo (2-for-3) and Karin Richter. Dever's home
run came on a 3-2 pitch and was hit over the left-field fence. Carpenter allowed
eight hits and three earned runs. Winning pitcher Melanie Parrent gave up only
three hits. A&M coach Bob Brock summarized the 3-0 Aggie loss perfectly: "If we
don't score, we can't beat anybody."

In the first game Thursday evening with about 850 in attendance, Arizona
pitcher Teresa Cherry faced Adelphi's Kris Peterson. After allowing a double with
two out in the first inning, Cherry retired nineteen consecutive batters and finished
with a splendid one-hitter in a 1-0 victory. Known for its team speed, Arizona went
for a big play in the fourth inning. It worked and won the game. Kristin Gauthier
was waved home from second by Arizona coach Mike Candrea at third. "With two
outs, I was going to take a chance on the arm," Candrea said. "I was relying more
on the outfielder having problems throwing on a strange field."

In the concluding first-round game, Nebraska started its ace, Lori Sippel, while
Cal Poly hurled Kris Rokosz. Through four innings the game was scoreless. But in
the fifth, Cal Poly loaded the bases and capitalized as Holly DeLuca had an RBI
single and Sippel walked in a run. The third and final Cal Poly run came in the

seventh when winning pitcher Rokosz singled home DeLuca. While the Broncos capitalized with two runs in the fifth and one more in the seventh, Nebraska had its chance and did not. The Huskers stranded seven base runners. "The turning point was when we got out of the inning (fifth) with the bases loaded," said Cal Poly head coach Carol Spanks. "They could have really busted loose."

With the first round completed, attention turned to the four games on Friday, May 27 — two elimination games and two winners-bracket games. After failing to score in its opening game, Texas A&M finally got its offense on track, collecting seven hits off losing Northern Illinois pitcher Beth Schrader. She had held the Aggies in check until the sixth inning when they scored three runs. First baseman Carrie Heightley led the Aggies with two hits in three at-bats and had a two-run single in the third inning. Center fielder Erin Newkirk also was 2-for-3 and had the other RBI in the third. Aggie Julie Carpenter allowed Northern Illinois five hits in getting her first win of the tournament, 3-0.

In the second losers-bracket game, Nebraska scored once in the first inning, and twice each in the third and seventh innings. Winning pitcher Donna Deardorff allowed one run in the sixth, and the Huskers sent Adelphi home with the 5-1 loss. Husker leadoff hitter and center fielder Margie Ogrodowicz led the offense, going 3-for-4 with a triple. Losing hurler Kris Peterson completed the year 25-8.

The first Friday night game featured a showdown between the No. 1-ranked UCLA Bruins and No. 2-ranked Fresno State Bulldogs, featuring two first-team All-American pitchers, Melanie Parrent and Lisa Longaker. The Bruins let Fresno off the hook twice early in the game, leaving the bases loaded in the third and fifth innings. But with the score tied at 1-1, UCLA scored five times in the top of the seventh inning, including a two-run home run on a 3-2 count by freshman second baseman Missy Phillips and a two-run shot by freshman walk-on Bea Chiaravanont. The home runs were the first for each player. Longaker got the win for UCLA, allowing three hits, including a solo home run by first baseman Gena Strang in the bottom of the second. Melanie Parrent took the 6-1 loss for the Bulldogs.

The second winners-bracket game followed, with each team starting the same pitcher who hurled in their respective opening games, Teresa Cherry for Arizona and Kris Rokosz for Cal Poly Pomona. Cal Poly scored a run in the first and managed to hold the one-run margin until the fifth inning when the Wildcats scored a pair of runs, then added two more in the top of the sixth for a 4-1 Arizona victory. Julie Standering led the Wildcats with a 3-for-4 performance. Cherry allowed six hits, and Rokosz gave up five hits and two runs before being replaced in the fifth inning by Lori Thompson. Thompson gave up three hits and two runs while concluding the game.

The first game Saturday morning matched Fresno State's Carie Dever against Nebraska's Lori Sippel, and both pitchers were on their games. They held their opposition scoreless through eight innings. In the top of the ninth, however, Fresno loaded the bases against Sippel, who appeared she would get out of the jam when her catcher picked pinch runner Geri Ciandro off third base for the second out.

**UCLA players savor the moment after winning the final championship game with Fresno State in Sunnyvale, Calif. The 1988 national championship was the fifth title for the Bruins since their first in 1978 and marked the first of three consecutive title match-ups between the two West Coast softball powers.** *(Photo courtesy of the UCLA Athletic Dept.)*

But pinch hitter Jill Rafel hit a grounder to third baseman Ann Halsne, who pulled first baseman Katy Wolda off first with the throw. This allowed Karin Richter, who had walked earlier, to score the game's only run. Sippel struck out nine and finished the season 22-11 as the Huskers became the third team eliminated in the first extra-inning game of the tournament.

Texas A&M and Cal Poly Pomona followed at 1:45 p.m., and A&M had one more hit than Poly in the afternoon contest. But Poly had the game's deciding blow—a solo home run on an 0-2 count by catcher Denise Correa over left field in the top of the seventh. The home run came at the expense of losing hurler Julie Carpenter, who walked one and struck out four in finishing the year 40-21. Cal Poly winning pitcher Nicky Luce fanned three batters and walked two in the 1-0 elimination of the Aggies, the fourth team sent home.

Unbeatens UCLA and Arizona met in the winners-bracket final that afternoon in a game that surprised even veteran UCLA coach Sharron Backus. The Arizona Wildcats did not help themselves and were out of contention early with a pair of errors in the second inning by third baseman Julie Standering, who allowed three unearned runs. UCLA also scored runs in the first and sixth innings, collecting seven hits off losing hurler Teresa Cherry, who was replaced by Ginnie Scheller in the third. The run in the seventh came on a solo home run by freshman Kerry Dienelt as the Bruins rolled to the 5-0 win. Longaker took her third win in the tournament.

Soon after their loss to UCLA, Arizona faced Fresno State in an elimination game Saturday night. The Wildcats appeared unrecovered from their earlier defeat. The Bulldogs jumped to an early lead, scoring four runs in the bottom of the third inning. Three of the runs came on a one-out, three-run shot over the left-field fence by Kathy Mayer. Gena Strang scored the other run in the inning on an error and also contributed two hits in three at-bats. It was Mayer's first home run of her college career. "I was sort of hyperventilating running around the bases," Mayer said. Winning hurler Carie Dever gave up only two hits. Ginnie Scheller was the losing hurler for the Wildcats, who finished third with the 4-0 loss. Wildcat ace Teresa Cherry did not pitch because of a nerve problem. "She has a problem with her ulnar nerve (in her arm)," said Arizona coach Mike Candrea afterward. "The lady's had a great career at Arizona, and I didn't want her out there getting pounded."

UCLA met Cal Poly in the nightcap, and the Broncos surprised the Bruins—at first. They led 1-0 after scoring a run on Dana Ramos's two-out RBI double in the first inning. The game remained that way until the Bruins finally got untracked, scoring three in the sixth inning and a single run in the seventh for the 4-1 win. Cal Poly was eliminated and finished fourth. The three runs in the sixth came on Kerry Dienelt's two-run single, and the run in the seventh came courtesy of a passed ball. UCLA pitcher Samantha Ford gave up only two hits. Cal Poly used two hurlers, Kris Rokosz, who hurled six innings in the loss, and Nicky Luce, who hurled the final inning.

With the field reduced to two teams, the undefeated Bruins would square off against the once beaten Fresno State Bulldogs in the championship. Fresno needed to beat the Bruins twice to win the title on Sunday. In the first game, UCLA scored a run in the third inning, and the score remained that way until the top of the seventh when the Bulldogs scored twice. Second baseman Kathy Mayer hit a double past a diving left fielder to score Martha Noffsinger with the tying run. Noffsinger had opened the inning with a bunt single. The Bulldogs loaded the bases against Longaker in the inning, with Karin Richter's sacrifice fly scoring Mayer with what proved to be the winning run, forcing the if-necessary game. Right fielder Richter played an outstanding game on defense, throwing out a pair of runners at home in the first and seventh innings in the 2-1 Bulldog win.

In the if-necessary game, Lisa Longaker and Carrie Dever again took the mound with a crowd of 1,750 on hand. The game was scoreless through three innings before UCLA tallied twice in the fourth and once in the seventh with an insurance run on Shanna Flynn's RBI single. Dever allowed only two earned runs in thirty innings Saturday and Sunday. The Bulldogs battled until the last out, loading the bases in the seventh. But the final two batters failed to hit, with Martha Noffsinger flying out to center and Kathy Mayer hitting into a dramatic shoestring catch by Flynn with two out and the bases loaded. "To tell you the truth," disappointed Fresno State coach Margie Wright said, "after we had loaded the bases, I thought we were going to win the second one."

Backus said after the 3-0 win that she was drained by the drama on the final

# 1988 Women's College World Series Bracket

### Sunnyvale, Calif. • May 25-29

# 1988 Final Standings

| | |
|---|---|
| University of California (Los Angeles) | 5-1 |
| California State University (Fresno) | 4-2 |
| University of Arizona (Tucson) | 2-2 |
| California Polytechnic Pomona | 2-2 |
| Texas A&M University (College Station) | 1-2 |
| University of Nebraska (Lincoln) | 1-2 |
| Adelphi University (Long Island, N.Y.) | 0-2 |
| Northern Illinois University (DeKalb) | 0-2 |

day of play. "The fact that we didn't respond offensively in the first game was real scary," she said. "It seemed like everything I tried came up wrong." Longaker shut out the Bulldogs and completed the year 31-4. Dever gave up nine hits in the loss. One of them was a two-run double to the fence in center field by UCLA third baseman Janice Parks in the fourth inning, scoring Stacy Sunny and Lorraine Maynez.

It was the fifth series title for the Bruins (previously 1978, 1982, 1984 and 1985), who finished the year 53-8. Fresno State finished runner-up for the second time and completed the season 55-17. Five Bruins were named to the all-tournament team, including Lisa Longaker (P), Stacy Sunny (C), Kerry Dienelt (1B), Missy Phillips (2B) and Shanna Flynn (OF). Joining them were Arizona's Julie Standering (3B) and Heidi Lievens (SS); Nebraska's Margie Ogrodowicz (OF); and Fresno State's Carie Dever (P), RaeAnn Pifferini (OF), Gena Strang (at-large) and Karin Richter (at-large). UCLA's Shanna Flynn led all batters with a .450 average.

Total attendance was counted at 8,500, 600 less than the 1987 attendance in Omaha. Tournament organizers had hoped for a warmer reception.

## Life After the WCWS...

Nebraska's **Lori Sippel** went on to an outstanding career pitching thirteen years for the Canadian National Team. She played for Canada in the 1996 Olympics, then coached the Canadian National Team in the 2008 Olympics to a fourth-place finish. In 2002 she became the associate head coach at the University of Nebraska. She is a member of the International Softball Federation Hall of Fame (2006), the Softball Canada Hall of Fame (1993), and the Nebraska University Hall of Fame (1997). Fresno State pitcher **Carie Dever** was twice named an Academic All-American. She served as head coach at the University of Arkansas from 1995 to 2004. In 2012 she was inducted into the Fresno State Athletic Hall of Fame.

# 1989: UCLA Sweeps the Field

With lackluster attendance the year before, the 1989 Women's College World Series hoped to improve fan support May 24-28 at the Twin Creeks Sports Complex. The field of eight teams included defending champ and No. 1-ranked UCLA, No. 2-ranked Oklahoma State, Cal Poly Pomona, South Carolina, Arizona, 1988 runner-up Fresno State, Toledo and Oregon. First-round action in the double-elimination event started Wednesday with UCLA facing South Carolina and Cal Poly opposing Oregon, which had last played in the tournament in 1980. The other first-round games were scheduled for Thursday, with Arizona facing Fresno State and Oklahoma State playing newcomer Toledo.

Wednesday evening, UCLA and South Carolina battled to a scoreless tie through five innings. With two out in the sixth inning, Bruin first baseman Kerry Dienelt dramatically broke the deadlock with a three-run shot over the left field fence. "I was surprised she (Charlene Manley) was pitching inside the whole game and that's my favorite pitch," said Dienelt, who accounted for all of her team's runs. South Carolina's Charlene Manley gave up ten hits and took the 3-0 loss. Winning pitcher Tiffany Boyd, a freshman, hurled a no-hitter and lost her perfect game in the top of the seventh when she walked third baseman Stacy Agee with one out. "The perfect game was in the back of my mind," Boyd said, "but it's not the first or the last performance for me. I'm here for one reason—to play for games and go home. I want that ring." She retired the first nineteen batters in order and finished with fifteen strikeouts.

In the second game, Cal Poly squared off against Oregon. It was scoreless until the bottom of the sixth inning, when Cal Poly loaded the bases against the Ducks' pitcher Katie Wiese with one out and scored the only run they would need. The run came off Holly DeLuca's sacrifice fly to center field, scoring Nicky Luce from third. Luce had walked to start the inning. "Once they walk somebody before you, you really want to hit it," said DeLuca. "I felt confident." Wiese allowed four hits. Winning pitcher Lori Thompson gave up three hits in the 1-0 Cal Poly victory.

The remaining four teams played Thursday evening with third-ranked Fresno State facing sixth-ranked Arizona in the first contest. The game was a surprise—especially for Fresno. The Wildcats scored twice in the first inning, once in the third, four times in the fourth, and five times in the fifth, collecting thirteen hits off the two Fresno hurlers, starter Terry Carpenter and Carie Dever. The game lasted only five innings with the ten-run rule invoked as Fresno was upset 12-0. Arizona freshman pitcher Doreen Juarez limited the Bulldogs to three hits in collecting her first win of the tournament. When asked about starting the freshman, Arizona coach Mike Candrea said: "She's done a very good job the last three or four outings, so I had no hesitation going in this tournament to start a freshman." For the Wildcats, Nicki Dennis doubled and drove in four runs, and Kristin Gauthier had three hits and three RBIs.

The Oklahoma State-Toledo game concluded the first round. The Cowgirls

**The second national championship in Sunnyvale seemed a lot like the first for the UCLA players. Just as they had the year before, they won the tournament after beating Fresno State in the final game.** *(Photo courtesy of the UCLA Athletic Dept.)*

and Mudhens were scoreless through the first five innings until the Cowgirls got to hurler Sheila Lotre in the bottom of the sixth inning. The Cowgirls scored three times, with center fielder Dee Brewer hitting a two-run single up the middle with the bases loaded and first baseman Debbie Mobius hitting an RBI single for the third and final run. Southpaw pitcher Michele Smith went the distance for the Cowgirls in the 3-1 win, striking out fifteen batters and allowing three hits, including a leadoff home run by Toledo's Rhonda King in the top of the seventh.

The losers-bracket games were played first, starting at 1 p.m. Friday with Oregon facing South Carolina. Oregon scored in the first inning when Julie Cavanaugh bunted for a single. Kathy Gray next hit a ground rule double over the left center-field fence with Cavanaugh stopping at third. Kim Manning then singled up the middle, scoring Cavanaugh. The early score was the game's only run. Katie Wiese kept South Carolina scoreless, hurling a four-hitter with three strikeouts. Angie Lear was the losing pitcher, allowing six hits. South Carolina was the first team eliminated.

After its opening game rout, Fresno State faced Toledo in the second elimination game. A pair of errors by Toledo catcher Lynn Szczypka allowed two runs in the second inning, and a wild pitch by Toledo's Patty Barnett in the third inning brought across Shelly Stokes. This would be the game's third and final run. Winning hurler Carie Dever allowed three hits in the 3-0 elimination of Toledo.

The first of the two winners bracket games was played at 6 p.m., with Cal Poly Pomona pitcher Lori Thompson hoping to add to her streak of seventy-four scoreless innings. But it did not take UCLA long to end the streak, scoring two runs in the first inning and knocking Thompson out of the game after only two innings. The Bruins added a pair of runs in the third and fourth innings and closed out their scoring with three runs in the sixth for a 9-0 shutout. Cal Poly pitchers Thompson, Nicky Luce and Caryn Askey allowed eleven hits. Only three of the nine runs were earned as Cal Poly hurt itself with seven errors. Samantha Ford hurled the shutout for the Bruins, allowing three hits. UCLA center fielder Lorraine Maynez had a perfect evening (4-for-4, with four scores), and second baseman Missy Phillips added a pair of hits in four at-bats to drive in two runs.

Oklahoma State and Arizona followed in the second winners-bracket game. It figured to be a battle and it was. Neither team could bring runs across the plate until the top of the eighth inning when OSU scored four times, with first baseman Debbie Mobius hitting a bloop single to right field to bring in the first run. Michele Smith also scored on the play when the outfielder bobbled the ball. Next, losing pitcher Ginnie Scheller hurled a pair of wild pitches to score the last two runs. Each pitcher allowed six hits in the 4-0 Cowgirl win.

The first game Saturday morning was an elimination game with Cal Poly facing Fresno State. During the regular season, Cal Poly had beaten the Bulldogs three times. Fresno banged out nine hits off two Cal Poly hurlers, Nicky Luce and Lori Thompson. The Bulldogs scored three times in the third, and once each in the fifth and sixth innings. Bulldog second baseman Kathy Mayer had a two-run single in the third inning, and catcher Shelly Stokes also scored in the inning on an error. Terry Carpenter hurled the 5-1 Bulldog win, allowing just one hit. Designated player Gina LoPiccolo scored the Fresno run in the fifth on an error by the left fielder, and Martha Noffsinger's ground out scored the run in the sixth. The Bulldogs got redemption with the win. Cal Poly's only hit was an RBI single by Shellie McCall in the fourth inning, scoring Luce.

Arizona and Oregon played the next elimination game Saturday afternoon, and the Wildcats got a splendid two-hit pitching performance from Lisa Bautista. The Wildcats scored a run in the third inning on a sacrifice fly by Kristin Gauthier, added another run in the sixth on Trish Boutin's RBI single and closed out the scoring on a two-run single by Nicki Dennis in the seventh inning. The 4-0 loss eliminated Oregon. Katie Weise was the losing hurler, pounded for eleven hits. Shortstop Julie Standering led the Wildcats with three singles in four at-bats.

That evening unbeatens UCLA and Oklahoma State met, and the Cowgirls took an early lead with a run in the fourth inning on Michelle Shean's fielder's choice. OSU clung to this 1-0 lead going into the top of the seventh inning. But the Bruins' Janice Parks opened the inning with a bunt single, and Julie Poulos went in as pinch runner for Parks. After Yvonne Gutierrez grounded out, pinch-hitter Monica Tourville walked and pinch runner Karen Walker entered to run for Tourville. OSU pitcher Dena Carter had allowed only two hits in the first six innings, but now faced freshman designated hitter Kelly Inouye with two runners on base. Carter's first pitch to Inouye was a ball, and OSU coach Sandy Fischer replaced Carter with Michele Smith. At 3-2, Inouye doubled to left center field, scoring Poulos and Walker for the 2-1 final score. "I just wanted to come through for the team," said Inouye. "I love to be in that kind of situation." Winning pitcher Tiffany Boyd allowed three hits and fanned eight batters. "So that one hurt," said OSU coach Sandy Fischer reflecting on the loss years later. "We thought that it was our year."

The Cowgirls were emotionally spent after the loss but had to pump up quickly to face Fresno State in the next game. The Bulldogs scored twice in the third and fourth, and three times in the seventh inning. Shelly Stokes's two-run home run highlighted the seventh inning. Carie Dever hurled a five-hit shutout for the Bulldogs. Michele Smith and Dena Carter split the pitching for the Cowgirls, allowing seven hits in the 7-0 loss. Stokes, Gina LoPiccolo and Dionne Ewing each had a pair of RBIs for the Bulldogs.

Arizona looked to upset the Bruins in the final game Saturday night, and the Wildcats would need to beat the Bruins again the next day to capture their first national title. UCLA scored single runs in the first, third and seventh innings, and Bruin pitcher Lisa Longaker was on her game. She limited the Wildcats to only a pair of hits. So the Bruins collected seven hits and three runs off losing hurler Doreen Juarez and advanced to the championship round on Sunday with the 3-0 victory.

UCLA needed only one win Sunday against archrival Fresno State for its sixth

# 1989 Women's College World Series Bracket
### Sunnyvale, Calif. • May 24-28

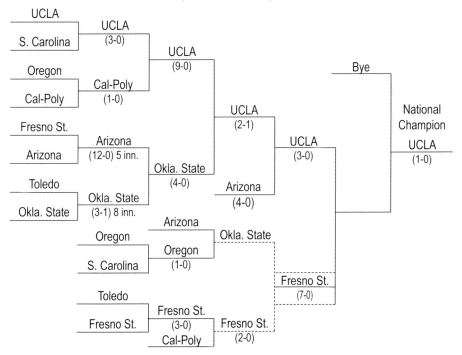

## 1989 Final Standings

| | |
|---|---|
| University of California (Los Angeles) | 5-0 |
| California State University (Fresno) | 3-2 |
| University of Arizona (Tucson) | 2-2 |
| Oklahoma State University (Stillwater) | 2-2 |
| California Polytechnic Pomona | 1-2 |
| University of Oregon (Eugene) | 1-2 |
| University of Toledo (Ohio) | 0-2 |
| University of South Carolina (Columbia) | 0-2 |

title in eleven years. The Bruins went with Tiffany Boyd on the mound and Fresno State named Carie Dever. Boyd got into trouble in the first inning when the Bulldogs had runners on first and third with two out. But the Bruin ace struck out Kathy Mayer to end the inning. The Bruins scored in the third inning when Erica Ziencina led off with an infield single and Kerry Dienelt followed with a sacrifice bunt to advance pinch runner Julie Poulos to second. Poulos went to third on Shanna Flynn's infield out, and then Lorraine Maynez hit a line-drive single off the glove of Bulldog first baseman Kerri Donis. "It was hit on a line to my right," Donis said. "I was making an attempt to catch it and it just went in and out." Poulos scored the only run of the game in the 1-0 Bruin victory. Boyd finished with six strikeouts and retired eighteen of the last twenty she faced. "I just wanted to win," the UCLA freshman pitcher said. "Considering the situation, I think I did the job just fine."

Joining Boyd on the all-tournament team were Bruin teammates Kerry Dienelt (1B), Janice Parks (3B), Lorraine Maynez (OF) and Missy Phillips (2B). Fresno State players selected were: Carie Dever (P), Martha Noffsinger (SS), Jill Polanco (OF) and Shelly Stokes (C). Others named were Oklahoma State's Michele Smith (utility), Arizona's Kristin Gauthier (OF) and Nicki Dennis (utility). UCLA's Lorraine Maynez led all hitters (.588).

Attendance of 9,260 was a slight improvement over the year before. But it was down a bit from the 1987 figures in Omaha and far from the record 16,200 in the 1985 championship. The women's series had received a cool reception in Sunnyvale—both from the fans and the weather. Some attendees never took their jackets off at the tournament. The NCAA announced soon after the 1989 tournament that it would relocate to Oklahoma City for the 1990 championship.

## Life After the WCWS...

Oklahoma State hurler **Michele Smith** compiled a record of 82-20 and a .343 career batting average. She was named a first-team NCAA All-American in 1988 and 1989. She was a member of the U.S. national team from 1991-2002. In 2006, she was inducted into the ASA National Softball Hall of Fame and is a member of four other halls of fame. In 2012, Smith was working as part of the ESPN broadcasting team for the Women's College World Series. After pitching UCLA to the title in 1989, **Tiffany Boyd** transferred to Cal State-Fullerton where she won eighty-two games and lost twenty-eight during the 1991-1993 seasons. While at Cal-Fullerton she pitched thirty-eight shutouts in 125 games and was a two-time, first-team NCAA All-American (1991-92).

# Six

# A Warmer Welcome in Oklahoma City

IN MAY 1989, A SMALL GROUP OF OKLAHOMANS WATCHED the competition at the Women's College World Series at Twin Creeks Sports Complex in Sunnyvale, Calif. These observers were interested in more than supporting the Oklahoma State University team that had won a berth in the national championship that year. The four members of this Oklahoma delegation were taking in the administration of the tournament with the anticipation that this event would be moved to Oklahoma City.

Soon after the group returned to Oklahoma, NCAA officials announced acceptance of the University of Oklahoma's bid to serve as host school for the tournament in 1990 and 1991. Play would be held at the recently constructed ASA Hall of Fame Stadium in northeast Oklahoma City. The stadium adjoined the national office of the Amateur Softball Association and the National Softball Hall of Fame.

"The city of Omaha is dying to get this tournament again," said an excited Marita Hynes, an official with the University of Oklahoma athletic department and a member of the Oklahoma delegation to the 1989 tournament. "But coaches were unhappy there because of the questionable weather, and it was usually cold." Omaha had been the site of most of the championships from 1969 to 1987. During these late spring tournaments, the wet, chilly Nebraska weather had not been popular with the coaches and players. Perhaps more disappointing to the NCAA, the attendance had leveled off to around 12,000 for the five-day event. Hynes had heard much about the wet, cool Omaha tournaments as coach of the Sooner softball team in the 1980s. Neither the weather nor the attendance improved much with the event's move to Sunnyvale in 1988 and 1989. Hynes recalled that during her visit to the northern California tournament in 1989 "there was never a day I took my jacket off."

News of the event's relocation to Oklahoma City may have surprised many of the city's locals in 1989. But members of the Oklahoma delegation to the Sunnyvale championship were well aware of the planning and efforts over a number of years that had gone into bringing this increasingly attractive event to Oklahoma

City. Working with the Oklahoma City Chamber of Commerce, the local All Sports Association had coordinated the bid that finally brought the championship to Oklahoma City in 1990. The organization had a good reputation for attracting and overseeing college and amateur sports events to Oklahoma City, including the long-running, annual All College Basketball Tournament, the national NCAA Wrestling Tournament (1983, 1985 and 1989), and the U.S. Olympic Festival in 1989.

Oklahoma City Councilman Pete White, who was on the executive committee of the All Sports Association in 1989, provided some of the needed clout with Oklahoma City administration for the bid. "You can't go after sports events with just sports people," White said as he recalled the efforts to bring the event to Oklahoma City in 1990. City officials have to provide support and cooperation, he said. White also emphasized the key role Hynes played in Oklahoma City's winning the bid from the NCAA. Hynes had directed this national championship from 1980 to 1982 at Reaves Park in Norman before the NCAA began sanctioning the tournament. "She had the institutional memory of the event," White said.

Hynes had been integral in winning the bid, but the visionary who had first promoted Oklahoma City's efforts to serve as host site of the Women's College World Series was a local businessman, Glenn Boyer. One of the Oklahoma delegates at the 1989 Sunnyvale championship, Boyer first began efforts to bring the women's series to Oklahoma City in the mid-1980s. He had been introduced to competitive fastpitch softball through his daughter, Candi, who had played shortstop for the University of Kansas in the early 1980s. President of the city's All Sports Association in the 1980s, Boyer had put together the one-time All College Women's Softball Tournament in fall 1983 in west Oklahoma City. A number of major college softball teams participated in the tournament, including 1983 national champion Texas A&M. Boyer's All Sports Association sponsored the tournament and Oklahoma City University served as host school.

In the mid-1980s, Boyer began working with the executive secretary of the Oklahoma City Chamber of Commerce, Stanley Draper Jr., to bring the increasingly prestigious Women's College World Series to Oklahoma City. Amidst these efforts by All Sports to attract the Women's College World Series, the association also started planning a bid to the U.S. Olympic Committee to host a U.S. Olympic Festival. In its bid to host the 1989 Olympic Festival, Oklahoma City was helped by a well-connected insider—city resident Don Porter. Porter served as a member of the U.S. Olympic Committee, a role that was related to his duties as executive director of U.S. softball's governing body, the Amateur Softball Association (ASA). The softball association had its national office in Oklahoma City and maintained the National Softball Hall of Fame at the same location in northeast Oklahoma City. The ASA, along with the Division of Girls' and Women's Sports, had sanctioned the first Women's College World Series in 1969 in Omaha, Neb.

Porter provided a connection to something else that proved key in Oklahoma City's bid for the women's softball championship: a world-class softball stadium.

ASA Hall of Fame Stadium had been completed by Porter's organization in 1987 and was considered the "Taj Mahal" of softball facilities. It was located on the grounds of the ASA in northeast Oklahoma City. After Oklahoma City was awarded host site for the 1989 Olympic Festival—with help from Porter—the city provided funding to enhance the stadium. The parking lot was expanded and improvements were made to the facilities. The first showcase event at the relatively new stadium was the Olympic Festival softball competition in 1989.

Soon after competition ended at the May 1989 tournament in Sunnyvale, the NCAA announced that All Sports Association had won the bidding for the 1990 and 1991 softball championships and both the University of Oklahoma and Oklahoma State University would serve as host schools for the tournament. From the beginning, Draper and Boyer planned to make Oklahoma City the permanent home for the national softball championship. With her past experience directing the tournament from 1980-1983, Hynes was an obvious choice for tournament director. Already busy with her responsibilities at the University of Oklahoma in 1990, Hynes would share her duties as tournament director with Cindy Bristow, the U.S. Junior Olympic softball program director at the Amateur Softball Association in Oklahoma City.

The first few years of the women's series in Oklahoma City saw little improvement in attendance from the peak years in Omaha in the mid-1980s. From 1990 to 1992 attendance averaged 12,650 over the five days of the event. "We'd do everything we could short of stopping people out on I-35 and detouring them into the Hall of Fame (Stadium)," Hynes later remembered. "It was really frustrating." But the facilities were first rate, Hynes and Bristow competently administrated the tournament, and the spring weather was warmer than in Sunnyvale or Omaha. The NCAA extended the tournament contract with Oklahoma City through 1995.

Along with good administration and excellent playing facilities, the city's hosting of the women's softball series had something else going for it in the 1990s—the gender revolution sweeping American sports. Propelled by changing attitudes and increased funding mandated by the 1972 federal Title IX legislation, teenage girls and their mothers were fueling an explosive growth in women's athletics by the 1990s. When the first national softball championship came to Oklahoma City in 1990, 178 Division I softball programs were competing. The number of these Division I programs would double over the next two decades.

This surge in women's sports participation also closed the traditional disparity in spectators. For the first time, women's sports events were drawing large crowds. As the site of the Women's College World Series, Oklahoma City would ride this wave in women's athletics that was changing the sports landscape of the nation. In 1993 attendance suddenly climbed to nearly 22,000. This upward trend continued in 1994 and 1995. Feeling more assured of keeping the championship event in Oklahoma City, tournament sponsors and local officials began to relax. But only a little—and not for long.

# 1990: UCLA Wins in the Championship's New Home

In May 1990, Oklahoma City became the third site for the Women's College World Series since the 1987 farewell tournament in Omaha. Sponsor for the championship would be the local All Sports Association, which had worked hard to bring the event to the city. Two state schools served as hosts: the University of Oklahoma and Oklahoma State University, which also had landed a berth in the 1990 tournament. The event would be co-directed by Marita Hynes, director of promotions at the University of Oklahoma, and Cindy Bristow of the Amateur Softball Association (ASA) national staff. Play would be held at the impressive ASA Hall of Fame Stadium. Just three years old, the state-of-the-art facility was built specially for major softball events and was nestled in the tree-lined Remington Land tourist area. Between games, tournament attendees were within walking distance of a zoo, a golf course, a science exhibition center, several museums and halls of fame, including the nearby ASA National Softball Hall of Fame. The NCAA guaranteed the tournament for two years in Oklahoma City, but whether the city kept the event beyond 1991 would depend largely on fan turnout. Omaha was working for the championship's return.

Ranked No. 1 all season, the UCLA team provided major star power for the event's debut in Oklahoma City. The Bruins had won the last two national titles and counted on making it three in a row in 1990. The defending champs were scheduled to play newcomer Kent State the first day of the May 23-27 tournament.

**Called the Taj Mahal of softball stadiums, ASA Hall of Fame Stadium provided a first-rate facility for softball's national championship. The stadium and Oklahoma City's usually mild spring weather helped to secure the city's bid to serve as host for the women's series. *(Photo courtesy of the Amateur Softball Association.)***

Also paired in the first day's play was fourth-ranked Cal State-Long Beach against another debutant, Nevada-Las Vegas. The remaining four teams would complete the first round on Thursday, May 24, with No. 3 Arizona facing No. 6 Oklahoma State and Florida State playing No. 2 Fresno State, which had finished runner-up to UCLA the last two years.

Undefeated in championship play the year before, UCLA started veteran right-hander Lisa Longaker against the Kent State Golden Flashes. Longaker was on her game, striking out nine and allowing only three hits, two of them by Kent State catcher Kim Henzler. Kent State pitcher Darby Seegrist allowed six hits, and half were in the bottom of the first inning after two outs. Missy Phillips doubled home Lisa Fernandez, and Yvonne Gutierrez homered on a 3-1 pitch to left center field to bring across Phillips. Kent State coach Sue Lilley watched her team commit four errors in the game. "I think we can contribute that to nerves," she said. UCLA added another run in the fourth on an RBI single by Fernandez as Kent State was shutout for only the third time in the season with the 4-0 loss. Some 1,350 were in attendance for ASA Hall of Fame Stadium's debut in women's series play.

In the second game Wednesday evening, pitchers Lori Harrigan of UNLV and Mary Letourneau of Long Beach State allowed six hits apiece, but the 49ers made theirs count, especially shortstop and leadoff hitter Kim Kostyk. She had two hits and scored a pair of runs. Kostyk scored the first run in the bottom of the third when the UNLV left fielder misplayed Speedy Mendoza's single, then came across in the sixth on Steffani Everett's RBI single. UNLV got a runner to third three times against Letourneau but didn't score, leaving four runners on base in the 2-0 loss.

In the first game on Thursday, Oklahoma State pitcher Dena Carter, who had hurled a no-hitter at the regional tournament, retired nineteen batters, one over the minimum, through six innings against Arizona. Only two Arizona runners reached base against Carter through six innings—Vivian Holm in the first inning and Julie Standering in the third—both resulting from OSU errors. But in the seventh, Arizona's Kristin Gauthier singled to spoil Carter's bid for a no-hitter. Nicki Dennis's bloop single loaded the bases before the Cowgirls ended the threat with a double play. Losing pitcher Julie Jones allowed eight hits and struck out one. For the Cowgirls, Shannon Kimberling had an RBI single up the middle in the second inning; Michelle Shean's sacrifice bunt back to Jones scored Dawn Lange in the third inning; and Sharon Sodano's single to left scored pinch-runner Christi Smith in the seventh inning. OSU notched a 3-0 victory.

In the second Thursday game, Florida State's Debbie DeJohn and Fresno's Carie Dever pitched scoreless ball through four innings. In the top of the fifth, Leslie Barton scored for the Seminoles on an error by the third baseman. DeJohn finished with a three-hit shutout, while Dever fanned five and allowed one unearned run in the 1-0 Fresno loss. Julie Smith had two hits in three at-bats for the Bulldogs.

In Friday's first game, UNLV had only one more hit than Kent State's three, but that extra hit proved to be the difference in the ball game. It was a bases-loaded double off the left field fence by UNLV's Kim Harris in the bottom of the fourth inning, which expanded the UNLV lead to 4-0. But Kent State fought back with a run in the top of the fifth when MeMe Vencl hit her sixth home run of the season. UNLV tallied once in the bottom of the fifth to lead 5-1 before Kent State closed out the scoring on first baseman JoAnn Gordon's third home run of the season in the top of the seventh. Both home runs came off winning pitcher Lori Harrigan, who fanned eight batters in the 5-2 UNLV win. Pitcher Darby Seegrist hurled a four-hitter in the loss for Kent State, the first team eliminated.

Next on Friday afternoon, Arizona and Fresno State faced off in a game that started with a controversial call in the first inning. Doreen Juarez had retired the first two Bulldog batters before RaeAnn Pifferini smacked a triple to right-center. Moments later Pifferini crossed the plate after an illegal pitch (leaping) was called by home plate umpire Marty Makar against Juarez. It was the only run scored in the 1-0 Fresno State win. Arizona coach Mike Candrea was livid: "I thought we got hammered with a call that was pathetic." Fresno's Marcie Green allowed three hits and struck out six while Arizona's Doreen Juarez gave up six hits. Arizona finished in a tie for seventh.

With the conclusion of the two afternoon losers-bracket games, the two winners-bracket games began with UCLA facing Long Beach. The game was scoreless through four innings, with Long Beach hurler Ruby Flores allowing only a pair of hits. But in the fifth, the Bruins' offense generated three runs. Yvonne Gutierrez brought home a pair of runs with a double and scored moments later on a double to left by Kerry Dienelt. Flores remained in the game, but the Bruins chalked up three more runs in the sixth. In the seventh, Flores was replaced by Karrie Schott. Bruin freshman pitcher Lisa Fernandez got

**UCLA's multi-talented freshman Lisa Fernandez made her national championship pitching debut against Cal-Long Beach at the 1990 women's series. Fernandez played most of the tournament at third base and hit her first home run as a college player in this series.**

the 6-0 win, allowing only four hits in her national championship pitching debut. Three of the six runs Flores gave up were unearned.

In the nightcap, OSU coach Sandy Fischer started Australian freshman Melanie Roche to keep Florida State off-balance with change-ups. The strategy worked well, excepting the leadoff home run by Toni Gutierrez in the fifth inning. It was the first run off OSU pitching in thirty-four innings. Gutierrez' home run only reduced the OSU lead to 3-1, however, as the Cowgirls had earlier scored three times in the bottom of the fourth. Dena Carter's two-run single keyed the inning. The Cowgirls added another run in the sixth inning en route to a 4-1 win. Roche finished with a four-hitter, striking out nine. "Roche mixed her speeds well, and we didn't adjust to it quick enough," said Florida State coach JoAnne Graf. Debbie DeJohn was the losing hurler.

A losers' bracket game started the competition at 11 a.m. Saturday, with Fresno State facing Long Beach. Pitcher Terry Carpenter started for the Bulldogs and survived a Long Beach threat in the second inning when Fresno center fielder RaeAnn Pifferini fired a strike to catcher Shelly Stokes, who did a good job of blocking the plate to tag out Steffani Everett. "Long Beach is a very momentum-oriented team," Fresno coach Margie Wright said after the game. "I thought that play took the wind out of their sails." Losing pitcher was Mary Letourneau, who allowed a pair of Fresno runs in the first inning of the 2-0 Bulldog win. A single by Gina LoPiccolo brought home Julie Smith with the first run, and LoPiccolo scored the second run on an error by right fielder Carrie Smith. Long Beach tied for fifth.

In the afternoon, UNLV took an early 1-0 lead on Kim Harris's RBI single off Seminole pitcher Debbie DeJohn. Lori Harrigan gave up a run to Florida State in the fourth after Penny Siqueiros singled and scored on Lisa Barton's triple. Barton also scored when the relay throw to home was off the mark. Holding a one-run margin, the Seminoles added a pair of insurance runs in the sixth on a sacrifice fly by Siqueiros and a solo home run over center field by Barton. "I just try to hit the ball hard," said Barton in her first year of fastpitch. "I don't even think about hitting it far." She hit it far enough to advance the Seminoles in the tourney and to eliminate UNLV, which finished tied for fifth after the 4-1 loss. DeJohn finished with a five-hitter.

The 3 p.m. winners-bracket game featured UCLA against Oklahoma State, who had been beaten 2-1 in the winners-bracket by the Bruins in last year's championship. The Cowgirls hoped for some redemption, but fell behind 2-0 against pitcher Heather Compton, sister of former UCLA star Tracy Compton. UCLA loaded the bases against Dena Carter and scored twice when Yvonne Gutierrez's grounder was misplayed by shortstop Lee Anne Ketcham. It remained that way until the seventh inning when the Cowgirls' Shannon Kimberling singled down the first base line, scoring pinch runner Melanie Roche. OSU then got runners to second and third with two out. UCLA head coach Sharron Backus did not hesitate, bringing in right-hander Lisa Longaker. The senior hurler fanned Shawn Gilbert on three pitches to preserve the 2-1 win. Compton allowed five hits and fanned five batters.

After their afternoon loss, the Cowgirls turned right around and played Fresno State in an elimination game that night. Marcie Green and Dena Carter were the rival pitchers in the do-or-die situation with the loser going home. Fresno State's Julie Smith left the game in the third inning with a broken nose and concussion after she fouled off a pitch that bounced off home plate and into her face. But the weatherman was not on either team's side, and the game was suspended after nine innings because of severe storms. When play stopped, Fresno State had six hits to the Cowgirls' three, but neither team had scored.

The game was supposed to resume at noon Sunday, but the wet conditions delayed it. Following a twenty-minute blow-dry by local television station KFOR-TV's helicopter, play finally resumed a little after 3 p.m. The scoreless pitcher's dual was broken in the top of the tenth inning when Fresno's Carie Dever walked, then moved to second on Michelle Gardiner's bunt. Shelly Morrison's single moved Dever to third. Wearing a face shield, the injured Julie Smith hit a hard grounder to OSU shortstop Lee Anne Ketchman, who threw home to catcher Shannon Kimberling. The ball fell free when Dever's arm hit Kimberling's mitt for the game's only run. Losing pitcher Carter allowed eight hits, and winner Green gave up four. OSU finished third for the second year in a row. "The best I can say is we were happy to be in the final four," said OSU coach Sandy Fischer afterward. "But we are definitely tired of finishing third."

Next, UCLA played Florida State, and Bruin pitcher-third baseman Lisa Fernandez, who had not hit a home run all season, got one in the first inning with Kerry Dienelt aboard. The Bruins added another run in the seventh on a single by Missy Phillips against losing hurler Debbie DeJohn, who gave up ten hits. Bruin hurler DeDe Weiman allowed three hits in the 3-0 win that eliminated the Seminoles, who finished tied for third. Fernandez led the Bruins with a perfect 3-for-3.

Sunday night, Fresno State and UCLA met in the championship round for the third consecutive year. Little had changed—the Bulldogs needed to beat the Bruins twice to win the national title. The Bulldogs loaded the bases against Lisa Longaker with one out in the sixth inning, but they could not capitalize. The inning included a double by Michelle Gardiner, the only hit Longaker allowed. Scoreless through six and one-half innings, the Bulldogs opened the bottom of the seventh with a walk to Gina LoPiccolo. Dina Lopez was sent in to run for LoPiccolo. Longaker got the next two batters, then Dever got aboard on an error by left fielder Shelly Montgomery. Lopez had advanced to third base and scored moments later on a wild pitch by Longaker. Fresno State squeaked out a 1-0 win. Winning Bulldog pitcher Terry Carpenter had replaced Marcie Green in the sixth inning.

Playing in the if-necessary championship game that evening, the Bruins and Bulldogs finished the top half of the second inning before rain suspended play at 10:30. Terry Carpenter had started for the Bulldogs and gave up a pair of singles before Carie Dever replaced her and threw a wild pitch. This gave UCLA an early 1-0 lead before play was suspended. Play resumed Monday in the bottom of the

## 1990 Women's College World Series Bracket
Oklahoma City • May 23-27

## 1990 Final Standings

| | |
|---|---|
| University of California (Los Angeles) | 5-1 |
| California State University (Fresno) | 4-2 |
| Oklahoma State University (Stillwater) | 2-2 |
| Florida State University (Tallahassee) | 2-2 |
| California State University (Long Beach) | 1-2 |
| University of Nevada-Las Vegas | 1-2 |
| University of Arizona (Tucson) | 0-2 |
| Kent State University (Kent, Ohio) | 0-2 |

third. UCLA's Shelly Montgomery singled to left field and advanced to second on Shanna Flynn's sacrifice. Kerry Dienelt then brought Montgomery home, with a single to right field. Heather Compton was almost perfect for the Bruins, allowing only one hit—a single by Kerri Donis in the fifth inning. Compton finished with five strikeouts for her eighteenth win against one loss. Carpenter took the 2-0 loss for the Bulldogs with Dever and Marcie Green finishing up. It was Fresno State's fourth runner-up finish in the women's series. "I know there are one hundred other teams who would like to be in our spot," heartbroken senior Dever said, "but this is so hard. But I wouldn't trade my time at Fresno for all the money in the world." Despite her disappointment, Fresno coach Margie Wright graciously praised Oklahoma City's initial hosting of the tournament. "I felt it was run very well," she said. "I thought the committee did a good job."

Five Bruins were named to the all-tournament team, including Kerry Dienelt (1B), Lisa Fernandez (3B), Shanna Flynn (OF), Yvonne Gutierrez (OF) and Lisa Longaker (P). Fresno State players named were: Martha Noffsinger (SS), Julie Smith (2B) and Marcie Green (P). Also named were Florida State's Leslie Barton (OF) and Debbie DeJohn (P); and OSU's Shannon Kimberling (C) and Dawn Lange (2B). Leading hitter was UCLA's Missy Phillips at .467.

Attendance for the five-day event was 12,550—a considerable improvement over the 9,260 at Sunnyvale the year before. Oklahoma State's win over Florida State on May 25 was watched by a crowd of 2,526—a single-game record at the time for ASA Hall of Fame Stadium.

## Life After the WCWS...

UCLA's **Lisa Longaker** compiled an 89-12 record for a winning percentage of .881. She had a career ERA of 0.40, allowing only forty-two earned runs in 725 innings. The three-time, first-team NCAA All-American (1987-88, 1990) was named the Honda Award winner for softball in 1990. She is a member of the UCLA Athletic Hall of Fame (2001) and was named to the NCAA Div. I Softball 25th Anniversary Team in 2006. A mother of two boys, Longaker was teaching physical education at an elementary school in Santa Monica, Calif., in 2013. "Softball taught me so much, it made me think about life and my place in it," she said in a 2013 interview. "It gave me tools that I am forever grateful for." Co-tournament director **Cindy Bristow** played in three national championship tournaments for Cal Poly Pomona (1978-1980) and went on to serve as head coach of softball at New Mexico State University and Wichita State University. She worked for ten years at the Amateur Softball Association national office, including duties as director of Junior Olympic Softball and co-tournament director for the women's series in Oklahoma City for six years (1990-1995). She worked with the U.S. and several other countries' Olympic softball teams, provided color analysis for ESPN college softball broadcasts, and is a member of the National Fastpitch Coaches Association Hall of Fame. In 2013 she was the owner and operator of Softball Excellence, an online source for softball instruction.

# 1991: Arizona Wins Its First National Championship

The University of California at Los Angeles strutted into Oklahoma City for the Women's College World Series ranked No. 1 and heavily favored to win the national championship for the fourth consecutive year. The Bruins were 8-1 in regular-season play against the other seven teams in the tournament, with the Arizona Wildcats having handed them that single loss in a four-game series. Perhaps coach Mike Candrea's Wildcats could again be good enough or lucky enough to control the Bruin juggernaut in the championship. But as the teams readied for tournament play May 22–26 at ASA Hall of Fame Stadium, Bruins co-head coach Sharron Backus believed that the "good" and the "luck" were both on UCLA's side. "I guess we're like the cliché: 'I'd rather be lucky than good,'" she said. "We've been fortunate to be both lucky and good."

After the tournament's debut in Oklahoma City the year before, tournament sponsor All Sports Association hoped to improve on the first year's modest beginning. Another impressive eight-team field was poised for action, but on opening day Mother Nature had plans of her own. After three hours of intermittent rain on Wednesday, tournament play was postponed until 1 p.m. Thursday. Seven-time champion UCLA (52-5) would face twelfth-ranked Florida State (61-10) in the opening game.

The UCLA-Florida State game was indeed played on Thursday, but was delayed for five hours and came only after a dedicated effort from the grounds crew and the drying power of television station KFOR-TV's helicopter. The field was finally deemed playable for the 6 p.m. start. After six innings, neither team had crossed home plate, and UCLA managed only frustration against Seminole pitcher Christy Larsen. She had limited the Bruins to only one hit while her teammates had three off UCLA's Heather Compton. But in the seventh, Yvonne Gutierrez singled and came home on Missy Phillips's triple, which went over the head of FSU left fielder Leslie Barton. Barton was playing unusually shallow, almost to the infield. Seminole coach JoAnne Graf called it a "defensive mistake," and the miscue cost FSU the 1-0 game. Larsen allowed only three hits. Compton gave up four and struck out eight.

Because of the earlier delay, the Arizona-UNLV game did not start until 8 p.m. and was still underway more than three hours later. With the score still 0-0 in the top of the thirteenth, Arizona's Kristin Gauthier walked but was forced at second with Julie Jones safe at first. After Suzie Lady grounded out, catcher Jody Miller singled to right field and scored Jones. Miller had been hitless in four previous at-bats. "The ball just finds a hole sometimes," Candrea said after the 1-0 Wildcat win. Wildcat hurler Debby Day retired UNLV in the bottom half of the inning in order and finished with a seven-hitter. Loser Lori Harrigan gave up eight hits. UNLV twice got runners to third but couldn't capitalize, stranding ten altogether.

While Arizona and UNLV were battling on the stadium field, Missouri and Long Beach State were on the back diamond. Through three innings the game was scoreless. But with one out in the fourth, Linda Lunceford doubled, and Kellie Kane reached first base on an error by Missouri right fielder Jill Brent, allowing Lunceford to score. Missouri had a chance to tie the game in the bottom of the seventh with runners on first and second with one out. But pinch runner Terry Young was picked off at second for the second out, and Karen Schneider grounded out to end the game. The 49ers Mary Letourneau got the win, allowing three hits, one less than Tiger Karen Snelgrove in the 1-0 Long Beach win.

The tournament resumed at 11 a.m. Friday with the final first-round game, Fresno State versus Utah. Bulldog pitcher Terry Carpenter retired the first eighteen batters through six innings before Utah leadoff hitter Amy Timmel singled to left field in the seventh inning. Timmel never got beyond first as Carpenter retired the side, finishing with seven strikeouts and giving up one hit. "I didn't know I had a perfect game going until (third baseman) Gina (LoPiccolo) came up to me after the game and told me she should have had it (Timmel's hit)," said Carpenter after the 2-0 Fresno win. Utah hurler Janet Womack allowed six hits and struck out two. The two runs Womack allowed came in the third inning when Donna McDaniel scored on RaeAnn Pifferini's grounder and Dina Lopez scored on a wild pitch.

Florida State and UNLV followed at 1 p.m. in the first second-round game. The Seminoles got behind 1-0 after UNLV's Michelle Moreno hit an RBI double off Seminole starting hurler Toni Gutierrez with two out in the first inning, scoring Tricia Reimche. But the Seminoles came back quickly with two runs in the bottom of the second on a two-run double by Becky Harrison. The Seminoles added another run in the third inning when Penny Siqueiros scored on Lora Migliaccio's single to center. Gutierrez hurled two and one-third innings before being replaced by Larsen, the winning pitcher, who hurled four and two-thirds innings and went two-for-three at bat. Losing pitcher Kim Smith started but completed only the first two innings in the 3-1 FSU win. UNLV was the first team eliminated from the tourney.

The second elimination game followed at 3 p.m., and the Missouri and Utah hurlers hooked up in an old-fashioned pitchers duel. After a twenty-minute rain delay in the fourth inning, Utah's Janet Womack had a no-hitter through six innings and a one-hitter after eight. Both Womack and Karen Snelgrove eventually gave up five hits, but Womack allowed four of hers in the top of the ninth inning. The Tigers loaded the bases on an error and two singles before Rechelle Johnson doubled, scoring Karie Kearns for the first run. The second run came on a single by Kellie Leach, scoring Jill Brent, who led the Tigers with two hits in four at-bats. Snelgrove got the 2-0 Missouri win, which eliminated Utah.

Unbeaten Pac-10 archrivals UCLA and Arizona met in the Friday evening winners bracket, and the Bruins wasted a golden opportunity in the top of the first inning when leadoff batter Shanna Flynn doubled against Arizona hurler Susie Parra. But Parra got the next three batters in order. UCLA started sophomore Lisa Fernandez in the circle, who gave up hits grudgingly. Parra was pulled after hurling the fifth, bringing in Debby Day to finish the game. With the game scoreless, Wildcat Julie Jones opened the ninth inning with a double before advancing to third on a walk and a sacrifice. Jones scored on Lisa Guise's grounder to shortstop for the 1-0 Arizona win. Day allowed only one hit. Fernandez completed the game, walking two and striking out five. She allowed five hits, with Jones getting two of them. The Bruins stranded 10 runners to seven for Arizona. "This is the kind of game you dream of," Arizona coach Candrea said. "I told our kids to keep believing that defense and pitching will win for you and that's exactly what happened tonight."

In the second winners-bracket game Friday night, Marcie Green started for the Bulldogs against Long Beach and lasted only two and one-third innings before being replaced by Terry Carpenter. Long Beach scored their first run in the third inning when pinch runner Gina DiCorpo scored on third baseman Gina LoPic-colo's error. Long Beach pitcher Stacy Van Essen helped her cause on offense by contributing a two-run single to left field, also in the third inning in the 3-0 Long Beach win. Van Essen hurled a complete game, allowing four hits and striking out three batters. Although it was Fresno's second game Friday, Bulldog coach Margie Wright would not blame the loss on fatigue. "We made some ridiculous mistakes," she said. "That's the fourth time this year we've beaten ourselves against them."

Saturday morning UCLA found itself in a rare situation—facing elimination by Missouri in the 11 a.m. game. But also saddled with a loss, the Tigers faced the same. Having stranded ten on base in their previous game, the Bruins were determined to bring runners across the plate. Bruin designated player DeDe Wei-man batted only once, but she drove in two of four runs in the fourth inning with a double down the right-field line. Two additional Bruin runs in the inning were scored on a fielder's choice and an error. Heather Compton hurled a four-hitter for the Bruins, striking out two. Karen Snelgrove and Melissa Skow shared the Missouri pitching duties. Snelgrove hurled the first six innings, allowing five hits, with Skow hurling the last inning. The Tigers made three of their four errors in the game-breaking fourth inning. UCLA made it 5-0 on Kerry Dienelt's RBI single in the top of the seventh inning.

Another elimination game followed, matching Fresno State and Florida State at 1 p.m. Terry Carpenter pitched for the Bulldogs against Seminole hurler Christy Larsen. Kim Maher's two-out solo homer over left field in the first inning gave the Bulldogs a 1-0 lead. Fresno's second baseman Julie Smith had two hits in the game and scored the second Fresno run on a Larsen wild pitch in the third inning. Lars-en also had a costly error in the seventh inning when she overthrew first base on a bunt by Dina Lopez, who went all the way around to score as the ball rolled into the right field corner. The Seminoles suffered a 3-0 defeat and became the fourth team eliminated. Carpenter allowed only three hits, just one in the last six innings.

With the field cut in half, Arizona and Long Beach met in the winners-bracket final Saturday afternoon. The Wildcats had relied on defense and pitching, record-ing two 1-0 extra-inning wins. Although Long Beach pitcher Mary Letourneau allowed six hits through the first seven innings, she had not given up any runs. Nei-ther had her pitching rival, Debby Day, who gave up only three hits through eight innings, retiring seventeen of nineteen batters. But in the bottom of the eighth, Arizona's Stacy Redondo opened with a bunt single and later scored on a grounder to second by Julie Jones. Redondo beat the throw to home for the game's only run, advancing the undefeated Wildcats to the championship round following their third consecutive 1-0 extra-inning game.

After the loss, Long Beach played a determined UCLA team Saturday night with both teams facing elimination. The game was scoreless until the bottom of the

eleventh when UCLA's Lisa Fernandez singled to left center, and Yvonne Gutierrez singled up the middle for her third hit in five at-bats. Missy Phillips was intentionally walked, loading the bases. Long Beach replaced starter Stacy Van Essen
with Letourneau to face Lorraine Maynez. Maynez singled on an 0-1 pitch down
the right-field line, scoring Fernandez for the game's only run and eliminating
the 49ers. DeDe Weiman got the Bruin win, hurling nine innings with Heather
Compton finishing up.

The last game Saturday night matched Fresno State against Arizona. The Wildcats and Bulldogs battled through a scoreless seven innings before Fresno scored a
run with one out in the bottom of the eighth inning. Julie Smith got aboard on an
error by the shortstop and stole second base. After an out, Kim Maher singled to left
field, scoring Smith with what proved to be the only run in Arizona's first defeat.
Susie Parra took the Arizona loss, allowing four hits. Terry Carpenter got the 1-0
win for the Bulldogs, giving up three hits.

With three teams still alive on Sunday, play resumed early that afternoon with
UCLA facing Fresno State. The two teams traded runs with UCLA scoring in the
fourth and Fresno scoring in the bottom of the fifth. It remained that way until
UCLA broke the game open with four runs in the top of the thirteenth off losing
pitcher Terry Carpenter. Carpenter had pitched twenty-nine consecutive scoreless
innings until giving up the run in the fourth. Lorraine Maynez brought home
the first two runs in the thirteenth with a double. The third was scored on Kristy
Howard's sacrifice fly, and the fourth and final run came on DeDe Weiman's single
down the left field line. Fresno went down in order in the bottom of the thirteenth
and finished third in the tournament.

With one loss each, Arizona and UCLA played for the title late Sunday afternoon. UCLA started Heather Compton, who held a 4-0 tournament record and
had allowed just one run in twenty-nine innings. The Wildcats put Debby Day
in the circle. Arizona jumped out to a 2-0 lead in the third inning on Julie Jones's
bases-loaded triple, which was Arizona's first extra-base hit in the tournament. The
Wildcats added a pair of runs in the fourth on RBI singles by Susie Parra and Day
before the Bruins closed the margin to 4-1 on a leadoff home run by Lisa Fernandez in the fourth inning. The Wildcats closed out the scoring in the fifth when
Fernandez experienced control problems, throwing three wild pitches. Her third
wild pitch scored Suzie Lady, giving the Wildcats a convincing 5-1 win. Day finished with a 4-0 record, allowing one earned run in thirty-two innings, and led the
tournament in batting (.385). Arizona finished the year 56-16. Arizona coach Mike
Candrea was overjoyed with his first national title and the university's first national
championship in any female sport. "It's a culmination of four years of hard work
for some of our kids," he said. "We came out and beat a very good UCLA team."

The championship game drew a crowd of 1,880, bringing the overall attendance for seven sessions to 11,950, which was slightly below the year before. The
all-tournament team included Arizona's Julie Jones (1B), Julie Standering (SS),
Kristin Gauthier (OF) and Debby Day (P); UCLA's Lisa Fernandez (3B), Lorraine

# 1991 Women's College World Series Bracket
### Oklahoma City • May 22-26

## 1991 Final Standings

| | |
|---|---|
| University of Arizona (Tucson) | 4-1 |
| University of California (Los Angeles) | 4-2 |
| California State University (Fresno) | 3-2 |
| California State University (Long Beach) | 2-2 |
| Florida State University (Tallahassee) | 1-2 |
| University of Missouri (Columbia) | 1-2 |
| University of Utah (Salt Lake City) | 0-2 |
| University of Nevada-Las Vegas | 0-2 |

Maynez (OF), Yvonne Gutierrez (OF), Kerry Dienelt (C) and Heather Compton (P); and Fresno State's Terry Carpenter (P), Julie Smith (2B) and Kim Maher (at-large).

## Life After the WCWS...

UCLA's **Kerry Dienelt** made the women's series all-tournament team four times (1988-91). A native of Australia, she played on the Australian Olympic team in 1996 and 2000, as Australia won bronze medals. In 2004 she was inducted into the Softball Australia Hall of Fame. Fresno State's **Julie Smith** originally began her college softball career at Texas A&M before finishing at Fresno State, where she was twice an NCAA first-team All-American (1990-91). In 1996, she was named to the U.S. national team for its Olympic debut. She was also a member of three USA gold-medal Pan American teams and two ISF World Championship teams. As of 2013 Smith was the head softball coach and assistant athletic director at the University of La Verne, a private research university east of Los Angeles. UCLA's **Heather Compton** won sixty-seven games, fanned 540 batters in 538.2 innings, and compiled an ERA of 0.52. She was a first-team NCAA All-American in 1991. She played pro softball with the Tampa Bay Firestix and the Ohio Pride before being named an assistant softball coach at Florida State in 1999, where she remained in 2013. Fresno State's **Kim Maher** starred in amateur softball, earning ASA All-American honors four times and most valuable player of the Women's Major Fast Pitch National Championship in 1994. She holds the record for most home runs in a Women's Major Fast Pitch National Championship with five in 1994. She is Fresno State's all-time leader in home runs (31), RBIs (182), runs (162) and doubles (49). As of 2013, she was head softball coach at Purdue University.

## 1992: Bruins Get Revenge Against Wildcats

As teams gathered for the 1992 national championship in Oklahoma City, discussion began about softball's approval by the International Olympic Committee in 1991 as a medal sport for the 1996 Olympic Games in Atlanta. This had been a longtime dream of Amateur Softball Association executive director and International Softball Federation president Don Porter, who had worked diligently over many years in hope of the sport's Olympic approval. In just four years the sport would be on the international stage, and most of the players on the future U.S. Olympic softball team would be former participants in at least one of the Women's College World Series tournaments. Fastpitch softball's admission into the Games of the XXVI Olympiad was just another indication of how far both the sport and women's sports in general had come in the previous two decades.

Diane Milutinovich, associate athletic director at Fresno State University and chairman of the six-member NCAA softball selection committee (which assigned twenty teams to the eight regional qualifier tournaments), said that she believed softball needed more marketing and exposure nationally. In Oklahoma City for the 1992 tournament, Milutinovich told local media that moving the national championship to Georgia in 1995 and 1996, where the Olympic Games would be held that summer, would give the sport some much-needed outside exposure.

Although Milutinovich's advice would eventually be followed for the 1996 tournament, nothing had been decided about this move when the 1992 Women's College World Series began a five-day run from May 21-25 with another star-spangled field of teams. Schools at the tournament included: defending champion Arizona, four-time runner-up Fresno State, Cal State-Long Beach, Florida State,

Cal-Berkeley, Massachusetts, Kansas, and seven-time winner UCLA. The opening round of games Thursday had UCLA facing Massachusetts at 6 p.m., followed by Florida State and Cal-Berkeley.

Although UCLA finished second to defending champion Arizona in the Pac-10, the Bruins were seeded No. 1 owing to their winning fourteen of their last fifteen games against the other seven teams in the tournament. UCLA star hurler Lisa Fernandez brought an undefeated record (25-0) to the opening game against Massachusetts, including a streak of thirty-nine scoreless innings. UCLA third baseman Joanne Alchin put the Bruins in front 1-0 in the bottom of the third inning when she scored on the first of two wild pitches by the Minutewomen's hurler Holly Aprile. Leading 1-0, the Bruins pulled away by scoring three more runs off Aprile in the sixth inning. Fernandez faced twenty-two batters—one over the minimum—and struck out ten in the 4-0 shutout.

The second Thursday game matched Florida State's Toni Gutierrez against Cal-Berkeley's Michele Granger. The Golden Bears struck quickly in the first inning with two out when catcher Lidia Stiglich hit a double scoring Gillian Boxx. Janeen LaGrace scored another Cal-Berkeley run in the same inning on a passed ball. The Golden Bears added an insurance run in the bottom of the sixth inning when Lisa O'Connor scored on an error by second baseman Lisa Davidson attempting a double play. Although entering the tournament with the highest team batting average (.318), the Seminoles only managed two hits off left-handed, power pitcher Granger. She fanned seven and walked one in the 3-0 Cal-Berkeley win.

On Friday, No. 4-ranked Fresno State faced No. 11 Kansas, and Jayhawk starting pitcher Stephani Williams had a four-hit shutout and a 1-0 lead in the bottom of the seventh when the Bulldogs scored a run to tie the game. Fresno dramatically struck again in the bottom of the eighth when Michelle Bento hit a rise ball from Williams over the left-field fence for a three-run home run—her third of the season. Williams had not given up a home run in 254 innings, and only one her entire career. "I expected the pitch to be right there, actually," Bento said, "because my previous times up she was throwing high on the first pitch." Terry Carpenter limited Kansas to four hits and struck out eleven in the 4-1 Fresno win.

Late Friday, defending champion and No. 2-ranked Arizona contrived a new way to give up a run against Long Beach with two outs in the third inning. Amy Geldbach had gotten on base with a single, then tried to steal second. Arizona catcher Jody Miller's attempted throw to second hit the helmet of batter Sandra Ross, and the ball ricocheted into left field as Geldbach raced around to score. "Sometimes I guess it's better to be lucky than good," said Long Beach coach Pete Manarino. "I've been in softball a long time and I've never seen a play quite like that before." The Wildcats' attempt to tie the game came up short in the bottom of the seventh when Stacy Redondo's headlong dive did not pay off. Catcher Lisa Wilson blocked the plate to make the game-winning tag. Long Beach pitcher Stacy Van Essen fanned ten in the 1-0 49er win.

With the first round of games completed, play resumed Saturday with a pair of losers-bracket games at 11 a.m. Massachusetts took an early 2-0 lead against Florida State, squeeze bunting home a run in the first inning and scoring the second run on an RBI single by Sherri Kuchinskas in the third inning. Florida State tied the game at 2-2 in the sixth inning on RBI singles by Susan Buttery and Jennifer Olow. But in the top of the seventh, Rachel Lawson's two-run single provided Massachusetts with a 4-2 win. "I was real nervous up at the plate, actually," Lawson said. "I was shaking. But I was really concentrating on hitting the ball somewhere, anywhere, and luckily I did." Holly Aprile was the winning pitcher, allowing nine hits with two walks and three strikeouts. Toni Gutierrez took the loss as the Seminoles stranded eleven runners and became the first team eliminated.

Kansas began play against Arizona at 1 p.m. Saturday, and three hours later the game was still scoreless. Finally, in the top of the seventeenth with one out, Wildcat Amy Chellevold doubled to left field and soon scored on a high throw from shortstop to first base. With the 1-0 loss, Kansas became the second team eliminated. Designated player Chellevold led Arizona with a 4-for-7 performance. The two starting pitchers, Arizona's Susie Parra and Jayhawk Stephani Williams, went all seventeen-innings and allowed just seven hits each. Parra struck out fourteen.

After sitting through the seventeen-inning marathon, fans watched UCLA against Cal-Berkeley Saturday afternoon in the winners bracket. This game was the reverse of the previous, with UCLA scoring four runs in the first, five in the fourth, and one in the fifth to combine for the ten-run lead to end the game by run-rule. Increasing her scoreless-inning streak to fifty-one, Lisa Fernandez allowed only two hits. Jennifer Brundage's two-run double and a bases-loaded error by the third baseman accounted for the Bruins' four runs in the first inning. In the fourth, Fernandez singled to drive in a run, then eventually scored on an error by the shortstop. Kelly Inouye's three-run double to center completed the inning. Fernandez drove in two runs and was a perfect 3-for-3 at bat. "Our kids, literally, were hungry, because we didn't feed them most of the day," said UCLA coach Sharron Backus.

Four-time women's series runner-up Fresno State met Long Beach in the other winners-bracket game Saturday night, and the Bulldogs jumped out to an early 2-0 lead in the second inning. Misty Poplawski's one out, two-run triple off the right center-field fence was at the expense of the 49ers' starting pitcher Mary Letourneau. The Bulldogs increased the lead to 3-0 with a run in the sixth when Kim Maher led off with a solo homer to left field and added another score in the top of the seventh on Rhonda Schwebach's run-scoring single. Marcie Green allowed only a pair of singles while going the distance in the 4-0 Fresno win. Letourneau hurled three innings, followed by Ruby Flores and Stacy Van Essen. The loss dropped the 49ers into the losers bracket.

Pac-10 rivals Arizona and Cal-Berkeley closed out play Saturday evening, with each team throwing its ace, Debby Day for Arizona and Michele Granger for the Golden Bears. The Wildcats jumped out to an early 2-0 lead after Day drove home the first run with an RBI double down the third-base line. Pinch runner Valeria Zepeda scored the second run in the sixth inning when Susie Parra's fly to center field was dropped. Kari Kropke had California's only hit—a two-out single in the third inning—but it did not contribute to the Bears' only run. The Golden Bears picked up their score on a ground out in the seventh inning in the 2-1 loss, finishing 1-2 in the tournament and the third team eliminated.

Sunday's competition with Long Beach against Massachusetts started at 1 p.m., with the Minutewomen scoring a run in the first inning. Long Beach evened the score with a run in the third. From then until the tenth inning, the game remained tied at 1-1. But in the bottom of the tenth, UMass's Angyla Brumm, who had been hitless in three previous at-bats, dropped a double into right field, scoring Stacey Nichols with the deciding run in the 2-1 win and eliminating Long Beach. Talking about her game-winning hit, Brumm said: "I was very nervous, but I had to get relaxed or I couldn't see the ball. So I just took a deep breath, saw the ball, and swung." Holly Aprile got the win, allowing nine hits, and losing hurler Mary Letourneau gave up four hits. Amy Geldbach (4-for-5) and Sandra Ross (3-for-4, RBI in third inning) had seven of the nine Long Beach hits.

The winners-bracket final at 3 p.m. featured archrivals UCLA and Fresno State. The Bruins wasted no time, scoring three runs in the first inning and add-

ing another run in the fifth inning. The three runs in the first came on a three-run homer by Yvonne Gutierrez off Terry Carpenter, who went the distance allowing eight hits. UCLA's Lisa Fernandez continued to be a double threat for the Bruins. She limited the Bulldogs to only a pair of singles and had two hits in three at-bats. Fernandez drove in the fourth and final UCLA run in the fifth with a single, scoring Kristy Howard. Fresno had only four base runners in the 4-0 defeat.

Jennifer "Twiggy" Brewster is welcomed home by celebrating UCLA teammates after the slender freshman hit the championship winning home run in the bottom of the seventh inning against Arizona. *(Photo courtesy of UCLA Athletic Dept.)*

Arizona faced Fresno State at 6 p.m. Sunday evening. The

Wildcats took a 1-0 lead with a run in the third inning with two outs when Jamie Heggen brought Steph Salcido home with a single to right field. In the sixth inning it appeared the Bulldogs might blow the game open when they loaded the bases with no outs, but they failed to capitalize. Fresno eventually lost 1-0, the fifth team eliminated. "We just got too anxious," said Fresno State coach Margie Wright. "You don't ever predict something like that to happen, but it did." Arizona coach Mike Candrea knew his team had dodged a bullet in the sixth inning. "I think I was doing the sign of the cross during that inning," he said. Susie Parra hurled the win for the Wildcats, fanning six. Marcie Green took the Fresno loss. Heggen led Arizona with two hits in three trips. Donna McDaniel was 2-for-3 for Fresno.

The surprising survivor Massachusetts and powerhouse UCLA closed out Sunday night's competition at 8 p.m., and for a while the Minutewomen stayed with the Bruins. They trailed only 2-1 entering the bottom of the fifth inning after UCLA had scored single runs in the second and third innings on a two-out RBI single by Kristy Howard and a two-out solo home run by Yvonne Gutierrez. The Minutewomen had reduced the deficit to a run with Barb Marean's home run leading off the fourth inning. But their hopes of pulling a shocker crashed in the bottom of the fifth when the Bruins tallied nine runs on five hits to register a 11-1 run-rule victory. Gutierrez had her second home run of the game—a three-run blast—to conclude the scoring in the fifth. This eliminated the Minutewomen, who had distinguished themselves with a third-place finish in their women's series debut. Heather Compton struck out ten batters and allowed four hits for the win, which advanced the Bruins to the championship Monday against archrival Arizona.

With a crowd of 2,500 watching, UCLA and Arizona met for the national championship on Monday with pitcher Debby Day opposing Lisa Fernandez. Through six and one-half innings neither team had scored, and each pitcher had allowed only four hits. But in the bottom of the seventh, UCLA's only senior, Gutierrez, singled and was bunted to second. Slender freshman Jennifer "Twiggy" Brewster stepped to the plate, carrying a 2-for-15 slump in the tournament. "I wanted to get it out of the infield," she said later, "because I knew Yvonne was going to score if I did." Brewster scored along with Gutierrez after she connected on a screwball from Day for a dramatic line-drive home run to end the game. With the 2-0 win, the Bruins capped a 54-2 season and won national championship No. 8.

Day, who had beaten the Bruins 5-1 in the title game the year before, allowed six hits to Fernandez's four. Amy Chellevold had a perfect day against Fernandez (3-for-3), but her teammates were only 1-for-18. Fernandez was 4-0 in the tournament with twenty-nine shutout innings, and she also batted .500 (8-for-16). Gutierrez led the tournament with three home runs and eight RBIs with her .429 batting average. For the tournament, UCLA tallied thirty-one runs and sported a robust .333 batting average. "We've never hit like this before," said Backus. "But fortunately our senior (Gutierrez) really rose to the occasion."

The all-tournament team featured UCLA's Lisa Fernandez (P), Kathi Evans (OF), Yvonne Gutierrez (OF) and Kelly Inouye (C). Also, Fresno's Kim Maher

## 1992 Women's College World Series Bracket
Oklahoma City • May 21-25

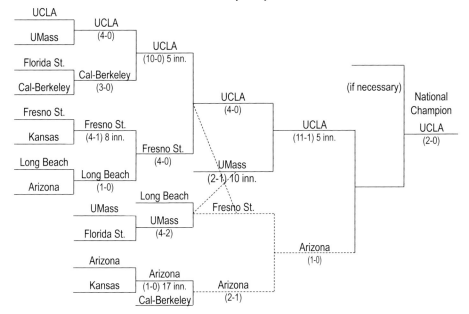

## 1992 Final Standings

| | |
|---|---|
| University of California (Los Angeles) | 5-0 |
| University of Arizona (Tucson) | 3-2 |
| University of Massachusetts (Amherst) | 2-2 |
| California State University (Fresno) | 2-2 |
| California State University (Long Beach) | 1-2 |
| University of California (Berkeley) | 1-2 |
| University of Kansas (Lawrence) | 0-2 |
| Florida State University (Tallahassee) | 0-2 |

(SS) and Michelle Bento (2B); Arizona's Debby Day (P), Susie Parra (at-large), Amy Chellevold (1B) and Susie Duarte (3B); and Massachusetts's Holly Aprile (at-large). Long Beach's Amy Geldbach was leading hitter at .467.

The seven-day attendance was 13,940, the best in the tournament's three years at Hall of Fame Stadium in Oklahoma City.

## Life After the WCWS...

UCLA's **Kelly Inouye** followed in the footsteps of UCLA coaches Sharron Backus and Sue Enquist when she was named the program's third head coach in

January 2007. Through 2012, she compiled a record of 255 wins and eighty-eight losses for a winning percentage of .743, including a national title in 2010. UCLA's **Yvonne Gutierrez** was named to the national championship's all-tournament team three years in a row (1990-1992) and finished her career with a .370 batting average, hitting nineteen home runs and driving in 149 runs. She was named an NCAA first-team All-American in 1991 and 1992.

## 1993: Wildcats Claw the Bruins Again

Although the adoption of a yellow, lively softball with a polyurethane center had a positive effect on hits and home runs during the regular season, it remained to be seen what effect this innovation would have in the 1993 Women's College World Series. For the fourth year in a row, the national championship would be held May 27-31 at ASA Hall of Fame Stadium in Oklahoma City. Cal State-Northridge coach Gary Torgeson did not hide his feelings about the new softball. "This ball is exactly what softball needs," he said. "You'll still see great-pitched games. But it used to be one run and it's over. Well, it's not over anymore." His team's home run production doubled to forty during the regular season.

All eight of the tournament teams increased their offense during the regular season and certainly hoped to continue that in the national championship. Veteran teams Arizona, UCLA, Oklahoma State, Connecticut, Cal State-Long Beach and Florida State were joined by women's series newcomers Southwestern Louisiana and Cal State-Northridge.

The No. 1-seed and defending champion UCLA Bruins faced Connecticut at 6 p.m. Thursday. This opening game matched the nation's leading earned-run pitchers, Lisa Fernandez of UCLA (0.28) and Pat Conlan of UConn (0.27). The Bruins gave Fernandez good support early, scoring twice in the first inning and adding another run in the fifth. Kristy Howard and Jennifer Brundage notched RBI singles for UCLA. Fernandez faced twenty-three batters—just two over the minimum—and hurled a no-hitter, with fourteen strikeouts and two walks in the 3-0 UCLA win. Conlan allowed four hits and gave up three runs.

In the second game, before a crowd of 4,300, Oklahoma State jumped out to a 5-0 lead with three runs in the fourth inning and two more in the fifth. Florida State countered with too little and too late, scoring a pair of runs in the seventh inning on Lisa Davidson's two-run double off Cowgirl pitcher Chrissy Oliver. Oliver hurled the last two innings for starter Melanie Roche, who pitched the first five innings, striking out seven, walking one, and giving up no runs. The two combined to pitch a four-hitter in the 5-2 OSU win. Toni Gutierrez and Marla Looper each hurled three innings for the Seminoles. Renee Cline, Kendra Hanes, Tonia Brown and Roche all had RBIs for the Cowgirls.

Despite occasional light drizzle, the final first-round games were played as scheduled on Friday. Arizona jumped out to a 2-0 lead against Cal State-Long

Beach with a pair of runs in the first inning, one in the second, and three in the fourth. Mary Letourneau hurled two and one-third innings for Long Beach before being replaced by Rae Rice, who finished the game. Susie Parra allowed five hits and fanned six in the 6-0 Wildcat win that avenged the previous year's bizarre 1-0 loss to the 49ers. "Revenge was probably in the back of our heads," Parra said. "It was sweet to come back and get all those runs and hits. But it didn't really seem like they were up. We were on fire though, and it's been a long time since we've been like that." Six Arizona players had at least two hits. Catcher Jody Pruitt was 3-for-4; DP Leah O'Brien was 2-for-3 and with two RBIs; shortstop Laura Espinoza was 2-for-4 with three RBIs. Amy Chellevold, Jamie Heggen and Stacy Redondo each had two hits.

In Friday's late game, Southwestern Louisiana and Cal State-Northridge battled to a scoreless tie through five innings in both team's debut in national championship play. In the sixth inning, the Lady Cajuns tallied four runs, with Lynn Britton and Kathy Morton delivering back-to-back RBI singles. Jen Fleming and Teri Pearson drove in a run each for Northridge in the bottom of the seventh inning. Winning Lady Cajun hurler Kyla Hall gave up four hits and struck out seven in the 4-2 USL win. Aptly named pitcher Amy Windmiller hurled five innings for Northridge, allowing six hits and four runs before Kathy Blake replaced her in the last two innings.

In the 11 a.m. Saturday elimination game between Connecticut and Florida State, the Seminoles had a 1-0 lead going into the bottom of the fifth inning after scoring on an RBI single in the third by Shamalene Wilson. But with two out, Connecticut's Andrea D'Innocenzo hit the tournament's first home run to tie the game. The Huskies had a chance to win the game in the seventh inning when D'Innocenzo singled, but Janna Venice tried to score from second and was tagged out at home. In the eighth Kim Staehle singled off FSU pitcher Rebecca Aase, was bunted to second, and reached third on Pat Conlan's single. She scored on Aase's wild pitch in the 2-1 UConn win that eliminated Florida State. Aase allowed eleven hits while winning hurler Conlan gave up four. Connecticut stranded eleven runners to FSU's six.

Cal State-Long Beach and Cal State-Northridge met in the second elimination game Saturday at 1 p.m., and the Northridge Matadors took a 2-0 lead in the first inning on RBI singles by Tamara Ivie and Scia Maumausolo. Northridge added another pair of runs in the fifth on two walks, an error, a sacrifice fly by Ivie, and Missy Cress's RBI single. The Long Beach 49ers closed the score to its final margin with two runs in the bottom of the fifth on Linda Lunceford's single. Kathy Blake hurled a four-hitter and was the winning pitcher in the 4-2 Northridge win that eliminated Long Beach, the second team sent home. Stacy Van Essen took the loss, allowing seven hits with two of the four runs unearned.

UCLA and Oklahoma State, no strangers in tournament play, faced off Saturday afternoon in a second-round game with a record crowd of slightly more than 5,000 on hand to watch what most figured to be one of the best games of the tournament. And it was. Pitchers Lisa Fernandez and Melanie Roche battled hard before the Cowgirls scored in the thirteenth inning. Kendra Hanes walked and was advanced on sacrifices by Renee Cline and Roche before Shyla Sick hit Fernandez' first pitch into center to drive in the game's only run. "You have to give it to Melanie," said UCLA co-head coach Sharron Backus," she pitched a whale of a ball game." OSU coach Sandy Fischer, who had been 0-3 against UCLA in previous women's series games, all narrow 2-1 losses, said about the win: "This is a big turning point for our team. It's a real shot for our program." In OSU's second game of the regular season, Fernandez had hurled a three-hit shutout in a 7-0 Bruin win with Roche allowing ten hits. Roche and Fernandez allowed five hits apiece Saturday, with Fernandez striking out thirteen and going 2-for-4 at the plate.

In the other second-round game Saturday, Southwestern Louisiana hurler Kyla Hall hit a solo home run off Arizona's Susie Parra in the fifth inning and the Wildcats trailed 1-0 going into the seventh. Then Arizona got back-to-back, one-out singles by Jenny Dalton and Krista Gomez. After a force-out, Amy Chellevold hit a high bouncer up the middle, scoring Gomez to tie the game at 1-1. The score remained tied until the tenth when Stacy Redondo scored on Leah O'Brien's sacrifice fly. The 2-1 win advanced the Wildcats to the winners-bracket final against Oklahoma State. Parra fanned sixteen batters and allowed only three hits, while Hall gave up seven hits and fanned five. Gomez had three of the seven hits.

In the final game Saturday, UCLA and Cal State-Northridge met in an elimination game. UCLA took a 2-0 lead in the fourth inning on a two-run triple by Janae Deffenbaugh, her only hit of the game. Her triple broke open the game and handed Northridge a 2-0 loss. Lisa Fernandez hurled another no-hitter and struck out thirteen. It was the eleventh no-hitter of her career. Kathy Blake was the losing hurler, allowing five hits while striking out three and walking two. Northridge became the third team eliminated.

On Sunday at 1 p.m., Southwestern Louisiana faced Connecticut in another elimination game. Through four innings the game was scoreless, but in the fifth Lady Cajun Vanessa Avant walked and first baseman Alyson Habetz smashed a run-scoring double into the right-field corner for the 1-0 USL win. This eliminated the Huskies. It was the only hit Habetz had in four at-bats and the only extra-base hit of the game. Connecticut finished 45-14. Losing hurler Pat Conlan gave up four hits, and winner Missy Skow allowed three.

The winners-bracket final with Arizona and Oklahoma State followed. It had all the intensity expected of two undefeated teams fighting for a spot in the championship round. After loading the bases in the third, fourth and seventh innings, Arizona stranded fourteen runners against Melanie Roche. "We were generating some offense," said Arizona coach Mike Candrea. "But the longer the game went, the more uneasy you get." Arizona catcher Jody Pruitt finally eased Candrea's mind, hitting a double over the head of right fielder K. K. McCoy in the bottom of the ninth inning and scoring Lisa Guise. This held as the game's only run in the 1-0 win. McCoy was playing in when Pruitt hit the ball into right center field off

Roche, who allowed twelve hits, walked one and hit two batters. Winning pitcher Susie Parra walked none, allowed three hits, and struck out thirteen. It was the second day in a row that OSU went extra innings, having played thirteen against UCLA the day before. "I think yesterday's game took something out of us," said OSU coach Sandy Fischer. "That's no excuse." OSU stranded seven base runners.

After the loss, the hardworking Cowgirls took the field again early that evening and met UCLA in an elimination game. The Bruins took the early lead with a run in the first before scoring twice each in the second and third innings. Jennifer Brundage had two RBIs with Joanne Alchin, Kelly Inouye and winning pitcher Lisa Fernandez driving in the other three in the 5-0 win. The Bruins had four hits to OSU's three. Melanie Roche hurled four and one-third innings, giving up the five runs, and Chrissy Oliver finished the game for the Cowgirls. OSU was the fifth team ousted, leaving Arizona, UCLA and a surprising Southwestern Louisiana team to battle it out for the championship.

Unbeaten Arizona faced once-beaten Southwestern Louisiana in the last game Sunday evening. Through four and a half innings, neither scored. But in the bottom of the fifth, the Lady Cajuns tallied a run on Vanessa Avant's RBI, bringing across Heather Neville with what proved to be the deciding run. Losing pitcher Susie Parra allowed only four hits and struck out ten. Winning pitcher Kyla Hall allowed six hits and struck out five. So the Lady Cajuns stayed alive to fight again on Monday against UCLA. The winner would face Arizona in the title game afterward.

After their 1 p.m. start on Monday, neither Southwestern Louisiana nor UCLA could manage a run through the first four innings. But in the bottom of the fifth, Janae Deffenbaugh hit a solo homer off Kyla Hall to put the Bruins on top 1-0. USL never managed to mount any kind of offensive threat in the pitching duel between Fernandez and Hall. The Lady Cajuns' only hit came from Vanessa Avant, who singled and eventually stole third with two out, but Fernandez then fanned Hall. The Bruin pitcher allowed only one more base runner the rest of the game, hurling a one-hitter and striking out seven. Hall fanned only

**Following the final game, Arizona Wildcats coach Mike Candrea made good on his promise to get a really close haircut if his players won a national championship in 1993. *(Photo by Doug Hoke)***

one batter and allowed three hits as Southwest Louisiana was eliminated 1-0 and finished in third place. "One pitch is really the difference in the game," said USL coach Yvette Girouard.

The championship game marked the third consecutive year Arizona and UCLA faced each other in the title game. Arizona struck early, getting a run in the bottom of the first inning off Lisa Fernandez. The Wildcats had only one hit in the final game—Leah O'Brien's one-out single up the middle that barely scored Amy Chellevold from second base. Chellevold had gotten on after an error by Bruin shortstop Kristy Howard. The Bruins had twice the number of hits that Arizona produced—but neither crossed home plate. Losing pitcher Fernandez (33-3) fanned four and walked one. In forty-eight innings pitched in the tournament, Fernandez allowed only eleven hits and two runs, and one of those runs won a national championship for Arizona. "I gave everything I had," said Fernandez. So did winning pitcher Susie Parra (28-3), who gave up only those two hits and fanned six going the distance. "Susie Parra proved today that she can throw with the best," said Arizona coach Mike Candrea, who forfeited his hair after the game to fulfill his promise to shave his head if the Wildcats won the title.

Arizona had five players on the all-tournament team: Parra (P), Jody Pruitt (C), Chellevold (1B), Krista Gomez (2B) and Stacy Redondo (OF). UCLA's selections were Fernandez (P) and Nichole Victoria (3B); USL's were Kyla Hall (P) and Kathy Morton (OF); Oklahoma State's were Melanie Roche (P) and April Austin (SS); and Connecticut's was Andrea D'Innocenzo (OF). UCLA's Fernandez led all hitters at .429.

The final session drew 3,150, bringing the five-day total to 21,963, a tournament record. And the new, yellow ball? In fifteen tournament games, forty-seven runs were scored, averaging 3.1 per game. But this was ten less than the year before when fourteen games were played. Five home runs were hit, and two no-hitters were pitched. And five of the last six games were 1-0 contests.

## Life After the WCWS...

**Lisa Fernandez** went on to an astounding amateur career, finishing at UCLA with a 93-7 pitching record and a .382 batting average. She led Division I colleges her senior year in ERA (0.25) and batting average (.510), the only player in the history of college softball to accomplish this feat. She was named an NCAA first-team All-American from 1990-1993. Fernandez won the Honda Sports Award in 1993 as the outstanding college softball player and went on to become the first softball recipient of the Honda-Broderick Cup, which is presented annually to the nation's top collegiate female athlete. In 2006 she was named to the NCAA Div. I Softball 25th Anniversary Team. A member of three U.S. gold-medal Olympic teams (1996, 2000 and 2004), she was inducted individually into the U.S. Olympic Hall of Fame in 2012. In 2013 Fernandez was an assistant softball coach at her alma mater, UCLA. A native of Australia, OSU's **Melanie Roche** was a two-time, first-team

## 1993 Women's College World Series Bracket
Oklahoma City • May 27-31

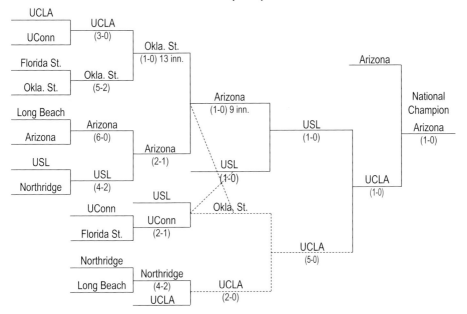

## 1993 Final Standings

| | |
|---|---|
| University of Arizona (Tucson) | 4-1 |
| University of California (Los Angeles) | 4-2 |
| University of Southwestern Louisiana (Lafayette) | 3-2 |
| Oklahoma State University (Stillwater) | 2-2 |
| University of Connecticut (Storrs) | 1-2 |
| California State University (Northridge) | 1-2 |
| California State University (Long Beach) | 0-2 |
| Florida State University (Tallahassee) | 0-2 |

NCAA All-American (1992-93) and played for Australia in four Olympic Games: 1996, 2000, 2004 and 2008. She was inducted into the OSU Athletics Hall of Honor in September 2011. She played in the Japan Softball League from 2001-2011 and is now a singer-songwriter in Australia.

## 1994: Wildcats Dominate Competition

By 1994, the Women's College World Series had become a popular event for attendees outside of Oklahoma as well as within. Although the field of eight teams would not be determined until May 22, the Oklahoma City All Sports Association received ticket requests from fifteen states more than seven weeks before the first pitch. These requests were even before the annual ticket-sales campaign had kicked off. Also, major changes in the tournament's format for play were implemented in 1994. There would be no winners-bracket final, no teams would play back-to-back games, and there would be only one "championship" game. So it was now a winner-take-all final game, which would be televised live by ESPN2 that year. All eight coaches in the tournament were satisfied with the new bracket. "I like it a lot," said UCLA co-head coach Sharron Backus. "It gives every team an opportunity to rest. ...There are all kinds of pluses."

The 1994 tournament was held May 26-30 and for the fifth consecutive year at the ASA Hall of Fame Stadium. The championship featured a mostly veteran field of teams, including: defending champion Arizona, UCLA, Fresno State, Oklahoma State, Utah State, Missouri, and Cal State-Northridge. The University of Illinois-Chicago was the only newcomer. All of the first-round games were played Thursday, starting at noon and continuing through the late evening.

In the first game, top-ranked Arizona, which had softball's version of Murderers' Row in 1994 (ninety home runs during the regular season), struck early against the Illinois-Chicago Flames. The Wildcats scored four runs in the second and two each in the fourth and fifth innings. Jenny Dalton had a two-run single in the second inning. Leah O'Brien's two-run blast highlighted the fourth inning, and she added a sacrifice-fly RBI in the fifth. Krista Gomez also had an RBI single in the fifth. Pitcher Nancy Evans allowed Chicago only three hits in the five-inning game, which was called because of the new eight-run rule in the 8-0 Flame loss. Chicago starting pitcher Destiny Mollison got the loss, one of four hurlers used against the hard-hitting Wildcats.

Archrivals Fresno State and fifth-ranked UCLA followed in the second game. Through six innings neither team could produce a run, and both had stranded numerous runners. But with two out in the top of the seventh, Bruin pitcher DeDe Weiman hit Fresno batter Jo Pini. Laura Berg singled, sending Pini to second, and freshman Robyn Yorke followed with another single to score Pini. Winning hurler Maureen Brady gave up eight hits, striking out five while handing UCLA its first opening-game loss (1-0) in women's series history. "The only job I was trying to do was hold UCLA to no runs so our team could score one," said Brady. "Every inning I just kept thinking: three more batters." Weiman fanned fourteen batters and allowed seven hits, with Yorke getting three of them. UCLA stranded twelve runners and twice loaded the bases against Brady with no results.

Oklahoma State and Utah began the evening session and almost duplicated the low scoring of the previous game. Going into the first extra inning, Utah scored two runs on two hits and two infield errors. Tammy Beer led off by getting on base on an error, stole second, and was singled to third by Amy Timmel. Stacie Reynolds singled home Beer with Timmel scoring on an infield error in the 2-0 Ute win. Utah pitcher Ali "Gator" Andrus limited OSU to only one hit—a single in the fourth inning by third baseman Brandi Stephenson. Ironically, Stephenson made both of the errors in the eighth inning. Losing hurler Amy Day allowed five hits and struck out eight, one more than Andrus.

Missouri and third-ranked Cal State-Northridge closed out the first-round of games in the nightcap. The teams were scoreless through three and one-half innings before Northridge hit three singles and a sacrifice-fly RBI in the bottom of the fourth to take a 4-0 lead. The Tigers, however, came back to cut the deficit in half with a pair of runs in the top of the fifth inning on Brandi Jones' RBI double and an error. Northridge's Tamara Ivie doubled in a run in the bottom of the inning to make it 5-2 before Missouri tallied a run in the seventh on Mary Babb's RBI double for the 5-3 Missouri loss. Pitcher Amy Windmiller went the distance in the win, striking out eleven and walking none.

Before an overflow crowd of 2,800 on Friday evening, the Wildcats jumped out to an early 2-0 lead against Fresno State in the opening second-round game. In the top of the first, Arizona scored on Leah O'Brien's RBI single and Nancy Evans's fielder's choice. Despite the early scores, Fresno played sensational defense and saved at least two and possibly three more runs in the inning. The Wildcats twice loaded the bases, in the third and sixth innings, but came up short. They scored their third run in the 3-0 win on Leah Braatz's home run leading off the seventh. Arizona had thirteen hits off losing hurler Maureen Brady. Susie Parra hurled a four-hitter and had her shutout saved in the fourth inning when O'Brien robbed Kim Maher of a home run by leaning over the fence next to the 220-feet sign in deep center field. "It was a great play at a great time," said Wildcat coach Mike Candrea, "because it kind of broke their back. If the ball goes out, it's a two-to-one game and the momentum has shifted."

In the second Friday game, Cal State-Northridge got a two-run home run from Beth Calcante to jump out to a 2-0 lead in the first inning against Utah. The Matadors expanded it to 3-0 on a walk, a single, and a sacrifice fly by Vicky Rios in the fourth inning. The Utes cut the deficit to two by loading the bases in the bottom of the fourth inning, scoring on a single by designated hitter Cyndee Bennett, who had three of the five hits given up by winning hurler Kathy Blake. Two unearned runs in the fifth inning finished the scoring in the Matadors' 5-1 win. Utah starter Ali Andrus allowed eight hits and five runs.

Facing elimination on Saturday, UCLA, which had beaten Illinois-Chicago 2-0 earlier in the year, scored a run in the second on Kari Robinette's RBI single, then added three more in the third and five more in the fourth. The Flames became the first team eliminated from the tournament with the five-inning, run-rule victory by the Bruins. DeDe Weiman and B'Ann Burns fanned ten and combined to no-hit Chicago, which also became the first team to lose its first two tournament games on the run-rule. In the 9-0 win, UCLA collected ten hits off four Chicago pitchers, with starter Jennifer Banas taking the loss.

Oklahoma State and Missouri met in the 2:30 p.m. Saturday elimination game, and OSU scored a quick run in the first. Missouri tied with a run in the bottom of the first. The Tigers increased their lead to 3-1 in the second before the Cowgirls, after a stern lecture from coach Sandy Fischer, tied the game at 3-all in the fifth. Cowgirl Karie Langelier's two-run home run in the sixth inning sealed the 7-3 win and eliminated Missouri. "The momentum really changed," said Langelier. "We were really on a high. People were diving for balls, hitting the ball better ..." Barb Wright absorbed the loss, allowing five runs in five and one-third innings. Kim Ward walked four and struck out five in her complete-game win. Cowgirl Michelle Kelly scored two runs and drove in a pair in a perfect game (4-for-4).

UCLA, playing its second game Saturday, faced Utah in an elimination game for both teams. Through three innings neither team scored. But in the top of the fourth, UCLA scored three runs on two hits, added four runs on four hits in the fifth, and closed out the scoring with four more runs on four hits in the top of the seventh in the 11-1 victory. Utah scored its only run in the sixth inning on three of its five hits with Deb DiMeglio's RBI-single. UCLA's DeDe Weiman fanned fourteen and allowed two hits, and B'Ann Burns gave up the three hits and the only run in the sixth. Utah's Ali Andrus hurled the first four and one-third innings with Amy Bigelow finishing. Nicole Odom (2-for-4, three RBIs) and Jennifer Brewster (1-for-3, two RBIs) led the Bruin offense.

Oklahoma State and Fresno State followed at 8:30 before a crowd of 3,500. The Cowgirls, who earlier had eliminated Missouri, broke a 0-0 deadlock through four innings with single runs in the bottom of the fifth and sixth innings. OSU got a break with its first run when Laura Quiroz's popup fell to the ground after a collision between shortstop Kim Maher and third baseman Erika Blanco. That brought up April Austin, who singled into center field to score Tonia Brown. The Cowgirls got an insurance run in the sixth when Michelle Kelly singled and later scored on April Ruedaflores' suicide bunt. The 2-0 OSU win eliminated the Bulldogs, and cut the field in half. OSU hurler Amy Day, a transfer from Southwest Missouri State, struck out seven and allowed four hits. Fresno's losing hurler Maureen Brady allowed six hits and struck out three.

Play resumed Sunday at noon with UCLA facing Arizona. The Wildcats were seeking their fifth consecutive win against the Bruins that season. After a scoreless first inning, Arizona broke on top for a 1-0 lead on an RBI single by pitcher Susie Parra in the second inning and increased it to 2-0 on an RBI single by Leah Braatz in the top of the third. The Bruins, however, countered in the bottom of the third and tied the game on a Jennifer Brundage sacrifice fly to left field and a Ginny Mike RBI single. Still, the tie did not last long as the Wildcats scored twice in the top of the fourth and added another run in the top of the seventh for a 5-2 win. Leah O'Brien and Jenny Dalton teamed up to bring across the last three Arizona runs, with O'Brien hitting an RBI single and Dalton a sacrifice-fly RBI in the fourth and a one-out solo home run in the seventh. "It was a very intense game," said Arizona coach Mike Candrea. "Usually is when we play UCLA." Susie Parra hurled a six-hitter to get the win for the Wildcats, striking out four and walking three. Weiman took the loss, allowing one more hit than Parra and fanning seven as UCLA finished the tournament in fourth place.

Cal State-Northridge and OSU followed at 2:30, and the Cowgirls took a 1-0 lead on Kim Ward's one-out double and Michelle Kelly's RBI single in the top of the fourth. The Matadors countered in the bottom of inning when Tamara Ivie walked, was bunted to second, and scored on Shannon Jones's single. OSU took a 2-1 lead in the fifth when Karie Langelier reached base on an error and scored on April Austin's two-out single. But Northridge fought back and tied it 2-2 in the sixth when Jones singled, went to third on Vicky Rios' single, and scored on a wild pitch. The game remained deadlocked until the top of the fifteenth when Kathy Blake, who hurled the last ten innings, gave up a pair of singles to April Ruedaflores and Langelier. Laura Quiroz advanced both runners with a sacrifice bunt, and Austin scored Koni Couts, pinch running for Ruedaflores, with the game-winner down the right-field line in the 3-2 Cowgirl win. Amy Day relieved Cowgirl starter Ward in the seventh and limited the Matadors to four hits and one walk to get the win. Blake also only allowed four hits, but two of them came in the fifteenth.

Sunday evening, the Cowgirls played Cal State-Northridge again with the loser to finish third and the winner to advance to the championship round. The Matadors exploded for four runs in the top of the fourth, with the first run scored on a sacrifice fly by Beth Calcante, and the last three runs courtesy of a booming three-run swat by Shannon Jones off OSU hurler Kim Ward. It was Jones's thirteenth home run of the season. Down 4-0, the Cowgirls reduced the game to its final margin with a pair of runs in the fifth inning on an RBI single by Ward and a

Celebrating after their title win in 1994, the Arizona Wildcats went 4-0 as they dominated the field. Arizona finished 64-3, breaking the NCAA record for wins in a season. *(Reprinted with permission from the Research Division of the Oklahoma History Center)*

# 1994 Women's College World Series Bracket
### Oklahoma City • May 26-30

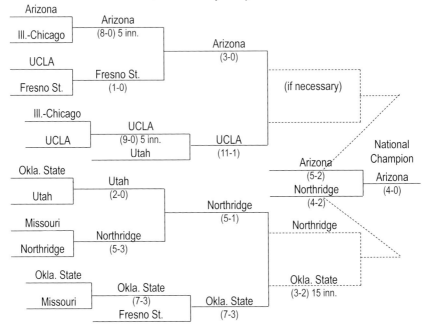

## 1994 Final Standings

| | |
|---|---|
| University of Arizona (Tucson) | 4-0 |
| California State University (Northridge) | 3-2 |
| Oklahoma State University (Stillwater) | 3-2 |
| University of California (Los Angeles) | 2-2 |
| California State University (Fresno) | 1-2 |
| University of Utah (Salt Lake City) | 1-2 |
| University of Missouri (Columbia) | 0-2 |
| University of Illinois (Chicago) | 0-2 |

solo homer by Laura Quiroz. OSU head coach Sandy Fischer summarized the 4-2 loss succinctly: "This game came down to one pitch and one catch." The one pitch was the Jones home run off Ward, and the catch was by Matador outfielder Beth Calcante, who robbed Karie Langelier of a game-tying home run in the sixth inning. Amy Windmiller got the complete-game win for Northridge, allowing seven hits. Cowgirls Ward and Amy Day combined to allow eight hits.

With the win, Cal State-Northridge advanced to the championship game Monday afternoon against the unbeaten Wildcats, eager to repeat as national champions. The Wildcats scored in each of the first three innings and added another run in the fifth inning. Laura Espinoza had a two-out RBI single in the first inning, Susie Duarte had the RBI in the second, Braatz had an RBI single in the third, and Jenny Dalton's fielder's choice scored the fourth and final run in the 4-0 win. Arizona collected seven hits off Jennifer Richardson and Amy Windmiller, who relieved Richardson in the fifth. Arizona's Leah O'Brien had three of Arizona's seven hits and scored two runs. Senior Susie Parra went out in style, allowing only two base runners, a first-inning single by Beth Calcante and a seventh-inning walk. She allowed only two runs in twenty-one innings in the 1994 tournament, and her earned-run average was 0.13 in 104 innings over four years of national championship play. "It was vintage Susie Parra," Candrea said after the win. "She has been phenomenal for the University of Arizona and the sport of softball."

With their repeat, the Wildcats finished the year 64-3, breaking the NCAA record for victories in a season, previously held by Florida State (sixty-three in 1992). The twelve all-tournament players selected were: Arizona's Leah Braatz (C), Amy Chellevold (1B), Jenny Dalton (2B), Leah O'Brien (OF) and Susie Parra (P); UCLA's Ginny Mike (at-large); Oklahoma State's Kim Ward (at-large), April Austin (SS) and Amy Day (P); Cal State-Northridge's Jen Fleming (OF), Shannon Jones (3B) and Beth Calcante (OF). O'Brien was also the leading hitter (.750).

The crowd of 4,000 for the championship game increased the overall attendance to 23,900, up from 21,960 in 1993. Just one week later, however, local organizers grew concerned over whether Oklahoma City would continue to serve as host for the tournament beyond 1995 and after the contract with the NCAA expired. The Division I softball committee was scheduled to meet in June 1994 to consider moving the event. Columbus, Ga., which would provide the softball venue for the 1996 Olympics, expressed an interest in serving as host for future women's series tournaments.

## Life After the WCWS...

Arizona pitcher **Susie Parra** compiled a four-year record of 101-9 with 61 shutouts, for a winning percentage of .918. She had a 9-1 record with eight shutouts in her four women's series tournaments. She was a two-time, first-team NCAA All-American (1993-94) and the 1994 Honda Sports Award winner for softball. In 2007, she was inducted into the Arizona Softball Foundation Hall of Fame.

# 1995: UCLA Takes Ninth Title (Temporarily)

In April 1995 the NCAA announced that the 1996 Women's College World Series would move to Columbus, Ga., the site for the 1996 Olympic softball competition that summer. Uncertainty over the return of the tournament to Oklahoma City hung like a dark cloud over local organizers and fans. "I was very disappointed," tournament co-director Marita Hynes said following the announcement.

"We've put a lot of heart into developing this championship. ... I hate to see it leave Oklahoma City." This was by far not the worst thing to happen to Oklahoma City that April. The Murrah Federal Building in downtown Oklahoma City, just a few miles southwest of ASA Hall of Fame Stadium, had been destroyed April 19 in a tragic and horrifying domestic terrorist attack. The city was still in shock over the loss of 168 lives. Still, advance ticket sales for the 1995 championship event were running nearly four times ahead of the previous year's purchases. Extra excitement was generated by the coming showdown May 25-29 at ASA Hall of Fame Stadium between No. 1-seed Arizona and No. 2 UCLA—Pac-10 rivals that between them had won the last seven national titles.

At noon on Thursday, May 25, Arizona (60-5) took on the unranked Princeton Tigers, a newcomer to the national tournament. Sporting the nation's leading batting average (.382) and averaging almost nine runs per game, the heavily favored Wildcats scored three runs in the bottom of the first on an error and a sacrifice fly. The Tigers struck back with a run in the top of the second. Princeton's Mandy Pfeiffer doubled to open the inning and eventually scored on Amy Whelan's RBI single. But Arizona added to its margin with a run in the third, two more in the fourth, and three in the fifth to emerge with a 9-1 run-rule victory. Arizona collected nine hits off losing hurler Maureen Davies, including back-to-back home runs by Leah Braatz (her sixteenth) and pitcher Nancy Evans in the fifth inning. It was Arizona's twenty-fourth run-rule win for the season. Evans allowed five hits in the win. "Any time you can get through the first ballgame of the College World Series in that fashion, you've got to be pleased," said Arizona coach Mike Candrea.

Fifth-seeded Cal State-Fullerton and No. 4-seed University of Nevada (Las Vegas) battled through six scoreless innings in the second game until the Titans scored a run in the top of the seventh. Julie Williams snapped out of an 0-for-9 slump with a two-out, run-scoring single bringing home Chris Zboril. Williams had two hits in three trips. "I knew I was due," said Williams after the 1-0 Fullerton victory. UNLV had only one hit off winning pitcher Jennifer Mortensen—a single by Sara Mallett to open the fourth inning. Mortensen fanned eight batters and walked four, besting the Rebels' Amie Stewart, who allowed three hits.

Thursday's night games—No. 9 Michigan versus No. 6 Southwestern Louisiana and unranked Iowa versus UCLA—were delayed by thunderstorms. The Michigan-USL game was scheduled to resume Friday morning with USL leading 1-0 in the bottom of the first, with two outs and runners on second and third. But rain delayed the restart until 2:30 p.m. Friday. USL finally scored a run on an RBI double by Stephanie DeFeo in the first inning. In the bottom of the second, the Lady Cajuns tallied twice, loading the bases on three consecutive singles before Lana Jimenez walked to bring across a run and Lynn Britton hit a sacrifice fly to bring in the second run. The Lady Cajuns added two more runs in the fifth on a two-run homer by DeFeo—her thirteenth of the season—en route to their final 5-0 win. USL hurler Cheryl Longeway fanned eight and walked three in blanking the Wolverines, her third no-hitter of the season. "All I want is a win," Longeway said.

"A no-hitter is a bonus, but all I want to do is win." The Lady Cajuns got eight hits off the two Michigan pitchers Sara Griffin and Kelly Kovach. DeFeo had three of those hits in a perfect performance.

UCLA and Iowa followed, and the Hawkeyes surprised the Bruins by taking a 1-0 lead on a Kari Knopf home run in the first inning. But the Bruins answered back in resounding fashion with a pair of back-to-back, two-out home runs by pitcher Tanya Harding and Alleah Poulson in the third inning. That ended the scoring. Harding gave up four hits and struck out six in the 2-1 win, while Iowa hurler Debbie Bilbao allowed eight hits. Iowa stranded six runners and UCLA eleven. Although the Bruins won, UCLA co-head coach Sue Enquist expressed some disappointment in her team's play: "In our huddle, I told the team: 'Bust out, bust out, just bust out. Don't be so tentative.'"

The Arizona versus Cal State-Fullerton game started around 6:30 p.m., and the Wildcats came out swinging with four runs in the first inning. They added three more runs in the third and four more in the fifth to register another run-rule win, 11-0, against the overwhelmed Titans. The Wildcats collected fourteen hits with Brandi Shriver's 3-for-3 and Jenny Dalton's three-run bomb in the fifth. Carrie Dolan got the win on a two-hitter, with Jennifer Mortensen and Brandi Isgar sharing mound duties for the battered Titans. "When Arizona is hitting on all cylinders, this is what they're capable of doing," said a beaming Mike Candrea.

Friday's round of competition concluded with UCLA facing Southwestern Louisiana. The Bruins took a 2-0 lead on a pair of RBI singles by Tanya Harding and Nicole Odom in the bottom of the first inning. The Bruins added a third run on an RBI single by Kathi Evans in the bottom of the fourth inning. Bruin hurler Harding retired the first thirteen batters in order before hitting Stephanie DeFeo in the fifth inning for the Lady Cajuns' only base runner in the 3-0 defeat. Cheryl Longeway absorbed the loss, giving up nine hits. "This game was all UCLA," said Southwestern Louisiana coach Yvette Girouard. "We looked intimidated the first four innings, which is unusual for us." Jennifer Brundage (2-for-4) and Odom (2-for-3) led the UCLA offense.

Princeton faced off against Nevada-Las Vegas at noon the next day, with both teams staring at elimination. The Tigers out hit UNLV eight to five and made no errors, while UNLV made three. But UNLV scored a run in the third and one in the sixth for a 2-0 lead. Kim Rondina and Sara Mallett had the RBI singles for UNLV, which split pitching between Amie Stewart and Teresa Branch. The Tigers battled to the end, scoring a run in the final inning, but stranding eight runners was hard for Princeton to overcome. Losing hurler Maureen Davies went the distance in the game, hurling a five-hitter as the Tigers became the first team eliminated. "The credit for this game goes to Princeton," UNLV coach Shan McDonald graciously remarked after her team's 2-1 win. "They played a helluva game, both offensively and defensively. ... We didn't play poorly, but we got the breaks."

Big Ten rivals Michigan and Iowa, who had split six games during the regular season, met that afternoon in another elimination game. Iowa jumped out to an early lead, scoring four runs in the top of the second before the Wolverines reduced the margin to one with three runs in the bottom half of the inning. In the fourth, Iowa scored again for a 5-3 margin, then Michigan took the lead with a four-run fifth inning. They couldn't hold it, however, as the Hawkeyes scored twice in the seventh to tie the game at 7-7. It remained that way through six more innings before the Hawkeyes tallied twice in the top of the fourteenth on a two-out, RBI double by Brandi Macias, who had a 5-for-7 performance. Kellyn Tate had a 5-for-7 showing for Michigan. Iowa's 9-7 win eliminated Michigan, the second team to pack. Each team used a pair of hurlers, Debbie Bilbao and Jenny McMahon for Iowa, and Sara Griffin and Kelly Kovach for Michigan. The two teams combined for thirty-one hits in a game that took three hours and fifty-three minutes. "People were on the edge of their seats the whole game," said Iowa coach Gayle Blevins. "The fans got their money's worth."

Nevada-Las Vegas and Southwestern Louisiana started at 6 p.m. Saturday, and the game remained scoreless until the bottom of the third inning. UNLV then exploded for five runs on six hits, featuring a three-run double by Kim Rondina and a two-run single by Cyndi Paris. Southwestern Louisiana scored its only run in the seventh inning on a two-out single by Lynn Britton. The 5-1 defeat eliminated the Lady Cajuns, the third team headed for home. USL's Amie Stewart hurled a complete game, allowing eight hits and striking out eight. Losing hurler Cheryl Longeway started and hurled into the fifth inning before Jennifer Clendenin finished up. Joni Podhorez had three hits in as many plate appearances to lead the Lady Cajuns.

Iowa and Cal State-Fullerton met at 8:30 p.m. in the last game Saturday, and the Hawkeyes got a solo two-out homer from Kari Knopf to take a 1-0 lead in the first. But the Titans tied the game in the second and took the lead with another run in the third. Fullerton expanded its lead to 5-1 with three runs in the fifth inning before the Hawkeyes tallied four in the seventh to tie the game at 5-5. Playing in the second extra-inning game of the tournament, Fullerton failed to score in the top of the ninth, but Iowa did in the bottom half on a fielder's choice by Tasha Reents for the 6-5 win. The Titans were the fourth team ousted. Debbie Bilbao hurled nearly eight innings to get the win, allowing eight hits. Jennifer Mortensen went eight innings in the loss, allowing six runs. In the losing effort, Fullerton out hit the Hawkeyes by double, twelve hits to six.

The final four—UCLA, Iowa, Arizona and UNLV—began play on Sunday, with Arizona and UNLV starting at noon. The Wildcats took an early 1-0 lead in the bottom of the first on a sacrifice fly by Jenny Dalton and increased it to 3-0 on RBI singles in the third inning by Brandi Shriver and Krista Gomez—with the help of two UNLV errors. UNLV loaded the bases in its half of the third, but couldn't capitalize, as Nancy Evans struck out Kim Rondina and Sara Mallett flied out. With UNLV trailing 3-0 in the fourth, the Rebels' Amie Stewart hit what would have been a two-run home run, but Arizona left fielder Alison Johnsen reached over the fence to make the grab and preserve the shutout. In the fifth, the Wildcats scored four more times on four hits, including a two-run single by Gomez and a two-run double by Leah O'Brien. With one more score in the sixth, the Wildcats' 8-0 run-rule win eliminated the Rebels, who had seven hits in the loss. Evans got the win and Stewart took the loss.

Perennial power UCLA and Cinderella-team Iowa met at 2:30 p.m. Sunday. UCLA took a 2-0 lead in the third on a two-run single by Tanya Harding and expanded it to 4-0 with another two-run single by Harding in the fifth. Jennifer Brewster upped the UCLA lead to 5-0 with a one-out, solo home run in the fifth. The 5-0 final score eliminated the Hawkeyes, who finished third and as the darling of the fans with their two remarkable comeback victories. "It was exciting to have tons of fan support," Iowa first baseman Kari Knopf said. "I mean people really started following us because we were the Cinderella team." Harding allowed five hits in the win and losing hurler Debbie Bilbao gave up eleven.

The big showdown between top-ranked Arizona and UCLA made for an All-Pac-10 final at 2 p.m. on "championship Monday." The Bruins had beaten the Wildcats in three of four games in regular season and were pitching Australian Tanya Harding, who had been imported by the Bruins in mid-season. With a crowd of 4,750 in attendance, Arizona struck first in the top of the second on Krista Gomez's RBI groundout, but the Bruins came back in the bottom half of the inning to take a 2-1 lead on Jennifer Brewster's two-run double. Each was scoreless in the fourth, but in the fifth the Wildcats tied it 2-2 on an RBI single by Leah O'Brien that scored Gomez from second. Then in the bottom half of the inning, the Bruins broke the tie—and the Wildcats' back—with a two-run home run by Kelly Howard after an error had put Ginny Mike on base. Final score: UCLA 4, Arizona 2. Howard's home run came off losing hurler Carrie Dolan, who allowed four runs (three unearned) and six hits. Harding got the win, scattering eight hits and frustrating the powerful Arizona lineup. Normally heavy-hitters Jenny Dalton, Laura Espinoza and Leah Braatz combined for a paltry 1-for-9.

"To win a championship you've got to execute perfectly," said Arizona coach Candrea. "Today we didn't help ourselves." UCLA made no errors while the Wildcats made several costly mistakes. In the second inning Jenny Dalton bobbled a grounder at second base that left two runners on with no outs. Three batters later, Brewster's drive was misplayed into a two-run double. In the fifth, Amy Chellevold dropped the throw at first base for an error before Howard connected on her game-winner. It was UCLA's ninth national softball title since 1978. "The sweetness is in beating a very, very talented team," said UCLA co-head coach Sue Enquist. But the sweetness for UCLA would not last. (Please see footnote after final standings.)

Harding was named the outstanding player for the tournament. She pitched four wins and had a .500 batting average (7-for-14 with six RBIs). The all-tournament team included: Arizona's Leah Braatz (C), Nancy Evans (P), Alison Johnsen (OF), Leah O'Brien (OF) and Brandi Shriver (at-large); UCLA's Tanya Harding (P), Jennifer Brundage (OF) and Kelly Howard (2B); Iowa's Brandi Macias (OF) and Kari Knopf (1B); UNLV's Amie Stewart (P); and Cal State-Fullerton's Julie Williams (SS). Batting .667, O'Brien and Shriver led the tournament.

# 1995 Women's College World Series Bracket
### Oklahoma City • May 25-29

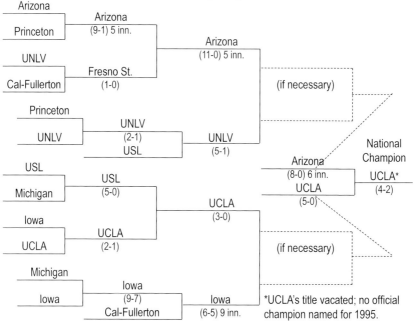

## 1995 Final Standings

| | |
|---|---|
| University of California (Los Angeles)* | 4-0 |
| University of Arizona (Tucson) | 3-1 |
| University of Iowa (Iowa City) | 2-2 |
| University of Nevada-Las Vegas | 2-2 |
| California State University (Fullerton) | 1-2 |
| University of Southwestern Louisiana (Lafayette) | 1-2 |
| University of Michigan (Ann Arbor) | 0-2 |
| University of Princeton (New Jersey) | 0-2 |

*In 1997 UCLA's first-place finish was vacated because of scholarship violations. Three softball players had been granted soccer scholarships, putting the Bruins three over the limit for softball. Although the three players involved were not identified, many believed that one of them was Tanya Harding. No official champion was named for 1995.*

The championship-game crowd increased final attendance to slightly over 22,000. With the 1996 national tournament traveling to Columbus, Ga., Oklahoma City organizers kept their fingers crossed for the event's return in 1997.

## Life After the WCWS...

UCLA's **Sharron Backus** retired from coaching in 1996 after compiling a record of 854-173-3. She is a member of the ASA National Softball Hall of Fame, the Women's Sports Foundation Hall of Fame and the NFCA Hall of Fame. She coached the Bruins to one AIAW national title and eight NCAA national titles. Arizona's **Laura Espinoza** smashed eighty-five home runs from 1992-1995, third best in NCAA history. She holds the University of Arizona single-season home-run record of thirty-seven (1995). She was named an NCAA first-team All-American in 1994 and 1995. UCLA's **Tanya Harding** left school two days after winning the 1995 national championship to return to play in the 1996 Olympics for her native country of Australia. She played in four Olympics, winning three bronze medals and one silver medal. Her school's first four-time, all-Pac-10 selection, Arizona's **Amy Chellevold** played in four national championship games and helped to win two of them. She stole 113 bases and left Arizona with a career batting average of .415, sixth best in school history. She batted .504 in 1994, third best season in Wildcat history. She was named an NCAA first-team All-American in 1994 and 1995.

# Seven

(1996-2004)

৯৶৶৶

# The Women's Series on the Olympic Stage

MOVING THE 1996 WOMEN'S COLLEGE WORLD SERIES to Columbus, Ga., and closer to the limelight of the Games of the XXVI Olympiad in Atlanta highlighted the connection between the growth of women's college softball and the sport's acceptance as an Olympic event. As host city for the national championship from 1990 to 1995, Oklahoma City had ridden the swelling wave of women's college softball. But behind this wave was an even stronger current—the growing acceptance of women's competitive sports. This worldwide tide swept women's fastpitch and larger numbers of female athletes into the 1996 Olympics. This tide also swept softball's national collegiate championship right out of Oklahoma City—at least temporarily.

The relocation of the women's series to Georgia disappointed and unnerved Oklahoma City tournament organizers. "It was a very big decision we did not make easily," said Cindy Cohen, chair of the NCAA softball committee and coach of the Princeton Tiger softball team. Cohen and her team had competed at the 1995 national tournament in Oklahoma City. "We know Oklahoma City has been great to us and for us. We would love to come back. It's definitely sad to leave Oklahoma City." Arizona's Mike Candrea, who had coached his Wildcat softball team to three national titles in the early 1990s in Oklahoma City, supported the tournament's relocation to Columbus. "If you look at the sport overall," he told a reporter at the 1995 championship, "it's a very good move." The Arizona coach said that he believed moving the tournament near the bright lights of the Olympics was a great opportunity to showcase the college championship in Columbus, at the same facilities where the women's Olympic competition would be held just two months later. Candrea also hoped that the women's series would return to Oklahoma City after the Olympic lights had dimmed. "Truthfully, I'd like to see it get back here," he said. "People here do an exceptional job."

The tournament's move to Columbus in 1996 may have served better as a dress rehearsal for the Olympic competition at the site than as a promoter of women's college softball. Attendance at the national tournament in Columbus fell to about

154

half what it had been in Oklahoma City in 1994 and 1995. Still, many hoped that the U.S. national softball team's appearance on the world stage in Olympic competition might do more than the Columbus event to promote the sport of fastpitch softball. The women on the U.S. softball team did not disappoint.

The U.S. national softball team, largely assembled from past and present stars from the Women's College World Series, played a big role in the Olympic show. The U.S. women won the gold medal in 1996, but they also won the hearts of America—female and male. Many of the former softball players in Columbus had starred in competition with little national recognition in Omaha, Sunnyvale and Oklahoma City—but after their televised performance in Olympic participation at Columbus, some of these women athletes became recognizable heroines at airports and in checkout lines across America. While the U.S. softball athletes may have stood out among other female competitors in the 1996 Olympic competition, they were among some 3,800 other women invited to Georgia to compete in a variety of sports. This was about 1,100 more females than had competed in the 1992 Olympic Games. Paralleling the trend in the United States, women in the 1990s were increasingly accepted in the Olympics Games as competitive athletes.

The female softball players from the United States were of a different breed than many of the American women athletes in past international competitions. Most had been born in the late 1960s and early 1970s and grew up with access to leagues and teams. Dubbed "Title IX babies," they had received college athletic scholarships and usually played on the best college softball teams. Almost all had been tempered in the heated competition of past Women's College World Series tournament play. In Georgia, they competed with skill and determination against the best teams in the world. Those who watched the U.S. softball team live in Georgia or on television at home in the summer of 1996 thrilled at the athleticism and competitiveness of the U.S. players.

Even before the somewhat disappointing crowds at the women's college championship in Columbus, the NCAA had already determined to return the national tournament to Oklahoma City. Meeting in July 1995 in Lake Tahoe, Nev., the NCAA softball committee entertained bids for the 1997 national tournament from Fresno, Calif., Columbus, Ga., and Oklahoma City, and perhaps others. But the committee chose to return the event to Oklahoma City, where it had begun to thrive in the early 1990s and where it would truly blossom throughout the rest of the decade.

Upon its return to Oklahoma City, a part of the tournament's increasing success was owed to the women softball stars of the 1996 Olympics. The college championship's move to Columbus that year may have been largely irrelevant, but the gold-medal performance of the U.S. national softball team brought the women's game to national and international prominence. When the 1997 college championship returned to Oklahoma City, the difference was palpable. Several of the teams in the women's series had players who had spent the most memorable summer of their lives the year before in Olympic competition. The Daily Oklahoman, the state's largest daily newspaper, ran a special feature on these Olympic veterans who were coming to town to compete in the national softball championship. The second game of the tournament—Arizona versus Fresno State—gave attendees the opportunity to watch three of the former Olympians in action.

Unsurprisingly, the 1997 national tournament set a record for attendance. The one year the event had snubbed Oklahoma City for the Olympic limelight was forgiven by the locals, who for the most part were just glad to get the tournament back. The 25,700 in attendance in 1997 beat the old record set in 1994 by nearly 8 percent. This upward trend in attendance would continue throughout the decade and beyond. Softball fans at the tournament enjoyed viewing many stars of both past and future Olympics in live competition.

Olympic glitter aside, the women's series also continued to reap benefits throughout the late 1990s from the growing number of college softball teams and increasing level of competition. With the continuing increase in college programs, the NCAA in 1999 expanded the number of team invitations to post-season regional tournament play from thirty-two to forty-eight. The new teams added excitement to the regionals and to the national tournament.

Continuing to upgrade its facilities for the burgeoning women's series, some $500,000 was spent on improvements to ASA Hall of Fame Stadium in 1998 and 1999. Continuing these efforts on a much grander scale in 2003 and 2004, another $6 million was invested in the stadium, raising fixed-seating capacity to 6,000 and adding 500 more parking spaces. Local organizers continually strived to provide a suitable home for the Women's College World Series in Oklahoma City.

ESPN television network's increased coverage of the tournament, especially after 2001, brought the national tournament to a mass audience across the country. Eleven games were televised by ESPN in 2002, and the ratings were good. By 2002 ESPN was televising all the games in the tournament. Women's college softball and its national championship were on a roll.

## 1996: Arizona Beats Upstart Washington in Columbus

Located about 100 miles southwest of Atlanta, the town of Columbus, Ga., served as the host site for the 1996 Women's College World Series. The eight teams gathered in the western Georgia city for competition at Golden Park Stadium, home of Class A baseball's Fire Sticks. The stadium would serve as the site for Olympic softball competition later that summer. Several of the college players in the women's series would compete for the U.S. women's national softball team just two months later, and the tournament competition provided an Olympic dress rehearsal for the Columbus facilities. The Fire Sticks played their home games at a nearby location while the women's competition took precedence that summer.

Columbus State University served as host school for the 1996 women's series, which started May 23 and concluded May 27. Mostly familiar teams from previous championships were on hand, including UCLA, Arizona, Michigan, Iowa, California-Berkeley, Princeton and Southwestern Louisiana. The only newcomer was the University of Washington, which made its debut as the tournament's top seed. All teams played on Thursday, May 23, with the precocious Huskies facing No. 8-seed Princeton at noon. Washington's rise to softball prominence had truly been meteoric under coach Teresa Wilson. Starting the Huskies' program from scratch four years earlier, the former Missouri Tiger star pitcher had guided Washington to a 56-8 record.

Washington jumped out to an early lead on a two-run home run by Sara Pickering in the bottom of the first. The Huskies increased their margin to 3-0 in the second when Mindy Williams scored on an error by the third baseman. The powerful Husky lineup added four more runs on four hits in the bottom of the sixth to hand Princeton its third consecutive loss in series play, with the Tigers winless in the previous year's championship. Princeton had only two hits off winning hurler Eve Gaw. The Tiger's Mandy Pfeiffer had both of the hits, including a one-out, solo home run in the top of the fourth inning. Losing hurler Maureen Davies gave up three runs on five hits in just over one inning, ending her twenty-eight-game win streak. Lynn Miller finished up in the Tigers' 7-1 loss.

Cal-Berkeley and Southwestern Louisiana met in the second game, and the Golden Bears surged ahead, scoring a run in the second and third innings. Jessica Parker opened the second inning with a double to left field, and Katie May followed with a run-scoring single to right field. In the third, Megumi Takasaki singled to left field, was sacrificed to second, and scored on Melanie McCart's single to left field. The Lady Cajuns collected seven hits, just two less than the Golden Bears, but could not bring across any runs in their 2-0 loss. USL stranded seven base runners in the shutout, only their fourth shutout of the year. Cal-Berkeley's Whitney Floyd struck out seven and hurled her twenty-seventh complete game of the season. Cheryl Longeway took the loss. "It was an obvious slow start for us," said USL coach Yvette Girouard. "We didn't make things happen and Berkeley did."

That evening, UCLA scored two runs against Michigan in the bottom of the second on a bases-loaded RBI single by Christie Ambrosi and a groundout by Laurie Fritz. Michigan twice got a runner to third base against Bruin hurler B'Ann Burns but couldn't capitalize, stranding five base runners during the game. Burns hurled her twelfth shutout of the season in the 2-0 game, her twelfth win in a row. She allowed only four hits—the second lowest total of the year for Michigan. Losing pitcher Sara Griffin hurled two innings, giving up two hits and two runs. Kelly Holmes hurled the last four innings for Michigan, allowing five hits. Right fielder Christie Ambrosi had three of UCLA's seven hits in a perfect evening at bat.

Arizona, runner-up the year before, closed out the first round of competition against the Iowa Hawkeyes, the Cinderella team of the 1995 tournament. The Wildcats seized the lead early, scoring twice in the second and three times in the third inning. Krista Gomez tallied the first run in the second on an error by left fielder Lea Twigg. Julie Reitan's RBI double to left center brought home Lisa Pitt.

The Wildcats went up 5-0 when Lety Pineda hit a two-run double to center field, and Tanya Farhat scored on an error by the second baseman. The double was Pineda's seventeenth of the season and extended her consecutive-game hitting streak to fifteen. The Hawkeyes avoided a shutout by scoring twice in the top of the seventh on RBI singles by Brandi Macias and Melissa Wielandt. Lisa Pitt hurled the 5-2, complete-game victory, allowing eight hits. Alison Johnsen had two hits in four trips to lead the Wildcats. Macias led the Hawkeyes with a 2-for-3 performance. Losing hurler Deb Bilbao hurled just over three innings, giving up seven hits and five runs. Jenny McMahon allowed one hit in remaining play.

The winning teams met on Friday, first with Washington facing Cal-Berkeley. The Golden Bears broke out early in the bottom of the first on a two-out RBI single by Jessica Parker that scored two runs. But the Huskies stormed back with three runs each in the third and fourth innings, two in the fifth, and one in the sixth to lead 9-2. Behind by seven runs, the Golden Bears mounted a furious rally in the bottom of the seventh, scoring five times on three hits and two errors—only to lose 9-7. Cal-Berkeley scored its last on a three-run home run by Jenny Ackley. After Ackley's long ball, winning hurler Heather Meyer got the final two outs, including left fielder Mindy Williams' robbing Parker of a home run. "It was redeeming for me," said Williams, who had missed a catch the day before. "Whether I had to climb the fence or not I was going to catch the ball." Williams also starred on offense (3-for-4). Whitney Floyd got the loss, allowing six runs on eight hits.

The evening concluded with archrivals UCLA and Arizona meeting at 8:30,

**Arizona pitcher and the tournament's most outstanding player, Jenny Dalton, holds high the 1996 championship trophy.** *(Reprinted courtesy of University of Arizona Athletic Dept.)*

and the Wildcats scored first on RBI singles by Julie Reitan and Michelle Churnock in the bottom of the second. The Wildcats increased their lead to 4-0 with a pair of runs in the sixth inning. Krista Gomez and Churnock had the RBI singles in the sixth as UCLA was shutout only for the second time of the season—and each time it had been the Wildcats. Carrie Dolan hurled the 4-0 win for the Wildcats without a base runner getting to third. She gave up five hits, walked one, and struck out three. Losing hurler B'Ann Burns gave up four runs in her seven-hitter. "We didn't play badly," Burns said, "They just put the ball in play when they had runners on base." Churnock had a perfect evening for the Wildcats (3-for-3), including a pair of RBIs.

Play resumed at noon Saturday with four losers-bracket games, starting with Princeton facing Southwestern Louisiana. Shutout in their opening game, the Lady Cajuns came back strong with three runs in the third and four more in the sixth en route to a 7-0 win, eliminating the Tigers. The Tigers collected only two hits off winning hurler Cheryl Longeway, who hurled her eighteenth shutout of the season and her fifth two-hitter. Her teammates collected thirteen hits off Maureen Davies and Lynn Miller, with Lynn Britton (3-for-5, one RBI), Lori Osterberg (2-for-4, two RBIs), and Kelli Bruce (2-for-3, two RBIs) leading the offense.

The Michigan-Iowa game followed, and the Hawkeyes scored three runs in the top of the fourth to start the scoring. The Hawkeyes tallied the three runs on four hits with Tammy Utley delivering an RBI double to left, and Melissa Young and Lea Twigg producing RBI singles. Young pinch-hit for pitcher Jenny McMahon, who hurled just more than five innings, allowed six hits, struck out five and gave up one of the two Michigan runs. The Wolverines scored their runs in the sixth and seventh innings to tighten the game to its 3-2 final margin. Losing pitcher Sara Griffin doubled to left center in the sixth and scored on Jessica Lang's single. In the seventh, Griffin singled to shortstop to drive in the second Michigan run. Griffin gave up seven hits in four innings, with Kelly Holmes finishing. Leticia Castellon got the save for Iowa.

Having won earlier in the day, Southwestern Louisiana met UCLA at 6 p.m., and the Lady Cajuns surprised the Bruins with a lead in the bottom of the first when Lori Osterberg's fielder's choice scored Vanessa Avant-Chapman, who had opened the inning with a single. The 1-0 lead held until the top of the fifth inning when the Bruins scored three runs, one on Julie Marshall's sacrifice-fly RBI and two on a single by Julie Adams. The game drew to its final 3-2 margin when the Lady Cajuns scored on Stephanie DeFeo's sacrifice-fly RBI to right field in the bottom of the sixth. B'Ann Burns limited the Lady Cajuns to seven hits as she won the thirteenth of her last fourteen games. Cheryl Longeway suffered the loss, allowing six hits and striking out seven. The Lady Cajuns became the third team eliminated.

Iowa played its second game of the day facing Cal-Berkeley in the final game Saturday night. The Hawkeyes seized the lead with a run in the bottom of the first inning when Lea Twigg singled to left field with one out and Christy Hebert doubled. Twigg scored on an error by the center fielder. That completed the scoring.

Pitcher Deb Bilbao hurled a three-hit shutout in eliminating the Golden Bears. Whitney Floyd absorbed the 1-0 loss, allowing four hits. It was the second consecutive tournament in which the Golden Bears had won their opener, then lost two straight. Berkeley was the fourth team headed home.

Action resumed at noon Sunday with Washington facing UCLA, and the Huskies scored first on Jennifer Cline's two-run single in the top of the third inning. UCLA tied the game on a two-out, two-run home run by designated hitter Kim Wuest in the bottom of the fourth. The tie was shattered when the Huskies scored six times on five hits in the top of the fifth to expand their lead to 8-2. The six-run fifth was highlighted by Sara Pickering's one-out solo home run and Jeanine Giordano's three-run double to right center. This drubbing eliminated the Bruins and handed them their worst defeat in women's series play. B'Ann Burns gave up eleven hits and eight runs (two unearned) in five innings before Kaci Clark finished up for the Bruins. Cline led the Huskies (4-for-4). Winner Heather Meyer allowed the Bruins eight hits and advanced the Huskies to the championship round.

Washington's opponent in the championship game would be determined in the next game at 2:30 p.m., with Arizona facing the never-say-die Iowa Hawkeyes. The Wildcats jumped ahead early, scoring three times in the first and once in the second before the Hawkeyes cut the deficit to two by scoring a pair in the bottom of the fourth. The Wildcats, however, tallied a run in the fifth and with five runs in the top of the sixth ended the game with the eight-run mercy rule—the first of the tournament. Jenny Dalton (3-for-3, 2 RBIs), Brandi Shriver (2-for-4, 2 RBIs), Alison Johnsen (2-for-4, 1 RBI), and Lety Pineda (1-2, 3 RBIs) led the fourteen-hit Arizona blitz. Dalton hit her twenty-fourth home run of the year to account for the run in the fifth, and Pineda hit a three-run home run (her fourteenth) to get the Wildcats off to the 3-0 lead in the first. Lisa Pitt allowed five hits in pitching the win, giving up the pair of runs in the fourth inning. Jenny McMahon, the first of three Iowa hurlers, took the loss. The win advanced the Wildcats to the championship for the sixth consecutive year and with three previous titles under their belt.

With a crowd of nearly 2,200 watching on Monday afternoon, the Wildcats came out swinging in the top of the first inning, scoring three on Jenny Dalton's home run. They added two more in the second and scored another in the fourth. Alison Johnsen's two-run double brought home the runs in the second and Pineda's two-out single scored the run in the fourth. The Wildcats looked on the verge of a rout with a 6-0 lead. But the Huskies answered in the bottom of the fourth, scoring four times on four hits to cut the deficit to 6-4. Michelle Church, Mindy Williams and Leah Francis all hit singles to drive in the Huskies' four runs. But the scoring ended there. Each team had eleven hits and two errors. Carrie Dolan went the distance to get the win for the Wildcats. Heather Myer lasted only an inning and two-thirds before Eve Gaw hurled the remainder of the game for the Huskies. Johnsen (4-for-4) led the Wildcats. Shelley Brown and Becky Newbry had two hits apiece to lead the Huskies, who finished the year 59-9 and with an impressive second-place finish in their first championship appearance.

# 1996 Women's College World Series Bracket
### Columbus, Ga. • May 23-27

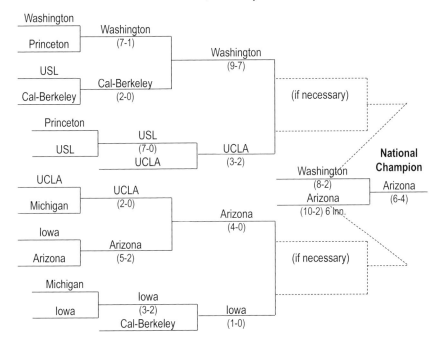

## 1996 Final Standings

| | |
|---|---|
| University of Arizona (Tucson) | 4-0 |
| University of Washington (Seattle) | 3-1 |
| University of Iowa (Iowa City) | 2-2 |
| University of California (Los Angeles) | 2-2 |
| University of California (Berkeley) | 1-2 |
| University of Southwestern Louisiana (Lafayette) | 1-2 |
| University of Michigan (Ann Arbor) | 0-2 |
| University of Princeton (New Jersey) | 0-2 |

"I am at a loss for words," Wildcat coach Mike Candrea said. "It is a great ending to a great year. Every kid over-exceeded my expectations." Dalton was named the tournament's most outstanding player. "What really pulled us through it is that nobody thought we could do it," she said. "I can't think of a better time when I have been so happy to prove everybody wrong."

Alison Johnsen led the tournament in batting (.533). The twelve named to the all-tournament team were: Arizona's Michelle Churnock (at-large), Carrie Dolan (P), Alison Johnsen (OF) and Krista Gomez (at-large); Washington's Jennifer Cline (C), Sara Pickering (2B), Tami Storseth (SS), and Mindy Williams (OF); Iowa's

Lyn Nance (at-large) and Lea Twigg (OF); Michigan's Traci Conrad (1B); and Southwestern Louisiana's Cheryl Longeway (P) and Lynn Britton (3B).

Attendance for the tournament in Columbus was not what many had hoped for or expected. It drew 10,000 less than the previous year in Oklahoma City.

### Life After the WCWS...

**Jenny Dalton** was named a three-time, first-team NCAA All-American (1994-96) and turned down the opportunity to play for the U.S. national softball team in the 1996 Olympics. She served as an assistant for the Kentucky Wildcats in the late 1990s. She was inducted into the University of Arizona Sports Hall of Fame in 2001. In 2013, the mother of three coached high school softball in Kentucky. A two-time, first-team NCAA All-American (1995-96), Southwestern Louisiana's **Cheryl Longeway**, was named the Louisiana Player of the Year in 1996. In 2011 she was inducted into the University of Louisiana-Lafayette Athletic Hall of Fame.

# 1997: Arizona Wins Post-Olympics Series

The 1996 U.S. women's Olympic softball team had been loaded with past and present stars of the Women's College World Series, and members of the gold-medal softball squad became celebrated heroes and household names across the nation. Three of these Olympians were in Oklahoma City to play in the 1997 women's series: Christa Williams (UCLA), Leah O'Brien (Arizona) and Laura Berg (Fresno State). "The experience is unbelievable," O'Brien said of the 1996 Olympic softball competition in Columbus, Ga. "Nothing else like it."

For these three former Olympians, the national championship tournament in which they were about to play may have lacked the thrill of the Olympic competition in Georgia. But for many softball fans, a seat at the 1997 tournament put them within shouting distance of some of the heroines of the U.S. softball team. The Olympic connection to the women's national championship had a noticeable effect on publicity and ticket sales. Advance sales were so brisk that more reserved seats were added to ASA Hall of Fame Stadium. "We have an awful lot of people coming from out of state," said Stanley Draper Jr., executive director of the event's local sponsor, the All Sports Association. "We've been constantly amazed at how many people come in. We're shooting for at least 25,000 with the interest we've seen."

A field of veteran teams gathered for the event, scheduled May 22-26, including defending champion Arizona, 1996 runner-up Washington, Massachusetts, Fresno State, UCLA, Iowa, Michigan and South Carolina. The teams had been seeded prior to the national tournament and assigned to different regional sites.

Beginning play at noon Thursday, top-seeded Arizona took a 1-0 lead in the first inning against Massachusetts when Alison Johnsen scored on former Olympian

Leah O'Brien's sacrifice fly to left field. UMass tied the game in the fourth inning on a one-out solo home run to left field by Sam Cardenas off pitcher Nancy Evans. In the bottom of the eighth, O'Brien singled Johnsen across with the game-winner for a 2-1 win. Each pitcher allowed five hits with Danielle Henderson absorbing the loss. Evans fanned ten batters in the win and would go on to pitch every inning for Arizona the entire tournament. Johnsen went 2-for-4 to lead the Wildcats. Cardenas and designated hitter Chris Martens led UMass with two hits apiece.

In the second game, fifth-seeded UCLA and fourth-seeded Fresno State battled through seven innings to a scoreless tie. Fresno State pitcher Amanda Scott was dominant in the middle innings, retiring twelve batters in a row at one point on grounders, including five in a row on bouncers back to the mound. But in the top of the eighth, the Bruins got to Scott for two runs on three hits with Alleah Poulson's two-run single the game-winner. Poulson (3-for-4) and Christie Ambrosi (2-for-4) had five of the seven hits Fresno's Scott allowed in her complete-game, 2-0 loss. UCLA's Christa Williams, who was a member of the USA 1996 Olympic team as a teenager, allowed only two hits, striking out ten. Fresno coach Margie Wright summed up the game from the Bulldogs' viewpoint: "It's pretty hard to win a game when you only have two hits."

No.-3 seed Iowa and Michigan began the evening session with the Wolverines taking a 2-0 lead in the top of the fourth on Melissa Gentile's two-out, two-run home run with Traci Conrad on base. "I really didn't know what pitch it was," Gentile said about her fifth home run of the season. "I just saw it coming and it was right down the middle." But the Hawkeyes tied the game an inning later on Tammy Utley's two-run double to left field. It remained 2-2 until the bottom of the seventh, when Iowa pitcher Deb Bilbao led off with a single, was sacrificed to second, and scored the winning run on Brandi Macias's single to left field. Michigan's Kelly Homes hurled six and two-thirds innings and gave up nine hits, which was two more than Bilbao.

Washington and No.-2 seed South Carolina closed out the first round Thursday evening, with the Huskies striking for three runs in the fourth inning and three more in the fifth. Leanne Rosser had a two-run home run off the top of the center-field bleachers in the fourth inning and added an RBI triple in the fifth inning. Sara Pickering had an RBI double to account for the other fourth-inning run. Becky Newbry's RBI double and a passed ball brought in the three runs in the fifth. The Gamecocks loaded the bases in the sixth inning with none out, but Sondra Hall's line drive down the third base line was caught by Heather Tarr, who tagged out Carolina's Tina Plew for a double play. The Gamecocks stranded seven runners in their 6-0 loss, ending their twenty-three-game win streak. South Carolina's Trinity Johnson allowed nine hits and struck out ten. Jamie Graves gave up five hits for the win, striking out three. "Sometimes pitchers win, and sometimes hitters win," South Carolina coach Joyce Compton philosophized. "Today it was the hitters."

Archrivals UCLA and Arizona played in the first winners game Friday evening, and neither team managed to score through thirteen tense innings. Finally, with two out in the top of the fourteenth, the Wildcats staged a rally. Chrissy Gil got aboard on a bunt single and stole second. Then Alison Johnsen walked before Katie Swan brought both runners home with a double to left field that bounced past Courtney Dale and rolled to the fence. In the bottom of the inning, UCLA loaded the bases before winning pitcher Nancy Evans took a bounce-back to her lip that she managed to toss to first for the final out. The 2-0 Bruin loss sent UCLA to the losers bracket. Evans hurled a five-hitter, striking out eight. Losing hurler Christa Williams fanned ten batters and gave up nine hits.

Iowa and Washington concluded the Friday winners games, starting late because of the earlier fourteen-inning contest. Washington jumped to the lead in the bottom of the first on a sacrifice-fly RBI by Becky Newbry. Iowa tied the game at 1-1 in the top of the third on Lyn Nance's single after Christy Hebert had tripled to open the inning. But the tie was broken in the bottom of the frame when the Huskies scored on Sara Pickering's RBI single. Washington scored two more runs in the fifth on Leah Francis' single and scored another in the sixth when Leanne Rosser drew a walk with the bases loaded. Jennifer Spediacci hurled the first two innings, allowing two hits for the Huskies before Jamie Graves came on to finish the game and get the 5-1 win. Deb Bilbao hurled the complete game for the Hawkeyes, allowing six hits, striking out nine and walking five. "To start at 10:45 after you have been here since 6:30 p.m. was a little bit difficult, to say the least," Washington coach Teresa Wilson said.

On "elimination Saturday" four games were scheduled, starting at noon with UMass facing Fresno State. The Minutewomen, who were 31-5 for the season in games when they scored first, went up 1-0 in the bottom of the first on Kim Gutridge's two-out single to left field. This scored Stephanie Mareina, who had singled to right with one out and advanced to second on a wild pitch. But the Bulldogs took the lead in the top of the third with two out when Angela Cervantez's hard grounder glanced off the glove of second baseman Mandy Galas with the bases loaded. This allowed Robyn Yorke and former Olympian Laura Berg to score. Neither team scored in the remaining four innings, so UMass was eliminated in the 2-1 loss. Each pitcher allowed four hits apiece with winner Lindsay Parker striking out six. Losing hurler Danielle Henderson fanned four.

Michigan and South Carolina met in the second game, and through five and one-half innings the teams were scoreless. In the bottom of the sixth with two out, Michigan's Traci Conrad got on base and Cathy Davie singled to right field. Michigan coach Carol Hutchins sent Conrad home when the right fielder booted Davie's hit. "I was trying to pull Conrad around the base and sneak it across," said Hutchins, who said she knew she was going to send her runner home "as soon as she left first base." The 1-0 loss eliminated the Gamecocks, who finished the season 63-5. Trinity Johnson took the loss, allowing four hits and finishing the year 34-4. Kelly Holmes gave up three hits and struck out five in her complete-game win.

With two teams eliminated, Fresno State faced Iowa at 6 p.m., and the Hawkeyes bolted to a 2-0 lead with runs in the first and third innings. Fresno State then erupted for four runs in the fourth inning to lead 4-2. But Iowa followed with their own four-run fifth inning, keyed by back-to-back homers by Tammy Utley and Brandi Macias. With Iowa leading 6-4 in the top of the seventh, Fresno State rallied for two runs on four consecutive singles. Iowa pitcher Debbie Bilbao steadied and retired the next two batters, bringing Laura Berg to the plate with runners on second and third. Iowa elected to walk Berg, loading the bases and setting the stage for Robyn Yorke's slap single between third and short. This capped the Bulldogs' dramatic rally and gave them a 7-6 win. Losing hurler Deb Bilbao hurled nearly four innings, giving up nine hits and six runs. Kim Peck got the win for Fresno State hurling just over two innings and allowing three hits. Both Brandi Macias of Iowa and Brooke Bernardoni of Fresno State went 3-for-4.

UCLA and Michigan followed in the last elimination game at 8:30 p.m., and the Wolverines took a 1-0 lead in the bottom of the second on Melissa Gentile's second home run of the tournament, a drive to left off Bruin starter B'Ann Burns. Michigan starting hurler Kelly Holmes blanked the Bruins the first three innings, but the UCLA offense finally came alive in the fourth inning with two runs. They added three more in the fifth and two more in the sixth. Michigan added single runs in the sixth and seventh innings in the 7-3 loss. They finished the year 56-16-1—best in school history. Holmes hurled six innings in the loss, allowing seven hits and seven runs. Burns hurled the first three innings, allowing two hits, and Christa Williams completed the game to get the win. Julie Marshall (3-for-4, 2 RBIs) and Alleah Poulson (2-for-3) led the UCLA offense, and Kellyn Tate (2-for-3) led the Wolverines.

Play resumed Sunday at noon with Arizona facing Fresno State. The Bulldogs took the lead in the bottom of the third on Nina Lindenberg's RBI single to left field, scoring Laura Berg. Berg had doubled and advanced to third on an error by Wildcat hurler Nancy Evans. The Bulldogs increased their lead to 3-0 with a pair of runs in the sixth inning courtesy of solo home runs by Lindenberg and pitcher Amanda Scott off Evans, who allowed five hits. Arizona's 3-0 defeat ended their twenty-six-game win streak. Scott gave up three hits—two to Leah O'Brien—and struck out five. She also contributed two hits in three at-bats. Lindenberg had a 2-for-3 performance with a pair of RBIs. It was only the second shutout suffered by Arizona that season.

Washington and UCLA followed at 2:30 p.m., and the Huskies' Shelley Brown scored on a passed ball in the top of the first. Sara Pickering's grounder brought home another Washington run in the same inning. Washington added to their lead when Leanne Rosser scored on a Christa Williams' wild pitch in the fourth inning, one of three in that same frame. Washington pitcher Jamie Graves, meanwhile, hurled just over four perfect innings as she throttled the Bruins, running her record in the series to more than sixteen scoreless innings. But in the fifth the Bruins ended her streak—and her perfect game—when Julie Adams hit a solo home run to left field. Then Stacey Nuveman hit a tremendous two-out, three-run blast to center field in the sixth inning to give UCLA the 4-3 win. "It wasn't a bad pitch,"

Graves said, "but to Stacey Nuveman it probably was." Freshman Nuveman's twentieth home run of the season helped Christa Williams get the win.

Fresno State and Arizona met in an elimination game at 6 p.m., and the Bulldogs jumped ahead on Nina Lindenberg's RBI single to center field in the first inning. They tallied again on Amanda Scott's RBI sacrifice fly with the bases loaded in the top of the third inning. But the Wildcats tied the game at 2-2 on Leah O'Brien's two-run round-tripper to left center in the bottom of the third. The Bulldogs regained the lead in the fourth inning on a solo home run to left field by Catalina Chavez, only to lose it in the fifth inning when the Wildcats scored on Leah Braatz's RBI single and again on a fielder's choice. Arizona closed out the game with two more scores on a home run in the sixth by Alison Johnsen in the Wildcats' 6-3 win. Amanda Scott got the loss, giving up five hits. Nancy Evans went the distance—again—allowing eight hits and striking out eight. Johnsen and O'Brien had two hits apiece in three at-bats for Arizona. The Wildcats advanced to the championship game.

Starting at around 8:30 p.m. Sunday, Washington and UCLA battled to face Arizona in the title game and neither scored through five innings. Washington pitcher Eve Gaw hurled a perfect game until the sixth inning when UCLA's Christie Ambrosi got on with an infield single. Laurie Fritz then got aboard on a fielder's choice, and Alleah Poulson singled to left field. With two runners on base, freshman catcher Stacey Nuveman lined an RBI double off Heather Tarr's glove at third base to score Fritz for the game's only run. The Huskies never threatened until the bottom of the seventh when Heather Tarr and Leah Francis blooped one-out singles. But pinch hitter Rochelle Rahal hit into a force-out at second, and UCLA first baseman Alleah Poulson threw to third to catch pinch runner Jamie Redd off the bag for a double play. Williams collected her third win of this tournament, striking out seven and giving up four hits—one more than Gaw. The 1-0 loss finished the Huskies for the year at 50-19 and in third place.

The championship final began at 1 p.m. Monday with both teams well experienced in the championship round. Pac-10 rivals Arizona and UCLA had won every championship between them since 1988, and had met earlier in the tournament when Arizona won 1-0 in fourteen innings. In the title game, Arizona scored two runs in the first and then added four more in the second inning for a quick 6-0 lead. UCLA's Julie Adams and Julie Marshall hit back-to-back homers in the bottom of the second to reduce the margin to four. But the Wildcats scored four more times in the fifth inning to end the game at 10-2 on the mercy rule—the first time the rule had been used in the championship game. The indefatigable Nancy Evans struck out three and walked one to get the win. She also helped out with three RBIs. UCLA's Christa Williams was battered for eleven hits and walked five as the Bruins finished the year 49-14. "That's Arizona softball," said Arizona coach Mike Candrea. "Get people on, get a key hit, and you can blow people out."

Evans was named the tournament's most outstanding player. The ten players named to the all-tournament team were Arizona's Leah O'Brien (1B) and Alison

## 1997 Women's College World Series Bracket
### Oklahoma City • May 22-26

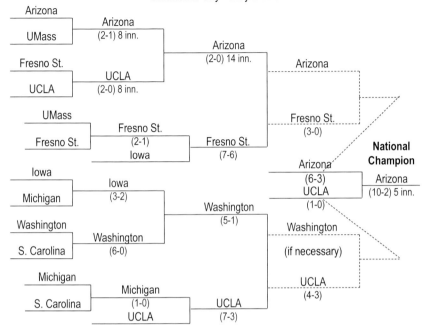

## 1997 Final Standings

| | |
|---|---|
| University of Arizona (Tucson) | 4-1 |
| University of California (Los Angeles) | 4-2 |
| University of Washington (Seattle) | 2-2 |
| California State University (Fresno) | 3-2 |
| University of Iowa (Iowa City) | 1-2 |
| University of Michigan (Ann Arbor) | 1-2 |
| University of Massachusetts (Amherst) | 0-2 |
| University of South Carolina (Columbia) | 0-2 |

Johnsen (OF); UCLA's Stacey Nuveman (C) and Alleah Poulson (1B); Washington's Sara Pickering (2B) and Jamie Graves (P); Michigan's Melissa Gentile (3B); Iowa's Christy Hebert (SS); and Fresno's Nina Lindenberg (2B). Leah O'Brien led the tournament in batting (9-for-15) with a .600 batting average and had six RBIs. It was the last women's series for senior O'Brien, who was 31-for-55 in four championship tournaments, including two home runs, twelve runs scored, and nineteen RBIs in her eighteen games.

Stanley Draper Jr., head of local sponsor All Sports Association, had hoped for attendance of at least 25,000 in the post-Olympic year. The official attendance figure came in at 25,694—a new record for the championship event.

## Life After the WCWS...

Arizona's **Leah O'Brien** was named to the women's series all-tournament team twice and was an NCAA first-team All-American in 1994, 1995, and 1997. She was a member of the U.S. national softball team in three Olympics (1996, 2000 and 2004) and was named to the NCAA Div. I Softball 25th Anniversary Team in 2006. O'Brien was inducted into the ASA National Softball Hall of Fame in 2009. In 2013 she provided color commentary for ESPN television and served as host for a religious sports show on Trinity Broadcasting Network. Following the 1997 tournament, UCLA's **Christa Williams** transferred to the University of Texas, where she completed her college career and was a first-team NCAA All-American in 1998. She was a member of the U.S. Olympic softball team in 1996 and 2000. In 2013, she was a softball coach at Manvel (Texas) High school. Washington's **Sara Pickering** was a two-time, first-team NCAA All-American and started at second base every game from 1994-1997. Pickering was diagnosed with Hodgkin's Disease and underwent a life-saving stem cell transplant in 2001. In 2013, she was an assistant coach at Fresno State.

# 1998: Fifth Title Game a Charm for Fresno State

An Oklahoma City sportswriter likened the Arizona Wildcats' appearance at the 1998 Women's College World Series with Godzilla's coming to dinner. The Wildcats' appetite had been hearty throughout their 64-3 regular season, and they returned to Oklahoma City having won four of the past five national championships. Coach Mike Candrea had built a softball dynasty on the desert, but Washington Husky coach Teresa Wilson offered hope for the tournament's other seven teams. "This is a game of inches," she said as tournament play began. "You can get ten hits and lose. Get two hits and win. It's a funny game."

Top-seeded Arizona would face a field of veteran teams at the tournament, scheduled May 21-25 at ASA Hall of Fame Stadium. The other contenders included Fresno State, Oklahoma State, Texas, Massachusetts, Nebraska, Washington and Michigan. With UCLA suspended from post-season play for scholarship violations, the 1998 tournament marked the first year a Bruin team had not played in the national softball championship since 1986. All the teams played in the opening round on Thursday, with two afternoon games and two evening games.

In the opener, Arizona faced the OSU Cowgirls, a team that had given the Wildcats some tough games in the past and that in the past few years had been a game or two away from the championship round. A crowd of 3,170 watched through five innings with neither team scoring. But in the bottom of the sixth with one out, Arizona third baseman Toni Mascarenas homered over left field to put the Wildcats ahead 1-0, snapping a twenty-six-inning streak of scoreless pitching by OSU hurlers. Wildcat pitcher Nancy Evans, named most outstanding player of the

1996 tournament, allowed only a two-out single by Kristi Bolle in the third and a leadoff single by Jaime Foutch in the seventh in the 1-0 win. Including Mascarenas's blast, OSU hurler Jenn Markert allowed only four hits while walking four and striking out five. "Couldn't ask for a tighter game," said OSU associate coach Margaret Rebenar, who filled in for ailing head coach Sandy Fisher. "It's not fun to lose the game on one pitch and one swing. We hope to see Arizona in the finals still."

In the next afternoon game, Washington took the lead in the first inning against Massachusetts when Kelly Hauxhurst walked, stole second, and scored on Eve Gaw's single to right field. Pitcher Jennifer Spediacci held UMass to one hit through five innings—a single in the third inning by Nikki Faessler. Spediacci was replaced by Jamie Graves, who hurled the last two innings and gave up a pair of hits in the seventh, including a double down the left field line by Faessler that sent Anne Smith to third base. But Graves got Kiley Scofield to ground out to end the threat in the 1-0 Washington win. Pitcher Danielle Henderson gave up three hits and struck out seven in the loss, ending her nineteen-game winning streak. Spediacci and Graves combined to hurl the Huskies' twenty-eighth shutout of the season. "We've started out with a couple of 1-0 games," said Washington coach Teresa Wilson. "There is a lot of parity in the tournament and a lot of quality teams."

In the first evening game, Michigan faced tournament newcomer University of Texas, thriving in only its second year of varsity softball under coach Connie Clark. The Wolverines got only four hits off Christa Williams, who had transferred from UCLA to Texas, but all came in the first inning and gave them a commanding 7-0 lead. Melissa Gentile's three-run home run (her thirteenth) to left center started the scoring, and Pam Kosanke's RBI single increased the lead to 4-0. Lisa Kelly then got aboard on an error to score another run, and two more errors brought home two more. Texas battled back with a pair of RBI singles by Autumn Eastes and Angie Scharnhorst to reduce the game to its final 7-2 margin. Williams lasted only a third of an inning for the Longhorns, giving up seven runs and yielding the mound to Christy Guidorizzi, who struck out eight. Sara Griffin got the complete-game win, allowing four hits and four walks while striking out three.

Four-time tournament runner-up Fresno State and Nebraska closed out the first round Thursday evening. In the second with two outs, Fresno's Angela Cervantez hit a solo home run, and in the third with two outs Fresno's Nina Lindenberg and hurler Amanda Scott hit run-scoring singles. The Huskers tallied a run in the bottom of the third on Ali Viola's RBI single to left center. The score remained 3-1 until the top of the fifth when the Bulldogs scored twice on Scott and Jamie Maxey's RBI singles. Carolyn Wilson's RBI double in the seventh completed the Bulldogs' scoring in the 6-1 victory. Scott struck out six and went 2-for-4 at-bat with a pair of RBIs. Jenny Voss allowed thirteen hits and took the loss, which ended her eleven-game win streak. Cervantez went 3-for-4 for the Bulldogs. Viola led the Huskers with three singles and an RBI.

With the first round completed, Friday's pair of games featured the winners of the four opening games. In the first game, Washington changed pitchers often

against Arizona, including one after only five pitches. They had three more changes in the fourth inning when starter Jamie Graves came back in for Jennifer Spediacci, who moments later replaced Eve Gaw. "We were trying to throw their hitters
off balance," said Washington's Wilson, who had coached the Huskies in one of
the three Arizona losses that season. By the third inning, however, the Wildcats had
piled up a 4-0 lead with single runs in the first and second innings, and two in the
third. Washington threatened in the third when they loaded the bases with one out,
but Evans retired the next two batters to end the threat. Arizona then scored four
times in the fourth for an 8-0 mercy-rule victory. Graves's single was the only hit allowed by Evans, who fanned four. Graves, Spediacci and Gaw allowed eleven hits.
Evans went 3-for-3 with two RBIs, followed by Alison McCutcheon with 3-for-4.

Fresno State faced Michigan in the second game, and the Bulldogs scored on
Amber Wall's two-run home run in the second inning. Fresno State then scored
four more runs in the fourth on three hits and an error, and two more in the fifth
on three hits. This gave the Bulldogs an 8-0 run-rule victory—the first time in
seventeen years that two consecutive games ended on a run-rule in the women's

**Flanked by several of her Fresno State players, coach Margie Wright hoists the 1998 na-
tional championship trophy.** *(Reprinted courtesy of FSU Athletic Communications)*

series. Amanda Scott had her drop-ball working and hurled her second no-hitter of the season. She faced fifteen batters—three struck out and twelve hit ground balls. Michigan had only one base runner against Scott, when Melissa Gentile got on base after an error by the shortstop in the second inning. Sara Griffin hurled four innings, giving up five hits and six runs in the loss. Jamie Gillies finished the game for Michigan, allowing three hits and the final two runs.

Noon on Saturday, Oklahoma State played the University of Massachusetts, and the Cowgirls hit three home runs in a span of three innings and thirteen batters against UMass hurler Danielle Henderson. Liz Silva started the assault with a line-drive home run into the left center field bleachers in the third inning. Shannon Sullivan followed with a one-out solo home run in the fourth, with Silva adding an RBI single in the inning. Kristi Bolle completed the homer assault with a two-run smash to left field in a three-run fifth inning in the 6-0 Cowgirl win, eliminating the Minutewomen. Henderson took the loss, giving up seven hits and six runs. "I've never had this happen to me my whole life," said a shell-shocked Henderson. "They hit the ball wherever it was." Henderson had allowed only one home run the entire regular season. The three home runs was an NCAA tournament record back to 1982. Leanne Tyler got the win for the Cowgirls, allowing a single by Kim Gutridge in the first inning for the first one-hitter of her career.

The next elimination game followed at 3 p.m. with Texas and Nebraska. The score was deadlocked at zero until the top of the fourth when the Huskers scored twice. Freshman Jamie Fuente doubled home Jennifer Lizama, and Jenny Smith's sacrifice fly to left field scored the second run. The Longhorns came back, how-ever, to narrow the game to its final 2-1 margin in the sixth on Nikki Cockrell's solo home run to left field, her tenth of the season. Jenny Voss went the distance in the win, allowing four hits and striking out eight. This extended her scoreless-inning streak to ninety-five for the season. Losing hurler Christa Williams fanned eleven and walked two, allowing only Fuente's double. "I was supposed to bunt the first pitch but I didn't," Fuente said. "So I tried to make contact, and I was fortunate enough to just slap it into the gap. She (Williams) is such a great pitcher that you have to be confident or that is one more notch she has against you."

Michigan and Oklahoma State played next at 6 p.m., and the Cowgirls took advantage of a second baseman's error to score twice in the first inning without any hits. Pam Kosanke's RBI single scored the lone Michigan run in the top of the fourth. OSU's Jaime Foutch then singled home Kristi Bolle from second base for another run in the bottom of the fourth. Michigan collected nine hits off two OSU hurlers, Amy Lopez and Jenn Markert, but had trouble bringing runners across in their 3-1 defeat. This eliminated the Wolverines, who tied for fifth place. Sara Grif-fin took the loss, allowing three runs (all unearned) on four hits with seven walks and two strikeouts. Traci Conrad had four of the nine Michigan hits in a perfect performance. So the Cowgirls advanced to the semifinals for the fifth time in ten women's series appearances.

Starting play shortly after 9 p.m., neither the Huskies nor the Huskers scored through the first four innings. In the top of the fifth, however, Washington tallied twice on Kelly Hauxhurst's two-out, two-run double off third baseman's Cindy Roethemeyer's glove. They added another run in the sixth on Eve Gaw's home run, her eighth of the season. Washington pitcher Jennifer Spediacci allowed no runs or hits until the seventh, when Ali Viola clubbed her twenty-second home run of the season. Until Viola homered, Spediacci had allowed only one base runner, Jennifer Lizama, who got on following an error by shortstop Rosie Leutzinger in the fourth. Spediacci struck out eight in her 3-1 win while eliminating Nebraska, pitching her twenty-third complete game of the season. Jenny Voss took the loss.

With the field reduced to four teams—Arizona, Oklahoma State, Fresno State and Washington—play resumed Sunday at noon with Arizona facing Oklahoma State. The Wildcats got away fast, scoring twice in the first inning on a two-run home run by catcher Leah Braatz over the left field fence—her twenty-fifth—and added three more runs in the third on a Braatz sacrifice-fly RBI and a two-run home run over left field by Leticia Pineda—her twentieth. The Cowgirls, meanwhile, could manage only two hits off stingy Wildcat hurlers Nancy Evans and Becky Lemke. Evans allowed two hits and struck out six in five innings, with Lemke finishing up the 5-0 win for Arizona. It was Evans's seventeenth consecutive win and her third shutout in the tournament, extending her overall women's series record to 10-1. Jenn Markert and Leanne Tyler combined to hurl the OSU loss, which eliminated the Cowgirls and advanced Arizona to the championship game.

The Fresno State-Washington semifinal match started at 2:45 p.m. and was scoreless through two innings. But in the third, Washington scored three runs on Jennifer Spediacci's RBI single, Becky Newbry's RBI double, and an error. Spediacci limited the Bulldogs to two hits through six innings before pitcher Amanda Scott homered leading off the bottom of the seventh. It was Fresno's only run. The 3-1 loss snapped Scott's twelve-game win streak, as she allowed eight hits in almost five innings. Lindsay Parker completed the game for the Huskies. Spediacci struck out six in her twenty-fourth complete game of the season. Kelly Hauxhurst and Spediacci had a pair of hits for the Huskies, who would then play the Bulldogs again for a berth in the championship game against Arizona.

In the rematch, the Bulldogs took a 2-0 lead with a pair of RBI singles by Jaime Maxey and Angela Cervantez in the top of the first inning. Eve Gaw's RBI double in the bottom of the inning cut the deficit to one. It remained 2-1 through the next three innings before the Bulldogs took advantage of two errors in both the fifth and sixth innings to score four more runs in the 6-1 win. Lindsay Parker limited the Huskies to only three hits, striking out three and walking two in her first start of the 1998 tournament. Jamie Graves hurled the first five innings, allowing eight hits and six runs before Jennifer Spediacci finished up. "As a coach you never expect any mistakes to happen," said Fresno coach Margie Wright, "but you've got to be able to capitalize on them. They did in the first game and we did in the second one." Washington completed its season with a third-place finish.

Four-time runner-up Fresno State and title-defender Arizona began play for

# 1998 Women's College World Series Bracket
## Oklahoma City • May 21-25

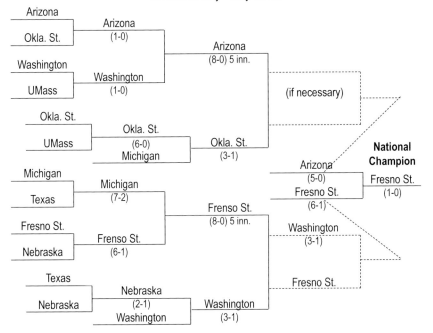

## 1998 Final Standings

| | |
|---|---|
| California State University (Fresno) | 4-1 |
| University of Arizona (Tucson) | 3-1 |
| University of Washington (Seattle) | 3-2 |
| Oklahoma State University (Stillwater) | 2-2 |
| University of Nebraska (Lincoln) | 1-2 |
| University of Michigan (Ann Arbor) | 1-2 |
| University of Texas (Austin) | 0-2 |
| University of Massachusetts (Amherst) | 0-2 |

the national championship at 1 p.m. Monday. Having held all its opponents scoreless in the tournament, Arizona had a twenty-nine-game win streak going. After eleven women's series appearances, Fresno could only hope its fifth try in the title game would be the charm. Through five innings, the game was scoreless. In the bottom of the sixth, Nina Lindenberg smacked a leadoff home run far over the bleachers—twenty-five feet beyond the left-field fence. Her thirteenth home run of the season gave the Bulldogs a 1-0 lead. Arizona got runners past first base only twice against Fresno hurler Amanda Scott. Toni Mascarenas was stranded at second after a two-out single and stolen base in the first inning, and

Alison McCutcheon failed to score from third with one out in the sixth. Scott at
one point retired fourteen Wildcats in a row and allowed only three hits from
twenty-four batters. The Bulldogs roughed up Nancy Evans for eight hits and the
one—and only—run needed for the national championship. Lindenberg was
perfect against Evans (3-for-3) as was winning hurler Scott (3-for-3), who hurled
her fourteenth shutout of the season and her second in the tournament. "Pretty
much all year, she (Evans) has thrown me the same pitch—the inside fastball,"
Lindenberg said about her game-winning home run. "It was time for me to take
one out."

Fresno's slaying of the Wildcat "Godzilla" brought home the school's first national title in any team sport—men or women's. In four of the past tournaments,
Fresno had lost to UCLA in the championship game without scoring a run. Their
one run in 1998 was all they needed against an Arizona team that had averaged 8.3
runs per game coming to Oklahoma City. In the post-game news conference the
moderator introduced "the 1998 NCAA champions from Fresno State." Perhaps
remembering her 4-3 loss in the sixteenth inning as a pitcher in the 1973 title game
in Omaha and her four title-game losses as a coach, a red-eyed Margie Wright
savored the moment. "Could you say that again, please?" she asked the moderator.

Scott was named the tournament's most outstanding player. The twelve mem-
bers of the all-tournament team included Fresno's Amanda Scott (P), Laura Berg
(OF), Nina Lindenberg (2B) and Angela Cervantez (1B); Arizona's Leah Braatz
(C), Nancy Evans (P), Leticia Pineda (1B), and Toni Mascarenas (3B); Oklahoma
State's Kristi Bolle (3B); Washington's Jennifer Spediacci (P) and Kelly Hauxhurst
(OF); and Nebraska's Ali Viola (SS). Evans was leading hitter (.600).

The crowd of 4,325 at the championship game pushed the overall attendance
to a record 27,535 for the tournament, topping the 25,649 the year earlier.

## Life After the WCWS...

Fresno State's **Laura Berg** was a four-time, first-team NCAA All-American
(1994-1998) and compiled a .414 career batting average. She was a member of
the U.S. national softball team and earned three gold medals and a silver medal
playing in four Olympic Games (1996-2008). In 2006, she was named to the 25th
Anniversary WCWS Team. In 2013, Berg was the head softball coach at Oregon
State University. Arizona catcher **Leah Braatz** was a four-time, first-team NCAA
All-American selection (1994-95, 1997-98). She completed her career by twice
winning Diamond Sports/NFCA Catcher of the Year honors. In 2003 she was inducted into the University of Arizona Sports Hall of Fame, and in 2006 named
to the NCAA Div. I Softball 25th Anniversary Team. A member of three national
championship teams, **Nancy Evans** compiled a pitching record of 124-8 at Arizona. She was a two-time, first-team NCAA All-American in 1997 and 1998. After
her graduation, she remained with Arizona as a coach from 1998-2007. In 2013
she was an assistant coach at DePaul University. Fresno's **Nina Lindenberg** was

a two-time, first-team NCAA All-American (1996 and 1998) and a member of the U.S. national softball team. She later coached as an assistant at Temple University.

## 1999: The Bruins Stage a Comeback

Defending champion Fresno State joined a quintet of Pac-10 title contenders in 1999. These West Coast softball teams had won the national championship every year since 1987, and these programs showed no signs of weakening. Yet continued growth in college softball teams was occurring across the country—even more no-ticeably in the South. Texas had made its debut in the women's series the year be-fore, and Southern Mississippi qualified for the first time in 1999. Remarkably, the Southern Mississippi Golden Eagles qualified in their initial year, emerging from the seventy teams in the nation's second-largest region. Southern Miss was just one of the nearly fifty new college softball teams initiated in the previous five years. This remarkable growth prompted the NCAA's expansion of the regional fields by sixteen teams, for a total of forty-eight in 1999. Joining Fresno State, UCLA and Mississippi State in the May 27-31 championship were: Washington, Arizona State, Arizona, Cal-Berkeley, and DePaul—another women's series newcomer.

Reflecting this growth in women's college fastpitch, improvements totaling a half-million dollars had been made to ASA Hall of Fame Stadium since the 1998 event. Additions included the field lighting that had been brought up to national television standards, a new sound system, and the renovation and enlargement of the pressroom for post-game interviews. A new $200,000-plus scoreboard had been installed prior to the 1998 tournament. The semifinal and final games would be televised live on ESPN2 in 1999.

All teams played Thursday, with No.1-seed UCLA starting the tournament play against No. 8 DePaul. DePaul surprised the Bruins with a 1-0 lead in the first in-ning, and the two teams battled back and forth throughout the opening game. DePaul held their one-run advantage until UCLA's Christie Ambrosi hit her tenth home run of the season leading off the sixth inning. DePaul regained the lead in the top of the seventh inning on a bunt-single by Yvette Healy, a Liza Brown sac-rifice, and a Julie Luna groundout RBI single. But the Bruins got a two-out RBI single from Ambrosi in the bottom of the seventh to tie the game at 2-2 and send it into extra innings. UCLA's Chrissy Buck put the game away in the ninth with a home run over the left field fence. Courtney Dale went the distance in the 3-2 win for UCLA, giving up five hits and one earned run while walking two and fanning five. Nicole Terpstra hurled the first seven innings for DePaul, and Liza Brown re-placed her, allowing one hit (Buck's home run) and taking the loss. "We definitely know we let one get away there," said DePaul head coach Eugene Lenti. "We know we had them on their heels a little bit."

Defending champion and fourth-seeded Fresno State and No. 5 Southern Mis-sissippi were scoreless through the first two innings, although the Bulldogs had loaded the bases in the bottom of the second. With two out in the third, Becky Witt opened with a single and scored for the Bulldogs on a single over third base by Angela Cervantez. In the fifth, Southern Mississippi threatened with two runners on with one out, but Bulldog pitcher Amanda Scott got a fielder's choice and a comebacker to the mound to end the threat. Neither team scored down the stretch, and the Bulldogs took the 1-0 win. Scott allowed four hits and struck out seven, while Courtney Blades—frustrated by the Bulldogs' patience at the plate—allowed six hits and fanned five. Fresno State left ten runners on base, Southern Mississippi five. Fresno's Witt (2-for-4) was the only player on either team with more than one hit.

With the two afternoon games completed, No. 3-seed Washington faced No. 6 Arizona State at 6 p.m. The two teams had played three 1-0 games earlier in the year, and it looked like it was headed that way again with a scoreless deadlock through five and one-half innings. But in the bottom of the sixth with two out, Washington's Erin Helgeland smacked a two-run double down the left-field line, Christie Rosenblad followed with an RBI single, and Jamie Graves knocked in the fourth run. ASU retaliated in the top half of the seventh on Jamie Hlebechuk's RBI, but scored no more in the 4-1 Washington win. Jamie Graves hurled the first three innings for the Huskies, allowing three hits. Jennifer Spediacci pitched the final four innings, allowing two hits and one run—all in the seventh. Losing pitcher Kirsten Voak hurled a complete game, allowing four runs on five hits with three walks and five strikeouts. Graves went 2-for-3 for the winners. Holly Smith had two of ASU's five hits.

Second-seeded Arizona and No.-7 Cal-Berkeley met in the final game of the first round Thursday evening, and neither scored through two innings. But the Wildcats tallied a run in the third, fourth and sixth innings. Catcher Lindsey Collins accounted for two of the scores with solo home runs, and Toni Mascarenas had an RBI single for the other. California collected four hits off winning pitcher Becky Lemke, who hurled a complete game, striking out six. Jocelyn Forest gave up five hits and three runs, and struck out ten in her complete-game, 3-0 loss. Collins and Lauren Bauer had two hits apiece for the Wildcats.

Fresno faced UCLA in the first winners-bracket game Friday evening, and pitching held the two teams in check through the first four innings. UCLA pitcher Amanda Freed maintained her composure even when it looked like the Bulldogs might score in the fifth inning with runners on second and third. Freed got the third out when Vanessa Czarnecki grounded to second base. The Bruin hurler again faced runners on second and third in the sixth inning before striking out Lindsay Fossatti. In the top of the seventh, UCLA's Julie Adams walked. Having dislocated her left shoulder in the opener against DePaul, Adams painfully ran to second on a bunt by Julie Marshall. Courtney Dale's grounder was then mishandled by the Bulldog first baseman, allowing Adams to score the only run in the 1-0 UCLA victory. Winning pitcher Freed allowed just five hits, one more than Bulldog losing hurler Amanda Scott. Christie Ambrosi (2-for-3) and Adams (2-for-

2) led the Bruins. Lovieanne Jung had two of Fresno's five hits.

The Washington and Arizona game followed, and neither team could manufacture a run through the first two innings. But in the third, Washington's Shannon Walsh drew a walk with two out and took second when Rosie Leutzinger smacked the ball over the head of the shortstop. Kelly Hauxhurst followed with a two-run double over the left fielder, scoring both runners for an early 2-0 Washington lead. The Huskies added another run in the fourth inning when Becky Newbry led off with a bloop double to center, which got away from Arizona's diving Nicole Giordano. With one out, Melissa Downs drove in Newbry with a single past third base. Washington pitcher Jennifer Spediacci, meanwhile, had retired sixteen batters in a row before her own throwing error allowed a runner on base in the sixth. But she retired the next three batters in order in the 3-0 Washington win to end the game. Lauren Bauer had Arizona's only hit—a double in the first inning. Losing freshman pitcher Jennie Finch hurled the first three and one-third innings for the Wildcats, allowing four hits and the three runs. Becky Lemke replaced her and pitched the remainder, allowing one hit.

At noon on "elimination Saturday," DePaul and Southern Mississippi hooked up, and in the second inning DePaul's Julie Luna hit a solo home run off Courtney Blades. Southern Mississippi had scoring chances in the fourth and fifth innings, but couldn't capitalize. The Eagles' Amy Berman hit what looked like a home run to left field in the fifth inning, but the umpire called the ball foul. Nicole Terpstra faced twenty-four batters in her complete-game performance, striking out ten and allowing three hits in her 1-0 win that eliminated Southern Mississippi. The Golden Eagles finished the year 52-9 and had not been shutout until reaching the

**Suspended from post-season play the year before, the UCLA Bruins came back strong in 1999 with a 4-0 sweep in the tournament. *(Reprinted courtesy of UCLA Athletic Dept.)***

tournament. Blades was displeased with her performance. "I probably could have pitched better," she mused, "but I had one bad pitch and she got a hold of it."

Arizona State and Cal-Berkeley were in a scoreless deadlock after three innings into the second Saturday game, when Golden Bear Lisa Iancin hit her sixth home run of the season with one out in the top of the fourth. It barely cleared the fence but gave Cal-Berkeley a 1-0 lead. The Golden Bears added another run in the sixth when Iancin smacked a two-out single that scored Amber Phillips, who had walked and been sacrificed to second. Both of Iancin's hits came off Erica Beach, who hurled five and two-thirds innings before Kirsten Voak finished up. Berkeley's Nicole DiSalvio allowed four hits in her complete-game performance, striking out two. She allowed no hits the final five innings in her 2-0 win that eliminated ASU. Missy Hixon had two of ASU's four hits.

Playing again at 6 p.m., DePaul faced off this time with Arizona. Neither team scored through the first three and a half innings. In the bottom of the fourth, DePaul senior Yvette Healy singled and advanced to second on Liza Brown's bunt. She scored on Julie Luna's double that hit the fence in the air. Arizona got a runner on in the seventh when Toni Mascarenas walked and advanced to second. But Felecity Willis struck out to end the game in the 1-0 Arizona loss, sending the Wildcats home early—a rarity in the 1990s. It was a big win for the DePaul program. Katie Swan and Lauren Bauer had the only hits for the Wildcats, who stranded three base runners against winning pitcher Liza Brown. Becky Lemke took the loss, striking out six.

At 8:30 p.m., Cal-Berkeley and Fresno began the last of Saturday's contests. The Bulldogs time and again had runners on base against Golden Bear pitcher Jocelyn Forest. She retired the Bulldogs in order only in the sixth inning, but in other innings she still managed nine outs with runners in scoring position. Fresno stranded ten base runners. The Golden Bears scored the game's only run in the second inning when Megumi Takasaki doubled down the left field line, advanced to third on a wild pitch, and scored on Kirsten Drake's single up the middle. "There was one out at the time," Drake said, "and I was just looking to drive the ball to the right side and score the run." Kristen Hunter went the first three innings for the Bulldogs, allowing two hits and the run, and Amanda Scott finished the game, allowing one hit. Vanessa Czarnecki had two of the five hits Forest allowed, and the 1-0 loss sent the defending champions packing.

With four teams remaining, play resumed Sunday at noon with UCLA facing DePaul. The Blue Demons, who had lost to the Bruins 1-0 in the opening game, took a 1-0 lead with a run in the second inning. Julie Luna got aboard on an error, and Molly Sircher was sent in as a pinch runner. After Sircher advanced to third on Katy Carter's hit, the Blue Demons attempted a double steal. UCLA threw to second on the play, allowing Sircher to score as Carter was tagged out between the bases. The next two innings were scoreless, but in the bottom of the fifth the Bruins tied the game at 1-1 on Courtney Dale's solo home run to center field. Still tied after seven, the Bruins scored in the bottom of the eighth on Stacey Nuve-

## 1999 Women's College World Series Bracket
### Oklahoma City • May 27-31

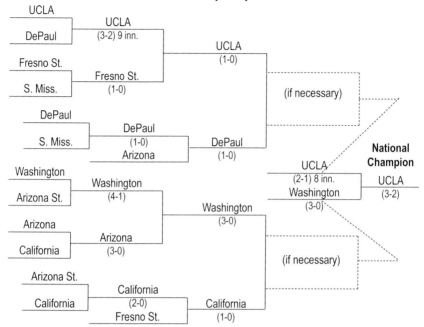

## 1999 Final Standings

| | |
|---|---|
| University of California (Los Angeles) | 4-0 |
| University of Washington (Seattle) | 3-1 |
| University of California (Berkeley) | 2-2 |
| DePaul University (Chicago, Ill.) | 2-2 |
| California State University (Fresno) | 1-2 |
| University of Arizona (Tucson) | 1-2 |
| Arizona State University (Tempe) | 0-2 |
| University of Southern Mississippi (Hattiesburg) | 0-2 |

man's one-out double, scoring Lyndsey Klein from first base. Nicole Terpstra went the distance for the Blue Demons, allowing eight hits and striking out six in her 2-1 loss. Amanda Freed struck out six and allowed four hits. The Blue Demons finished in a respectable tie for third. "We just ran into the best team in the country," said DePaul coach Lenti, "and we took them to extra innings twice." DePaul completed the season 54-14, the first time the team passed the fifty-win mark.

Washington and Cal-Berkley followed, and the Huskies tallied a run in the first followed by another in both the fourth and fifth innings. Kim DePaul had a pair of RBI singles to bring across Rosie Leutzinger for each of the first two runs, and

Christie Rosenblad hit a double in the fifth to score Melissa Downs. That was all the scoring in the game. The Huskies' Jennifer Spediacci allowed three hits in the first four innings, and Jamie Graves hurled the last three, allowing one hit. Nicole DiSalvio hurled four innings and allowed six hits in the Golden Bears' 3-0 loss and elimination. Washington advanced to Monday's championship game against UCLA, only the second time the Huskies had made it to the final round.

With a crowd of 4,470 on hand, UCLA struck fast for a 2-0 lead in the first inning on a double by Julie Adams. Courtney Dale's home run—her sixth of the year—made it 3-0 for the Bruins in the top of the second. In the bottom of the second, Erin Helgeland scored Spediacci, who had walked earlier. Trailing 3-1, the Huskies scored again in the seventh with two out when DePaul brought home Leutzinger. But the Huskies ran out of chances, coming up short in the 3-2 UCLA win. Adams (2-for-3, 2 RBIs), Amanda Freed (2-for-3), and Christie Ambrosi (2-for-4) led the eight-hit UCLA offense against the two Washington pitchers. UCLA's Dale hurled the first four innings, allowing three hits and one run, with Freed hurling the last three innings to get the save. Spediacci hurled six innings for the Huskies, allowing the three runs with no walks and six strikeouts. Jamie Graves hurled the last inning. "It's unbelievable, the road we've traveled this year to handle the pressure from day one," said Sue Enquist, who redshirted most of her club after the Bruins were banned from postseason play in 1998. "I couldn't be more proud of the way these kids played."

Julie Adams was named the most outstanding player and batted 6-for-9, despite missing most of the tournament opener after re-injuring her shoulder. She played errorless ball the last three games despite the injury. "Julie Adams is just a gamer, such incredible drive," said Enquist. "The world could be on her shoulders and she's going to get it done." The twelve players named to the all-tournament team included UCLA's Adams (3B), Amanda Freed (P), Christie Ambrosi (OF) and Courtney Dale (P); Washington's Jennifer Spediacci (P), Kim DePaul (3B) and Melissa Downs (1B); Fresno State's Lovieanne Jung (2B) and Amanda Scott (P); Cal-Berkeley's Lisa Iancin (2B); and DePaul's Katy Carter (C) and Julie Luna (3B). Ambrosi was leading hitter (.429).

It was the first national championship win for the Bruins (67-6) since 1992 and their ninth overall. The big crowd in the championship game brought the overall attendance to just more than 24,000.

## Life After the WCWS...

Fresno's **Amanda Scott** was a four-time, first-team NCAA All-American (1997-2000) and compiled a pitching record of 106-18. She was an alternate for the 2000 U.S. Olympic softball team and was named to the NCAA Div. I Softball 25th Anniversary Team in 2006. In 2013, Scott was head coach of softball at Roosevelt University in Illinois.

# 2000: Oklahoma Wins Title and Boosts Attendance

As the Women's College World Series moved into a new century of championship history in 2000, tournament competition was refreshed with new and improving softball programs. Representing the growing strength of the Southeastern Conference, Alabama made its debut at the women's series. And Big 12 champion Oklahoma returned to the tournament for the first time since 1982, when the old AIAW Division I national championship had been held in Norman with the University of Oklahoma as the host school. The Sooners had not won a berth to the tournament since the NCAA-sanctioned championship began eighteen years earlier. Increased attendance from local Oklahoma fans was anticipated by tournament organizers. Conference USA winner Southern Mississippi made its second consecutive appearance at the 2000 event, but most of the pre-tournament buzz centered on No. 1-seed and Pac-10 champion Washington, which was making its fifth consecutive appearance.

Perennial powers Arizona (No. 2 seed) and UCLA (No. 4 seed) came to town—but somewhat overshadowed by their growing Pac-10 rival, the Huskies. The other two teams rounding out the final eight qualifiers were California-Berkeley and DePaul, the surprise team in the previous national tournament. All eight teams played on the first day of the championship, May 25, with the title game scheduled for May 29. Two games would be played in the afternoon of the first day and two in the evening.

In the first afternoon game, the DePaul Blue Demons startled the crowd—and the top-ranked Huskies—by taking an early 2-0 lead in the top of the first inning. Liz Bouck led off with a single, and one out later, right fielder Shavaughne Desecki smashed a 2-1 pitch from senior right-hand hurler Jennifer Spediacci over the left-field fence. But Washington recovered and took the lead on three runs in the second inning. Jamie Clark led off the inning with a solo home run, her twenty-third that year, followed by a two-run double by Rosie Leutzinger. Spediacci settled down after the first inning and gave up no more hits to the Blue Demons the remainder of the game. The only other DePaul runners came off two walks. The 3-2 Washington victory marked the third win that season by the Huskies over the Blue Demons. Lindsay Chouniard hurled the first four and one-third innings for DePaul, and losing pitcher Vanessa Saavedra finished the game. "It wouldn't be the College World Series if DePaul didn't have a one-run game," said DePaul coach Eugene Lenti. "We felt like we validated ourselves today."

Newcomer Alabama faced UCLA in the second game, and the Tide got the Bruins' attention in the first inning with runners on first and third with no outs. Ginger Jones then knocked in the game's first run with a sacrifice fly. The 1-0 lead held through four innings, but in the bottom of the fifth UCLA scored twice with two outs when Natasha Watley's hard-hit ball was dropped by the left fielder. The two base runners scored, and the momentum of the game shifted. "I thought we went flat after that," Alabama coach Pat Murphy said later. The Bruins added another pair of runs on a two-run home run by Lyndsey Klein in the sixth inning in the 4-1 UCLA victory. Amanda Freed went the distance for the Bruins and allowed two hits, one by White and another by Jennifer Reach. Shelley Laird absorbed the loss, giving up four runs.

Oklahoma faced California-Berkeley in the first evening game, and a record 6,860 fans poured into the stadium, shattering the single-session mark of 5,020 in 1993. Through the first four innings, however, neither cheering section had much to celebrate with the 0-0 deadlock. But in the fifth, Candace Harper's two-out single gave the Golden Bears a 1-0 lead. The Sooners trailed 1-0 going into the bottom of the seventh but staged a rally when Andrea Davis walked and pinch-runner Jaime White advanced to second on Ashli Barrett's sacrifice bunt. Cal-Berkeley pitcher Jocelyn Forest hit the next two batters to load the bases. Forest struck out LaKisha Washington for the second out, but Leah Gulla then singled to score White, tying the game. With the Sooner fans roaring, Christy Ring hit a two-out single for the game-winner in the 2-1 victory. Forest allowed six hits as did the two OU pitchers. Sooner Lana Moran started and hurled the first five innings, allowing five hits and one run, and Jennifer Stewart finished. It was Sooner coach Patty Gasso's 300th win. "We didn't give 'em much to cheer about for a while," said Gasso. "But when we started making a little noise in the seventh, you could really feel the energy."

**Lisa Carey's two-run blast would supply all the runs the Sooners needed to beat UCLA for the 2000 women's series title.** *(Reprinted courtesy of The Oklahoman)*

Arizona and Southern Mississippi, featuring NCAA strikeout-leader Courtney Blades, closed out the first round of games. The Southern Miss Golden Eagles jumped out to a 1-0 lead in the first inning on Erin Johnson's RBI single. Blades showed outstanding control, going to a 3-2 count only three times and allowing only three balls out of the infield. She struck out eleven in the 1-0 perfect game, upsetting the second-seeded Wildcats and becoming the NCAA's career (150-53) and single season record holder (51-6). Becky Lemke took the loss for the Wildcats, allowing seven hits and striking out ten. It was the first opening-game loss for Arizona since 1992. The last pitcher to hurl a perfect game in the national tournament had been UCLA's Tanya Harding in 1995. Johnson and Jennifer Collins had two hits apiece for the Eagles.

With the winning teams competing Friday evening, UCLA took the lead against Washington in the second inning on an RBI by Julie Adams. The Bruins added to the margin with a two-run home run by Lyndsey Klein in the third for a 3-0 lead. But with lightning streaking across the sky, tournament officials suspended the game at 7:50 p.m. with one out in the bottom of the fifth inning—and with Washington runners on first and second. "You guys sure know how to kill a rally," Huskies coach Teresa Wilson told the officials. With play resuming at 9 a.m. Saturday, UCLA's Amanda Freed threw her first pitch outside, intentionally walking Jenny Topping. Jamie Clark then smacked the first pitch for a double that plated two runs and tightened the game to 3-2. Freed got the next two batters to end the inning and afterward retired the next seven Washington batters. Jamie Graves hurled six innings, giving up the three runs and striking out six before Jennifer Spediacci finished up in the 3-2 Washington loss. UCLA's Lyndsey Klein had two hits and two RBIs for the Bruins, including her home run, and Bruin Tairia Mims was 3-for-3.

Southern Mississippi and Oklahoma followed, with the Sooners opening the scoring in the top of the second inning. Right fielder Andrea Davis slammed a home run to left-center on her first pitch from Courtney Blades. The long ball upped Davis's season total to fourteen. In the fifth inning the Sooners again led off with a solo home run, this time by designated player Mandy Fulton. With the Sooners still batting, second baseman LaKisha Washington singled to second base later and then stole her twenty-first base of the season. Left fielder Christy Ring drove a single up the middle to plate Washington and give the Sooners a 3-0 lead. Southern Mississippi scored in the bottom half of the fifth inning on a solo home run by Amy Berman. Blades struck out thirteen batters for the Golden Eagles, allowing six hits and three runs in the 3-1 loss. Jennifer Stewart got the win for Oklahoma, also giving up six hits. Ring led the Sooners with a 2-for-4 performance.

With the suspended games completed, the regularly scheduled games began at 1:30 p.m., with DePaul facing Alabama in the first of four. The Blue Demons struck in the first inning on Shavaughne Desecki's RBI single to take a 1-0 lead. Alabama took the lead in the second inning when Jennifer Reach walked with the bases loaded, and Kelly Kretschman belted a three-run triple to right center to put Alabama out in front, 4-1. But the Blue Demons tied the game at 4-4 with three runs in the top of the fifth on Desecki's three-run triple to right center. The Crimson Tide fired back with two runs in the bottom of the sixth on a sacrifice-fly RBI by Jennifer Reach and an RBI single by Kelley Askew. The 6-4 Alabama win eliminated the Blue Demons. Shelley Laird went the distance for the win, allowing five hits and four runs (all unearned), while Lindsay Chouniard got the loss, allowing six runs and giving up seven hits. Christy Kyle led Alabama with three hits in three at-bats.

Arizona and Cal-Berkeley played next, and the Wildcats, who had been victim of a perfect game by Blades in their last outing, took control early with runs in the first and second innings. They stretched their lead to 4-0 with a pair in the third. The Wildcats added to their tally with a run in the sixth and another in the seventh for a 6-0 win, sending the Golden Bears home. Toni Mascarenas led the Wildcats with a perfect 4-for-4 performance including a solo home run in the seventh and RBI singles in the first and third innings. Allison Andrade and Chrissy Gil also hit solo home runs for the Wildcats. Becky Lemke scattered five hits and walked three batters to get the win. "Arizona was ready to hit the ball today," said Cal-Berkeley coach Diane Ninemire. "We left a lot of people in scoring position." The Golden Bears stranded ten runners. Nicole DiSalvio took the loss, hurling two and one-third innings, allowing six hits and four runs before Jocelyn Forest took over. Lisa Iancin had three of Cal-Berkeley's five hits.

Southern Mississippi and Alabama met in the 7 p.m. game and the Golden Eagles jumped out to an early 3-0 lead, scoring twice in the first inning and once more in the third. Jennifer Ford drove in all the runs with a two-run single in the first inning and a fielder's choice in the third inning. Courtney Blades held the Crimson Tide in check, allowing two hits in the fourth and one each in the third and sixth innings in the 3-0 elimination of Alabama. Blades walked one and fanned seven in the complete-game performance, and Alabama only twice got a runner as far as second base. Shelly Laird hurled six and two-thirds innings, replacing losing pitcher Melisa Bautista in the first inning.

Fierce rivals Arizona and Washington met in the 9:30 p.m. elimination game, and the Wildcats scored twice in the bottom of the second on an RBI double by Allison Andrade and Katie Swan's RBI single. Washington cut the lead in half with a run in the top of the third, scoring on an error by the Wildcat third baseman. But the Wildcats offset this with a run in the bottom of the third when pitcher Jennie Finch scored on an error by third baseman Kim DePaul. Washington again reduced the margin to one with a run in the top of the fourth on Erin Helgeland's solo home run to left field. Leading 3-2, the Wildcats added an insurance run in the bottom half of the fourth on a Toni Mascarenas sacrifice-fly RBI. Finch hurled the complete game, allowing five hits, striking out five and walking five. Jennifer Spediacci allowed four runs and struck out six in the 4-2 loss. Katie Swan (3-for-3) and Nicole Giordano (2-for-3) combined for five of Arizona's six hits.

With the field down to the final four, UCLA struck quickly in the first game

## 2000 Women's College World Series Bracket
Oklahoma City • May 25-29

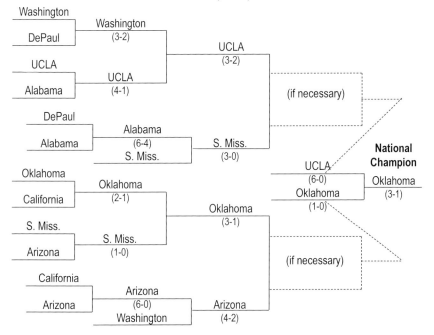

## 2000 Final Standings

| | |
|---|---|
| University of Oklahoma (Norman) | 4-0 |
| University of California (Los Angeles) | 3-1 |
| University of Southern Mississippi (Hattiesburg) | 2-2 |
| University of Arizona (Tucson) | 2-2 |
| University of Washington (Seattle) | 1-2 |
| University of Alabama (Tuscaloosa) | 1-2 |
| University of California (Berkeley) | 0-2 |
| DePaul University (Chicago, Ill.) | 0-2 |

Sunday against the Golden Eagles' Courtney Blades. The Bruins scored twice in the first inning on a two-run home run by Julie Adams. They added three more runs in the second inning on Tairia Mims two-run home run and pitcher Amanda Freed's solo shot. All the balls hit to left fielder Crystal Stevens may have dazed her, as she misplayed Mims's fly and helped it over the fence. Stevens and Erin Johnson had the only hits off winning pitcher Freed, who hurled five innings, striking out four before Courtney Dale finished. Blades took the loss, lasting two innings and giving up five runs in the 6-0 loss. Freed (2-for-3), Adams (2-for-3), Julie Marshall (2-for-4) and Mims (2-for-3) all had two hits apiece for the Bruins, who advanced to Monday's championship game.

Arizona and Oklahoma met in the second game Sunday to determine the Bruins' opponent in the title game. The Wildcats had defeated the Sooners 6-0 in Tucson earlier in the season, but neither scored through the first three innings before a record, partisan crowd of 7,400. Oklahoma got a break in the first inning with Wildcat runners on first and third with two outs when Nicole Giordano was tagged out at home. In the fourth, Oklahoma's Lisa Carey homered to left field off right-hander Becky Lemke. It was Carey's nineteenth home run of the season and ended an 0-for-7 hitless streak in her previous three games. Lemke had retired nine batters in a row before facing Carey with one out. "I just wanted to hit the ball hard somewhere," Carey said. "It was a great result." Jennifer Stewart held the hard-hitting Wildcats (team batting average of .342) to six singles to take the 1-0 win.

Fourth-seed UCLA and third-seed Oklahoma met in Monday's championship game in front of another record crowd of 8,050. The Sooners took the lead in the third when Lisa Carey got hold of an Amanda Freed screwball and sent it over the left field fence for a two-run home run. The Sooners were not yet done in the third. Freshman shortstop Kelli Braitsch nailed a single to left field to score Jaime White for a 3-0 lead. UCLA finally got on the board in the sixth inning when Natasha Watley tallied on a sacrifice fly by catcher Julie Marshall. Behind 3-1, the Bruins threatened again in the seventh inning with runners on first and second with one out. Chrissy Buck was on second, representing one of the tying runs. Then things turned bizarre. Amanda Freed popped to left field for the second out, and the ball was thrown back to Stewart. When OU third baseman Leah Gulla headed for the pitching circle, Buck bolted for third. Home-plate umpire Lisa Harvey called Buck out for leaving second base while Stewart was in the pitching circle ("look-back" rule). UCLA head coach Sue Enquist protested the call, but to no avail. With the 3-1 win, Oklahoma took the school's first national championship by a women's team. "For all of us, winning this national championship is a life-changing experience," said Sooner coach Patty Gasso. "Our lives are all going to be different from this point on."

Sophomore Jennifer Stewart, who won four games, was named the tournament's most outstanding player. The all-tournament team included: OU's Stewart (P), Lisa Carey (1B) and Kelli Braitsch (SS); UCLA's Amanda Freed (P), Julie Marshall (C) and Tairia Mims (1B); Southern Mississippi's Erin Johnson (3B) and Courtney Blades (P); Arizona's Toni Mascarenas (3B); DePaul's Shavaughne Desecki (OF); and Alabama's Kelly Kretschman (OF). Mims led the tournament in batting with a .600 average.

The 38,000 in attendance for the women's series smashed the old record by more than 10,000.

## Life After the WCWS...

Southern Mississippi's **Courtney Blades** transferred from Nichols State and played for the Golden Eagles her last two years of college. She compiled an over-all record of 151 wins and 34 losses with 1,773 strikeouts in 1,261.2 innings. She was a first-team NCAA All-American in 2000 and won the Honda Sports Award as college softball's top player that year. In 2006, she was inducted into the Southern Mississippi Golden Eagles Hall of Fame. Washington's **Jennifer Spediacci** was named to the all-tournament team twice. She was named first-team Pac-10 three times and was the 2000 Pac-10 Pitcher of the Year after leading the Huskies to four consecutive berths in the national championship. After leaving Washington, she played softball professionally in Italy and in 2004 played for the Italian national team in the Olympic Games. In 2010, she was inducted into the Husky Hall of Fame.

# 2001: Arizona Win Continues Pac-10 Dominance

Another Olympic year had passed since the previous Women's College World Series, and the U.S. softball team had added another gold medal to their collection. The 2000 gold-medal team had been loaded with former women's series stars, including two collegians returning to Oklahoma City for the 2001 national championship—UCLA's Amanda Freed and Stacey Nuveman. The participation of women's series players in the Olympics continued to enhance the reputation of college softball and the national championship event.

College softball programs continued their expansion and development, as clear-ly shown by the steady procession of debutants at the women's series. New to the 2001 tournament were the Stanford Cardinal and the Louisiana State Tigers—an-other team from the South. Just a year earlier two other southern teams—Alabama and Southern Miss—had made their initial appearances. And with Oklahoma de-feating perennial power UCLA in the 2000 title game, could the Pac-10 teams' grip on the national championship have been loosening? No. 1-seeded Arizona indicated not. The powerful Wildcats sported a 61-4 record coming to Oklahoma City in 2001 and averaged 7.1 runs per game. Starting a five-day championship run on May 24, other teams rounding out the "magnificent eight" included UCLA, Michigan, Iowa, defending champion Oklahoma, and California-Berkeley.

Arizona and Cal-Berkeley opened play at 11:30 Thursday morning, and de-spite the Wildcats' NCAA-record 121 home runs that season, they were stifled the first five innings by Cal-Berkeley pitcher Jocelyn Forest. But in the sixth, Wildcat Erika Hanson led off with a blooper into left-center, followed by a single by Nicole Giordano. Toni Mascarenas then turned on an inside rise ball and blasted it down the left field line. The ball did not clear the temporary television tower, but it eas-ily cleared the fence for Mascarenas' twenty-third home run of the season and a 3-0 Wildcat lead. In the top of the seventh, Cal-Berkeley first baseman Veronica Nelson tightened the game with a two-run home run with no outs. But winning pitcher Jennie Finch retired the next three batters in order to conclude the 3-2 win. Forest allowed three hits and struck out seven in taking the loss, while Finch fanned ten and allowed four hits. "When you're having trouble scoring runs, a good pitcher will hold the other team down," Arizona coach Mike Candrea said of Finch. "Jennie gave us an opportunity to make things happen."

Defending champion Oklahoma faced Michigan in the second game, and more than 5,000 watched Oklahoma's Jennifer Stewart and Michigan's Marie Barda battle through three scoreless innings. In the top of the fourth inning, Barda, who had retired the first ten Sooners, walked Christy Ring with one out. Ring ran all the way to third when Lisa Carey belted the ball past the Michigan second baseman Kelsey Kollen, who had been moving toward first in anticipation of a bunt. Barda intentionally walked Ashli Barrett to load the bases, but Ring scored on Jennifer Stump's sacrifice-fly RBI to left. Two innings later, Ring singled and scored again with two outs on Barrett's single. After a first-inning single by Michigan, Stewart retired twelve straight batters and allowed only three hits in the 2-0 win. Carey led the Sooners with a pair of hits in three trips to the plate. First baseman Melissa Young had two of Michigan's three hits. Barda allowed five hits in the loss, striking out five.

Newcomers Stanford and LSU met in the first evening game, with neither crossing home plate through the first three innings. In the top of the fourth, Sarah Beeson hit her twelfth home run of the season for Stanford. LSU's April Janzen got aboard in the bottom of the inning with an infield single, went to second on Stephanie Hastings' sacrifice, then beat the throw to home by center fielder Jessica Mendoza, who had reached over the fence for the grab. Neither team scored in the next three innings as pitchers Britni Sneed of LSU and Dana Sorensen of Stanford dominated. But in the eighth, Ramon Shelburne scored when Mendoza smashed a double into right field for the 2-1 Stanford win. Sneed allowed six hits and fanned seven batters, while Sorensen scattered seven hits and also struck out seven. April Janzen had three of LSU's seven hits. Mendoza led Stanford with two doubles in three trips to the plate, and she stole a base—her thirty-first of the year.

UCLA and Iowa concluded the first round Thursday evening in a game that developed into a pitcher's duel between Iowa's Kristi Hanks and UCLA veteran and former Olympian Amanda Freed. Iowa had a chance for a score in the fifth when Christina Schmaltz led off with a double, but Freed sandwiched two ground balls around a strikeout to end the threat. In the sixth, Bruin Claire Sua smacked a single to right field, scoring Stephanie Ramos and Tairia Mims. Ramos had started the rally with a one-out double—until then only the third UCLA hit—before Mims singled and Stacey Nuveman was intentionally walked, loading the bases. Freed allowed four hits in the 2-0 UCLA win, with one walk and five strikeouts. Hanks, who had held the Bruins hitless until the fourth, walked five and gave up five hits.

In the first winners game on Friday and with the second largest crowd in tournament history (7,420), Oklahoma's Jennifer Stump hit a ball over right center for a three-run home run in the fourth inning against Arizona. It was her twelfth of the season and only the sixth home run Jennie Finch allowed in 195 innings in

2001. Another Sooner run came in the fifth, courtesy of LaKisha Washington, who blasted the ball over the deepest part of center field for her second home run of the season. But Arizona closed the gap in the sixth inning with a three-run home run by Toni Mascarenas, and Mackenzie Vandergeest tied the game at 4-4 in the top of the seventh with a solo shot to right field. OU failed to capitalize on two hits in the bottom of the seventh, sending the game into extra innings. In the top of the eighth, Arizona's Nicole Giordano led off with a single to center field and three batters later scored from second with two outs after a bad throw to first base by the Sooner second baseman. Oklahoma loaded the bases in the bottom of the inning but could not score, ending their twenty-three-game win streak. Staying perfect on the year with the 5-4 Arizona win, Finch (31-0) gave up a season-high ten hits and struck out nine. Oklahoma's Jennifer Stewart took the loss, allowing five runs on seven hits. Giordano (3-for-4) led the Wildcats. Stump (3-for-4) led the Sooners.

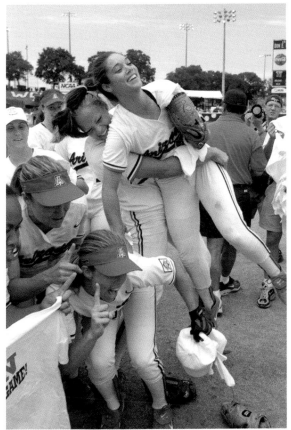

Arizona's stellar pitcher Jennie Finch celebrates the Wildcats' 2001 national championship with a power lift of teammate Toni Mascarenas. *(Reprinted courtesy of The Oklahoman)*

Pac-10 rivals Stanford and UCLA met in the second winners' game, and the Bruins scored five times in the fourth inning courtesy of Claire Sua's three-run home run and Toria Auelua's two-run shot. It was Sua's tenth home run of the season and Auelua's second. Neither team scored before or afterward. Keira Goerl hurled the first five innings for the Bruins and allowed three hits, with Courtney Dale pitching the last two innings for the 5-0 win. Dana Sorensen hurled the first three and one-third innings for the Cardinal, allowing the five runs, with Tori Nyberg finishing the game. Bruin shortstop Natasha Watley had two hits in four trips to the plate.

Four games were scheduled on "elimination Saturday" with Cal-Berkeley facing Michigan at 11 a.m. The Wolverines broke through for their first runs of the tournament in the fourth against pitcher Jocelyn Forest. Junior third baseman Stefanie Volpe followed a leadoff bunt single by Melissa Taylor with her fourth home run of 2001 over the right-field fence to score two runs. California immediately retaliated in the bottom of the inning. Michigan starter Marie Barda walked the first two batters, and Eryn Manahan singled to load the bases. Michigan coach Carol Hutchins replaced Barda with Marissa Young, who struck out the first batter she faced. But she hit the next, Amber Phillips, to force in a run before retiring the next two batters. Cal-Berkeley scored a pair of runs in the fifth, first on a sacrifice fly by Candace Harper that tied the game and then on an RBI single up the middle by Courtney Scott that took the lead. Barda re-entered the game in the sixth to try to keep the Wolverines within striking distance, but three Wolverine errors led to two more unearned runs by California and a 5-2 Golden Bear victory. Nicole DiSalvio threw the last three innings in relief, blanking Michigan on three hits and three strikeouts to get the win and eliminate the Wolverines.

Iowa and LSU followed in another elimination game and through four innings neither team scored. Erin Johnson got the Tigers going in the top of the fifth with a double to right center. Freshman Julie Wiese then stepped to the plate and launched a two-run home run to left field, her twelfth of the season. The ball landed in the seats and just beyond the glove of Hawkeye outfielder Erin Doud. "It was about an inch away from my glove," Doud said. "I'd gone about as far as I could without completely flipping over." The Hawkeyes came back to tighten the game when Alicia Gerlach's RBI single scored pinch-runner Melissa Stuber in the bottom of the seventh inning. But Iowa came up short in the final 2-1 score and was the second team eliminated. The Hawkeyes had eight hits off senior hurler Ashley Lewis, who allowed one run, walked two, and struck out three in the win. Losing hurler Kristi Hanks ended the season 39-9, allowing five hits and two runs.

After eliminating Michigan earlier, Cal-Berkeley began its second game of the day as it faced Stanford. The Golden Bears threatened to score in the first after they strung together a walk and two singles to load the bases, but a two-out groundout to second ended the rally. The Cardinal's Jessica Draemel scored from second base in the bottom half of the second inning when the shortstop failed to come up with a ground ball hit by Michelle Thiry. Cal-Berkeley's Veronica Nelson singled to left center in the fourth and senior Amber Phillips got a base hit in the fifth, but the Golden Bears failed to put anything else together. Candace Harper and Manahan had the only other hits for the Golden Bears. Dana Sorensen pitched the first five innings for the Cardinal for the win, and Jaime Forman-Lau finished up. Berkeley's Nicole DiSalvio allowed two walks and took the 1-0 loss. Jocelyn Forest took the mound in the third and finished with four strikeouts. The Golden Bears finished the season with a 54-18 record and became the third team eliminated.

In the fourth and final elimination game Saturday evening, Oklahoma faced LSU with another large partisan crowd watching. The Sooners scored in the first inning when shortstop Kelli Braitsch hit a ball over the right field fence on a 1-2 count. It was the second time in 2001 that she had led off with a home run. The Tigers came back in the fifth inning when Julie Wiese smacked a single that scored Sara Fitzgerald, pinch running for Christy Connor, who had singled to lead off the inning. The game continued on inning after inning with no score. Finally, with two outs in the bottom of the thirteenth, LSU pinch hitter Ashley Lewis hit a ball to shortstop Braitsch, who fielded the ball but sailed the throw past first base. That scored Jennifer Schuelke from third, and gave the Tigers the 2-1 win. The Sooners had failed to score on several ripe opportunities, leaving ten runners on base—nine in scoring position. LSU's Britni Sneed went the entire thirteen innings, giving up just one run on the Sooners' eight hits and fanning nineteen. Sooner junior Christy Ring went 4-4 and walked twice. Jennifer Stewart tossed nearly thirteen innings, giving up two runs on eight hits, never walking a batter, and striking out eight.

LSU joined Arizona, Stanford and UCLA for the two games on "survival Sunday." Stanford and Arizona met in the first game at noon, and the Wildcats wasted no time scoring. Toni Mascarenas ripped Tori Nyberg's high fastball over the left field bleachers with two out in the bottom of the first inning. It was Mascarenas's twenty-fifth home run of the season. Cardinal Sarah Beeson got a two-out single in the fourth inning, but it would be the only Stanford hit off pitcher Becky Lemke, who went the distance, struck out five, and walked one in the 1-0 win that eliminated Stanford. "That was a tremendous performance by Becky," said Arizona coach Mike Candrea. Nyberg was one of three Stanford pitchers, with Jaime Forman-Lau hurling two and one-third innings and Dana Sorensen one inning.

In the second Sunday game, the Bruins struck first against LSU in the opening inning as Tairia Mims scored from third on Courtney Dale's infield single off pitcher Ashley Lewis. UCLA struck again in the third. Amanda Simpson scored first when Claire Sua singled, and pinch runner Casey Haraiwa scored from third on Courtney Dale's single to left field. The Bruin rally continued when Monique Mejia, a pinch runner for Sua, scored on Amanda Freed's double down the right field line. The Tigers' Lewis was relieved by Britni Sneed, who promptly gave up a double to Toria Auelua to deep left field, scoring Freed and Julie Hoshizaki, who pinch ran for Dale. Sneed retired the next two batters, but the damage was done and gave UCLA the 6-0 win. Freed allowed just one hit by the Tigers and fanned five in five innings. Dale came on in the sixth to finish up, allowing one hit. The Tigers packed for home in third place and with a 59-11 record. Lewis took the Tiger loss after giving up six runs on five hits.

Arizona and UCLA, who together had won ten of the last thirteen national championships, met in the final for the sixth time since 1991. With a crowd of 4,460 watching on Monday afternoon, the game was scoreless in the top of the fourth when Arizona catcher Lindsey Collins snapped a string of thirty-eight scoreless innings by UCLA's Amanda Freed with a solo homer in the fourth. It was Collins's eleventh of the season and only the fourth home run Freed had allowed in more than 148 innings. That was all the scoring in the game. Arizona pitcher Jennie Finch struck out seven, including two of the last three Bruins she faced, and al-

## 2001 Women's College World Series Bracket
### Oklahoma City • May 24-28

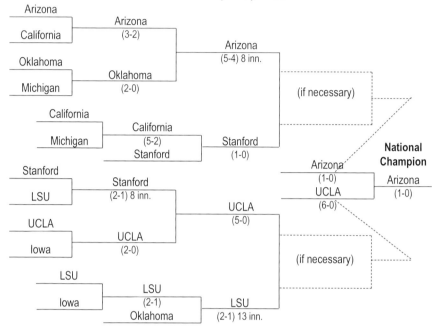

## 2001 Final Standings

| | |
|---|---|
| University of Arizona (Tucson) | 4-0 |
| University of California (Los Angeles) | 3-1 |
| Louisiana State University (Baton Rouge) | 2-2 |
| Stanford University (Palo Alto, Calif.) | 2-2 |
| University of Oklahoma (Norman) | 1-2 |
| University of California (Berkeley) | 1-2 |
| University of Iowa (Iowa City) | 0-2 |
| University of Michigan (Ann Arbor) | 0-2 |

lowed just four hits to finish the year undefeated (32-0). "A perfect end to a perfect season," Finch proclaimed after the 1-0 Wildcat victory. UCLA finished 62-6 and had runners on base in every inning but the first and seventh. Freed hurled a three-hitter, walking four and striking out six. Arizona (65-4) left seven runners on base.

Jennie Finch was named the most outstanding player and Oklahoma's Christy Ring was the leading hitter (.636). Named to the twelve-player all-tournament team were Arizona's Finch (P), Lindsey Collins (C), Nicole Giordano (OF) and Toni Mascarenas (3B); UCLA's Amanda Freed (P), Tairia Mims (1B) and Claire Sua (DH); LSU's Britni Sneed (P) and Julie Wiese (3B); Stanford's Jessica Mendoza (OF); and Oklahoma's Christy Ring (OF) and Jennifer Stewart (P).

College softball programs were spreading across the nation, but the West Coast and Pac-10 teams still showed dominance in 2001. The championship attendance of 34,740 in 2001 and 38,100 the year before convinced the NCAA that the women's series should stay put for another three years. NCAA officials informed local organizers that the tournament would remain at ASA Hall of Fame Stadium at least through 2004.

## Life After The WCWS...

Stanford's **Jessica Mendoza** was a four-time, first-team NCAA All-American (1999-2002) and a member of the U.S. Olympic softball team in 2004 and 2008. In 2012, Mendoza worked for ESPN as a color analyst during the Women's College World Series and as a sideline reporter for ESPNU. Arizona's **Toni Mascarenas** was a two-time, first-team NCAA All-American (1998, 2001) and was on the women's series all-tournament team twice (2000-01). She was a member of the U.S. national team when it won a gold medal at the U.S. Cup tournament in 2001. Mascarenas graduated with a bachelor's degree in political science and went on to play for the Arizona Heat in the National Pro Fastpitch league.

# 2002: Overdue Cal-Berkeley Gets Its Reward

ESPN's extensive televised broadcasts of the Women's College World Series was bringing the national championship to a mass audience across the country by 2002. After televising three games in 2000 and eleven games in 2001, ESPN and ESPN2 stepped up coverage and combined to televise all the games in 2002. The ratings for 2001 indicated that the event had been a hit—the championship game reached almost one million homes with a tournament-record 1.2 rating.

While television was certainly playing a major role in bringing the event to millions of people, the increasing athleticism and competitiveness on the field contributed to more exciting viewing. Although the South and other regions of the country were growing and improving their women's college softball programs, the Pac-10 still continued to dominate the event. Pac-10 schools had won fifteen of the previous twenty national championships. Four Pac-10 teams—UCLA, Arizona, Arizona State and California-Berkeley—had survived on the road in the 2002 regionals and would be among the eight finalists in Oklahoma City at the tournament, set for May 23-27. The rest of the field included Nebraska, Oklahoma, Michigan and Florida State.

Action began on Thursday at 10 a.m. with No. 1-seed UCLA against Florida State. The Bruins had dominated the Seminoles in the past. In the bottom of the first, UCLA's Claire Sua sent a slow roller up the middle that bounced off the second base bag and scored Natasha Watley. The game remained at 1-0 until the top of the fourth, when Florida State's Brandi Stuart sent a one-out single to right field and was sacrificed by Tatiana George. As Stuart stole third, a bad throw allowed her to keep running. She crossed home plate and tied the game. After several innings and a half-hour rain delay, the Seminoles' Monique Marier sent a shot over the fence down the left field line in the ninth inning to put the Seminoles ahead 2-1. In the bottom of the ninth with Bruin runners on second and third with two out, Marier made a diving catch in left field for the final out. Leslie Malerich went the nine innings for the Seminoles to get the 2-1 win, allowing six hits and walking nine. Losing hurler Keira Goerl allowed only four hits while striking out twelve and walking one. The Bruins stranded fourteen runners in their first opening-day loss since 1994.

Oklahoma and Cal-Berkeley followed in the next game. Just before play began, Sooner shortstop Kelli Braitsch had been taken to a local hospital for examination after taking a bad hop to the mouth during infield practice. Cal-Berkeley's Candace Harper singled home Kristen Bayless in the bottom of the third, following two errors by Braitsch's replacement at shortstop. With the Golden Bears still at bat, another Sooner error by the second baseman allowed two more Cal-Berkeley runs. Leading 3-0 in the fifth, Cal-Berkeley shortstop Chelsea Spencer singled across Veronica Nelson for another run. In the top of the sixth, OU cut the deficit in half when Erin Evans singled after two outs and Christina Enea hit a two-run home run—her ninth—over the left field fence off Jocelyn Forest. The scoring ended there, and the Golden Bears took a 4-2 win. Forest recorded fourteen strikeouts. Jennifer Stewart took the loss for the Sooners.

With the day games completed, Arizona State and Michigan met at 6 p.m. Thursday. Neither was able to muster much offense through the first three innings. In the fourth inning, Wolverine junior Meghan Doe reached first on a bunt single and was sacrificed to second by Stefanie Volpe. She scored on pitcher Marissa Young's looping double down the right field line. In the bottom of the sixth, Young walked the Sun Devils' Nicole Thompson, who was knocked in by Erin Wardein's single to right field. Kristin Farber followed soon after with an infield single to score Kari Reidhead. Michigan went down in order in the top of the seventh in the 2-1 loss. ASU collected four hits off losing hurler Young, with Farber and Wardein getting two each. Michigan had only two hits off Erica Beach, the fewest number of hits in a game their entire season. The loss ended Young's nine-game win streak. "Obviously we're disappointed," said Michigan coach Carol Hutchins. "I thought Marissa (Young) pitched a great game, but I think Erica Beach pitched a great game as well."

Arizona and Nebraska concluded the first round at 8:30 p.m. Thursday. In the top of the fourth, the Huskers threatened with runners on second and third with one out. But Arizona hurler Jennie Finch struck out Nebraska pitcher Peaches James and got Leigh Suhr to pop up to second base to end the inning. In the bottom of the fourth with one out, Arizona slugger Leneah Manuma hit her twenty-first home run of the season over the right field fence. Manuma had been hitless in her five previous women's series games before unloading on James. James took the 1-0 loss, giving up three hits and fanning nine. Winning pitcher Finch also gave up three hits and fanned nine. "I think the most important game in this tournament is the first one," said Arizona coach Mike Candrea. "And it was nothing fancy, but we got the job done."

Winners Cal-Berkeley and Florida State squared off in a winners-bracket game at 4 p.m. Friday, and their pitchers dominated the action. Cal-Berkeley pitcher Jocelyn Forest gave up no hits until a bunt single by Seminole Brandi Stuart in the top of the fourth inning. Forest would allow only one other hit as she struck out seven, with her teammates playing stellar defense. The Golden Bears collected five hits off Leslie Malerich, including a leadoff home run to left field by shortstop Chelsea Spencer in the top of the fifth inning that broke a scoreless tie. Spencer's third home run of 2002 gave the Golden Bears a 1-0 win and marked the first time they had won their first two games in the national championship. It also tied the school record for season wins (fifty-four). Florida State pitcher Leslie Malerich gave up five hits and walked two in the loss. "It wasn't the best pitch," Malerich said of Spencer's home run, "but it wasn't the worst pitch that I threw. It caught just a little too much of the plate."

In-state rivals Arizona and Arizona State met in the concluding game Friday. ASU had its chances against Wildcat starter Jennie Finch in the first three innings, stranding four runners with three in scoring position. After three rain delays, the game was postponed with no score through three innings. After play resumed Saturday morning, ASU starter Erica Beach gave up her first two hits of the game, but Arizona could not bring the runners across. But the Sun Devils were unable to generate any offense against Finch. She allowed only one hit in the game—an infield single by Kristin Farber in the second inning. Beach held the Wildcats scoreless until the eighth inning. Lovieanne Jung walked and scored from third when Mackenzie Vandergeest smacked a hard hit ball that clipped Beach's glove. It was the game's only run. Finch, who retired the last thirteen batters in order, hurled her fourth one-hitter of 2002, striking out nine in the 1-0 win. "The other pitcher is going through the same thing that you're going through," Finch said about the rain delay. "You just have to get through it and stay focused." Beach took the loss, allowing four hits and striking out seven.

Before a packed house of 6,645 at 1 p.m. on "elimination Saturday," Oklahoma loaded the bases in the bottom of the first inning against UCLA hurler Keira Goerl. Junior shortstop Kelli Braitsch, who had missed the Sooners' first game of the tournament with her pre-game injury, returned to the starting lineup and drew a one-out walk. She then stole second but was later gunned down at the plate by center fielder Amanda Freed. In the top of the second, Bruins' catcher Stacey Nuveman scored the game's first run with a solo home run off Sooner starter Jennifer Stewart. It was her twentieth home run of 2002 and the ninetieth of her career. But Stewart settled down and retired the next ten batters. In the fifth, UCLA's Jennifer Ramos led with a single. Amanda Simpson was sent in to pinch run and then moved to

third on a single by Toria Auelua. UCLA right fielder Monique Mejia delivered
a RBI-single to bring across Simpson with an insurance run for the 2-0 UCLA
win. That eliminated the Sooners (49-16), the first team to pack for home. Goerl
allowed only one hit and struck out three. Ramos had two hits in three at-bats to
lead the Bruins. Stewart gave up seven hits in five and two-thirds innings in her last
college game. Angela Foster finished the game.

The second elimination game matched Nebraska against Michigan, and as
both pitchers settled in, the game wore on with a growing sense that one run might
decide things. It was Nebraska that broke through with that run in the fifth. A one-
out double by Leigh Suhr was followed by a single up the middle by Cindy Roethemeyer that scored Suhr from second. Jessica Merchant ranged far to her left to
knock down the single but was unable to cut down Suhr at the plate. Michigan had
a golden opportunity in the sixth after Kelsey Kollen and Meghan Doe reached
base on Nebraska errors to lead off the inning, prompting Cornhusker coach Rhonda Revelle to bring Peaches James out of the bullpen. James responded by striking
out Stefanie Volpe and Monica Schock, and then getting Marissa Young to ground

**It was Golden Bear hugs all around after Cal-Berkeley won it all in the 2002 national cham-
pionship under coach Diane Ninemire. It was the Bears' tenth appearance in the women's
series since 1980. *(Reprinted courtesy of The Oklahoman)***

out to second base to end the threat. In the seventh, Courtney Betley popped out to the shortstop with the tying run on second, leaving the Wolverines one run shy for the second straight game. It was the first time in 2002 that Michigan had lost two consecutive games, and the run in the fifth snapped Nicole Motycka's string of twenty-eight consecutive scoreless innings and her seventeen-game win streak. Winning pitcher Leigh Ann Walker hurled five innings, allowed one hit and struck out eight, with James hurling the last two innings to earn a save.

Another elimination game followed at 6:30, with UCLA facing Arizona State. The Sun Devils got back-to-back singles from Kristin Farber and Kara Brun with two out in the top of the third. Then Phelan Wright hit a double that bounced on the right field line and scored Farber. Following an intentional walk of pitcher Erica Beach, Missy Hixon drove in Brun to give ASU a 2-0 lead. But in the sixth the Bruins got on the board when Amanda Freed hit a one-out single to right, followed by a single to left by Mims. Stacey Nuveman then stepped in and delivered an RBI double down the right field line. But the batters behind Nuveman were unable to produce more in the 2-1 Bruin defeat. The Sun Devils earned a berth in Sunday's semifinals against Cal-Berkeley. Winning pitcher Beach allowed six hits, struck out one and walked one. Amanda Freed was the losing hurler, giving up four hits in three innings. Goerl retired twelve batters in a row in relief, striking out five.

The final game Saturday evening matched Florida State and Nebraska, with the Cornhuskers playing their second game of the day. Nebraska took the lead in the bottom of the third when Amanda Bucholz scored Cindy Roethemeyer on a sacrifice fly. With the score 1-0 and the bases loaded in the top of the fifth, FSU's Kimmy Carter sent a drive through the left side of the infield driving in two runs, with a third score coming on two Nebraska fielding errors on the same play. With FSU leading 3-1 and still batting, slumping Jessica van der Linden sent a double to left center scoring Carter and putting FSU ahead 4-1. But Nebraska answered in the bottom of the inning with Nicole Trimboli's bases-loaded single that scored two runs. Trimboli was thrown out at second, however, ending the inning. The 4-3 defeat eliminated the Cornhuskers from the tournament, the fourth team eliminated. Leslie Malerich got the win for the Seminoles, allowing five hits and striking out six. Nebraska used two pitchers, with Peaches James hurling four and one-third innings and Leigh Ann Walker finishing up.

Action resumed Sunday with Cal-Berkeley facing Arizona State at noon. In the first inning, the Golden Bears' Kaleo Eldredge and Kristen Morley singled before Veronica Nelson walked to load the bases. Jennifer Deering pinch-ran for Nelson. With two outs, Jessica Pamanian hit a slow roller that ASU third baseman Phelan Wright charged, one-handed, and threw away—allowing all runners to score. ASU never mounted a threat against Jocelyn Forest, who struck out four and allowed only one hit, a single by Wright to open the second inning. Wright was ASU's only base runner. The 3-0 loss eliminated the Sun Devils, who finished third and 46-20 for the season. The win advanced the Golden Bears to Monday's championship game against the winner of the Arizona-Florida State contest that followed.

## 2002 Women's College World Series Bracket
### Oklahoma City • May 23-27

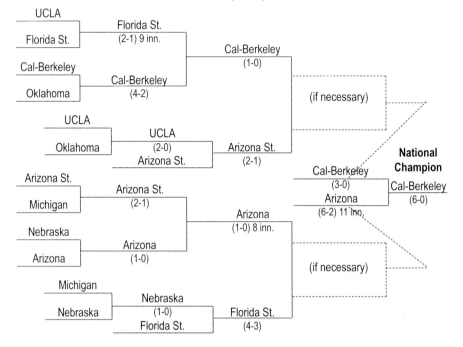

## 2002 Final Standings

| | |
|---|---|
| University of California (Berkeley) | 4-0 |
| University of Arizona (Tucson) | 3-1 |
| Florida State University (Tallahassee) | 2-2 |
| Arizona State University (Tempe) | 2-2 |
| University of Nebraska (Lincoln) | 1-2 |
| University of California (Los Angeles) | 1-2 |
| University of Michigan (Ann Arbor) | 0-2 |
| University of Oklahoma (Norman) | 0-2 |

Florida State scored an unearned run on Kimmy Carter's RBI single that scored Shundra Colzie to take a 1-0 lead against Arizona in the bottom of the third inning. Arizona answered in the top of the fourth when Mackenzie Vandergeest scored from third on a wild pitch by Jessica van der Linden. In the top of the fifth, the Wildcats scored an unearned run with two outs to take a 2-1 lead. But the Seminoles tied the game in the bottom of the fifth with a one-out solo shot by Colzie, the first off Jennie Finch in forty-two innings. The game remained tied until the eleventh when Finch hit a two-out solo home run onto the canopy covering the left field bleachers, and Jackie Coburn followed with an opposite-field, three-run shot over the wall in left-center for the 6-2 win. The home runs were Finch's nineteenth of the season and Coburn's fourteenth. Finch struck out the side in the bottom of the eleventh, finishing with seventeen strikeouts in her third win. FSU's Jessica van der Linden hurled the first six innings, allowing seven hits and two runs before Leslie Malerich finished the remaining five innings, giving up two hits and four runs.

Before a Memorial Day turnout of 5,055 for the championship game, neither Cal-Berkeley nor Arizona scored a run through six innings. But in the top of the seventh, the roof caved in on Arizona. Finch walked Kaleo Eldredge, and Kristen Morley singled to left field. Candace Harper singled to score Eldredge and advanced to second on a throwing error by the center fielder. After Veronica Nelson was intentionally walked, Courtney Scott walked with the bases loaded to force in another run. Jessica Pamanian then ripped a bases-clearing double. Jenny Gladding replaced the tiring Finch in her final college game. But Chelsea Spencer then hit an RBI double off Gladding. The shell-shocked Wildcats went down in order in the bottom of the seventh in the 6-0 loss. Jocelyn Forest fanned eight and got the win for the Golden Bears, allowing only a two-out single in the fourth by Mackenzie Vandergeest. Finch hurled six and two-thirds innings, allowing five hits, six runs, and eight walks. It was the first NCAA women's championship in any sport for the Golden Bears (56-19). "We've waited nineteen years to see this day," said Cal-Berkeley coach Diane Ninemire. "We worked so hard for this. We definitely deserve this championship." Pamanian had two hits in three trips to lead the Golden Bears and was the only player on either team with more than one hit.

Cal-Berkeley's Jocelyn Forest was named the tournament's most outstanding player and was joined on the all-tournament team by teammates Veronica Nelson (1B), and Chelsea Spencer (SS); Arizona's Leneah Manuma (1B), Jackie Coburn (3B) and Jennie Finch (P); Arizona State's Erica Beach (P) and Kristin Farber (OF); UCLA's Natasha Watley (SS), Stacey Nuveman (C) and Keira Goerl (P); and Florida State's Leslie Malerich (P). Watley was the leading hitter (.462).

## Life After the WCWS...

California-Berkeley's **Jocelyn Forest** compiled a pitching record of 103-42 at the school and later tried college coaching at Penn State and Boston College. She also played pro softball. In 2013, she owned CrossFit West Santa Cruz, a strength and conditioning center in Santa Cruz, Calif. Winning first-team NCAA All-American honors three times (2000-2002), Arizona's **Jennie Finch** went on to become one of the most publicized players of her era. Finch compiled a 119-16 record at Arizona, including a record sixty consecutive wins, and was twice named winner of the Honda Sports Award (2001 and 2002). She was a member of the U.S. Olympic softball team in 2004 and 2008, and was named to the NCAA Div. I Softball 25th Anniversary Team in 2006. She retired as a player following the 2010 season, and in 2013 she and her husband, Casey Daigle (a Major League baseball pitcher), were raising their three children. UCLA's **Amanda Freed** was a two-time, first-team

NCAA All-American (1999 and 2002). After serving as an alternate for the 2000 U.S. national team, she was a member of the 2004 U.S. Olympic softball team. In 2013 she worked with Special Olympics of Southern California. UCLA's Stacey Nuveman is the NCAA's all-time career leader in home runs (ninety) and slugging percentage .945 and was a four-time, first-team NCAA All-American (1997, 1999, 2001-02). She was a member of three U.S. Olympic softball teams (2000, 2004 and 2008). In 2013, she was an assistant softball coach at California State University (San Diego). **Jennifer Stewart** ended her career at Oklahoma with 115 wins and later coached at Coastal Carolina and Texas Tech before trying pro softball with the Philadelphia Force.

## 2003: Stadium Upgrade, Pitching Enhance Tournament

The ASA Hall of Fame Stadium had a new look in 2003. The home of the Women's College World Series for thirteen of the previous fourteen years had undergone a $5.1-million overhaul that doubled the permanent seating to more than 5,000. Other enhancements included more than 500 parking spaces and improvements to the concessions, rest rooms and walkways. Two new playing fields were undergoing construction adjacent to the two existing ones. All these enhancements were made to keep the national championship in Oklahoma City. Feedback from NCAA officials indicated that these efforts were bearing fruit.

"Now they've done all these amazing upgrades," said Lisa Vad Thorner, chair of the NCAA softball selection committee. "... It's a great facility." This was music to the ears of the tournament's sponsor, Oklahoma City's All Sports Association. All Sports executive director Tim Brassfield said that he believed the latest enhancements would make Oklahoma City's bid for the event difficult to surpass.

The field of teams announced for the May 22-26 tournament included Arizona, Alabama, Oklahoma, Washington, Texas, Louisiana-Lafayette (formerly University of Southwest Louisiana), UCLA and defending champion California-Berkeley. The 2003 contenders brought a bevy of noted pitching stars, including Cat Osterman (Texas), Alicia Hollowell (Arizona) and Keira Goerl (UCLA). Five of the pitchers in the tournament brought ERAs below 1.00.

Arizona, winner of six NCAA national titles, met Alabama in the opening game at 10 a.m. Thursday. The Wildcats jumped on top in the bottom of the third inning when Arizona RBI-leader Lovieanne Jung hit a two-run double in the right centerfield gap to score two runs. Wendy Allen then hit a one-out grounder to second to score Courtney Fossatti from third and put the Wildcats out in front 3-0. Alabama reduced the margin in the fifth when Ashley Courtney hit a double down the right field line scoring Staci Ramsey and Jackie Wilkins. The scoring ended there. The 3-2 Arizona win marked the eighth consecutive defeat of the Crimson Tide by the Wildcats. Winning pitcher Alicia Hollowell, making her first start in the women's series, fanned thirteen batters and walked four in her two-hitter. "I was nervous," she said, "but I'm nervous before every game. I was probably a bit more for this one, but I played through it." Stephanie VanBrakle took the loss, allowing three runs on six hits. Alabama head coach Pat Murphy was philosophical about the loss: "Like my good buddy (DePaul coach) Eugene Lenti said, 'There's no such thing as a bad day at the World Series.'"

In its fourth consecutive women's series appearance, Oklahoma took a 1-0 lead against Washington in the bottom of the third on a solo home run by designated player Jennifer Stump, her third of the season. But the Huskies countered in the next inning when shortstop Jaime Clark sent the ball over the left-field fence on a 1-1 count against pitcher Kami Keiter to tie the game at 1-1. It was Clark's seventeenth home run in 2003. Still tied in the top of the seventh, Washington's Amanda Oleson doubled to score Aimee Minor and Traci Tawney for a 3-1 lead. A Sooner rally fell short in the bottom of the seventh, giving Washington the 3-1 win. Winning pitcher Tia Bollinger got the complete-game victory, allowing three hits, but had her scoreless inning streak snapped at almost twenty innings by Stump's home run in the third. Clark went two-for-three for Washington and was the only batter on either team with more than one hit. Keiter struck out eight and allowed only four hits, but two came in the decisive seventh inning.

Veteran contender Louisiana-Lafayette surprised Texas and star pitcher Cat Osterman in the top of the first inning with Danyele Gomez's two-run home run to left field. The run ended Osterman's streak of sixty-five scoreless innings. In the fourth, the Longhorns' Tamara Poppe led off with a solo shot to left center to reduce the deficit to one run. Behind 2-1 in the bottom of the sixth with one out, the Longhorns got Poppe on with a walk. Then Amber Hall hit a home run to right field, allowing Texas to edge out Louisiana-Lafayette 3-2 and grab its nineteenth consecutive win. Hall (2-for-3) was the only player on either team with more than one hit. After the two-run home run in the first inning, Osterman retired the next twenty batters in order for her fifth consecutive one-hitter. She fanned eleven batters and did not give up a walk. "I threw a one-hitter," Osterman said, "but I would rather have given up ten singles than a home run." Losing pitcher Brooke Mitchell allowed three hits in the loss, striking out two and walking six.

Defending champion California-Berkeley and UCLA met in the concluding first-round game at 9 p.m. UCLA got on the board first in the bottom of the third inning when Natasha Watley scored on Tairia Mims' double to left—the first run Cal-Berkeley had allowed in nearly fifty innings of post-season play. The Golden Bears' Haley Woods led off the fifth with a single to center, and pinch runner LeAnna Hoglen scored on Kaleo Eldredge's double to left field. With the bases loaded, Vicky Galindo then hit a hard grounder that third baseman Mims could not handle, allowing Eldredge to score and giving the Golden Bears a 2-1 lead. Cal-Berkeley added another run in the sixth when Veronica Nelson led off with a solo home run—her twelfth of 2003. In the seventh, however, UCLA's Tairia Mims took the first pitch she saw over the left-field fence for a two-run home run that tied the score at 3-3 and sent the game into extra innings. In the top of the tenth, Courtney Scott scored on an error by Keira Goerl; Chelsea Spencer singled home Nelson from third; and Spencer and Eldredge scored after an error to give Cal-Berkeley the convincing 7-3 win. Cal-Berkeley's Kelly Anderson pitched eight strong innings, allowing three runs, only one of which was earned, on five hits. Kristina Thorson relieved her in the top of the ninth to get the win. Goerl, the Pac-10 Pitcher of the Year, gave up seven runs and eight hits over the ten innings with thirteen strikeouts. The win snapped UCLA's sixteen-game win streak against the Golden Bears dating back to April 1998.

The winners-bracket games began at 4:30 p.m. Friday, with Arizona's Mackenzie Vandergeest drawing a walk in the top of the second off Washington's Tia Bollinger and scoring on Jackie Coburn's single up the middle. But Washington tied the game in the bottom of the fourth inning when Kristen Rivera hit a one-out, solo home run down the left field line—her twenty-fifth of the season. Arizona had a prime opportunity in the top of the sixth with runners on second and third with one out, but came up empty. Tied 1-1 in the top of the seventh, Arizona's Lisha Ribellia scored when Autumn Champion's ground ball was thrown away by the Huskies' third baseman to give Arizona the 2-1 win. Winning pitcher Alicia Hollowell recorded her second consecutive thirteen-strikeout game, allowing four hits and one walk. Bollinger hurled the first five innings for Washington, with Ashley Boek hurling the last two innings and getting the loss. The two Washington pitchers allowed six hits. Lovieanne Jung (2-for-3) and Rivera (2-for-2) were the only players with more than one hit.

Texas and Cal-Berkeley met to conclude Friday's play, with the Longhorns seeking their twentieth consecutive win. The game was a scoreless deadlock through five innings, but in the sixth Longhorn Lindsay Gardner scored the game's first run on a groundout to third base by Chez Sievers. After another single and a walk, Golden Bear starter Kelly Anderson was replaced by Kristin Thorson, who struck out the next two batters to end the inning. The Bears got runners in scoring position twice, in the third and the seventh, but Osterman used a couple of her seventeen strikeouts to get out of trouble both times. So Texas got the 1-0 win and their twentieth consecutive victory. It was the eleventh time in 2003 that Osterman won a game 1-0. "She threw exceptionally well tonight," Texas coach Connie Clark said. "She mixed speeds more effectively tonight than she has all year and that was the difference." The Longhorns and Wildcats would get a day off with "elimination Saturday" on tap for the six other teams.

With Alabama facing Oklahoma in the first elimination game Saturday morning, the Sooners scored two in the top of the third when Tiffany Weight and April Valdez came across home plate on a wild pitch by Alabama pitcher Erin Wright. The Sooners added a run in the fourth when shortstop Kelli Braitsch hit her twelfth home run of 2003 over the right field fence. But Alabama fought back with Tide third baseman Staci Ramsey blasting a run over center field on a 2-1 count to lead off in the bottom of the fifth inning. Two batters later, center fielder Jackie Wilkins hit Kami Keiter's first pitch to her over the left field fence to pull Alabama to within a run, 3-2. Alabama tied the game at 3-3 in the sixth when Staci Ramsey's sacrifice fly to left scored Jackie McClain, who had reached base on an error. The game remained tied until the ninth inning when Oklahoma's Christina Enea scored on Jennifer Stump's double down the left field line, giving the Sooners a 4-3 lead. Next, Braitsch dashed home on a wild pitch by Tide relief hurler Stephanie Van-Brakle, followed by an RBI single by Erin Evans. Oklahoma got the 6-3 win and eliminated the Tide. Keiter finished with seven strikeouts and three walks, allowing four hits. The Tide's Stephanie VanBrakle allowed seven hits in five innings and took the loss, with Erin Wright hurling the remaining four frames. Stump and Christiana Enea led the Sooners with two hits apiece.

UCLA faced Louisiana-Lafayette in the 3 p.m. elimination game, and the Bruins pushed a run across in the top of the first when Caitlin Benyi scored on a fielder's choice hit by Claire Sua. The Bruins added a run in the third on a two-out solo home run by Tairia Mims, her twenty-first of the season and sixtieth of her UCLA career. In the fourth, Louisiana cut the lead in half after Becky McMurtry scored on Joy Webre's single to right center. UCLA added three more runs in the sixth inning, first with a two-run home run by Monique Mejia, scoring Emily Zaplatosch. Andrea Duran then doubled to left field and eventually scored on a double by shortstop Natasha Watley. The 5-1 win eliminated Louisiana-Lafayette, the second team ousted. Bruin hurler Keira Goerl got the win with her fourteenth one-hitter of the season, striking out eight. Watley led the Bruins with three hits in four trips to the plate. Losing pitcher Brooke Mitchell, who was bothered by a sore arm throughout the tournament, allowed nine hits in five and two-thirds innings with Afton Thoms hurling the remainder.

In the first evening elimination game, Oklahoma took an early 1-0 lead in the bottom of the first on a double by senior Leah Gulla that brought across Kelli Braitsch. Their lead vanished fast, however, as the Golden Bears Chelsea Spencer singled to right to start the second inning and eventually scored on Vicky Galindo's infield single. In the top of the fourth, Cal-Berkeley's Kaleo Eldredge reached first on a bunt and moved to second on a fielder's choice hit by Spencer. Galindo singled to left field to bring across Eldredge and Spencer. But the Sooners pulled to within one when Jennifer Stump hit a solo home run in the bottom of the fourth inning—her second of the tournament. With two out in the seventh, Eldredge walked before Spencer hit a home run over left field that gave the Golden Bears a 5-2 lead. Oklahoma was unable to rally in the bottom of the inning and took the 5-2 loss. Cal-Berkeley's Kristina Thorson allowed two hits and a run in the first inning before being replaced by Kelly Anderson, who fanned three batters, walked six, and allowed two hits and a run in six and two-thirds innings. Sooner hurler Kami Keiter walked five while allowing four runs on five hits. Galindo and Spencer had two hits apiece for the Golden Bears.

UCLA and Washington faced off in the final elimination game Saturday at 8:30 p.m. The Bruins took the lead when Natasha Watley singled and scored from second on a single by Tairia Mims in the bottom of the third inning. But Washington tied the game on a one-out solo home run by Aimee Minor in the top of the fifth inning before UCLA's Keira Goerl struck out the next two batters to end the inning. With the game tied, UCLA went up in the sixth inning on Tairia Mims's third home run of the tournament. The scoring ended there, and the 2-1 defeat eliminated the Huskies. Winning pitcher Goerl scattered four hits and fanned seven. Ashley Boek took the loss, striking out four and walking two while allowing four hits. Mims had two hits in two at-bats to lead the Bruins.

The first game at noon Sunday matched Arizona against Cal-Berkeley, and Arizona scored first when Lovieanne Jung scored on Wendy Allen's double to right center in the top of the fourth inning. The Wildcats remained in front until the seventh inning when Cal-Berkeley's Vicky Galindo reached first on a fielding error by Jung and scored on Courtney Scott's single to center field. The 1-1 score held until the twelfth inning when Cal-Berkeley's Chelsea Spencer singled down the left field line to bring Linzi Wescott across for the 2-1 win. Kelly Anderson pitched all twelve innings, allowing just one run on five hits while striking out nine. Losing pitcher Alicia Hollowell allowed eight hits and two runs while striking out sixteen. The two teams were to meet again later that day.

UCLA and Texas followed at 2:30 Sunday. The Bruins took a 1-0 lead in the top of the fourth when Toria Auelua hit her sixth home run of the season over the right-field fence off Texas southpaw Cat Osterman. In the seventh the Bruins' Monique Mejia walked and eventually scored on an RBI single by Natasha Watley. Claire Sua then stroked an RBI single to score Watley. Texas could not get a hit in their last at bats, giving the Bruins the 3-0 victory. Keira Goerl got the win, allowing only two hits while striking out nine. Osterman hurled four innings, allowing two hits before Amy Bradford replaced her and hurled three and two-third innings, giving up four hits. Lizi Sowers finished up.

Cal-Berkeley and Arizona faced off for the second time that day, with the Golden Bears' Kaleo Eldredge blasting a home run to left center in the top of the second inning. In the bottom of the inning, the Wildcats' Lisha Ribellia hit a two-out double to center field to score Jackie Coburn and tie the game. In the fifth and with one out, Courtney Scott singled to right field before Veronica Nelson unloaded a two-run shot to left center to up the Cal-Berkeley margin. In the top of the seventh the Golden Bears' Chelsea Spencer singled down the left field line to score LeAnna Hoglen and eliminate the Wildcats 4-1. Kelly Anderson allowed four hits in her complete-game win. Cal-Berkeley got seven hits off losing hurler Alicia Hollowell, who walked eight batters and struck out three. The Golden Bears advanced to the championship game Monday to play the winner of the UCLA-Texas game.

In the final game Sunday, Texas sought to qualify for the title game for the first time. In the top of the first, the Longhorns got Lindsay Gardner on base on a Bruin error, and she came home from third on an RBI single by Chez Sievers. Pitchers Cat Osterman and Keira Goerl kept both teams from scoring for the next five innings. In the bottom of the seventh inning, with Texas still up by the one earlier run, the Bruins' Monique Mejia scored from second when Natasha Watley drilled a single up the middle and just to the right of Osterman. With two outs, freshman

## 2003 Women's College World Series Bracket
Oklahoma City • May 22-26

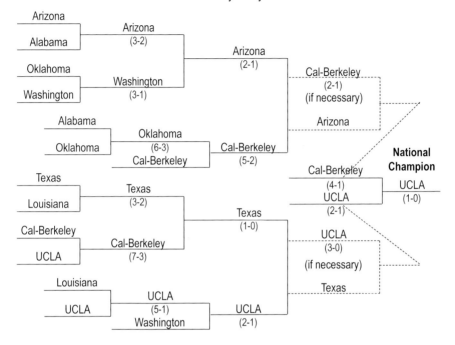

## 2003 Final Standings

| | |
|---|---|
| University of California (Los Angeles) | 5-1 |
| University of California (Berkeley) | 4-2 |
| University of Texas (Austin) | 2-2 |
| University of Arizona (Tucson) | 2-2 |
| University of Washington (Seattle) | 1-2 |
| University of Oklahoma (Norman) | 1-2 |
| University of Louisiana (Lafayette) | 0-2 |
| University of Alabama (Tuscaloosa) | 0-2 |

Caitlin Benyi, who had struck out in three previous at-bats, hit the first pitch into right field for a hit, scoring Watley from second base and eliminating the Longhorns from the tourney by a 2-1 score. UCLA's Goerl became the all-time winning pitcher in Bruin softball with her ninety-eighth career win. She allowed three hits, walked one and struck out three. Osterman walked two, struck out thirteen, and allowed six hits as the Longhorns finished 49-9 and tied for third.

UCLA and Cal-Berkeley met on Monday in a tournament rematch for the national championship. The Bruins threatened in the third inning but were unable to capitalize. In the fourth, Cal-Berkeley's Veronica Nelson was issued her second intentional walk of the game, but the Golden Bears' batters could not bring her home. UCLA again got runners on base in the sixth, seventh and eighth innings, but failed to score each time. The Golden Bears' biggest problem was getting a hit off Goerl. The game went into extra innings tied at 0-0. Finally, in the top of the ninth, UCLA center fielder Stephanie Ramos led off with a double to left center that hit the outfield wall. She advanced to third on a sacrifice bunt by Emily Zaplatosch and scored on a slow-moving single through the left side of the infield by Toria Auelua for a 1-0 lead. With hitless Cal-Berkeley at bat, Goerl retired all three batters, sealing the Bruins's win with the 1-0 no-hitter. Losing hurler Kelly Anderson hurled all nine innings, allowing six hits while striking out five. Anderson led all pitchers in the tournament with forty-eight innings—just one more than Goerl.

UCLA's victory was sweetened by their coming back from a first-game loss to win the national title, the tenth for the Bruins. "I have respect for all those championships that preceded this one," said UCLA coach Sue Enquist. "Each one is special. What will be defining for this team is we came back out of the losers bracket. This team refused to lose." Enquist then declared that parity had arrived in women's college softball and predicted an end to dynasties like those her Bruins and the Arizona Wildcats had maintained.

Keira Goerl pitched all forty-eight innings for UCLA in the 2003 tournament, striking out forty-four and allowing just four earned runs. With a gaudy 0.60 ERA, she was named the tournament's most outstanding player. The twelve players named to the all-tournament team included UCLA's Goerl (P), Natasha Watley (SS) and Tairia Mims (3B); Cal-Berkeley's Kelly Anderson (P), Vicky Galido (3B), Veronica Nelson (1B) and Chelsea Spencer (SS); Oklahoma's Jennifer Stump (DH); Texas's Cat Osterman (P) and Tamara Poppe (LF); Arizona's Alicia Hollowell (P) and Lovieanne Jung (2B). Watley was the leading hitter (.444).

## Life After The WCWS...

UCLA's **Natasha Watley** won the Honda Sports Award in 2003 as the outstanding college softball player and went on to become the second softball recipient of the Honda-Broderick Cup, which is presented annually to the nation's top collegiate female athlete. She was a four-time, first-team NCAA All-American (2000-03) and played for the U.S. national softball team in the 2004 and 2008 Olympic Games. She was named to the NCAA Div. I Softball 25th Anniversary Team in 2006. In 2013, Watley played for Team Toyota of Japan after playing professionally in the National Pro Fastpitch League (2005 and 2006) and the PFX Tour in 2007. Oklahoma shortstop **Kelli Braitsch** in 2001 earned NCAA first-team All-American honors and was Big 12 Player of the Year. In 2000 she was named to the women's series all-tournament team. As of 2013, Braitsch was a police officer for the Tulsa (Okla.) Police Department.

# 2004: Goerl Pitches UCLA to 11th Series Title

With attendance at more than 37,000 for the women's series in 2003, local tournament organizers continued improvements at ASA Hall of Fame Stadium. The $6-million upgrade before the 2004 event had increased seating capacity to 6,000, but amenities to the facility were ongoing. The NCAA would review bids for the tournament in summer, and Oklahoma City hoped for a five-year extension, at least. "(The future site) will be reviewed this summer, but I know the committee is very happy with what Oklahoma City has done," NCAA championships director Sharon Cessna said that year. "There's a good fan following, and they've really upgraded the stadium."

Facilities changes aside, continuing changes on the field of play had taken a noticeable toll on pitching statistics by 2004. Top college fastpitch hurlers once had ERAs below 0.50. But by the early 2000s, even many of the best pitchers had ERAs higher than 1.00. The changes that had aided batters included: moving the pitching rubber back in 1988, overhauling the ball in 1993, advances in bat technology, and weight training for players. Still, even with improved batting statistics, the name of the game was pitching. Six of the eight regional tournaments leading up to the 2004 tournament had crowned pitchers as their most outstanding players. "You live and die with your pitching," Michigan coach Carol Hutchins said. "The success here will be determined by pitching."

The teams that won a berth in the May 27-31 tournament were all veterans of past national championship play and included: Michigan, LSU, Stanford, UCLA, Washington, Oklahoma, Cal-Berkeley and Florida State. In the opening game Thursday, pitchers Kristin Schmidt of LSU and Nicole Motycka of Michigan matched zeroes through eleven innings. Then in the twelfth, the Wolverines finally broke through with Grace Leutele's two-run home run. But in the bottom of the twelfth, LSU rallied to tie the game at 2-2 after Leigh Ann Danos's RBI single drove in LaDonia Hughes, followed by Leslie Klein's score on a throwing error. In the bottom half of the thirteenth inning, LSU's Sara Fitzgerald singled and eventually scored on a throwing error. Schmidt got the 3-2, complete-game win for LSU, striking out thirteen and allowing six hits. Motycka, replaced by Jennie Ritter in the twelfth, hurled eleven and two-thirds innings, allowed eight hits and a pair of runs. Ritter hurled one inning, allowing two hits and one run.

UCLA and Stanford met in the second game, and the Cardinal opened the scoring with a run in the top of the first inning on an RBI single by Jessica Allister. The Bruins countered with a run in the bottom of the inning on a double by Andrea Duran and Lisa Dodd's RBI single. The teams traded zeros in the second and third innings before Stanford's Leah Nelson hit a solo home run in the top of the fourth. Trailing 2-1, the Bruins rallied in the bottom of the fourth, sending eleven batters to the plate and collecting seven hits. The six-run rally was capped by a three-run shot by Caitlyn Benyi, her twenty-third home run of the year. This increased the UCLA lead to 7-2, and Lisa Dodd's RBI double in the sixth secured the 8-2 UCLA win. Bruin pitcher Keira Goerl struck out seven batters in her complete game and allowed six hits. Stanford starter Dana Sorensen hurled the first two innings, allowing one run on three hits, and was replaced by Laura Seversen, who gave up eight hits and seven runs to get the loss. UCLA had eleven hits with Lisa Dodd going 3-for-4 with two RBIs.

Thursday evening Washington and Oklahoma met before a crowd of more than 6,000. Washington took a 1-0 lead in the top of the first inning on Dena Tyson's run-scoring single, but Oklahoma answered in the bottom of the inning with a bases-loaded, RBI single by Christina Enea. Jessica Leslie and Mariee Mena followed with run-scoring singles to give the Sooners a 4-1 lead. But Washington cut the deficit to two on Amanda Oleson's RBI single in the third inning. The game progressed quickly until the bottom of the sixth when OU's Kristin Vesely scored pinch runner Jade Prather and Norrelle Dickson with a double to left-center. Sooner pitcher Kami Keiter got the 6-2 win, giving up eight hits and striking out five. Losing pitcher Ashley Boek allowed six runs on nine hits and struck out five. Enea led all batters, going 3-for-4.

California-Berkeley and Florida State met late Thursday to conclude the opening round. FSU jumped out to a 2-0 lead in the bottom of the first inning on a two-run home run by pitcher Jessica van der Linden. Golden Bear hurler Kristina Thorson kept her composure, and Cal-Berkeley fought back in the top of the third inning when Lindsay James scored on Kaleo Eldredge's two-out single. California added two more in the inning on Jessica Pamanian's two-run triple, putting the Golden Bears ahead 3-2. California increased its lead and closed out the scoring with a solo shot by Roni Rodrigues in the top of the fourth inning over the left center field fence. Thorson got the complete-game win in her two-hit performance, striking out twelve and retiring seventeen straight batters from the first through the sixth inning. Losing pitcher van der Linden struck out nine and allowed nine hits in the 4-2 loss. The Seminole pitcher had the only two hits off Thorson. Vicky Galindo, Haley Woods and Pamanian had two hits apiece for the Golden Bears.

With the winners playing on Friday, UCLA faced LSU in the first contest at 2 p.m. The Bruins scored twice in the top of the first inning on four hits. Stephanie Ramos singled to the right center-field wall to score Andrea Duran, and Jodie Legaspi followed with a single to score Lisa Dodd. Trying to overcome the 2-0 deficit, LSU's best scoring chances came in the fourth and sixth innings when the Tigers had runners at second and third with no outs. But UCLA hurler Keira Goerl got out of both jams for the 2-0 victory. Goerl struck out five and gave up four hits in the shutout. LSU losing hurler Kristin Schmidt gave up two runs on seven hits. Lisa Dodd had three hits in four at-bats to lead the Bruins.

With nearly 6,500 in attendance in the second winners game, California-Berkeley took a 1-0 lead against Oklahoma in the bottom of the third on a Vicky Galindo home run. But the Sooners erased the deficit with a run in the fifth when Golden Bear catcher Haley Woods threw the ball into center field after a strike-out with the bases loaded, allowing Kristin Vesely to score. The game remained tied through seven innings, but in the bottom of the eighth Cal-Berkeley's Vicky Galindo scored the game-winner. Galindo tallied after Kaleo Eldredge lined out to OU center fielder Vesely, who overthrew second base getting the ball back into the infield. The ball rolled through the infield into foul territory as Galindo raced home with the deciding run for the 2-1 Cal-Berkeley victory. Golden Bear starter Kristina Thorson hurled five and one-third innings, allowing five hits before being relieved by Kelly Anderson, who allowed one hit and struck out two for the win. Kami Keiter was the losing hurler, allowing four hits and two runs. "When it's all over you remember the last play," Oklahoma coach Patty Gasso said. "But that's unfair to Kristin Vesely. We had opportunities." The Sooners stranded ten runners.

The first game on "elimination Saturday" was Stanford versus Michigan at 11 a.m. Stanford took the lead in the top of the second when Jessica Allister hit her twelfth home run of 2004. With the bases loaded, Wolverine pitcher Jennie Ritter then walked in a run to hand the Cardinal a 2-0 lead. Michigan answered in the bottom of the same inning when Jennifer Olds hit a two-run home run to tie the game 2-2. Michigan's Monica Schock's sacrifice-fly RBI in the bottom of the fourth gave the Wolverines a go-ahead run. But the Cardinal came back in the top of the fifth when Leah Nelson scored Catalina Morris with a single to left, and Lauren Lappin scored on a groundout by Elizabeth Bendig. Michigan tied the game 4-4 in the sixth on a groundout by Grace Leutele that scored Tiffany Haas. In the seventh inning, Stanford's Meghan Sickler won the seesaw contest with a sacrifice fly to right field to score Shoney Hixson. Dana Sorensen picked up the 5-4 win for Stanford, allowing four runs on four hits. Ritter hurled two innings, allowing three hits and two runs. Nicole Motycka took the loss for Michigan in relief, allowing three runs on eight hits over five innings. Michigan became the first team eliminated from the tournament, finishing the year 54-13.

Mid-afternoon, Washington played Florida State in another elimination contest. The game's only score was in the top of the fourth, when FSU's Tatiana George hit a two-run home run down the left-field line. Seminole pitcher Jessica van der Linden allowed the Huskies four hits but no runs through seven innings, while striking out ten. Van der Linden also had two hits in two at-bats. The Huskies stranded nine runners in the 2-0 loss. Losing hurler Boek hurled a four-hitter with two strikeouts and one walk. Amanda Oleson led the Huskies with a 2-for-3 performance. "I didn't have my A game with me," van der Linden said after the game. But she had enough to advance the 'Noles.

Oklahoma and Stanford followed, with the Sooners getting a score from Kristin Vesely in the top of the first when Cardinal first baseman Leah Nelson dropped a throw from shortstop. The Sooners' Christina Enea also scored in the first on Mariee Mena's RBI single. Stanford closed to within one in the third when Katherine Hoffman scored on an RBI single by Lauren Lappin. With lightning threatening, the game was delayed until 9 a.m. Sunday. When play resumed the next day in the sixth inning, Stanford's Lappin hit a solo shot over the left field fence in the bottom of the inning to tie the game at 2-2. Still batting in the sixth with two outs,

the Cardinal's Meghan Sickler sliced a triple down the right field line to score
pinch runner Jacki Hansen and give Stanford a 3-2 win. Dana Sorensen recorded
the complete-game win for the Cardinal, allowing two unearned runs on ten hits
with four strikeouts. Kami Keiter took the loss for Oklahoma, allowing three runs
on six hits with six strikeouts.

Florida State and LSU followed in another elimination game that had been
postponed by the Saturday evening storm. Before a crowd of more than 6,400, the
Tigers Lauren Castle scored in the top of the first on a single up the middle by Camille Harris. Then Leigh Ann Danos was hit by a pitch to load the bases. But the
LSU rally ended when LaDonia Hughes was called for interference after colliding
with the Seminole catcher at home. FSU tied it in the bottom of the first when
leadoff hitter Veronica Wootsen smacked her eighth home run of the season. The
Tigers regained the lead in the top of the fourth when pinch runner Lauren Uhle
scored on Sara Fitzgerald's single through the left side. Kristin Schmidt got the 2-1
win for LSU, allowing one run on four hits with thirteen strikeouts. She struck out
seven of the final eleven batters she faced. Casey Hunter took the loss, allowing two
runs on eight hits. Jessica van der Linden came on in relief in the sixth.

With the field reduced to four teams, Stanford and UCLA played next at 1
p.m. UCLA's Caitlin Benyi opened the game with a leadoff home run, taking a 1-0
pitch over the left field fence. It was the seventh time in 2004 she had led off the

**The UCLA team poses after the 2004 title game with their newest of eleven national cham-
pionship trophies for softball. The 2004 win marked the second consecutive title for the
Bruins and their third consecutive appearance in the championship game. *(Reprinted
courtesy of UCLA Athletic Department)***

game with a home run. Stanford countered in the bottom half of the first as Catalina Morris came around to score on Jessica Allister's single. For the next ten innings, starting pitchers Dan Sorensen for Stanford and Keira Goerl for UCLA matched zeros. But in the twelfth, UCLA's Benyi walked with two outs and scored on Lisa Dodd's RBI double for the 2-1 Bruin victory. UCLA advanced to the championship for the nineteenth time since 1978. After the win, Bruin coach Sue Enquist disdained comparisons with legendary UCLA basketball coach John Wooden. "With all due respect, I can never be compared to John Wooden," she said. "More importantly, it's these kids who are the reason we continue to have this type of success."

LSU and California-Berkeley followed at a little after 5 p.m. The Golden Bears took the early lead in the bottom of the first when Lindsay James scored on a single by Kaleo Eldredge. The Tigers countered in the top of the second with Leslie Klein's leadoff home run to right field—her fourteenth of 2004 and a single-season school record. In the top of the third, Camille Harris doubled with two out, scoring Lauren Castle and LaDonia Hughes to give LSU a 3-1 advantage. The Tigers added another run in the sixth when Lauren Delahoussaye doubled to score Stephanie Hill, giving LSU a 4-1 lead that held. Kristin Schmidt was the winning pitcher, allowing one run and striking out eight batters. Cal-Berkeley used two pitchers, with Kristina Thorson taking the 4-1 loss after two and two-thirds innings, allowing three runs on four hits. Kelly Anderson came on in relief in the third and allowed one unearned run on three hits with three strikeouts. The LSU win forced the if-necessary game—a rematch against the Golden Bears.

In the 8 p.m. rematch, LSU took the lead in the bottom of the second as Sara Fitzgerald doubled-in pinch runner Lauren Uhle. LSU kept the 1-0 lead for several innings. In the fifth with the bases loaded, Tiger pitcher Kristin Schmidt walked Jessica Pamanian and forced in the game's tying run. Chelsea Spencer then knocked in another run, followed by Alex Sutton's two-run RBI single that extended the Bears' lead to 4-1. Kelly Anderson got the 4-1 win for California, allowing four hits and one run. Schmidt, who hurled 358 pitches in three games on that long Sunday, was relieved in the top of the seventh and got a standing ovation from the crowd. She gave up twelve hits as LSU (57-12) finished third.

With the win, the Golden Bears advanced to the championship game for the third consecutive year and faced the Bruins, their opponent a year earlier. California got on the scoreboard in the first inning when Jessica Pamanian singled down the left field line, scoring Lindsay James. Cal-Berkeley pitcher Kelly Anderson retired the first twelve UCLA batters in order, but in the bottom of the fifth the Bruins' Claire Sua homered to left field to tie the game at 1-1. With UCLA still batting, freshman Kristen Dedmon delivered a single up the middle, scoring Amanda Simpson and Tara Henry after obstruction was called on the Cal-Berkeley catcher. Winning pitcher Keira Goerl retired the last six batters in the 3-1 win, becoming only the third pitcher since 1982 to win more than one title game. Goerl allowed seven hits and struck out four. It was UCLA's eleventh national softball championship, including their 1978 AIAW title. Losing pitcher Kelly Anderson hurled five

## 2004 Women's College World Series Bracket
Oklahoma City • May 27-31

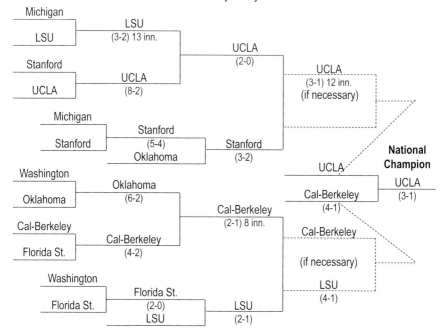

## 2004 Final Standings

| | |
|---|---|
| University of California (Los Angeles) | 4-0 |
| University of California (Berkeley) | 3-2 |
| Louisiana State University (Baton Rouge) | 3-2 |
| Stanford University (Palo Alto, Calif.) | 2-2 |
| Florida State University (Tallahassee) | 1-2 |
| University of Oklahoma (Norman) | 1-2 |
| University of Michigan (Ann Arbor) | 0-2 |
| University of Washington (Seattle) | 0-2 |

innings, allowing one hit, with Kristina Thorson finishing up. The Golden Bears (53-13) finished runner-up for the second year in a row. "But those are some big shoulders that carried this team," UCLA's Enquist said of Goerl. "Keira is the best we've ever had."

Kristin Schmidt of LSU was named the tournament's most outstanding player after winning three games, leading in strikeouts (44), and throwing an incredible 634 pitches in five games. Joining her on the all-tournament team were teammate Camille Harris (RF); UCLA's Lisa Dodd (1B), Keira Goerl (P), Caitlin Benyi (2B) and Jodie Legaspi (SS); Cal-Berkeley's Kelly Anderson (P), Vicky Galindo (3B) and Jessica Pamanian (2B); Florida State's Jessica van der Linden (P); Stanford's Lauren Lappin (SS); and Oklahoma's Christina Enea (1B). Enea led all batters with her average of .545.

An attendance record of just over 41,000 was set for the 2004 women's series. The year also marked the end of the tournament's tradition of crowning a champion on Memorial Day. Future title games would be played in early June.

## Life After the WCWS...

UCLA's **Keira Goerl** compiled a pitching record of 130-21 during her college career and is one of three pitchers to win two NCAA national title games. She was a two-time, first-team NCAA All-American (2002-03). After completing her master's degree in management-organizational leadership in 2010, Goerl was working as a recruiter at Aerotek Commercial Staffing in the Los Angeles area in 2013. LSU pitcher **Kristin Schmidt** compiled a college pitching record of 116 wins and twenty-nine losses for a winning percentage of .800. She struck out 1,154 batters in 986 innings for an average of 8.2 batters per game. Cal-Berkeley's **Vicky Galindo** earned first-team NCAA All-American honors twice (2004-05) and was named to the U.S. national team for the 2008 Olympics. In 2013 Galindo played for the Chicago Bandits in the National Pro Fastpitch league. Florida State's **Jessica van der Linden** was named the USA Softball National Collegiate Player of the Year in 2004 after compiling a pitching record of 28-7 and batting .389. She twice earned NCAA first-team All-American honors (2003-04). In 2013, van der Linden and her husband, former National Football League player Michael Boulware, provided softball training and conditioning at their company, All Out Training, in Lugoff, S.C.

# Eight

(2005-2012)

৵৶৵৶

# Living Dreams in a Series of Their Own

The growth, competitiveness and popularity of the Women's College World Series that had increased incrementally throughout the 1990s flowered dramatically in the middle of the first decade of the new century. Moving the tournament's schedule into June facilitated this maturation of the championship event in Oklahoma City. The 2005 tournament left behind the traditional Memorial Day championship game and began first-round play the Thursday after the holiday. The new titleholder would be decided in a best-of-three final format, eschewing the winner-take-all national title game in the previous quarter century of championships.

The calendar change for the women's series was driven by officials at ESPN television network. The cable giant had done much to spread the popularity of softball nationally, and the programming change would promote the sport even more. Airing only one game ten years before, ESPN had expanded its coverage of the tournament since this meager beginning. In the three years before 2005, the sports network aired every game live. With the calendar change and championship format change, ESPN planned to air most of the 2005 tournament in prime viewing time. Using recognizable Olympic softball stars like Michele Smith and Jessica Mendoza as broadcast analysts, ESPN's 2007 television ratings for the women's series proved comparable to their ratings for the men's baseball College World Series in Omaha.

Of profound importance, televised national coverage of the women's series had done much in the decade before 2005 to inspire a desire to excel in budding female athletes. These broadcasts of the women's national championship provided young softball players across the country with sports heroines. Caitlin Lowe recalled watching Arizona win the 1997 women's series on television as a twelve-year-old in Tustin, Calif. "I grew up idolizing (Wildcat center fielder) Alison McCutcheon," Lowe told an Oklahoma City news reporter at the 2007 national championship. "I wanted to be just like her. That's when I decided I wanted to win a national championship." Lowe would live out her dream in 2007 as a standout for the Arizona team that won the national title. The NCAA All-American center fielder batted 4-4 in the title-clinching Wildcat victory over Tennessee. Later that same year she was named to the U.S. national softball team for the 2008 Olympic Games in Beijing, China. While federal legislation had given college softball a generation of athletic "Title IX" babies in the 1990s, more and more "ESPN babies" like Lowe were emerging in the first decade of the new century. These twenty-first-century college athletes had found their role models in sports as adolescents a decade earlier while viewing the women's series and dreaming of their own futures.

National television coverage of the series had both contributed to and reflected the growing national popularity of college softball. With this increased popularity, new college programs continued to battle their way to the national championship. The colleges of the South in particular began to challenge the traditional powers, with five of the eight teams in the 2008 national tournament from southern schools. The long-discussed "parity" in college softball became a reality late in the decade. Previously dominant Pac-10 and California schools began to scramble with the rest of the field for a berth in the national title game. In 2011, for the first time in a quarter century, neither of the two perennial Pac-10 powers—UCLA and Arizona—qualified for the tournament. And in 2012, for the first time since 1986, no Pac-12 team would participate in the title game of the women's series.

The increased popularity and competitiveness of college softball was clearly reflected in the mushrooming attendance figures at the tournaments throughout the decade. For the tournament's first three years (1990-1992) in Oklahoma City, series attendance averaged 12,650, and local tournament organizers worried that the NCAA might try a new location. "I can remember a (session) when we didn't have even 200 people when we first started hosting the world series in Oklahoma City," longtime tournament director Marita Hynes reminisced in 2006. Hynes could laugh about those early lean attendance figures by 2006, the year after she stepped down as tournament director. In her last year overseeing the tournament in 2005, attendance had risen to almost 42,000. A decade after the championship's debut in Oklahoma City, the three-year average (2000-02) had spiked to almost 35,000. Astonishingly, the three-year average (2010-12) a decade later climbed steeply to nearly 70,000—about double that of ten years earlier.

The escalating attendance figures were accompanied by continuous expansion and improvement to ASA Hall of Fame Stadium. Permanent seating was more than doubled in 2002 to 5,000, with additional bleacher seating behind the outfield increasing total capacity to 8,000. By 2010, the stadium's seating capacity had been increased to 9,000, and new locker rooms for the players had been built. The contract for the tournament was on a two-year renewal cycle, but the local sponsor, the All Sports Association, was working for a longer-term arrangement with the NCAA. This kind of agreement might require a newer, larger stadium in the future. All Sports executive director Tim Brassfield believed the tournament was on sound footing in Oklahoma City and had found a home. "But we're still doing everything we can to make sure everyone benefits," he said in 2009. NCAA officials seemed comfortable with local efforts to keep improving the event. In Oklahoma City to view his first softball national championship in 2009, NCAA executive director Myles Brand had only positive things to say about the tournament and Oklahoma City. "This is a great event," Brand said. "The Women's College World Series, frankly, is one of our growth sports. .... Oklahoma City has done a great job. We like the idea of coming back to the same place."

While women's fastpitch softball continued to experience increasing growth and popularity in college athletics, many were surprised and dismayed when it was dropped as an Olympic sport after the 2008 Games in Beijing. The reasons for this were complex, but softball's parting with the Olympics probably only elevated the standing of the Women's College World Series. No longer an Olympic sport and lacking a strong professional league, fastpitch softball's pinnacle in the United States moved from the Olympics to the college national championship. Fittingly so, as most of the players on the U.S. national softball team in the Olympics had previously been steeled in competition at the women's series in Omaha, Sunnyvale and Oklahoma City.

By 2012, women's college softball and the Women's College World Series had risen to a level of popularity and competitiveness that its early organizers and promoters had only dreamed of in the late 1960s. The pioneers of college softball could only be thrilled at all that had been gained, and just as important, gratified at what had not been lost from the early years of women's college softball—a spirit that is often sadly missing in competitive sports. Berry Tramel, a longtime follower of the national championship in Oklahoma City and a sportswriter for The Oklahoman newspaper, best expressed this spirit in a column he wrote while observing the teams at the tournament in June 2007:

> ... Then they took the field and, without losing the spirit, still clapping and chanting on every batter and celebrating every out, competed like Michael Vick pit bulls. It's this way every year in the World Series. Softball players sing and sweat, dance and dive, chant and, yes, curse ... They play hard and they fight well and they lose tough. But they don't forget to pack their joy. That's my favorite thing about the series. It's an ode to joy.

## 2005: Michigan Takes National Title Back East

The Women's College World Series entered a new frontier in 2005 with the best-of-three format to determine the national champion and with tournament play starting after Memorial Day. The traditional Memorial Day championship game would be in the past. Some were worried that attendance would be hurt by this move away from the holiday weekend. These worries proved needless, as by 2005 softball's popularity had reached a new high and would only increase in the years ahead. ESPN television network planned to air in prime time as many as eleven games. The championship's new best-of-three final format could make for even more compelling viewing than in years past. "A few years ago we found a diamond in the rough," said Carol Stiff, ESPN's director of programming and acquisitions. "We noticed a trend where a lot of eyeballs were watching softball." So for the fourth consecutive year, ESPN and ESPN2 would air every game live. ESPN also added a "skycam" to enhance coverage in 2005.

The return of Texas pitcher Cat Osterman to the 2005 series provided real star power for television viewers at home and for spectators at ASA Hall of Fame Stadium. The 6-foot-2 Osterman had pitched for the U.S. national softball team a year earlier in the Olympic Games and was one of the most recognizable players across the nation. Another tall pitcher drawing media attention before the action started was Tennessee's Monica Abbott. The 6-foot-3 hurler led the nation in strikeouts in 2005, and she, too, would earn a spot on a future U.S. national softball team in the Olympics.

With the new tournament format, the eight teams were first divided into two brackets of play and the winning pair of teams emerging from those brackets would compete in a best-of-three series for the national championship. The opening game in the upper bracket began at 11 a.m. Thursday, June 2, and featured a pitching duel between Tennessee's Abbott and Arizona's Alicia Hollowell. The Lady Vols finally scored the contest's only run with two-out in the top of the sixth inning when Katherine Card drove in Ashley Cline from first base. Arizona right fielder Adrienne Acton fielded Card's drive but her throw into the infield was off target. Cline raced home under the tag of Hollowell for the game winner in the 1-0 Tennessee win. "When I saw the ball bounce off (catcher Jackie Coburn's) chest protector, I thought I had a shot," Cline later said of her winning gamble. "It was close, but I knew I was safe." Southpaw Abbott limited Arizona to only a single by Callistra Balko while striking out twelve. Losing hurler Hollowell also struck out twelve but gave up four hits.

In the second game of the upper bracket at 2 p.m., Cal-Berkeley's Vicky Galindo scored on a throwing error by UCLA's Anjelica Selden in the bottom of the third inning to give the Golden Bears the lead. But the Bruins evened the score on Ashley Herrera's solo blast in the fifth inning. Then, UCLA's Krista Colburn's two-out, RBI single in the sixth inning scored Emily Zaplatosch with the winning run for the 2-1 Bruin win. UCLA pitcher Selden allowed only three hits in the victory. Losing pitcher Kelly Anderson hurled five innings, allowing three hits and two runs, with Kristina Thorson finishing up. "They have a terrific team," said UCLA coach Sue Enquist. "But today it was our turn to get a win."

In the lower bracket, No. 1-ranked Michigan and DePaul met in the first of two night games on Thursday. Michigan designated player Nicole Motycka singled across Alessandra Giampaolo and Jessica Merchant in the first inning to put the Wolverines in front 2-0. In the fourth inning, Wolverines pinch runner Michelle

Weatherdon scored on a sacrifice fly by Tiffany Haas to extend the Michigan lead to 3-0. Michigan pitcher Jennie Ritter did not allow a hit after the third inning, finishing with a three-hitter with two walks and twelve strikeouts in the 3-0 win. DePaul starter Tracie Adix hurled three and one-third innings for the loss, with Megan Huitink hurling the remaining two and two-third innings.

The first round concluded Thursday evening with Texas facing newcomer Alabama in front of 4,250 spectators. With no score through the first five innings, Longhorn Jacqueline Williams walked to open the bottom of the sixth, and Melanie Jarrett entered as pinch runner. After two outs, Tina Boutelle blooped a double into left field, scoring Jarrett. Chez Sievers then beat out an infield single on a ball hit back to Alabama pitcher Stephanie VanBrakle to score Boutelle. Finally, Desiree Williams hit a shot back up the middle to score Sievers in the decisive sixth inning. Texas southpaw Cat Osterman threw her ninth one-hitter of 2005 and got her twenty-first shutout. She struck out seventeen batters, which tied the women's series record for strikeouts in a seven-inning game. VanBrakle took the 3-0 loss, giving up four hits while walking one and striking out seven. She had the only hit off Osterman—an infield single in the second inning—as Texas won its thirteenth game in a row. "We're used to it, but we don't like it," said Osterman of the Longhorns' low-scoring games. ... But we did feel like it was just a matter of time until we strung something together."

Thursday's winners played on Friday with UCLA and Tennessee starting the action at 7 p.m. UCLA got to Lady Vols' ace Monica Abbott in the bottom of the first inning when Tara Henry scored on Emily Zaplatosch's single. But the Lady Vols evened the score in the fourth on a solo homer by Tonya Callahan. Henry gave UCLA the lead back in the fifth when she scored on Jodie Legaspi's single. The Bruins added an insurance run in the bottom of the sixth when Krista Colburn scored on an error by Abbott. The Tennessee pitcher allowed seven hits and fanned only four. "I think UCLA came in with a game plan to get me out of my rhythm," Abbott said. "They took a lot of time-outs and they were really long." UCLA coach Sue Enquist disagreed, calling it merely "respect for the batter's box." Winning pitcher Anjelica Selden posted ten strikeouts without walking a batter and surrendered three hits in the 3-1 Bruin win.

Michigan and Texas played the second evening game before a crowd of nearly 4,700. In the fourth inning, the Wolverines' Samantha Findlay doubled in Alessandra Giampaolo and Jessica Merchant. In the sixth, Merchant scored on Nicole Motycka's single, sliding around the sweeping tag by the catcher to up the lead to 3-0. Michigan added another run in the seventh inning when Tiffany Haas singled in Stephanie Bercaw. Pitcher Jennie Ritter got the 4-0 win on a one-hit shutout. Losing hurler Osterman, who fanned ten of the first twelve batters she faced, allowed six hits and three runs while striking out twelve in five and two-thirds innings. Meagan Denny finished the game. The two runs in the fourth ended Osterman's streak of scoreless innings at sixty. Before Friday's game, she had allowed only eleven earned runs in 251 innings. Michigan coach Carol Hutchins was overjoyed with the win. "We had our 'A' game tonight," she said. "To beat Texas and score four runs off that team and Cat Osterman is incredible."

Competition resumed at 11 a.m. on "elimination Saturday" with Arizona against Cal-Berkeley. In the bottom of the second inning, Arizona's Jackie Coburn led off with a home run, her tenth of the year. Two batters later, Callistra Balko sent the ball over the outfield fence for her fifth homer of the year. Kristina Thorson then replaced Cal-Berkeley pitcher Kelly Anderson. Trailing 2-0, the Golden Bears' Julie Meyer scored Chelsea Spencer with an RBI single to center field in the top of the fifth. Erika Racklin ran for Meyer and tied the game when Alicia Hollowell mishandled Kaleo Eldredge's grounder back to the mound. The score remained tied until the twelfth inning when Allyson Von Liechtenstein's single scored Adrienne Acton as the ball bounced away from Golden Bear left fielder Lindsay James for the 3-2 Arizona win. Wildcat pitcher Hollowell went the distance, giving up one earned run on eight hits in eliminating the Golden Bears. Allowing just three hits, Thorson shut down the Wildcats for eight and one-third innings before tiring in the eleventh when Anderson re-entered.

DePaul and Alabama followed in another elimination game, with the Tide striking first on Dani Woods's RBI single in the bottom of the fourth inning. Her hit scored Dominique Accetturo. In the sixth inning, DePaul's Jessica Evans singled and eventually scored on a wild pitch by Alabama's Stephanie VanBrakle. With a 1-1 score, lightning forced a suspension in the bottom of the eighth inning. The game resumed Sunday at 10 a.m. and remained tied until the bottom of the twelfth when Alabama's Capper Reed singled to score Michelle Menningmann and end the game. The 2-1 loss eliminated the Blue Demons (45-21), the second team ousted. VanBrakle recorded seventeen strikeouts, a school record in a national championship game, allowing five hits in the win. Megan Huitink allowed nine hits in the loss and struck out six.

Texas and Arizona played Sunday afternoon in another elimination game. After a scoreless game in regulation, the two teams battled into the eleventh. Then Longhorn MicKayla Padilla was hit by a throw during a rundown between third and home, putting Texas up 1-0. In the bottom of the eleventh, Arizona loaded the bases against Osterman, but Jennifer Martinez struck out to end the game and eliminate the Wildcats (45-12). Osterman threw the complete game, striking out nineteen batters in the four-hitter to take the 1-0 win. Loser Alicia Hollowell hurled a five-hitter and registered eleven strikeouts in the final nine and two-thirds innings in relief of starter Leslie Wolfe. Osterman and Hollowell combined for thirty strikeouts—a tournament record by two teams in a single game. "It was just one of those games that was a grind," Texas coach Connie Clark said. "Cat was fresh at the beginning of the game, but we wore out pretty good today."

Alabama and Tennessee followed Sunday afternoon before a crowd of more than 6,000. In the bottom of the first, Tennessee's Lindsay Schutzler scored on a perfect suicide bunt by Kristi Durant. Tonya Callahan scored next when Katherine Card hit a one-hop double over the left fielder and off the fence. With Tennessee leading 2-0 in the bottom of the second, the Lady Vols' Stacey Jennings scored on an RBI single by Schutzler. Tennessee added to its lead in the sixth on Natalie Brock's RBI single. Alabama got two runners on in the seventh, but Monica Abbott completed the 4-0, four-hit win with a strikeout, her eighth of the game. Losing pitcher Jennifer Wright allowed seven hits in four innings, and Chrissy Owens gave up two hits while finishing for Alabama, the fourth team eliminated.

UCLA and Texas followed at 5 p.m., with the winner to advance to the best-of-three final on Monday. Texas started Meagan Denny instead of southpaw standout Cat Osterman, and the Bruins roughed Denny up in the bottom of the first. Jodie Legaspi singled, scoring Henry, then Zaplatosch scored on Texas shortstop Desiree Williams's bad throw. Krista Colburn's single scored Legaspi for UCLA's third run of the inning. So the Longhorns put in Osterman, who retired the next sixteen batters she faced in five and one-third innings, striking out six. Texas got runners on second and third in the sixth inning before UCLA pitcher Anjelica Selden struck out the last two batters to finish with twelve strikeouts in the 3-0 UCLA win. It was UCLA's twelfth consecutive win in the women's championship series, a record. Asked about Texas's pitching Denny instead of Osterman, UCLA's Enquist said: "I think the (UCLA) team sensed a possible opportunity." Texas finished 49-13 and tied for third in the tournament.

Michigan played Tennessee Monday afternoon with the winner qualifying for

**Michigan's Samantha Findlay celebrates her three-run home run in the tenth inning of the 2005 title game as she passes the somber UCLA dugout.** *(Reprinted courtesy of The Oklahoman)*

the best-of-three final. The Wolverines jumped on the Lady Vols early, scoring Alessandra Giampaolo on Samantha Findlay's ground-ball single in the bottom of the first. Stephanie Bercaw increased the Michigan lead in the fourth, drilling an 0-1 pitch over the left-field fence for two runs, her seventh home run of the season. Trailing 3-0, Tennessee reduced the game to its final 3-2 margin in the fifth on a two-run single by pinch hitter Natalie Brock, scoring Stacey Jennings and Kenora Posey. The Lady Vols (67-15) tied for third. Jennie Ritter was the winning pitcher, giving up four hits while striking out eight in the Michigan win. Monica Abbott suffered the loss, allowing four hits with four strikeouts.

Michigan advanced to face UCLA in the best-of-three final Monday evening, trying to become just the second team east of the Mississippi to win the women's series. After a stellar five innings by Michigan pitcher Jennie Ritter, UCLA's Emily Zaplatosch laced a 2-2 pitch to left center with the bases loaded. This gave the Bruins a 2-0 lead. Ritter was then replaced by Lorilyn Wilson, who hurled a wild pitch that scored Caitlin Benyi. Pinch runner Alissa Eno scored the fourth run in the inning on a Kristen Dedmon single. Lisa Dodd's RBI single scored Jodie Legaspi for the fifth and final run of the inning. UCLA pitcher Anjelica Selden closed the game by retiring five of the final six batters, allowing four hits and striking out eleven in the 5-0 Bruin win. Losing pitcher Ritter hurled five innings, allowing two hits and four runs, with Lorilyn Wilson hurling the last two innings.

In the second of the best-of-three series Tuesday, UCLA's Lisa Dodd scored on Andrea Duran's two-out double in the bottom of the third inning. The Bruins added to their lead with a leadoff home run by Caitlin Benyi in the fourth inning, her fourteenth of 2005. Held to one hit through four innings, Michigan scored its first two runs in the fifth on Becky Marx's sixth home run of the year, tying the game at 2-2. Later in the inning, Jessica Merchant doubled to give the Wolverines a 4-2 lead. Michigan added a fifth run in the seventh as Giampaolo scored on a single by Samantha Findlay. Ritter got the 5-2 win for Michigan, allowing two runs on four hits while striking out five. She allowed only one base runner after the fourth inning. Losing pitcher Anjelica Selden fanned thirteen and gave up eight hits.

Tied at one game apiece, UCLA and Michigan met Wednesday at 6:30 p.m. in the if-necessary game with the national title on the line. UCLA struck in the second inning, taking a 1-0 lead with a two-out solo home run by Lisa Dodd over the left field fence. The 1-0 UCLA lead held until the top of the sixth when Michigan's Tiffany Haas singled, Alessandra Giampaolo walked, and Jessica Merchant singled to load the bases. Findlay then singled to score Haas and tie the game, but the Bruins limited the Michigan rally to the one run. From there, neither team was able to mount much of a threat until the top of the tenth. Haas again started the one-out Michigan rally, reaching base on an error. Giampaolo singled, and after the second out the reliable Findlay smashed a dramatic three-run home run to give Michigan a 4-1 lead. The Bruins got a runner on base in their last at-bat, but Ritter got the final two outs to secure the first national softball championship for the Wolverines. Ritter got the 4-1 win, giving up five hits and the one run. UCLA's

# 2005 Women's College World Series Bracket
Oklahoma City • June 2-8

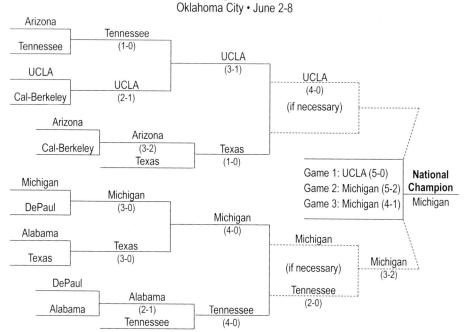

## 2005 Final Standings

| | |
|---|---|
| University of Michigan (Ann Arbor) | 5-2 |
| University of California (Los Angeles) | 4-2 |
| University of Tennessee (Knoxville) | 3-2 |
| University of Texas (Austin) | 2-2 |
| University of Arizona (Tucson) | 1-2 |
| University of Alabama (Tuscaloosa) | 1-2 |
| University of California (Berkeley) | 0-2 |
| DePaul University (Chicago, Ill.) | 0-2 |

Selden took the 4-l loss, striking out ten but giving up nine hits. "Obviously, it's a great moment for Michigan, Michigan softball, for all our alums and the Big Ten Conference," Wolverine coach Carol Hutchins said. "I'm just so proud. But I'm most proud of these kids, they were incredible here all week."

Leading all hitters at .409, Samantha Findlay became the first freshman to win the tournament's most outstanding player award. She joined teammates Stephanie Bercaw (RF), Jennie Ritter (P) and Jessica Merchant (SS) on the all-tournament team. Also selected were UCLA's Krista Colburn (RF), Anjelica Selden (P), Emily Zaplatosch (C) and Jodie Legaspi (SS); Tennessee's Monica Abbott (P), Tonya Callahan (1B) and Katherine Card (LF); and Texas's Cat Osterman (P).

Concerns that attendance would be hurt by the tournament's move away from the traditional Memorial Day championship game proved groundless. The crowds were not deterred, and a new attendance record of nearly 41,700 was recorded.

## Life After the WCWS...

Michigan pitcher **Jennie Ritter** was a two-time, first-team NCAA All-American (2005-06) and compiled a record of 98-22 in her college career. Ritter was the 2005 USA National Player of the Year. In 2013, she was a softball analyst on ESPN and the Big Ten network, and the coach of the Florida Select 18-under softball team. Michigan's **Samantha Findlay** earned NCAA first-team All-American honors (2008) and is her college's all-time leader in career home runs (62) and RBIs (219). In 2013 she was an assistant coach at DePaul. **Marita Hynes** was named the University of Oklahoma's second softball coach in 1976 and became the driving force behind the women's national championship in Oklahoma City, directing the tournament from 1990 to 2005. Including the three years (1980-82) she oversaw the AIAW national softball championship in Norman, Hynes directed nineteen of the women's series events from 1980 through 2005. She retired from the university in 2003. In April 2004, Oklahoma named the playing field at its softball complex in her honor. Hynes managed a golf course in Ruidoso, N.M., in 2013.

# 2006: Arizona Wins Battle of the Wildcats

Record ratings for ESPN broadcasts of the 2005 women's series had been noted by the television network's executives. ESPN's eight telecasts averaged 959,000 households, up a remarkable 61 percent over 2004. So by 2006, ESPN and its cable network were showing more women's softball games than ever. Moving the championship game from Memorial Day and into the first week of June had helped boost ratings. "It was a home run for us," ESPN senior director of programming Carol Stiff said. "It's an exciting sport to watch. It's seven innings in a two-hour window."

The 2006 tournament was the twenty-fifth anniversary of the first NCAA women's series in Omaha, and the first championship in Oklahoma City without Marita Hynes directing the event. Hynes had recently retired and moved to New Mexico, but she of course came back to watch the action in 2006—strictly as a spectator. In her last year as tournament director just the year before, the championship had set another record in attendance. She could now reminisce about the earlier lean years and smile about them. "It really was an uphill battle for a long time," she mused. "But now it's just a huge event. It's better, I think, than most any of us (imagined) years ago."

College softball programs from the South continued to show strength in 2006, with Tennessee and Alabama returning to the national championship for the second year in a row. The tournament saw the return of former contenders Northwestern and Oregon State, both absent from the tournament for several decades. The Northwestern "Wildcats of the North" had played twice in Omaha (1985-1986) but had fallen back for many years thereafter. The June 1-7 national tournament included four veteran teams in 2006: Arizona ("Wildcats of the Southwest"), Arizona State, top-seeded UCLA, and Texas. Again this year, the teams would be divided into upper and lower brackets.

In the upper bracket, No.-2 seed Arizona met Oregon State in the opening game at noon on Thursday, June 1. Scoreless after two innings, the Wildcats' Adrienne Acton scored in the bottom of the third inning on Autumn Champion's infield single. Kristie Fox also hit an RBI single to center, giving Arizona a 2-0 lead. Oregon State pitcher Brianne McGowan reduced the deficit by one with a fifth-inning solo homer. Rain and lightning halted the game in the bottom of the fifth for an hour and a half. Upon resumption, the Beavers' Adrienne Alo scored in the sixth on Stefanie Ewing's nubber down the first-base line when pitcher Alicia Hollowell overthrew first. Still tied 2-2 after eight innings, Arizona's Caitlin Lowe opened the ninth inning with a single and scored on a hit by Fox to end the game. Hollowell surrendered one earned run in nine innings, fanning ten in the 3-2 Arizona win. McGowan scattered ten hits and walked six. Fox finished 2-for-4 with two RBIs, and Lowe went 3-for-5.

Arizona State and Texas began at 2 p.m., and the Longhorns took a 1-0 lead in the bottom of the fourth on Amber Hall's RBI double that scored Chez Sievers. The Longhorns' Desiree Williams smashed her thirteenth home run in the fifth inning—a two-out solo shot off the left field foul pole—to increase the Texas lead to 2-0. Texas pitcher Cat Osterman, meanwhile, allowed only a leadoff single by Bianca Cruz in the second inning and fanned a record eighteen batters in the 2-0 Texas win. Osterman and Northwestern's Lisa Ishikawa (in 1984) had shared the previous women's series record for strikeouts in a seven-inning game. "I could tell from my warm-ups I was having a good day," Osterman said after the win. "My ball was spinning well and I felt really in command." Losing pitcher Katie Burkhart allowed six hits, walked two and fanned nine.

Starting play in the lower bracket Thursday evening, Alabama faced Northwestern in the first game. In the bottom of the third inning, the Northwestern Wildcats loaded the bases against Alabama before pitcher Stephanie VanBrakle hit Kristen Amegin in the back, forcing in a run that gave the Cats a 1-0 lead. But VanBrakle helped her own cause in the top of the fourth with a two-run RBI single. Northwestern reclaimed the lead in the bottom of the inning on a three-run home run by Garland Cooper to go up 4-2. Alabama reduced the Northwestern lead by one in the top of the fifth when Darcy Sengewald threw wildly to first base in an attempt to get Jordan Praytor, allowing Mandy Bruford to score. In the top of the sixth, Alabama tied the game with three consecutive hits followed by Brittany Rogers' hit off the knob of the bat, scoring Kelley Montalvo. Jordan Praytor then walked, scoring

Dominique Accetturo to put Alabama ahead 5-4. But in the bottom of the seventh, Northwestern's Erin Dyer whacked a two-out, two-strike solo home run over center field to tie the game. The game remained tied until the bottom of the tenth when Wildcat Darcy Sengewald scored on Tammy Williams's single and an error by the center fielder. Senior Courtnay Foster earned the 6-5 Northwestern win with four and two-thirds innings in relief, allowing one run with her thirteen strikeouts. Chrissy Owens took the loss in relief, allowing one run on six hits. "The game was back and forth and you just can't play yo-yo softball at the World Series," Alabama coach Pat Murphy said. "You have to make a statement and keep the lead."

Beginning just past 11 p.m., tournament-favorite UCLA and Tennessee matched up to conclude the first round of play. In the bottom of the first, UCLA's Krista Colburn scored on Caitlin Benyi's single to put the Bruins up 1-0. Andrea Duran tripled to open the third inning for the Bruins and scored on Colburn's RBI single to increase the lead to 2-0. But in the top of the sixth, Tennessee hit five consecutive singles and scored three runs to take a 3-2 lead. In the seventh, Tennessee loaded the bases before Kristi Durant singled home India Chiles, upping the Lady Vols' lead to two runs. In the Bruins' last at bats, Lisa Dodd's RBI single to left made it a one-run game, 4-3, but the UCLA rally ended there. Tennessee's Monica Abbott allowed nine hits and three runs (two earned) with eleven strikeouts to get the win. Anjelica Selden also gave up nine hits and fanned nine in taking the 4-3 loss, a rare opening-game defeat for UCLA.

In the first winners game on Friday night, the Arizona and Texas teams were held scoreless through the first five and one-half innings by the pitching duel between Cat Osterman of Texas and right-hander Alicia Hollowell of Arizona. Osterman fanned ten of seventeen during that span. But in the sixth with one out, the Longhorn hurler hit Caitlin Lowe and walked Kristie Fox to put runners on first and second. Lowe scored when Wildcat catcher Callistra Balko singled. With runners on first and third, Arizona executed a double steal, and Texas catcher Megan Wills's throw to second allowed another Wildcat score for a 2-0 lead. Hollowell registered the 2-0 win with a four-hit shutout, walking none and striking out nine. It was the first hit for Balko off Osterman, having struck out in eight previous at bats. Osterman gave up only one run and struck out thirteen in the losing effort.

In Friday's second game, Northwestern and Tennessee began as advertised with a pitchers' duel between Wildcat Eileen Canney and Lady Vol Monica Abbott. Through five innings, the score remained 0-0. But in the top of sixth Northwestern's Katie Logan led off with a single and four batters later scored on Kristin Amegin's two-out single up the middle. In the top of the seventh, Wildcat sophomore Darcy Sengewald turned on an inside pitch and crushed it over the left-center fence for a 2-0 Northwestern lead. Canney allowed only one hit, walked two and struck out ten in the 2-0 Northwestern win, getting the twenty-ninth shutout of her career while stopping the nation's top-hitting team. The only hit she gave up was a double by Jennifer Griffin. Abbott fanned fifteen batters in the loss. "We ran into a buzz saw," Tennessee coach Ralph Weekly said, "and it was wearing purple."

Four games were scheduled on "elimination Saturday" with six of the eight teams in action. Arizona State and Oregon State met in the first game at 11 a.m., and in the third inning ASU's Heidi Knabe hit a solo shot over the left field fence to put the Sun Devils out front. ASU scored again soon after when Oregon State's center fielder threw a wild ball into the Beaver dugout, scoring Jessica Mapes. In the top of the fifth, ASU loaded the bases on a pair of walks and a hit-batter before Rhiannon Baca's sacrifice fly to left scored Mapes again to give ASU a 3-0 lead. In the bottom of the inning, Beaver pitcher Brianne McGowan hit a towering home run over the left-field fence to reduce the deficit to 3-1. But that completed the scoring. Winning ASU pitcher Katie Burkhart fanned twelve and allowed two hits in eliminating Oregon State. Losing hurler McGowan gave up six walks and four hits in her complete game.

UCLA and Alabama followed at 1 p.m. in the next elimination game. Andrea Duran opened the game for UCLA with a triple on the first pitch of the game and scored on Krista Colburn's single. In the second inning, Alabama's Dominique Accetturo tied the game on a two-out, first-pitch home run. UCLA took back the lead in the third inning when Duran led off the inning with her fourteenth home run of 2006, a shot to left center. Krista Colburn followed with a single to right, stole second, and scored on a throwing error by third baseman Staci Ramsey. With UCLA up 3-1, Alabama brought in pitcher Chrissy Owens to replace Stephanie VanBrakle. But the Bruins scored in the sixth inning on Tara Henry's single to shallow left field, upping the UCLA advantage to 4-1. Bruin pitcher Anjelica Selden fanned five in going the distance to eliminate Alabama, the second team sent home. VanBrakle picked up the 4-1 loss, allowing three runs on five hits in just over two innings. Owens hurled the final five innings, allowing one run on two hits.

After having eliminated Oregon State earlier in the day, ASU played Tennessee in another elimination game at 6 p.m. After four scoreless innings, the Lady Vols took the lead in the top of the fifth after India Chiles drilled a shot back to the circle that pitcher Katie Burkhart misplayed, allowing Lillian Hammond to score. In the bottom of the fifth, ASU catcher Heidi Knabe smacked Abbott's first pitch over the left field wall for a one-out solo home run to even the game at 1-1. The game remained tied until the top of the ninth inning when Tennessee's Jennifer Griffin blasted a two-run shot deep over the left center-field wall to give the Lady Vols the 3-1 win. "I'm not going to say I expected a certain pitch," said freshman Griffin, "but I knew I had taken a first-pitch strike all day, so I knew going up there I was swinging at that first pitch." Tennessee hurler Monica Abbott allowed four hits and struck out ten in her complete-game win. ASU's Katie Burkhart also went all nine innings, striking out fourteen and giving up eight hits.

The final elimination game on Saturday matched UCLA against Texas at 8 p.m. In the third inning with two out, UCLA's Andrea Duran smashed an inside-the-park home run that bounced off the right-field fence and out of play long enough for her to score the first run. With one out in the fourth, catcher Emily Zaplatosch blasted her seventh home run that year to put the Bruins up 2-0. Zaplatosch also had a single and a double in a perfect performance. She was the only player in the tournament to get three hits off Texas southpaw Cat Osterman, who allowed five hits in the 2-0 Longhorn defeat. Osterman struck out nine in the last college game of her career. Anjelica Selden got the win for the Bruins, allowing three hits and striking out twelve. The Bruins advanced to Sunday's semifinal against Northwestern, needing to beat the Wildcats twice to advance to the best-of-three championship series starting Monday.

Sunday's first game at noon matched Monica Abbott of Tennessee and Alicia Hollowell of Arizona, and the two engaged in another pitchers' duel. With the score at 0-0 in the bottom of the fifth inning, Lady Vol Katherine Card hit a leadoff home run. Arizona outfielder Caitlin Lowe made a tremendous effort to catch the ball, crashing into the outfield fence and tumbling over the other side. The Wildcats had scoring opportunities in the third, sixth and seventh innings, but couldn't capitalize. Hollowell allowed only three hits—one of them the fatal home run— while striking out six in the 1-0 defeat. Monica Abbott limited Arizona to two hits, with her win forcing the if-necessary rematch of the two teams late Sunday night.

The Cinderella team of the 2006 women's series, Northwestern led UCLA 1-0 after a solo home run from catcher Jamie Dotson in the second inning. The Wildcats held the 1-0 lead for more than five innings before UCLA, down to its

last strike, tied the game in the seventh on a single from pinch-hitter Kristen Dedmon off pitcher Eileen Canney to send the game into extra innings. But in the eighth, Northwestern's Tammy Williams launched a home run to left field to put the Wildcats ahead before first baseman Garland Cooper followed with another solo home run to left in the 3-1 win, eliminating the Bruins. Anjelica Selden took the loss, allowing nine hits and three earned runs with eight strikeouts. Canney allowed six hits and fanned six.

Pitching in the title game against Northwestern, Wildcat Alicia Hollowell set a women's series record sixty-four strikeouts and was named the 2006 tournament's most outstanding player. *(Photo by Richard T. Clifton)*

Arizona and Tennessee played again on Sunday night in the if-necessary game, with the winner to play Northwestern for the national championship. Jenae Leles and Autumn Champion both hit two-run singles in the first and second innings, respectively, to give the Wildcats a 4-0 lead. Laine Roth's RBI single in the third inning added another run followed by another Wildcat run in the sixth. Hollowell got the two-hit, 6-0 win and fanned fourteen batters. Abbott allowed nine hits in the loss. Hollowell had a change of strategy in the rematch with Tennessee that day. "I basically just tried to mix my pitches more," she said. "I just wanted to keep them off-balance as much as possible."

Arizona and Northwestern met on Monday in the first game of the "all-Wildcat" three-game final format. Arizona sought its seventh national championship, while Northwestern hoped for its first. Scoreless through two innings, Arizona broke through convincingly in the third with Adrienne Acton scoring on Autumn Champion's RBI. Caitlin Lowe came in on a Northwestern error, and Champion scored on a bloop single from Callistra Balko. Taryne Mowatt then hit a two-run double to make it 5-0. Arizona added another run in the fourth. Chelsie Mesa hit a solo homer in the top of the seventh, and Mowatt followed with a towering home run just inside the left field foul pole for the final 8-0 score. Arizona pitcher Alicia Hollowell picked up where she left off the game before on Sunday, allowing only one hit—a fifth inning single by Jamie Dotson—along with twelve strikeouts in her nineteenth shutout of 2006. Eileen Canney hurled two innings for the loss, with Courtnay Foster hurling the last five innings and allowing six runs on five hits. Arizona's Mowatt batted 3-for-4 with three RBIs.

In the second and deciding game on Tuesday, the Arizona Wildcats jumped on Northwestern starting pitcher Eileen Cannery in the bottom of the first. Lowe and Champion hit-back-to-back singles, and both advanced on Kristie Fox's sacrifice. Callistra Balko's RBI groundout scored Lowe to put Arizona up 1-0. Arizona pitcher Alicia Hollowell worked out of jams in the third and fifth innings before Arizona's Lowe led off the bottom of the fifth with an infield single and moved to second on a throwing error by Ashley Crane. After Canney hurled a wild pitch moving Lowe to third, Champion singled Lowe home for Arizona's second run. Balko's RBI double then scored Champion for a 3-0 Arizona lead. Arizona loaded the bases in the top of the seventh with three one-out singles, setting the table for the top of the order. Lowe's blistering shot to first, ruled an error, scored pinch runner Danielle Rodriguez. Champion then singled home Roth, increasing the lead to 5-0. Northwestern loaded the bases in the bottom of the seventh, but Hollowell ended the game by striking out Jamie Dotson. The celebration was on.

"She (Hollowell) promised me when I recruited her she was going to win a national title," said Wildcat coach Mike Candrea. "I just didn't think it would take four years." Hollowell, named the tournament's most outstanding player, fanned thirteen in the game to finish with a tournament-record sixty-four strikeouts, breaking the old mark by Debbie Doom in 1982. Eileen Cannery took the loss, allowing five runs on twelve hits and striking out four. Autumn Champion led the Arizona offense with a 3-for-4 performance, driving in a pair of runs and scoring once.

## 2006 Women's College World Series Bracket
### Oklahoma City • June 1-6

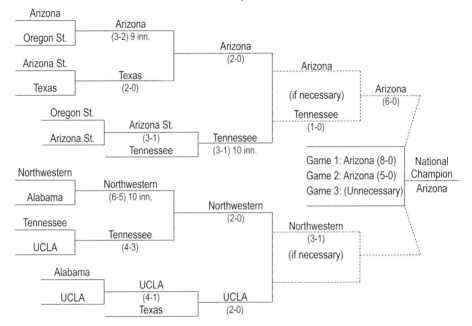

## 2006 Final Standings

| | |
|---|---|
| University of Arizona (Tucson) | 5-1 |
| Northwestern University (Evanston, Ill.) | 3-2 |
| University of Tennessee (Knoxville) | 3-2 |
| University of California (Los Angeles) | 2-2 |
| University of Texas (Austin) | 1-2 |
| Arizona State University (Tempe) | 1-2 |
| University of Alabama (Tuscaloosa) | 0-2 |
| Oregon State University (Corvallis) | 0-2 |

Hollowell was also named to the all-tournament team with teammates Caitlin Lowe (OF), Taryne Mowatt (DH) and Autumn Champion (LF); Northwestern's Tammy Williams (SS), Garland Cooper (1B) and Eileen Canney (P); Tennessee's Monica Abbott (P) and Kristi Durant (DH); Arizona State's Heidi Knabe (C), UCLA's Andrea Duran (3B); and Texas's Cat Osterman (P). Katie Logan of Northwestern and Jodie Legaspi of UCLA shared leading-hitter honors (.400).

### Life After the WCWS...

University of Texas pitcher **Cat Osterman** was a three-time, first-team NCAA

All-American (2003, 2005-6) and compiled a record of 136 wins and twenty-five losses. She was a member of the U.S. national softball team (2001-08) and compiled a 59-4 record, pitching in two Olympics. In February 2013, Osterman was inducted into the Texas Sports Hall of Fame and soon announced her retirement as a player afterward. Arizona pitcher **Alicia Hollowell** was named an NCAA first-team, All-American twice (2003-04) during her college career and won 112 games. She was named to the U.S. national team for the 2008 Olympic Games. As of 2013, she was an assistant softball coach at Arizona. Arizona outfielder **Caitlin Lowe** earned NCAA first-team All-American honors three times (2004-06) and had a career .446 batting average. She was a member of the 2008 U.S. Olympic softball team. In 2013, Lowe was playing with the National Pro Fastpitch league's USSSA Pride. Tennessee's **Monica Abbott** earned all-tournament honors at three women's series and was a three-time, first-team NCAA All-American (2005-07). She holds six NCAA career-pitching records, including most wins, strikeouts, shutouts and innings pitched. She played for the U.S. national softball team in the 2008 Olympics. The University of Tennessee retired her jersey number in 2013. She was playing pro softball in 2013 for Team Toyota in Japan and the Chicago Bandits.

## 2007–Arizona Wildcats Win No. 8

For the first time in thirty years, no California team would play in the Women's College World Series. Eight teams representing five different conferences came to compete in 2007, and three of the schools—Northwestern, DePaul and Washington—were from way north of the Sun Belt. College softball had been talking about the coming parity since the late 1990s, and it appeared to have made it in 2007—without Golden Bears, Bulldogs or Bruins in Oklahoma City for the tournament. ESPN's televised broadcasts of the national championship across the country in the 1990s may have contributed to the growing parity in the sport, promoting teenage dreams of softball stardom across the nation. The annual national championship had become the linchpin of ESPN's coverage of college softball.

While funding from Title IX legislation had promoted an increase in female athletic programs and "Title IX babies" throughout the last decades of the twentieth century, a new generation of "ESPN babies" was now appearing at softball's national championship. These athletes, like Texas A&M's Amanda Scarborough in 2007, had idolized some of the players while watching the Women's College World Series on television in the 1990s. "My mom would have all the games on and I would see all these amazing players playing in the Women's College World Series," Scarborough told a local reporter at the tournament, "and I knew then when I got to college that was the big dream I wanted to fulfill." These college stars of the early 2000s were now living their dreams from childhood. "Finally, young female athletes have a role model that they can follow and they can see on TV, which is something I had for years as a young man growing up," Arizona coach

Mike Candrea told a local reporter at the 2007 tournament.

In addition to the three northern teams above, debutant Baylor University earned a berth in the May 31-June 6 national tournament, along with veteran competitors Arizona, Arizona State, Texas A&M and Tennessee. Once again the eight teams were divided into two brackets with all the teams playing on Thursday in the first round.

The opening game in the upper bracket at noon Thursday paired DePaul with Washington, under third-year coach Heather Tarr. The Blue Demons struck first in the top of the third. Linda Secka scored on a throwing error by Danielle Lawrie on a comebacker to the mound hit by Stephanie Blagaich. But Washington went up 2-1 in the bottom of the third on a two-run home run by Dena Tyson, and the Huskies added another run on a solo shot in the fourth inning by Ashlyn Watson for a 3-1 lead. Except for her errant throw to first base in the third inning, Washington's Lawrie performed magnificently, fanning nine batters in her 3-1 no-hitter—the first in the women's series since 2003. "It was awesome," said an exhilarated Lawrie afterward. "It's something I'm always going to remember." Tracie Adix took the loss, hurling three and one-third innings, allowing three runs on five hits. Becca Heteniak was effective in relief, holding Washington scoreless in the final two and two-thirds innings.

Arizona State and 2006 runner-up Northwestern met in the second game at 2 p.m., with Northwestern taking the early lead in the bottom of the third inning. The Wildcats' Kelly Dyer singled just off the top of the third baseman's glove and scored on Katie Logan's double into right field. Northwestern made it 2-0 in the bottom of the sixth inning on Tammy Williams's fifteenth home run of the season down the left-field line and off the foul pole. Wildcat pitcher Eileen Canney, meanwhile, allowed only two Sun Devil base runners and no hits through the first five innings before giving up a bunt single by Michelle Smith in the sixth inning. Canney fanned eleven in the one-hit, 2-0 Northwestern win. Katie Burkhart took the loss for ASU. Dyer batted 2-for-2.

In the first evening game in the lower bracket, three-time national champion Texas A&M met Tennessee, with the game developing into a pitchers' duel between Tennessee's celebrated Monica Abbott and A&M's Amanda Scarborough. Neither team scored through the sixth inning. In the seventh, however, Tennessee's Kenora Posey scored on India Chiles' two-strike single into left field for a 1-0 lead. Tennessee then loaded the bases, and Shannon Doepking ripped a single into left center to increase the lead to 2-0. Monica Abbott threw the second no-hitter of the day, fanning sixteen batters in the 2-0 Lady Vols win. With her performance, Abbott also became the NCAA single-season record holder for strikeouts with 665. Scarborough took the 2-0 loss, allowing eleven hits and two runs with twelve strikeouts. Chiles's winning RBI in the seventh was hit in her first game since tearing her anterior cruciate ligament (ACL) on May 19. Tennessee coach Ralph Weekly had left the decision up to Chiles whether to play in the tournament. "I feel normal," said Chiles. "I just felt like I could do whatever I was doing before with it, so why not play?" Doepking, Lindsay Schutzler and Anita Manuma each posted a 2-for-4 effort for Tennessee.

Thursday's final game matched seven-time and defending national champion Arizona against newcomer Baylor at 8 p.m. The starting pitchers, Arizona's Taryne Mowatt and Baylor's Lisa Ferguson, stayed in control until the fourth inning when the Wildcats scored on Laine Roth's RBI ground-out to shortstop, scoring Kristie Fox. But Baylor answered in the top of the fifth when Kirsten Shortridge scored on the second of two passed balls by catcher Callistra Balko. The score remained tied 1-1 until the bottom of the ninth when Fox lifted Ferguson's first pitch inside the left-field foul pole for a solo home run to end the game. Fox finished with a 3-for-3 performance, and Wildcat Caitlin Lowe was 2-for-4. Wildcat hurler Mowatt allowed one unearned run on two hits in nine innings with fifteen strikeouts in the 2-1 Arizona win. Losing hurler Ferguson allowed two runs on six hits with seven strikeouts in her eight innings.

After a rain delay and with a crowd of more than 7,700 at the first winners-bracket game Friday evening, Washington's Ashley Charters was walked by North-western's Eileen Canney and scored on a single by Dominique Lastrapes in the top of the third. Marnie Koziol then added another run on Dena Tyson's grounder to the right side to give the Huskies a 2-0 lead. After adding an insurance run in the fourth, Washington sent twelve batters to the plate in the fifth, collecting three hits and scoring six runs to end the game at 9-0 on the run rule. Lawrie earned the win and her eleventh shutout of 2007, with her eleven strikeouts holding Northwestern to one hit—a leadoff double by Nicole Pauly in the bottom of the second. Canney took the loss, allowing seven runs on five hits and five walks in five innings. Charters and Lastrapes had two hits apiece for the Huskies.

Because of the earlier rain delay, Tennessee and Arizona did not start playing until after 11 p.m. Pitchers Monica Abbott and Taryne Mowatt battled through five innings with neither team scoring. In the sixth inning, the Lady Vols appeared to have a run on a single by India Chiles, but Arizona's Caitlin Lowe came up throwing on Chiles' hit and threw out Liane Horiuchi at home for the second out. But this was followed by the bobbling of Tiffany Huff's infield grounder for an error, allowing Lindsay Schutzler to race home for a 1-0 Lady Vol advantage. The one run was all that was needed in the pitching duel. Abbott fanned sixteen and allowed six hits in her 1-0 win, escaping two loaded-bases jams. Mowatt gave up only a pair of hits, striking out ten and walking four in the Arizona defeat. Chiles went 2-for-3 for the Lady Vols, with Lowe 2-for-4 for the Wildcats. "Well, this is where you want to be, and it really does not matter how you get there," said Lady Vol co-head coach Karen Weekly. "Arizona is a very tough team and they played a fantastic game."

The first game at 11 a.m. on "elimination Saturday" saw DePaul facing Arizona State. The Blue Demons' Sandy Vojik slammed a two-run home run in the fifth inning to break open a scoreless pitchers' duel. Vojik added an RBI single in the seventh inning, scoring Shea Warren. In the bottom half of the seventh, the Sun Devils got a double from Michelle Smith and an RBI single from Rhiannon Baca but could only reduce the game's margin to its final 3-1 score. Tracie Adix hurled a five-hitter the first five innings and allowed only one extra base hit after DePaul had built a 3-0 lead. Becca Heteniak and Stephanie Blagaich hurled the remaining innings. Katie Burkhart took the loss for ASU, allowing six hits. The Sun Devils finished the season 54-17 and became the first team eliminated.

Baylor and Texas A&M followed in another elimination game at 1 p.m., and the Aggies took a 1-0 lead in the first inning on Megan Gibson's fourteenth home run of 2007. But Baylor's Chelsi Lake smacked a two-run double in the bottom of the first, and Ashley Monceaux scored on a throwing error by Amanda Scarborough in the bottom of the third to put Baylor up 3-1. Courtney Oberg then smashed a three-run home run over the bleachers in left center field, her seventh of 2007, to give Baylor a 6-1 lead after three innings. In the top of the fifth, the Aggies reduced the margin to 6-3 on Jamie Hinshaw's two-run, RBI double that scored Macie Morrow and Joy Davis. A&M added its fourth and final run in the sixth on a sacrifice fly by Morrow, scoring Scarborough. The Lady Bears added another run in the sixth with pinch hitter Jordan Daniels scoring to give Baylor a 7-4 advantage. Lisa Ferguson picked up the 7-4 Baylor win, allowing three earned runs on seven hits while going the distance. Scarborough took the loss, allowing six runs on six hits in two and two-third innings. Megan Gibson entered in relief and worked the remaining three and one-third innings, allowing one run on three hits. The Aggies became the second team eliminated.

Arizona and DePaul were next in another elimination game, and the game remained scoreless through the first four innings. Then in the top of the fifth inning with the bases loaded, the Wildcats' Caitlin Lowe hit a double over the heads of the drawn-in outfielders, scoring a pair of runs. In the seventh, Wildcat K'Lee Arredondo singled and scored on Chelsie Mesa's single for an insurance run and a 3-0 Arizona advantage. Taryne Mowatt allowed no hits until the sixth inning and finished with a two-hitter, striking out six. DePaul's Tracie Adix took the 3-0 loss after throwing five innings, giving up two runs on seven hits. The Blue Demons finished the year 47-14 and as the third team eliminated in the tournament.

The final game Saturday evening matched Baylor and Northwestern before a crowd of more than 8,000. The Wildcats started fast in the top of the first inning, loading the bases against Baylor pitcher Kirsten Shortridge. Erin Dyer's two-run single to left center scored Tammy Williams and Garland Cooper and gave Northwestern a 2-0 lead after one inning. In the second inning, Tammy Williams's three-run homer over the left field fence and Garland Cooper's solo home run put the Wildcats ahead 6-0 after just two innings. Northwestern increased their lead to 7-0 in the fourth on Nicole Pauly's solo home run. The long balls by Williams and Cooper came off Lisa Ferguson, who replaced Shortridge in the second inning and allowed four runs on two hits. Eileen Canney earned the 7-0 win giving up five hits and striking out nine. The game's official attendance of 8,222 established a single-session record, topping the previous record of 8,049 set during the 2000 championship game between Oklahoma and UCLA.

Play began 11 a.m. Sunday with Washington facing Arizona. Arizona had just one hit off Danielle Lawrie until the sixth inning. After an out, Arizona's Sam Banister drove a pitch to right center field to score Jenae Leles and Laine Roth. The runs were the first two earned runs off Lawrie in eighteen innings, and she had held her tournament opponents to a .069 batting average with twenty-eight strikeouts. Washington had its chances but could not capitalize, stranding eight, including runners on third base in both the fifth and sixth innings. Lawrie took the 2-0 Washington loss, allowing two hits and striking out eight. Taryne Mowatt got the win with four hits and eight strikeouts. The Arizona win forced an if-necessary game later Sunday evening.

Tennessee and Northwestern followed at 2 p.m., and the contest was decided early. After the Lady Vols loaded the bases in the bottom of the first inning, Wildcat shortstop Tammy Williams fielded Tonya Callahan's ground ball, reached up and tagged Lillian Hammond between second and third for the first out, and quickly threw home to Wildcat catcher Erin Dyer. Dyer mistakenly treated Williams's throw to the plate as a force instead of a tag play, allowing India Chiles to score Tennessee's initial run. Next, Lady Vol catcher Shannon Doepking drilled a grounder to first, which ricocheted off Garland Cooper's first baseman's mitt and back toward the pitching circle for a two-out error. This allowed Lindsay Schutzler to score the second Tennessee run. That would be all the help Lady Vol ace Monica Abbott would need. She fanned seventeen batters and allowed only two hits in the 3-0 shutout that eliminated the northern Wildcats (52-13), who tied for third. Eileen Canney took the loss, allowing three runs on three hits.

Arizona faced Washington in the if-necessary game Sunday, with the winner advancing to the best-of-three championship series on Monday. The Wildcats started fast against pitcher Danielle Lawrie. Caitlin Lowe and Chelsie Mesa hit back-to-back singles in the top of the first, and both scored on Jenae Leles' double down the left field line. In the third inning, Sam Banister singled home Kristie Fox for the third Wildcat run. Washington broke Taryne Mowatt's shot at a shutout with a run on three singles in the bottom of the fourth. In the fifth, Mesa singled and eventually scored on Leles's sacrifice fly to give Arizona a 4-1 advantage. In the sixth with the bases loaded, Mesa doubled home a pair of runs for the Wildcats. Then Fox's sacrifice fly scored Adrienne Acton, and Leles's RBI single plated Mesa for an 8-1 Arizona lead. Mowatt got the win, allowing four hits and striking out nine in seven innings. Lawrie took the 8-1 loss after getting roughed up for four runs on eight hits in five innings. Caitlin Noble relieved her and allowed four runs on as many hits over the last two innings. For the Wildcats, Mesa was 3-for-4 and Leles 2-for-4 with four RBIs. Washington finished tied for third.

Arizona faced Tennessee on Monday in the best-of-three series, the twelfth time in seventeen years the Wildcats played for the title. With aces Monica Abbott and Taryne Mowatt hurling, neither team managed much in the first inning. But with two outs in the top of the second, Lady Vol Alexia Clay smashed a solo home run just beyond Arizona center fielder Caitlin Lowe for a 1-0 Tennessee advantage.

It was Clay's fourth home run of 2007. The Lady Vols doubled their lead in the fourth when catcher Shannon Doepking, who had been 0-for-8 against Arizona, smacked her sixth home run of 2007. After an insurance run by Tennessee in the top of the seventh, Monica Abbott got the 3-0 win with a three-hit shutout and eight strikeouts. Mowatt took the loss, allowing three runs on six hits and six strikeouts.

In the second game of the best-of-three series on Tuesday evening, Abbott again faced off with Mowatt. Both pitchers held their opponents in check through the first five innings. Tennessee loaded the bases with no outs in the sixth inning but could not capitalize as Mowatt got a force-out and two pop-ups to end the threat. In the top of the tenth, the scoreless tie was finally broken when Arizona's Danielle Rodriguez, pinch running for Sam Banister, scored on hitter Adrienne Acton's fielder's choice to score the only run in the game and force an if-necessary game to decide the championship. Tennessee catcher Shannon Doepking had blocked the plate and swiped at Rodriguez. But she missed as the runner slid around her. "I thought I had her," said Doepking. "... But no matter what, that's not what lost the game to me. We've got to bring runners across when we've get runners in scoring position." The Lady Vols stranded fourteen runners. Despite a blister on the index finger of her pitching arm, Mowatt had tossed her seventh complete game in six days, allowing seven hits and striking out eleven. Losing pitcher Abbott allowed the one run on four hits and struck out eleven.

With one win each, the teams squared off Wednesday night before a crowd of 5,530. Again Abbott and Mowatt dueled, holding their opponents scoreless through the first four innings. But the fifth inning was decisive. The Wildcats

scored on Jenae Leles' two-run double and on Chelsie Mesa's three-run round-tripper for a 5-0 advantage. All the runs were earned against Abbott, who allowed ten hits and fanned seven in the 5-0 loss. Mowatt gave up seven hits and struck out eleven to get the win and give the Wildcats their eighth national championship since 1991. Caitlin Lowe had four of Arizona's hits in a perfect performance. Mowatt's seventy-six strikeouts set a tournament record, and she tallied 1,035 pitches while hurling every game. "I can't remember seeing a grittier

Most outstanding player of the 2007 tournament, Arizona's Taryne Mowatt displays the 2007 championship trophy and her bandaged right index finger after hurling 1,035 pitches in eight games. *(Photo courtesy of Arizona Athletic Dept.)*

## 2007 Women's College World Series Bracket
Oklahoma City • May 31-June 6

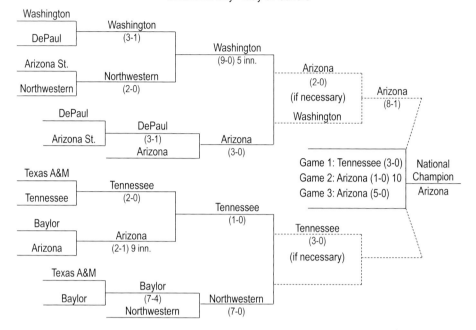

## 2007 Final Standings

| | |
|---|---|
| University of Arizona (Tucson) | 6-2 |
| University of Tennessee (Knoxville) | 4-2 |
| University of Washington (Seattle) | 2-2 |
| Northwestern University (Evanston, Ill.) | 2-2 |
| Baylor University (Waco, Texas) | 1-2 |
| DePaul University (Chicago, Ill.) | 1-2 |
| Texas A&M University (College Station) | 0-2 |
| Arizona State University (Tempe) | 0-2 |

performance than this young lady gave us," Arizona coach Mike Candrea said.

Mowatt was named the tournament's most outstanding player. She was also named to the all-tournament team and was joined by Arizona teammates Kristie Fox (SS), Caitlin Lowe (OF) and Jenae Leles (3B); Tennessee's Monica Abbott (P), India Chiles (OF) and Lindsay Schutzler (SS); Washington's Danielle Lawrie (P), Dena Tyson (1B) and Ashley Charters (SS); Northwestern's Tammy Williams (SS); and Baylor's Ashley Monceaux (LF). Both Arizona's Fox and Baylor's Ashley Monceaux batted .500 to lead all hitters.

The new attendance record of 62,460 was the first time the women's series had totaled more than 60,000.

## Life After the WCWS...

Arizona's **Taryne Mowatt** compiled a pitching record of 100 wins and thirty-three losses during her college career and was named to two women's series all-tournament teams. In 2013, she was an assistant softball coach at California Baptist College in Riverside, Calif.

# 2008: ASU Takes Title After 35-Year Drought

Five teams from the softball-flourishing South qualified for the 2008 Women's College World Series, two of them newcomers—Florida and Virginia Tech. Florida made its tournament debut as the top seed, coming to Oklahoma City with a sparkling 67-3 record under third-year coach Tim Walton. Other southern teams included Louisiana-Lafayette, Texas A&M and Alabama, with the rest of the field made up of perennial college softball powers UCLA, Arizona and Arizona State.

The eight teams would begin competition on May 29 in an upgraded ASA Hall of Fame Stadium. Massive, portable bleachers encircled the outfield for the 2008 tournament, thus making way for a new video board. The additional 3,000 outfield seats brought the Hall of Fame Stadium's seating capacity to almost 8,000. In addition, home-plate umpires were again "miked" for taped segments, and ESPN field reporter Holly Rowe visited the dugouts to help track game strategy.

The noon Thursday opener pitted top-seed Florida against Louisiana-Lafayette. In the bottom of the second inning, the Gators' Corrie Brooks doubled down the right-field line to score Tiffany DeFelice. In the bottom of the fourth, Aja Paculba doubled to score Brooks and up the Gators' lead to 2-0. But Ragin' Cajun Vanessa Soto's two-run double off the center-field fence tied the game at 2-2 in the fifth inning. It remained tied until the eighth inning when Holly Tankersley hit a home run into the center-field bleachers to put Louisiana ahead 3-2. "It just happened," Tankersley said of her twenty-second home run of 2008. "I just took my chances—closed my eyes and swung—if you want to know honestly." Freshman Louisiana hurler Ashley Brignac scattered six hits in eight innings and fanned a career-high fifteen in the 3-2 win. Florida ace Stacey Nelson surrendered three runs on eight hits and fanned six. She had allowed only one home run during the season before Tankersley's game-winner.

Virginia Tech and Texas A&M met in the second game, which figured to be a battle between two of college softball's top pitchers—the Aggies' Megan Gibson and the Hokies' Angela Tincher, USA Softball College Player of the Year. The anticipated pitching duel did not disappoint, with neither team able to score through the first five and a half innings. But with two out in the bottom of the sixth, Megan Gibson hit a liner at third baseman Charisse Mariconda, who fielded the ball cleanly but threw wide of first base, allowing Andrea Tovar to score the game's only run. Gibson allowed five hits and fanned nine for the shutout. Tincher allowed only a pair of hits and also struck out nine. "It feels great to get that first win," said A&M coach Jo Evans. "Last year we exited early and we have been talking about getting back here ever since." It was A&M's first win in the national tournament since 1988.

At 6 p.m. Thursday, third-seeded Alabama opposed sixth-seeded Arizona State, and this game turned into a pitching duel like the previous contest. ASU's Katie Burkhart and Alabama's Kelsi Dunne held both teams scoreless through four and one-half innings before Alabama's Jordan Praytor scored on Charlotte Morgan's RBI-double. With the Crimson Tide leading 1-0 in the top of the seventh, ASU's Kaitlin Cochran walked and scored on Leslie Rogers's double to tie the game at 1-1. ASU's Mandy Urfer then ripped the first pitch past third baseman Kelley Montalvo and down the left field line, allowing Rogers and Renee Welty to score. After some controversy, home plate umpire Linda Hoover ruled that Montalvo had touched the ball in fair territory and pushed it foul. This upped the ASU lead to 3-1, where the scoring ended. Burkhart allowed three hits and struck out thirteen in the 3-1 ASU win. Dunne gave up four hits and fanned ten in the loss.

Two schools with twenty national championships between them—Arizona and UCLA—met in the fourth and final opening-round game Thursday evening. In the bottom of the first, UCLA freshman Katie Schroeder got aboard on a throwing error by pitcher Taryne Mowatt and continued to second. Krista Colburn bunted her to third, and Amanda Kamekona singled to score Schroeder with the first run of game. From that point the game turned into a pitchers duel between Anjelica Selden and Mowatt. Selden struck out two in the second, fourth and sixth, finishing with nine strikeouts. She walked two and allowed three hits in the 1-0 Bruin win. Mowatt allowed only two hits—just one after the first inning. She finished with five strikeouts and two walks, giving up just the unearned run.

At 6 p.m. Friday in the first of two winners-bracket games and before a record crowd of 8,230, Texas A&M's Jamie Hinshaw bunt singled to open the fourth inning against Louisiana and advanced to third on Holly Ridley's single. Jami Lobpries' sacrifice fly to left field then scored Hinshaw to give the Aggies a 1-0 lead. In the bottom of the sixth, Louisiana loaded the bases and tied the game at 1-1 on Gabriele Bridges' sacrifice-fly RBI that scored Vallie Gaspard. In the top of the seventh, Lobpries singled up the middle and stole second with Rhiannon Kliesing at bat. An errant throw back to the mound by Cajun shortstop Brooke Brodhead allowed Lobpries to swipe third. She scored on Kliesing's single to put A&M ahead, 2-1. "That's definitely my biggest highlight," Kliesing said afterward. "I was just trying to put the ball in play and make something happen ..." Megan Gibson, who worked out of a bases-loaded jam in the sixth and retired the side in the seventh, got the 2-1 win, allowing one run on four hits with six strikeouts. Ashley Brignac took the loss, allowing five hits, striking out four.

UCLA and Arizona State met in the second winners-bracket game, and the

Sun Devils took an early 2-0 lead in the bottom of the third. Leslie Rogers singled to center, scoring Kaitlin Cochran and Jackie Vasquez after the ball got by Bruin center fielder Katie Schroeder. In the fifth ASU's Cochran was intentionally walked, and Vasquez reached first on a fielder's choice. Krista Donnenwirth then singled in Cochran, and a throwing error allowed Vasquez to score on the play as well, increasing the ASU lead to 4-0. ASU pitcher Katie Burkhart struck out eight in the four-hit shutout to get the 4-0 win. She allowed only one hit after the third inning and completed the game. Anjelica Selden took the UCLA loss, allowing four runs on three hits and five walks.

On "elimination Saturday" newcomers Florida and Virginia Tech met at 11 a.m. The teams battled through a scoreless tie through eight innings before the Gators rallied in the top of the ninth. Virginia Tech pitcher Angela Tincher had scattered just five hits through eight innings and had seventeen strikeouts. Tincher struck out two more Gators in the top of the ninth before Ali Gardiner got aboard and Francesca Enea singled to short. Tincher loaded the bases after hitting Tiffany DeFelice. Senior Mary Ratliff then laced a double through the left side, scoring two runs. The Hokies came up empty in their last at bats, and Florida took the 2-0 win. Gator hurler Stacey Nelson, who escaped a bases-loaded, no-out jam in the seventh, allowed only two hits in her shutout, striking out seven and walking three in her 104 pitches. Tincher took the loss, surrendering eight hits with no walks and nineteen strikeouts, one shy of the tournament's single-game record held by UCLA's Debbie Doom since 1982. The Hokies were the first team eliminated.

The second Saturday game matched Arizona and Alabama, which had never beaten the Wildcats in their ten past encounters. In the top of the third inning, Alabama's Charlotte Morgan smashed her nineteenth home run of the season on a towering shot down the left-field line for a 1-0 Alabama lead. The Wildcats, however, came back quickly in the bottom of the same inning to tie at 1-1 on Stacie Chambers's RBI single. The Crimson Tide broke the game open in the sixth, scoring on Brittany Rogers's RBI double, Charlotte Morgan's bases-loaded two-RBI single, and an RBI double by Kelley Montalvo. Alabama went up 5-1, and that is where the scoring ended. Alabama's Kelsi Dunne allowed four singles, striking out five in her win that eliminated the Wildcats, the second team eliminated. Pitcher Taryne Mowatt, who had won it all the year before, took the loss, giving up five runs on ten hits with seven walks. Charlotte Morgan (3-for-3, three RBIs) led the Alabama offense. Alabama coach Pat Murphy was pleased with his team's offensive performance. "We talked about if our offense showed up the rest of the tournament," Murphy said, "I didn't think anyone could match us."

UCLA and Florida followed at 6 p.m. Saturday. The Gators took a 1-0 lead in the first inning when Kim Waleszonia walked, stole second, and scored when UCLA pitcher Anjelica Selden tried to scoop up Ali Gardiner's slow roller and shovel the ball to first. The ball got by first baseman GiOnna DiSalvatore, allowing Waleszonia to score. The Gators increased their lead to 2-0 in the sixth inning on a two-out single by Ali Gardner. Pinch runner Le-Net Franklin stole second and scored on Francesca Enea's single. Florida junior pitcher Stacey Nelson tossed her second shutout of the day, allowing the Bruins only five hits. Florida coach Tim Walton talked about what the win meant to the Gator softball program: "This is a huge win for our program," he said. "The name UCLA and College World Series go hand-in-hand." UCLA's Selden allowed three hits, striking out nine in the 2-0 loss. So the Bruins became the second consecutive Pac-10 power eliminated by a team from the South.

The final elimination game followed at 8 p.m. Saturday with Louisiana facing Alabama before a crowd of 7,660. Alabama scored a run in the first inning without the benefit of a hit. Brittany Rogers walked, stole second, advanced to third on a passed ball, and scored on a wild pitch. The Tide added two more runs in the bottom of the fifth, one from a throwing error by the pitcher and the second on Jordan Praytor's sacrifice-fly down the third-base line in foul territory. With Alabama up 3-0, Holly Tankersley got Louisiana on the scoreboard with a tremendous solo shot to straightaway center field to lead off the top of the sixth—her twenty-third home run of the season. In the bottom of the sixth, lightning delayed the game for an hour and thirty-seven minutes. With no runs scored in the seventh, Alabama pitcher Charlotte Morgan got the 3-1 win, allowing one run on five hits with three strikeouts. Donna Bourgeois took the loss for the Ragin' Cajuns, working five and one-third innings and allowing three runs on four hits.

Florida and Texas A&M played at noon Sunday, with Francesca Enea blasting

**Mindy Cowles trots home after her three-run blast put the Sun Devils out of the Aggies' reach in the final game of the 2008 tournament. (Photo by Richard T. Clifton)**

a line drive over the left field fence in the top of the second to give the Gators a 1-0 lead. A&M tied the game in the bottom of the inning when Rhiannon Kliesing walked to force in a run. In the fourth, the Gators took command. Pinch runner Danyell Hines scored on an error; Mary Ratliff doubled home Enea; and Corrie Brooks singled home Ratliff. The Gators took a 4-1 advantage. Florida added two more runs in the top of the seventh when Enea slammed her second homer of the game, this one over the center-field fence to up the Gator lead to 6-1. Stacey Nelson allowed one run on three hits and struck out six. Relief hurler Stephanie Brombacher, who replaced Nelson in the fourth, earned the 6-1 win hurling four innings. Losing hurler Megan Gibson allowed four runs on five hits in three and two-third innings before being replaced by Rhiannon Kliesing in the fourth. The win forced the if-necessary game later Sunday.

Arizona State and Alabama followed at 2 p.m. Sunday, and the Crimson Tide scored first with a run in the top of the third inning on an RBI single by Jordan Praytor that scored Kellie Eubanks. But the Sun Devils rocketed back in the bottom of the inning. Rhiannon Baca reached base on a fielder's choice before Kaitlin Cochran was hit by a pitch. Jackie Vasquez then launched her fourth home run of the season to put the Sun Devils into the lead 3-1. Katie Burkhart struck out nine and gave up two hits in the 3-1 ASU win that sent her team to Monday's championship series. Alabama packed for home in third place.

Texas A&M and Florida played their rematch Sunday night to determine the second team for the championship series. For eight innings, Megan Gibson of A&M and Stacey Nelson of Florida dueled from the mound. Finally, with two outs in the ninth inning, A&M's Macie Morrow singled and scored moments later on Kelsey Spittler's triple just inside the first base bag into the right-field corner. It was Spittler's first hit after going 0-for-10. The 1-0 loss eliminated Florida (70-5), which finished tied for third. Disappointed in her loss and early exit in the first game earlier Sunday, A&M's Megan Gibson had come back strong, hurling her twenty-first shutout of the season. She scattered seven hits while striking out six. Stacey Nelson was charged with the loss, allowing one run on six hits with two strikeouts and three walks. The Aggies became the first Big 12 team to reach the championship series since Oklahoma in 2000.

In the opening game of the best-of-three series on Monday, ASU took an early lead in first the inning when Jackie Vasquez walked, went to second on a wild pitch, and scored on Krista Donnenwirth's RBI single. The Sun Devils increased their lead to 2-0 in the bottom of the third, and again it was Donnenwirth who came through. She hit a deep shot to left field for her fifteenth home run of the year and a 2-0 ASU lead. But Donnenwirth was not yet done—in the fifth she singled home Kaitlin Cochran to increase the Sun Devil lead to 3-0. Katie Burkhart won her fourth game of the series for ASU, hurling a two-hit shutout with eleven strikeouts in the 3-0 win. Megan Gibson took the loss, allowing seven hits and three runs. Donnenwirth's 3-for-3 performance led the Sun Devils, who needed only one more win for the championship.

## 2008 Women's College World Series Bracket
### Oklahoma City • May 29-June 3

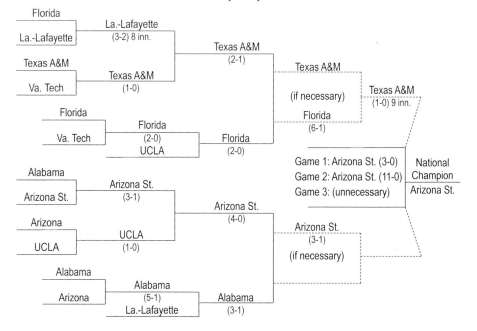

## 2008 Final Standings

| | |
|---|---|
| Arizona State University (Tempe) | 5-0 |
| Texas A&M University (College Station) | 3-3 |
| University of Florida (Gainesville) | 3-2 |
| University of Alabama (Tuscaloosa) | 2-2 |
| University of California (Los Angeles) | 1-2 |
| University of Louisiana (Lafayette) | 1-2 |
| University of Arizona (Tucson) | 0-2 |
| Virginia Polytechnic Institute (Blacksburg) | 0-2 |

In the second game of the championship series, ASU jumped out to an early 1-0 lead on an RBI single by Jackie Vasquez in the third inning. Two innings later, Kaitlin Cochran, who had been intentionally walked six times in the tournament, smashed a three-run homer—her fourteenth—to the opposite field to up the ASU lead to 4-0. Mandy Ufer had reached on an error and Rhiannon Baca had singled off the third baseman's glove before Cochran's three-run homer. The sixth-seeded Sun Devils (68-5) turned the game into a rout with seven runs in the seventh inning, including a two-run single by Caylyn Carlson and a three-run blast by Mindy Cowles that caromed off a canopy over the seats in left field. Katie Burkhart struck out thirteen to win her eleventh straight decision, allowing four hits. A&M's Gibson took the loss, allowing ten hits and eleven runs as the Aggies finished 57-10 and advanced only one runner as far as third base against Burkhart. It was ASU's first national championship under coach Clint Myers. "This is a tradition we're trying to build," Myers said. "This year's team put it on the map." The championship victory was ASU's third women's series national title, having won back-to-back titles under coach Mary Littlewood in 1972 and 1973 in Omaha.

Burkhart was named the most outstanding player and was joined on the all-tournament team by teammates Krista Donnenwirth (3B), Leslie Rogers (LF/DP), Jackie Vasquez (OF) and Kaitlin Cochran (OF). Other selections included Texas A&M's Megan Gibson (P) and Jami Lobpries (CF); Louisiana-Lafayette's Holly Tankersley (RF); Virginia Tech's Angela Tincher (P); Florida's Stacey Nelson (P) and Francesca Enea (LF); and Alabama's Charlotte Morgan (1B). Amanda Kamekona of UCLA was the leading hitter (.444).

## Life After the WCWS...

ASU's **Kaitlin Cochran** was a four-time, first-team NCAA All-American (2006-2009). She is only the second player in Pac-10 history to be named the Pac-10 Newcomer of the Year in her freshman year and then go on to earn Pac-10 Player of the Year honors in her sophomore, junior and senior seasons. She played on the U.S. national softball team in 2011, helping to win the 2011 World Cup. ASU's **Katie Burkhart** twice was named an NCAA first-team All-American (2007-08) and as of 2013 was playing professional fast pitch for the Carolina Diamonds. UCLA pitcher **Anjelica Selden** was twice a first-team NCAA All-American (2006 and 2008) after earning all-tournaments honors at the 2005 women's series. In 2012, Selden debuted her handcrafted jewelry line, Bell'Anima Maria. As of 2013, she was playing for Des Caserta, a professional team in Italy.

# 2009: Washington Road Queens Take Title

Softball teams from the South continued to show strength, with the Southeastern Conference matching the Pac-10 in teams at the 2009 national championship. Both qualified three teams, with the SEC sending top-seeded Florida and newcomer Georgia. "Everybody is ultra-competitive," said Alabama coach Pat Murphy of his SEC rivals. "If you don't catch up ... you're left as road kill."

The 2009 tournament actually had good geographic distribution, with teams from four conferences from coast to coast. With no California teams at the 2009 championship, it was left to Arizona, Arizona State and Washington to carry the Pac-10 banner. And the Huskies had been carrying the Pac-10 flag far and wide on the long road to the national championship. Washington left Seattle for a regional tournament in Massachusetts more than two weeks before arriving in Oklahoma

City. From Massachusetts, the team had gone to Atlanta, Ga., for a super regional. From there, these softball queens of the road were on to Oklahoma City.

As the teams had begun to vary more in the national tournaments, so varied the fan base watching the competition. By 2009, tournament officials estimated that more than half of ticket sales were from fans outside Oklahoma. And many returned each year, with an estimated 85-percent renewal rate in 2009 and more than 4,200 all-session tickets sold.

All eight teams were in action in the first round on Thursday, May 28, with No. 3-seed Washington welcoming newcomer and No. 6-seed Georgia in the opening game. Despite base runners from both teams in the opening innings, the game remained scoreless though the first three-and-a-half innings. Finally, Washington freshman Niki Williams scored two runs on a home run in the bottom of the fourth inning. Georgia partially closed the gap in the top of the fifth when Kristin Schanke doubled to lead off and scored on Taylor Schlopy's double. But the Huskies added an insurance run in the seventh when Kimi Pohlman ripped a two-out RBI single to center to score Bailey Stenson. Washington pitcher Danielle Lawrie allowed one run on six hits and struck out five for the 3-1 win. Christie Hamilton took the loss, allowing seven hits and three runs.

Missouri, returning to the national championship after a fifteen-year hiatus, and defending champion Arizona State met in the second upper-bracket game. ASU loaded the bases in the bottom of the first inning and got RBI singles from Krista Donnenwirth, Talo Haro and Katelyn Boyd to grab a 3-0 lead. Loading the bases in the second inning, the Sun Devils increased their lead to 6-0 on RBI singles by Kaylyn Castillo, Haro and Katie Crabb. Missouri got a run back in the third on Rhea Taylor's RBI double to left center. But ASU's Haro smacked an RBI single to score Michelle Turner in the fourth, increasing her team's lead to 7-1. Missouri got another run back in the sixth on Micaela Minner's groundout RBI scoring Rhea Taylor. The Tigers reduced the game to its final four-run margin in the top of the seventh on a solo home run by Marla Schweisberger off winning hurler Hillary Bach. Bach allowed four hits and three runs in the 7-3 ASU win. Chelsea Thomas hurled the first two innings for the Tigers, allowing six hits with Stacy Delaney hurling the remainder of the game, giving up seven hits. Jessica Mapes and Haro led the Sun Devils with four hits apiece.

In the first lower-bracket game Thursday evening, Michigan struck first against Alabama. The Wolverines took a 1-0 lead in the top of the second when Teddi Ewing walked with the bases loaded, forcing in pitcher Nikki Nemitz. In the third, freshman designated player Amanda Chidester smashed a solo home run—her eighth of 2009—over the center-field fence to give the Wolverines a 2-0 advantage. Michigan added another run in the fourth on Ewing's RBI single, scoring Kristin Larsen for a 3-0 advantage. The Wolverines scored three times on four singles and an Arizona error in the top of the sixth to go up 6-0. Alabama narrowly avoided a shutout when Whitney Larsen's double scored Ashley Holcombe in the bottom of the seventh. Michigan's Nemitz allowed one run on three hits to get the 6-1 win.

Alabama's Kelsi Dunne gave up six runs and allowed six hits in the loss. "We were able to capitalize on some good at-bats and drew some great walks, and the bottom of the order got it done for us today," said Michigan coach Carol Hutchins.

The last of four opening-round games matched perennial power Arizona against top-seeded Florida. With a crowd of 6,500, the Gators jumped to a 2-0 lead in the bottom of the first inning on a two-run home run by Francesca Enea—her eighteenth of 2009—over the center-field fence. Florida increased its advantage to 3-0 in the second inning on Megan Bush's fifteenth home run of the season over left center. After Bush's shot, Arizona starter Lindsey Sisk was replaced with ace Sarah Akamine, who hurled five innings and allowed three hits but no more runs. Pitcher Stacey Nelson got the 3-0 Florida win, allowing only two hits and striking out twelve. It was Florida's thirty-eighth shutout of the season. The stymied Wildcats had entered the game averaging more than eight runs per game.

In the first of the two winners bracket games on Friday, pitching by Arizona State and Washington kept the batters at bay through regulation play. Washington's Danielle Lawrie and ASU's Hillary Bach dueled from the mound and kept the bases mostly empty until the Huskies last bats in the bottom of the eighth. The Huskies' Kimi Pohlman doubled and Morgan Stuart knocked her in to win the game. Washington hurler Danielle Lawrie, who had played on the Canadian national softball team in the 2008 Olympics, allowed two hits in eight innings and struck out three in the 1-0 Washington win. Pohlman batted three-for-four. ASU losing hurler Bach gave up eight hits. With her team idle until the semi-final on Sunday, Husky coach Heather Tarr hoped to guard against rust. "We'll try to stay in motion, get some swings in and run around a little bit," she said, "but we're gonna keep everybody loose and relaxed and ready to play our game."

In the second Friday evening game, Florida and Michigan were scoreless through five innings before Florida's Megan Bush hit a solo home run in the top of the sixth to score the game's only run. Stacey Nelson limited Michigan to one hit, a single in the fourth inning by Bree Evans, to get the 1-0 win. It was Florida's twenty-eighth consecutive victory. Nelson fanned nine batters for her twenty-second shutout of the season. Losing pitcher Nikki Nemitz hurled two and two-thirds innings in relief, allowing two hits and the one run. Lauren Taylor pitched the first four and one-third innings for Michigan, allowing three hits and striking out five.

Georgia faced Missouri in the first game at 11 a.m. on "elimination Saturday." The Bulldogs took a 1-0 lead in the bottom of the first inning on an RBI ground-out by Alisa Goler, scoring Taylor Schlopy. Georgia extended its lead to 3-0 in the fourth on Kristyn Sandberg's two-run home run—her ninth of 2009. The Bulldogs added two more in the fifth on a two-run double from Kristin Schnake for a 5-0 lead. Avoiding the shutout, Missouri scored twice in the sixth on Marla Schweisberger's two-run single to left center to cut the deficit to three runs. Senior Christie Hamilton earned the 5-2 win for the Bulldogs, allowing five hits and two runs with four strikeouts. Missouri pitcher Chelsea Thomas allowed five runs on three hits in four innings to take the loss. Stacy Delaney closed out the game for Missouri, striking out three in two innings. Despite the Tigers' elimination from the tournament, their 50-12 record was the best in Missouri softball history.

Alabama and Arizona followed, and the Tide wasted no time scoring, putting across two runs in the first inning. They stacked up eight more in the second inning and two more in both the third and fifth innings. The game was ended there by the run rule. Charlotte Morgan tossed a five-hitter with a walk and three strikeouts to get the stunning 14-0 Alabama win. Every Alabama starter had at least one hit and an RBI as the three Arizona pitchers gave up sixteen hits. Morgan and Kelley Montalvo (both 3-for-4) led the Alabama offense. Wildcat starter Sarah Akamine gave up six runs on seven hits in three and two-third innings before Jennifer Martinez and Lindsey Sisk finished up. "The parity spread much quicker, kind of what (college) baseball experienced twenty years ago," Arizona coach Mike Candrea said afterward. "It's not a surprise. It was just a matter of time."

Georgia played its second game Saturday facing Michigan at 6 p.m. in front of a single-game record crowd of 8,475. Michigan scored three times in the top of the first on a two-run home run from Roya St. Clair and an RBI single from Nicole Nemitz. Georgia cut the deficit to two in the bottom of the first on Taylor Schlopy's solo home run. The Bulldogs then tallied four runs to pull ahead 5-3 in the bottom of the second on an RBI single by Ashley Pauly and a three-run home run by Taylor Schlopy. The Bulldogs added another run in the bottom of the fourth on Ashley Pauly's solo shot. But Michigan answered with two runs in the top of the fifth on RBI singles by Angela Findlay and St. Clair to reduce the deficit to 6-5. The Bulldogs continued to score, however, with a solo home run by Brianna Hesson to left center in the bottom of the sixth—the fourth Georgia home run, which set a single-game tournament record. Christie Hamilton collected the win for Georgia in relief of starter Sarah McCloud. Hamilton pitched six innings, allowing two runs on seven hits. Losing pitcher Nikki Nemitz gave up six hits and five runs in two innings before Jordan Taylor replaced her to finish the game.

The fourth and concluding game Saturday matched Alabama against defending champion Arizona State University. After a slow start by both teams, the Sun Devils struck in the top of the fourth on Katie Crabb's two-run home run. In the bottom of the inning, Alabama roared back and scored four times on a pinch-hit grand slam run over the left-field fence by freshman Jazlyn Lunceford. Alabama added two more runs in the bottom of the fifth when Whitney Larsen smacked a ball off the glove of the ASU second baseman, scoring Cassandra Reilly-Boccia, followed by pinch runner Jessica Smith's score on a double steal. This put the Tide up 6-2 and ended the scoring. Sophomore Kelsi Dunne hurled the Alabama win, allowing two earned runs and two walks, and striking out nine. Hillary Bach was tagged with the loss, giving up six runs. Alabama became the third SEC team to advance to the semifinals of the tournament and would face conference-rival Florida on Sunday afternoon. "It's not often you beat Mike Candrea and Clint Myers on the same day," said Alabama coach Pat Murphy, "and that could be the best day in the history of our program, especially since our backs were against the wall."

Georgia and Washington met in the opening game at noon Sunday, and the Huskies jumped out to a 3-0 advantage in the top of the second inning on a three-run home run by Niki Williams. But Georgia scored twice in the bottom of the inning on an RBI single by Krystyn Sandberg and a sacrifice fly by Tori Moody. Washington reclaimed the lead with a run in the top of the third only to see Georgia tie it 4-4 on Alisa Goler's two-run home run in the bottom of the third. Georgia pulled ahead with four runs in the bottom of the fourth on an RBI single by Taylor Schlopy and a three-run home run by Kristin Schnake. With the Bulldogs leading 8-4, Washington tied the game in the top of the fifth on a grand slam by Niki Williams. The game remained tied until the bottom of the ninth when Georgia's Brianna Hesson drew a bases-loaded walk to bring across the winning run. Danielle Lawrie took the tough 9-8 loss for Washington, allowing a career-high nine runs. Georgia used a quartet of pitchers with freshman Erin Arevalo getting the win, allowing four hits and no runs in four innings. Morgan Stuart of Georgia went 5-for-5 to tie the tournament single-game record while Williams's seven RBIs for Washington set another single-game record. The Georgia win forced an if-necessary game later that evening against Washington.

Florida and Alabama followed next at 2 p.m., and the Tide took a 1-0 lead in the top of the third on an RBI bloop single by Kelley Montalvo, scoring Jennifer Fenton. The Gators took the lead in the fourth on a two-run home run by Kelsey

**The Washington Huskies celebrate at the end of a long road trip that culminated in their taking home their first national championship trophy. *(Reprinted with permission of The Oklahoman )***

Bruder, her sixteenth of the season. Alabama, however, regained the lead in the fifth, scoring four runs on RBI singles by Lauren Parker and Montalvo, and a two-run double by Ashley Holcombe. The 5-2 Tide lead held until the bottom of the seventh when Florida loaded the bases and Ali Gardiner hit a two-out grand slam to give the Gators a storybook 6-5 victory. Stephanie Brombacher got the win for Florida, striking out four and allowing one hit in two innings. Florida's Stacey Nelson started, allowing eight hits in five innings. Kelsi Dunne shouldered the loss for Alabama, giving up seven hits and six runs as the Tide tied for third. The win advanced Florida to the best-of-three championship series pending the outcome of the Washington-Georgia game, which followed.

The Washington-Georgia rematch Sunday evening started the way Florida's win against Alabama just ended. Danielle Lawrie hit a first-inning grand slam to put the Huskies ahead 4-0. Remarkably, Lawrie's grand slam was the tournament's fourth in a twenty-four-hour span, after only one since the 1982 championship. The Huskies added a single run in the bottom of the second on an RBI triple by Ashley Charters to lead 5-0, before Georgia staged a three-run rally in the top of the third. The Bulldog scores came on an RBI single by Alisa Goler and a two-run double by Brianna Hesson. Still up 5-3, Washington padded their lead with another run in the bottom of the third on a solo shot by Morgan Stuart. The Huskies scored three insurance runs in the bottom of the sixth on an RBI single by Niki Williams and a two-run double by Jenn Salling to conclude the scoring. Lawrie cruised to the 9-3 win, allowing three runs on five hits and striking out twelve. Erin Arevalo took the loss for Georgia, allowing five hits and five runs, with Christie Hamilton finishing the last four and one-third innings, allowing four runs and six hits. Salling and Charters led the Huskies with 3-for-4 hitting.

The Huskies advanced to the three-game championship series against Florida, on a roll with their twenty-nine-game winning streak. In the first game of the championship series on Monday, neither team scored until the top of the third inning when the Huskies suddenly turned a bases-loaded single by Jenn Salling and an errant throw to second by the Florida catcher into a 4-0 lead. The Huskies extended the lead to 6-0 in the fifth on a two-out, two-run double by Morgan Stuart, scoring Salling and Lawrie. Florida changed pitchers in the sixth, but Washington greeted Stephanie Brombacher with a two-run home run by Ashley Charters, extending the lead to 8-0. It was Charters' ninth home run of the season and Washington's sixth in the series. Lawrie allowed the Gators only two hits in her 8-0 shutout, which ended Florida's twenty-nine-game win streak. Stacey Nelson was the Florida loser, giving up six runs.

In the second game Florida came out hot in the top of the first, taking a lead when leadoff batter Aja Paculba tripled and quickly scored on a passed ball. Megan Bush's sacrifice fly then scored Francesca Enea to make it 2-0. Washington answered immediately, however, scoring in the bottom of the first inning on Danielle Lawrie's RBI single and again on a wild pitch. With the score 2-2, Washington loaded the bases in the third inning with only one out. The Huskies' Morgan Stuart

## 2009 Women's College World Series Bracket
### Oklahoma City • May 28-June 2

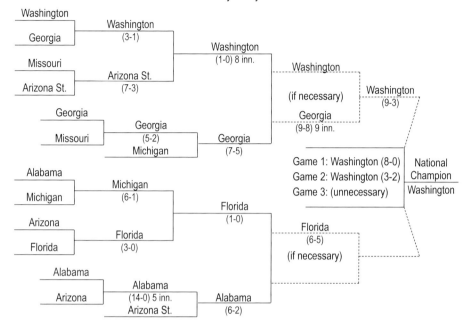

## 2009 Final Standings

| | |
|---|---|
| University of Washington (Seattle) | 5-1 |
| University of Florida (Gainesville) | 3-2 |
| University of Georgia (Athens) | 3-2 |
| University of Alabama (Tuscaloosa) | 2-2 |
| Arizona State University (Tempe) | 1-2 |
| University of Michigan (Ann Arbor) | 1-2 |
| University of Arizona (Tucson) | 0-2 |
| University of Missouri (Columbia) | 0-2 |

hit a dribbler back to the mound, which pitcher Stacey Nelson mishandled, scoring Kimi Pohlman and giving the Huskies a 3-2 advantage. Lawrie took care of the Gators from there, hurling the 3-2 win to give the Huskies their first national championship. She struck out eight and gave up seven hits. Stacey Nelson took the loss, allowing six hits. Washington coach Heather Tarr, who had been a player on the Washington national runner-up team in 1990, praised Lawrie. "I can't say enough about Danielle and her ability to carry a team on her back," Tarr said. "Coaching someone like her is a gift because she works so hard." After three weeks on the road, the Huskies could go home—with a national championship trophy in tow.

Lawrie was named the most outstanding player after her fifth win of the series. She was joined on the all-tournament team by teammates Ashley Charters (2B), Kimi Pohlman (LF), Morgan Stuart (3B) and Niki Williams (1B); Florida's Megan Bush (SS) and Stacey Nelson (P); Alabama's Kelley Montalvo (3B), Charlotte Morgan (1B/P) and Brittany Rogers (CF); Georgia's Taylor Schlopy (CF) and Alisa Goler (3B). Leading hitter was Marla Schweisberger of Missouri (.600).

### Life After the WCWS...

Florida pitcher **Stacey Nelson** was named a first-team NCAA All-American twice (2008-09) and had a college record of 136-36. As of 2013, she was attending Loyola Law School in Los Angeles, Calif.

# 2010: Bruins Make a Strong Statement

The Washington Huskies, the previous year's queens of the road, came to the Women's College World Series with new standing. Returning as the team to beat, the defending champions brought their ace Danielle Lawrie to ward off attempts to dethrone them. Lawrie had recently been named college softball's player of the year for the second straight season and had posted a gaudy 40-3 record for the regular season. The UCLA Bruins also came to the tournament as a strong contender and hoped to add to their past success, which had faded somewhat since winning their last national championship in 2004.

The Huskies' status as queens of the road in 2009 would be passed in 2010 to a tournament newcomer, the University of Hawaii Rainbow Wahine. The Hawaiian squad had been on the road for twenty-four days before arriving in Oklahoma City, following conference and regional tournament competition in California, New Mexico and Alabama. Other teams hoping to replace Washington on softball's throne were veterans Florida, Arizona, Tennessee, Missouri and Georgia.

The opening game at noon on Thursday, June 3, had the Hawaii Wahine facing the Missouri Tigers at noon in the upper bracket of four teams. Hawaii gamely jumped out to a 1-0 lead in the top of the second inning on a solo home run to right center field by Alexandra Aguirre. Missouri evened the score with a run in the third on an RBI double by Nicole Hudson. Missouri got its first lead of the game in the bottom of fifth on Rhea Taylor's opposite field home run, her eighth of the season. Missouri led 2-1 going into the top of the seventh inning when the Wahine's Katie Grimes singled, setting up a two-run blast by Traci Yoshikawa. This gave Hawaii a 3-2 lead and concluded the scoring. Wahine pitcher Stephanie Ricketts retired the Tigers in the bottom half of the seventh for the victory. Ricketts allowed six hits, walked three and fanned six, while Kristin Nottelmann took the loss, allowing nine hits and three runs. Kelly Majam and Kanani Pu'u-Warren had two hits apiece for Hawaii. "If someone told me Hawaii would only score three runs, I'd say, 'Sweet, we can win that game,'" disappointed Missouri coach Ehren Earleywine said. "But we didn't. ... We just have to a better job of hitting."

In the second game, UCLA met Florida, runner-up in 2009. Andrea Harrison put the Bruins out in front in the first inning with a three-run home run before the Gators tied the game 3-3 in the bottom of the second on a bases-clearing double by Tiffany DeFelice. UCLA regained the lead in the top of the third with three runs and added one more in the fourth. The Bruins ended the contest convincingly with a nine-run sixth inning, sending twelve batters to the plate. Andrea Harrison's three-run home run and Megan Langenfeld's two-run home run highlighted the sixth inning in the 16-3 win. Langenfeld was the winning pitcher, allowing four hits in five innings with three strikeouts. She also went 4-for-4 at-bat and drove in four runs. Losing hurler was Stephanie Brombacher, who hurled two and one-third innings, allowing three hits and five runs.

The third game featured Tennessee and Arizona. The Lady Vols took a 4-0 lead in the third inning, highlighted by Erinn Webb's two-run double, and expanded the lead to 7-0 in the fourth with three more runs. Jessica Spigner's two-run double in the fifth ended the game on the run-rule. Tennessee's Ivy Renfroe hurled the 9-0 win, allowing three hits with six strikeouts and no walks. Bedeviled by illegal-pitch calls and walked batters, Kenzie Fowler took the loss, allowing three hits and seven runs with Sarah Akamine finishing up. This marked Arizona's fifth consecutive loss in the women's series since winning the title in 2007.

The fourth and concluding game of the first round matched defending champion Washington against Georgia. Washington took a 3-0 lead in the bottom of the first inning on an RBI double by Niki Williams and a two-run single by Hooch Fagaly. The Bulldogs got a two-out solo home run from Kristyn Sandberg in the fourth for their first run. Georgia opened the fifth with four consecutive singles, with the fourth by Megan Wiggins cutting the lead to 3-2. Taylor Schlopy then beat the throw to the plate on a fielder's choice by Brianna Hesson to tie the game at 3-3. Georgia rallied again in the sixth with Wiggins hitting her sixteenth home run of the season and putting the Bulldogs ahead, 6-3. Erin Arevalo hurled four and one-third innings to get the Georgia win in relief of starter Sarah McCloud. Washington's ace hurler Danielle Lawrie was roughed up for eleven hits and six runs, all earned. The Bulldogs were led by Ashley Pauly (3-for-3), Laura Trout (2-for-3) and Wiggins (2-for-4).

With the first round completed, Thursday's winners would play on Friday with Hawaii facing UCLA at 6 p.m. followed by Tennessee against Georgia. In a battle of two of the nation's top home-run hitting teams, UCLA took a 3-0 lead in the top of the second on a two-run shot by Samantha Camuso—her fourteenth home run of the season—and an RBI single by GiOnna DiSalvatore. In the fourth inning, the Bruins increased the advantage to 4-0 on Julie Burney's seventeenth home run of the season. Hawaii rallied, however, with two out in the bottom of the fourth on a two-run home run by Alex Aguirre to cut the deficit to 4-2. The Bruins got one of the runs back in the fifth when Andrea Harrison hit her sixteenth home run of the season to push their lead to 5-2. Senior Megan Langenfeld earned the 5-2 win in the circle for the Bruins, striking out six and giving up two runs. "She loves to compete," UCLA coach Kelly Inouye-Perez said of Langenfeld. "If you could cut her open ... I always say I wish I could take some of that and give it to everyone." Stephanie Ricketts took the loss for Hawaii, lasting only one inning and giving up two hits and three runs.

The second winners-bracket game on Friday matched SEC rivals Tennessee and Georgia. With a single-session record crowd of 8,695 in attendance, the Lady Vols' Jessica Spigner scored the first run in the top of the second on a wild pitch. This was followed by another wild pitch that scored Lauren Gibson for a 2-0 Tennessee lead. Tennessee expanded its lead to 6-0 with four runs in the third on a grand slam by Erinn Webb, her second of the season and the sixth of the tournament since 1982. The Lady Vols scored again in the fourth inning when Raven Chavanne tripled and scored on a slap single by Kat Dotson. The Bulldogs cut the lead to 7-1 in the bottom of the fourth on Ashley Pauly's two-out infield single and scored again in the fifth when Ashley Razy drove in Megan Wiggins to make it 7-2. Georgia kept scoring with a rally in the bottom of the seventh that led to a three-run home run by Razy, but the Bulldogs fell short in the 7-5 loss. Ivy Renfroe hurled the Tennessee win, allowing five runs on ten hits with ten strikeouts. Georgia starter Sarah McCloud was the losing pitcher with Erin Arevalo and Alison Owen finishing up. The three allowed eight hits.

The first of four games on "elimination Saturday" matched Florida against Missouri. Scoreless through three and a half innings, Brittany Schutte put the Gators ahead 2-0 in the bottom of the fourth with a two-run home run—her seventeenth of 2010—into the center-field bleachers. Florida expanded the lead to 3-0 an inning later on a solo home run by Kelsey Bruder. Missouri replaced pitcher Kristin Nottelmann with Jana Hainey in the sixth, and Schutte promptly smashed her second home run of the day to make it 4-0. Corrie Brooks' sacrifice fly later that inning scored pinch runner Ensley Gammel to give the Gators the final 5-0 win. Stephanie Brombacher recorded the win with her twelfth complete-game shutout. Kristin Nottelmann took the loss for the Tigers, allowing three hits and three runs in five innings.

Arizona and Washington followed in the next elimination game. Bruised by the Bulldog hitters earlier in the tournament, Washington ace Danielle Lawrie struck out seven of the first eight Wildcat batters she faced. But in the top of the third, Arizona's Karissa Buchanan scored on Lauren Schutzler's infield single and Brittany Lastrapes scored on an infield error. The Huskies cut the deficit to one on Niki Williams's RBI single in the fourth, which was helped earlier by an illegal pitch. But Arizona got the run back in the top of the fifth when K'Lee Arredondo smashed a line-drive single to right, scoring Schutzler and giving Arizona a 3-1 lead. In the sixth, the Huskies got back to within a run when Danielle Lawrie scored after a deep fly to right field by Hooch Fagaly. Arizona's K'Lee Arredondo's RBI single scored pinch runner Becca Tikey in the top of the seventh upped the

Arizona advantage to 4-2. In the bottom of the seventh, Jenn Salling's sacrifice fly scored a run to tighten it to 4-3, but the Huskies scored no more. With her illegal pitches under control, Wildcat freshman Kenzie Fowler got the win, allowing three runs (one earned) on seven hits while striking out eight. Lawrie hurled a complete game and allowed four runs (only one earned) on five hits while striking out twelve. "Defensively, we broke down today, which is disappointing but part of the game," said Washington coach Heather Tarr. "We just didn't peak at the right time, so we are sitting here two and out."

Georgia and Florida followed in the next elimination game before a record crowd of just more than 9,000. Georgia took the early lead in the bottom of the first inning on Alisa Goler's two-run home run over the right field fence. Florida's Brittany Schutte cut the lead in half with a solo blast leading off the fourth. The Gators briefly tied the game in the fifth with pinch runner Lauren Heil scoring on a wild pitch. Georgia regained the lead in the bottom of the inning on an RBI single by Brianna Hesson that scored Megan Wiggins. Erin Arevalo earned the 3-2 win for the Bulldogs in relief of starter Alison Owen. Arevalo pitched two and two-thirds innings, allowing two hits and striking out six. Stephanie Brombacher took the Florida loss, giving up eight hits and three runs.

**As she rounds third base in the final game, UCLA pitcher and tournament most outstanding player Megan Langenfeld waves three fingers for each of her three home runs at the 2010 women's series. *(Photo by Richard T. Clifton )***

Arizona faced Hawaii in the final game Saturday and scored in the bottom of the first inning on a throwing error by Hawaii pitcher Stephanie Ricketts on K'Lee Arredondo's bunt. Hawaii tied the score in the third inning on a solo homer by Traci Yoshikawa. But Arizona responded in its half of the frame with a double by Arredondo scoring Buchanan and Stacie Chambers's sacrifice fly scoring Brittany Lastrapes. This upped the Arizona lead to 3-1. In the fourth Arizona added two more runs when Kristen Arriola and Lastrapes scored on an error by Yoshikawa. Wildcat pitcher Kenzie Fowler got her second win of the day, 5-1, striking out thirteen in a two-hit performance. Ricketts took the loss for Hawaii, hurling three and two-thirds innings, giving up seven hits and five runs.

Before the opening game Sunday, UCLA observed a moment of silence to remember former UCLA basketball coaching legend John Wooden, who had passed away two days earlier. Then the Bruins struck first against Georgia with a two-run home run by B. B. Bates in the second inning. The Bruin lead expanded to 5-0 with three runs in the bottom of the third on Samantha Camuso's three-run smash to center. This was the eighth home run for the Bruins, a women's series record. Georgia got on the board in the top of the fourth, scoring two runs on Alisa Goler's bloop single to left. But winning pitcher Megan Langenfeld allowed no more Bulldog runs, while getting her third win in the series by a 5-2 score. She fanned three in seven innings and allowed two runs on two hits. Losing pitcher Erin Arevalo hurled the first four and one-third innings, allowing two runs and two hits before Alison Owen finished up. The Bruins waited for their opponent in the championship finals.

Arizona and Tennessee followed with the Wildcats needing to beat the Lady Vols to force an if-necessary game. The Wildcats took a 3-0 lead in the top of the third, highlighted by Lini Koria's RBI single that scored K'Lee Arredondo and Kristen Arriola's walk with the bases loaded. In the top of the fifth, Arizona's Karissa Buchanan scored Lini Koria and Kristen with a two-run double. Three more Wildcat runs followed that inning, giving Arizona an 8-0 run-rule win. Kenzie Fowler hurled four innings, allowing no runs and no hits with three strikeouts. Losing pitcher Ivy Renfroe allowed three runs and four hits in her two and two-thirds innings. Cat Hosfield finished the game for Tennessee.

The Arizona win forced a rematch to determine who would play UCLA in the championship series. Tennessee got on the scoreboard in the top of the first inning, loading the bases before Lauren Gibson's walk forced in Raven Chavanne. The Lady Vols expanded the lead to 2-0 in the third on an RBI double by Tiffany Huff. In the bottom of the third, Stacie Chambers hit Arizona's first home run since May 23—a two-out, two-run shot to even the score. In the fifth, Wildcat Brigette Del Ponte's RBI single gave the Wildcats a 3-2 lead. Arizona expanded the lead to the final 5-2 score on K'Lee Arredondo's two-run home run in the sixth inning. Plagued with numerous illegal-pitch calls earlier in the tournament, freshman Kenzie Fowler hurled the Arizona team to another win, scattering six hits and striking out eight. Renfroe allowed five runs on twelve hits in the loss. This eliminated the Lady Vols, who finished tied for third. Arizona coach Mike Candrea praised his pitcher Fowler for her poise. "I don't know of many freshmen that can go through what she has," he said. "She gave us an opportunity to win."

With the win, the Wildcats advanced to the championship series at 7 p.m. Monday to face archrival UCLA—a match-up of two of the nation's most honored programs. The game would be a women's series classic. Arizona scored first with Brigette Del Ponte's bloop single to left scoring K'Lee Arredondo in the top of the first inning. But the Bruins came back in the bottom of the inning with Megan

## 2010 Women's College World Series Bracket
### Oklahoma City • June 3-8

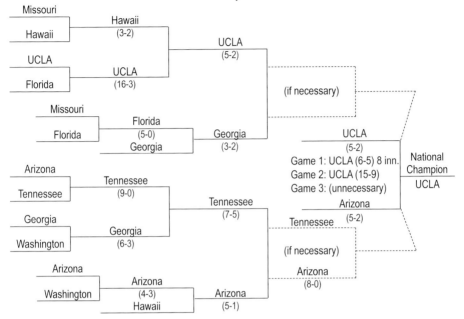

## 2010 Final Standings

| | |
|---|---|
| University of California (Los Angeles) | 5-0 |
| University of Arizona (Tucson) | 4-3 |
| University of Georgia (Athens) | 2-2 |
| University of Tennessee (Knoxville) | 2-2 |
| University of Florida (Gainesville) | 1-2 |
| University of Hawaii (Honolulu) | 1-2 |
| University of Washington (Seattle) | 0-2 |
| University of Missouri (Columbia) | 0-2 |

Langenfeld's eighteenth home run to even the game. UCLA took the lead in the bottom of the third on a bloop single by Langenfeld, scoring GiOnna DiSalvatore. But the Wildcats tied the game in the top of the fifth on a single by Stacie Chambers. The Bruins took the lead again with yet another two-out rally in the bottom of the sixth on a two-run double by Monica Harrison that scored Kaila Shull and B. B. Bates. With the Bruins leading 4-2 in the top of the seventh, Arizona scored three runs to go up 5-4, highlighted by Arredondo's two-run home run to left. In the bottom of the seventh, UCLA's Dani Yudin hit a fly to left-center that should have ended the game, but it fell between a colliding Brittany Lastrapes and Lauren

Schutzler for a double. Soon after the misplay, Kaila Schull hit a double, scoring pinch-runner Marti Reed to tie the game at 5-5. In the eighth inning, the Wildcats failed to produce a run, but the Bruins Langenfeld hit a two-out home run to end the game at 6-5. Langenfeld went 4-for-5 and said she considered the game a peak experience in her life. "Tonight was one of the greatest nights of softball I've ever been a part of," UCLA's Inouye-Perez said. Langenfeld started and pitched six innings, but sophomore Aleah Macon picked up the win in relief. Losing pitcher Kenzie Fowler allowed six runs on twelve hits and struck out twelve.

The next day, almost in anticlimax, Megan Langenfeld continued her heroics in the top of the first with a two-run home run. In the second inning, the Bruins expanded their lead to 6-0 on a grand slam by Andrea Harrison over center field, Harrison's seventeenth home run of the season and fourth of the tournament. The Wildcats fought back gallantly, eventually cutting the deficit to 7-4 after four innings. But UCLA broke the game open in the fifth, sending twelve batters to the plate and scoring seven times. Arizona continued to fight but could never close the gap, and UCLA scored a resounding 15-9 win for their twelfth national title since 1978. Sophomore Aleah Macon got the win and Donna Kerr closed out the game. Starting pitcher Fowler left early for the Wildcats, and Sarah Akamine and Ashley Ralston finished up. It was the first title for Inouye-Perez, following in the footsteps of UCLA coaching icons and mentors, Sharron Backus and Sue Enquist.

Langenfeld was named the tournament's most outstanding player and led all hitters with a stunning .706 average. Named to the all-tournament team, she joined Bruin teammates Andrea Harrison (LF) and Samantha Camuso (DP/RF). Arizona's selections were K'Lee Arredondo (SS), Karissa Buchanan (RF), Brittany Lastrapes (LF) and Kenzie Fowler (P); Tennessee's Ivy Renfroe (P) and Erinn Webb (1B); Missouri's Rhea Taylor (CF); Florida's Brittany Schutte (C); and Hawaii's Traci Yoshikawa (2B).

### Life After the WCWS...

Washington pitcher **Danielle Lawrie** earned NCAA first-team All-American honors three times (2007, 2009-10) during her college career, compiling a record of 136 wins and forty-one losses. A native of Burnaby, British Columbia in Canada, Lawrie played in the 2008 Olympics for the Canadian national team. In 2013, she was a member of the USSSA Pride in the National Professional Fastpitch league. UCLA pitcher **Megan Langenfeld** graduated in March 2011 with a degree in economics and in August 2012 received a master's of science degree in recreation and sports management from the University of Arkansas.

## 2011: Sun Devils Hold Pac-10 Banner High

Although it seemed like old times a year earlier with UCLA and Arizona battling in the women's series final game, the strong 2010 showing of these two Pac-10 softball powers was somewhat misleading. Significantly, neither qualified for the 2011 Women's College World Series, the first time since 1986. Six of the eight qualifiers for the 2011 women's series indicated how other teams from other conferences were challenging college softball's elites. For the first time, half of the field at the national championship was made up of Big 12 teams—Missouri, Oklahoma, Baylor and Oklahoma State. Also, for the seventh year in a row at least two teams from the Southeastern Conference—Alabama and Florida in 2011—had made it to the women's series. Twice since 2007, a Southeastern Conference team had played in the final game of the tournament.

Reflecting the still booming popularity of college softball, attendance for the tournament at ASA Hall of Fame Stadium had nearly doubled over the last decade. A spike in these rising attendance figures had been seen in 2000 with the strong showing of the University of Oklahoma in the championship. The school is just a half-hour drive south of Oklahoma City. This year, both Oklahoma and Oklahoma State—about a one-hour drive north of Oklahoma City—had qualified for the tournament, so local organizers were excited about the record pace of advance ticket sales.

Title-hungry Big 12 and SEC teams notwithstanding, two veteran Pac-10 teams—Cal-Berkeley and top-seeded Arizona State—were ready to play softball on June 2 in Oklahoma City. Cal-Berkeley squared off against Alabama at noon to begin play. The Tide's Kaila Hunt drove in a run with a single to left field to take a 1-0 lead in the bottom of the second inning. Alabama threatened again in the third, fourth and sixth innings, but Cal-Berkeley hurler Jolene Henderson worked out of the jams. The Golden Bear batters struggled, however, and Berkeley suffered a 1-0 loss. Alabama senior Kelsi Dunne hurled eighty-three pitches for the win, striking out eleven and allowing only a one-out single by Britt Vonk off the shortstop's glove. Jackie Traina pitched the seventh inning for Alabama for a save. Henderson fanned nine and walked one. "That's a big 'ol monkey off our back," said Alabama coach Pat Murphy of the Tide's first opening-round championship win. "At the World Series, you need great pitching, great defense and timely hitting. Today, we had all three." Amanda Locke and Kayla Braud had two hits apiece for Alabama.

Big 12 rivals Baylor and Oklahoma State met in the second game before a crowd of 7,300, the largest first-session attendance at the tournament since 1982. The game progressed through seven innings as a pitchers' duel between OSU sophomore Kat Espinosa and Baylor sophomore Whitney Canion. In the first extra inning, Baylor scored the game's only run on a line-drive home run down the left-field line by catcher Kelsi Kettler, who filled in for injured starter Clare Hosack. Canion allowed only three hits and fanned ten for the 1-0 Baylor win. Espinosa took the loss, striking out five and giving up four hits. Baylor's Kathy Shelton went 2-for-4.

The first Thursday evening game matched Arizona State against Oklahoma. Scoreless until the bottom of the fourth inning, Mandy Ufer singled to score Kayla

Ketchum and Bailey Wigness for a 2-0 lead by the Sun Devils. Oklahoma cut the deficit to one with a run in the fifth inning on an RBI double by Haley Nix that hit the top of the fence in right center. Arizona State got that run back in the bottom of the inning when Katelyn Boyd led off with a solo home run to left center, her 18th of the season. Dallas Escobedo struck out six and allowed five hits in the 3-1 ASU win. Oklahoma pitcher Keilani Ricketts gave up six hits, walked three, and struck out four. Oklahoma put a runner on base every inning but stranded all seven of them. Leslie Rogers and Sam Parlich led the Sun Devils with two hits apiece. Nix went 3-for-3 for the Sooners.

Florida and Missouri met in the nightcap of Thursday's first round before a crowd of more than 8,100. The Gators seized the lead in the bottom of the first after Kelsey Bruder singled in a run, then scored on a sacrifice bunt by Brittany Schutte. Leading 2-0, the Gators increased their lead on Michelle Moultrie's lead-off home run in the third, followed by Megan Bush's two-run shot (her 21st of the season) over left field. Florida led 5-0 until the top of the sixth when Missouri's Lisa Simmons smacked a two-run double to make it 5-2. But the Gators closed out the scoring and the game in the bottom of the sixth on Ensley Gammel's RBI single for a final score of 6-2. Gator pitcher Hannah Rogers replaced starter Stephanie Brombacher in the third inning and allowed only two hits the final four and two-thirds innings to get the win. Brombacher allowed two hits and no runs. Losing pitcher Chelsea Thomas allowed six runs on eight hits and four walks. Moultrie, Bush and Gammel had two hits each for Florida.

In the first winners-bracket game Friday evening, Alabama's Amanda Locke drove in Jennifer Fenton on an RBI sacrifice fly in the bottom of the first inning against Baylor. The Tide added a run in the fourth on an RBI grounder by Whitney Larsen, and went up 3-0 in the fifth when an error by the center fielder allowed Locke to score. The Bears got only five hits off the combined pitching of Kelsi Dunne and Jackie Traina. Dunne allowed four hits and Traina one in the 3-0 win, giving Alabama thirty consecutive innings of shutout pitching. Kayla Braud and Kaila Hunt had two hits apiece to lead Alabama's six-hit attack. "I thought it was a great defensive performance by our team," said Alabama's Murphy. "Kelsi (Dunne) is in a zone right now. It just warms my heart to know a senior is in that position when it comes to her final performance of her career."

The second and concluding winners-bracket game matched Arizona State and Florida before a crowd of 8,630. The Sun Devils struck in the bottom of the first frame, stringing together four hits before Annie Lockwood's single scored a run. ASU got two runs in the second on an error for a 3-0 lead. Mandy Ufer homered in the third to extend the lead to 4-0. But the Gators stormed ahead in the fourth with Tiffany DeFelice's two-run home run, another two-run shot by Michelle Moultrie, and Brittany Schutte's RBI double. Suddenly the Gators led 5-4. But ASU tied the game in the bottom of the inning on a solo home run by Lockwood. The tie held until the seventh inning when the Sun Devils' Lockwood hit a ball to third base with the bases loaded, scoring the deciding run. Dallas Escobedo went the distance to get the 6-5 ASU win, throwing a career-high 174 pitches, allowing eight hits with twelve strikeouts. Senior Stephanie Brombacher gave up three runs on six hits in one inning before Hannah Rogers closed the game, allowing three runs on five hits while walking eight. Lockwood led ASU with her 3-for-3, while Moultrie was 3-for-4 for the Gators.

Cal-Berkeley and Oklahoma State met in the first of four losers-bracket games at 11 a.m. on "elimination Saturday." Shutout in their first game, the Golden Bears tallied their first run of the tournament in the bottom of the second when Victoria Jones singled up the middle with two out to score Lindsey Ziegenhirt from second. OSU took a 2-1 lead in the top of the fourth on five straight singles with Ashley Boyd and Tamara Brown each driving in a run. But the Bears came back with four runs in the bottom of the fifth, highlighted by Ashley Decker's two-out, three-run triple and an error by the shortstop. Cal-Berkeley's Elia Reid smashed her ninth home run of the season in the bottom of the sixth to close out the scoring. Jolene Henderson hurled the complete-game, 6-2 win for the Golden Bears. Right-hander Kat Espinosa started and suffered the loss, allowing five runs on nine hits in five innings of work. Sarah Odom came on in relief in the bottom of the sixth. The Cowgirls became the first team to pack, finishing the year 42-20.

Big 12 rivals Missouri and Oklahoma met in the second elimination game, with the Bears scoring first on a throwing error by the catcher in the second inning. They added another run in the fourth courtesy of another Sooner error. Missouri closed out their scoring with two runs in the sixth inning on an overthrow to home. Trailing 4-0, OU tallied its only run in the top of the seventh on Dani Dobb's solo home run, her ninth of the season. Pitcher Chelsea Thomas got the 4-1 win, giving up six hits with six strikeouts. It was Missouri's first win in the women's series since 1991. Pitcher Keilani Ricketts took the error-plagued Sooner loss, allowing six hits and four runs (one earned) while striking out five. Catherine Lee and Nicole Hudson led Missouri with two hits apiece.

Florida and Cal-Berkeley followed. The Golden Bears grabbed the lead in the top of the first when Britt Yonk scored on a double by Jace Williams. Williams then scored on a Lindsey Ziegenhirt single to give the Golden Bears a 2-0 lead. Florida came back in the bottom of the third on an RBI single by Cheyenne Coyle, with Brittany Schutte scoring on the same play following a Golden Bear throwing error. Aja Paculba's RBI single then put the Gators in front 3-2 after three innings. The Gators added an insurance run in the fourth and fifth innings with Tiffany DeFelice's RBI single in the fourth and Michelle Moultrie's infield RBI single in the fifth. The scoring concluded with Florida leading 5-2. Freshman right-hander Hannah Rogers earned the win for Florida, working the first four innings and giving up just one earned run. Stephanie Brombacher came on in the fifth to hurl the final three scoreless innings for her first save of the season. Jolene Henderson worked a complete-game loss for the Golden Bears, allowing ten hits and five earned runs. For the Gators, Kelsey Bruder and Paculba each went 2-for-3 while Schutte and Moultrie were 2-for-4.

Baylor and Missouri met in the final game Saturday night with a raucous crowd of 8,480 in attendance. Dueling late, Chelsea Thomas for the Tigers and Whitney Canion for the Bears held both teams scoreless for twelve innings. Finally, Baylor's Holly Holl brought play to an abrupt end with a home run in the bottom of the thirteenth. This gave Baylor the 1-0 victory and eliminated Missouri (53-10). Canion allowed just two hits through thirteen innings, walking two and striking out eleven in her ninth complete-game shutout of the season. Thomas hurled twelve and two-thirds innings, allowing eight hits while striking out nineteen. "Whitney threw one of the best games I have seen and Holly (Holl) came through in the clutch," Baylor coach Glenn Moore said. "I am so proud of this team." Kathy Shelton, Megan Turk and Canion each collected two hits apiece for Baylor.

Alabama and Florida met in Sunday's first game—a contest that was over before it really got started. The Gators erupted for an incredible eleven runs on five hits in the bottom of the first inning, sending fourteen batters to the plate. The Gators added two runs in the second and three in the third in the five-inning, run-rule game that ended 16-2—setting a record for most runs in one inning. The first inning featured a leadoff home run by Florida's Michelle Moultrie and a grand slam by Brittany Schutte. Alabama pitcher Kelsi Dunne, who hadn't allowed a run since game one of the super regional against Stanford—thirty consecutive innings earlier—was pounded for six earned runs in one-third of an inning. Stephanie Brombacher got the win for Florida, allowing only three hits with seven strikeouts and no walks. The Florida win forced an if-necessary game between the same two teams later that evening.

The second game Sunday matched Arizona State against Baylor. The Sun Devils started with two runs in the top of the second inning on Mandy Ufer's two-run shot over the center-field fence. While Sun Devil pitcher Dallas Escobedo remained unscathed through four innings, her teammates added another run in the fifth on Annie Lockwood's RBI double to right center to make it 3-0. ASU added an insurance run in the seventh on Leslie Rogers's RBI single. Escobedo, meanwhile, hurled the shutout, allowing five hits with eight strikeouts for the 4-0 win. Whitney Canion took the Baylor loss, giving up seven hits and four runs with six strikeouts. The win advanced ASU to the best-of-three championship series against the winner of the second Alabama-Florida game that followed.

In the if-necessary game between Alabama and Florida, the Gators' hot batters picked right up where they left off earlier. A two-run home run from Kelsey Bruder and a solo shot from Brittany Schutte gave Florida a 3-0 lead in the top of the first inning. The Gators expanded the lead in the third with a pair of runs on Cheyenne Coyle's two-run single, then scored their sixth run in the fourth on Bruder's sacrifice fly that brought in Kasey Fagan. The Gators scored three insurance runs in the top of the seventh on a three-run home run by Aja Paculba. Behind 9-0 in the bottom of the seventh, Alabama gamely scored twice to avoid a shutout. The runs came on Jennifer Fenton's RBI triple down the right-field line and a walk to Jackie Traina, forcing in Cassie Reilly-Boccia. The 9-2 Florida win eliminated the

Tide (53-11) and left them in third-place. Gator pitcher Hannah Rogers allowed four hits and two runs while fanning seven to get the win. Kelsi Dunne hurled the first two innings for the Tide, allowing six hits and five runs, with Traina finishing up the effort. "There's been a lot of talk about the Pac-10 dominating," Bruder said afterward. "We just want to show everybody we play the brand of ball they do."

Bruder and her Gator teammates got that chance on Monday against Arizona State in the first game of the best-of-three championship series. But the Sun Devils did all the showing, scoring in the bottom of the first inning when Michelle Moultrie let Kaylyn Castillo's single get by her, bringing home Leslie Rogers with the first ASU run. In the bottom of the second, Castillo smashed a two-out, two-run single, Breanna Kaye an RBI single, and Krista Donnenwirth a three-run shot to up the lead to 7-0. Things only worsened for the Gators when Arizona added three runs in the third on RBI singles by Castillo, Rogers and Talor Haro. A solo home run by Sam Parlich in the fourth, three runs in the fifth on a two-run home run by Annie Lockwood, and a solo blast by Donnenwirth combined for a 14-0 Sun Devil lead. Florida gamely tallied a run in the top of the sixth on Kelsey Bruder's solo home run and three runs in the top of the seventh to conclude the scoring. The game's seven home runs tied a women's series record set in 1982. Pitcher Dallas Escobedo hurled the 14-4 win, allowing five hits and four runs with seven strikeouts. Hannah Rogers took the loss for the Gators, allowing nine runs on ten hits, with Stephanie Brombacher finishing up.

**Previously red hot but ineffective against Arizona pitcher Dallas Escobedo and the Sun Devils, the Florida bats produced only a total of two runs in the two championship series games. *(Photo by Richard T. Clifton)***

# 2011 Women's College World Series Bracket
### Oklahoma City • June 2-7

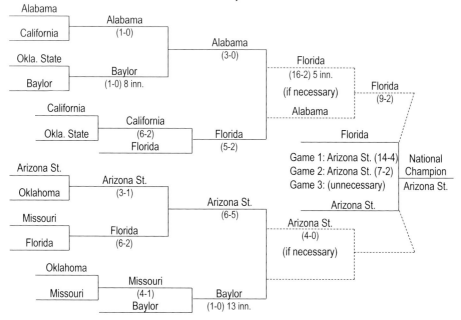

## 2011 Final Standings

| | |
|---|---|
| Arizona State University (Tempe) | 5-0 |
| University of Florida (Gainesville) | 4-3 |
| University of Alabama (Tuscaloosa) | 2-2 |
| Baylor University (Waco, Texas) | 2-2 |
| University of Missouri (Columbia) | 1-2 |
| University of California (Berkeley) | 1-2 |
| University of Oklahoma (Norman) | 0-2 |
| Oklahoma State University (Stillwater) | 0-2 |

With this win, the unbeaten Sun Devils needed to take only one game to capture their second women's series title in four years, and fourth overall. Florida surprised with a 1-0 lead in the bottom of the first inning on Brittany Schutte's sacrifice fly, scoring Michelle Moultrie, who had doubled. But the Sun Devils came back quickly in the second inning when Gator starter Stephanie Brombacher walked Alix Johnson to force in a run, and Katelyn Boyd added a two-run single to put the Sun Devils ahead 3-1. Johnson blooped in a two-run single to right in the third, and Boyd tacked on an RBI single in the fifth inning to make it 6-1 for Arizona State. Annie Lockwood added another run for Arizona State with a solo shot in the sixth inning. Florida scored its second and final run on Tiffany DeFelice's

RBI single in the seventh inning. ASU hurler Dallas Escobedo allowed four hits and five walks in the 7-2 win, becoming only the fourth freshman to hurl her team to the national title. Brombacher took the loss, going the first three innings, giving up five runs in six hits before Rogers closed out the final four innings.

The top-seeded Sun Devils from the Pac-10 Conference came to Oklahoma City as the team to beat, and they only got better against the nation's best college teams. "They played their best softball of the year here," ASU coach Clint Myers said. And they did it on offense and on defense. Arizona State became only the third team since 1982 to win the women's series without a single fielding error. Finishing 60-6 on the year, the Sun Devils made 105 putouts and fifteen assists in their undefeated run in the national championship tournament. With ASU carrying the banner, Pac-10 softball still appeared alive and well, regardless of other conferences' ambitions.

Escobedo and Moultrie shared most outstanding player honors. Florida's selections on the all-tournament team included Kelsey Bruder (LF), Cheyenne Coyle (SS), and Brittany Schutte (RF). Other selections included Arizona State's Krista Donnenwirth (3B), Annie Lockwood (RF) and Mandy Ufer (1B); Baylor's Whitney Canion (P) and Holly Holl (1B); Missouri's Chelsea Thomas (P); and Alabama's Whitney Larsen (SS). Lockwood batted .563 to lead all hitters.

The crowd of 6,314 at the final game Tuesday upped total attendance for the tournament to just more than 67,600, despite both OU and OSU's two-and-done fizzles. This broke the attendance record of 65,560 from the year before.

## 2012: Alabama and SEC Win Their First

For the second straight year, UCLA and Arizona had not qualified for the Women's College World Series. But their conference, realigned as the Pac-12 in 2011, was still well represented at the 2012 tournament with three teams—Cal-Berkeley, Arizona and Oregon. But with five teams from the South—including newcomer South Florida—filling the other tournament berths, the unmistakable scent of national parity was in the air. "With parity across the country, the rivalries between conferences, the toughest part is getting here," said Arizona State coach Clint Myers. "The regionals are getting a lot more quality teams." The absence of UCLA and Arizona attested to that.

Still, the Pac-12's Cal-Berkeley, a veteran of women's series play since 1980, came to town as the tournament's top seed. In her twenty-fifth season as head coach, Diane Ninemire had led the Bears to the national tournament eleven times, including a championship title in 2002. Emphasizing the growing rivalry between the South and West Coast softball powers, Alabama was seeded No. 2 at the tournament. Although the Southeastern Conference had been well represented at recent national championships, no SEC school had taken the top prize. Making its eighth consecutive bid for the national title, the Crimson Tide yearned to be the first SEC national softball champion. Oklahoma, Tennessee and Louisiana State rounded out the field.

South Florida and Oklahoma met in the opening game on Thursday, May 31. In the top of the fourth, South Florida's Kourtney Salvarola scored Courtney Goff with a single. With the USF Bulls leading 1-0 in the bottom of the fourth, Oklahoma freshman Lauren Chamberlain smashed a two-run home run, her twenty-eighth, to put the Sooners ahead 2-1. Oklahoma took a 5-1 lead in the sixth with an RBI triple by pitcher Keilani Ricketts, an RBI single by Brianna Turang, and a bases-loaded walk. USF changed pitchers four times in the sixth inning. Winning pitcher Ricketts gave up three hits, fanned twelve, and walked one in her complete-game, 5-1 win for the Sooners. Bulls starter Sara Nevins worked four and two-thirds innings, allowing four of the Sooner's five hits. Lindsey Richardson and Sam Greiner also hurled for the Bulls. Chamberlain went 2-for-3 to lead the Sooners.

No.1-ranked Cal-Berkeley and Louisiana State met in the second game, and the Golden Bears fell behind 2-0 in the second inning on a bases-loaded, two-run single by LSU's Morgan Russell. Berkeley's Frani Echavarria cut the margin to one with an RBI single in the bottom of the third that scored Britt Vonk, and the Bears evened the score on a sacrifice fly in the fifth inning that brought home Jamie Reid. Gaining momentum in the sixth, the Bears' Elia Reid scored her sister Jamia on a comebacker to the mound, Vonk tallied Cheyenne Cordes with a single to right, and Echavarria's RBI single completed the Berkeley scoring. In the seventh, LSU's Ashley Langoni doubled to score Cassie Trosclair, who had singled to short and advanced around on groundouts. Jolene Henderson pitched the complete-game, 5-2 win for Cal-Berkeley, allowing eight hits and fanning five. Rachele Fico took the LSU loss, allowing two runs on five hits and four walks in five and one-third innings.

SEC rivals Tennessee and Alabama hooked up Thursday evening, and the Tide wasted little time, scoring in the bottom of the first inning on a bases-loaded three-run double by Cassie Reilly-Boccia, who scored on a walk later in the inning. After Tennessee cut the lead in half in the second with a two-run home run by Melissa Davin, Alabama added some insurance in the bottom of the fourth on Jennifer Fenton's RBI single up the middle, scoring Kayla Braud. Trailing 5-2, the Lady Vols added one run in the seventh to conclude the scoring. Alabama's Jackie Traina threw a complete game five-hitter, giving up three runs while striking out eight in the 5-2 win. Braud had three of Alabama's five hits off losing pitcher Ivy Renfroe, who allowed four runs on three hits in two and two-thirds innings. Her sister Ellen finished the game, allowing one run and two hits in three and one-third innings.

Defending champion Arizona State and Oregon, both veterans of women's series play since the 1970s, concluded the first round Thursday evening. Oregon was poised to score early in the first inning when Samantha Pappas doubled to left on the first pitch of the game and advanced to third on a sacrifice bunt. Pappas appeared to score on Kelsey Chambers' sacrifice fly, but was called out for leaving third base too early. ASU took a 1-0 lead in the bottom of the first on an RBI double by Haley Steele, and a two-out rally in the third gave ASU a 3-0 cushion. Both runs in the third were scored on an error by the shortstop. Oregon's lone run came in the seventh inning when Christie Nieto doubled to left and scored on an error by the second baseman. ASU sophomore pitcher Dallas Escobedo struck out four, walked one and allowed five hits in the complete-game, 3-1 Sun Devil victory. Oregon losing hurler Jessica Moore struck out three, walked four and allowed only three hits.

In the first winners-bracket game at 6 p.m. Friday between Cal-Berkeley and Oklahoma, Lauren Chamberlain doubled in the third to score the Sooners first run. In the fourth inning, Oklahoma pitcher Keilani Ricketts walked with the bases loaded to bring in the second run, and the Sooners scored in the sixth on Georgia Casey's tenth home run of the season. Ricketts allowed only two hits and fanned sixteen in the complete-game, 3-0 win, extending her consecutive scoreless inning streak to forty. Cal-Berkeley pitcher Jolene Henderson gave up five hits. The frustrated Golden Bear hitters were impressed with Ricketts's pitching performance. "Her changeup was on," Jace Williams said. "It was dropping off the table."

In the second game with a record crowd of more than 9,200, second-seeded Alabama met defending champion Arizona State. In the bottom of the fourth inning, ASU's Elizabeth Caporuscio singled to right to score a run. Alabama tied it in the fifth on Jennifer Fenton's RBI single, driving in Courtney Conley. In the sixth, Amanda Locke hit a mammoth home run to straightaway center field to put the Tide up 2-1. That would be all Alabama needed for the win. Tide hurler Jackie Traina walked five and struck out eleven in her three-hitter as Alabama advanced to the semifinals for the fourth time. The win brought Traina's record to 39-2, a single-season pitching record for Alabama. Pitcher Dallas Escobedo took the ASU loss, allowing seven hits and two runs with nine strikeouts.

Louisiana State and South Florida met in the first game on "elimination Saturday" before a crowd of 8,500. Neither team could put a run across until the bottom of the sixth inning when LSU's A. J. Andrews tagged from third base and went home on Allison Falcon's popup to shortstop. The throw to home was high and toward the first-base line, enabling Andrews to slide around the tag. "I've been in softball for a long time, seen a lot of things," said LSU coach Beth Torina. "I don't remember if I've ever seen that before, but it was a pretty amazing, gutsy play by A. J.—not me." The gutsy play paid off, and the 1-0 LSU lead held up. LSU winning pitcher Brittany Mack hurled a two-hit shutout and recorded eight strikeouts against four walks. South Florida pitcher Sara Nevins took the 1-0 loss, hurling five and two-thirds innings, allowing two hits and the one run.

Oregon and Tennessee followed in the next game. It took only two pitches for Oregon to get on the scoreboard in the top of the first inning as lead-off batter Samantha Pappas drove her tenth home run of the season just over the glove of leaping center fielder Tory Lewis. Second baseman Kaylan Howard continued the early outburst with a double into the left center gap and scored on Kailee Cuico's single down the left field line. In the bottom of the second with Oregon up 2-0, the

Lady Vols cut the deficit in half on an RBI single by Tory Lewis, scoring Ashley Andrews. Tennessee's Ivy Renfroe entered in relief of her sister Ellen in the top of the third, and an inning later Oregon's Christie Nieto scored on an RBI double off the center field wall by Alexa Peterson, giving the Ducks a 3-1 lead and concluding the scoring. The Lady Vols managed just four hits off Oregon pitcher Jessica Moore, who walked one and struck out four. Ellen Renfroe took the loss for the Lady Vols, allowing two runs on three hits.

Arizona State and LSU followed in the next elimination game, and ASU jumped on top with a three-run home run by Alix Johnson in the top of the third. The Sun Devils expanded their lead to 6-0 in the top of the fifth when an LSU throwing error platted the fourth run and Sam Parlich singled to left to score two more. Freshman Hillary Bach tossed a four-hit shutout on an efficient eighty-three pitches to get the 6-0 ASU win. Pitcher Rachele Fico took the LSU loss, giving up six runs on seven hits, which included allowing her first home run of the year. Brittany Mack finished the pitching for the Tigers.

Saturday's final elimination game matched Cal-Berkeley against Oregon. The Golden Bears grabbed a 3-0 lead in the top of the first inning on a two-out, three-run home run to center field by Jace Williams, her eighth of the season. The Golden Bears added two more runs in the second on Britt Vonk's two-run double. Oregon's Samantha Pappas cut Cal's lead to four with a solo home run in the third inning. Victoria Jones, however, piled on more for Berkeley when she crushed the first pitch of the fourth inning for a home run, putting the Bears up 6-1. A bases-loaded, two-run double by Oregon's Sara Goodrum in the sixth inning plated Kailee Cuico and Christie Nieto for the 6-3 final score. Golden Bear hurler Jolene Henderson scattered six hits and allowed the three runs. Jessica Moore took the loss for Oregon as the Ducks became the fourth team sent home.

With the original field of eight cut in half, Oklahoma faced Arizona State at noon on Sunday. The Wildcats started swiftly in the first inning with Annie Lockwood's two-run double to right center scoring Alix Johnson and Amber Freeman. Down 2-0, the Sooners chipped at the lead in the bottom of the second when Katie Norris hit a solo shot over the center field fence. Oklahoma moved ahead in the third with a four-hit, four-run rally to go up 5-2, highlighted by a two-run double by catcher Jessica Shults. The Sun Devils closed the game to 5-3 with a run in the fourth inning by Elizabeth Caporuscio, who scored on a fielder's choice by Katelyn Boyd. The scoring stopped there as Sooner pitcher Keilani Ricketts allowed three runs on eight hits and struck out thirteen in the Sooner's eleventh consecutive win. ASU pitcher Dallas Escobedo struck out eight and gave up five runs on nine hits. ASU stranded nine runners, with five left in scoring position.

After Oklahoma punched its ticket for the championship series, top seeds Alabama and Cal-Berkeley faced off to determine the Sooners' opponent. The Tide took a 1-0 lead in the bottom of the second on a solo home run by pitcher Jackie Traina, her tenth of the year. Alabama added to its lead in the third inning when Kayla Braud scored on Kaila Hunt's infield single. The Golden Bears, however, tied the game in the top of the fourth on a two-run home run by third baseman Danielle Henderson. The Tide continued to produce runs, regaining the lead in the bottom of the fourth on Kendall Dawson's RBI single, scoring Jazlyn Lunceford. Leading 3-2, Alabama added single runs in the fifth and sixth inning on home runs by Hunt and Lunceford. Alabama pitcher Jackie Traina threw a complete-game two-hitter for the 5-2 win, striking out six and allowing two runs. Jolene Henderson took the loss, allowing nine hits and five runs with eight strikeouts.

Alabama advanced to the three-game championship series for the first time, while Oklahoma sought its second national championship. With play beginning at 7 p.m. Monday, the game was scoreless through three and one-half innings. In the bottom of the fourth, Alabama pitcher Jackie Traina scored on a sacrifice fly by Kendall Dawson. Trailing 1-0 in the top of the fifth, the Sooners tied the game with a run on a sacrifice fly by catcher Jessica Shults and moved ahead on a run-scoring grounder by Brianna Turang. Oklahoma added two more runs in the sixth inning on an RBI single by Shults and a surprise squeeze bunt by Katie Norris that scored Keilani Ricketts. Alabama's attempted rally in the bottom of the sixth ended with a strikeout and a runner on second, and neither team scored in the seventh. Ricketts allowed five hits and fanned twelve in the 4-1 Sooner win. Traina allowed eleven hits and four runs (two earned) for her first loss since May 4—and an end to Alabama's eleven-game win streak.

In the second game on Tuesday evening, Oklahoma took a 1-0 lead in the bot-

**The hour is late but the smiles are bright as Alabama celebrates its first national softball title following a hard-fought victory over the Oklahoma Sooners in the third game of the championship title series. (Photo by Richard T. Clifton )**

tom of the first on Jessica Shults's bloop single, scoring Georgia Casey from second base. But Alabama scored four times in the second inning on Jennifer Fenton's fielder's choice and a three-run double by pitcher Jackie Traina. The Tide scored four more in the top of the fourth on a sacrifice fly by Kaila Hunt and a three-run double by Amanda Locke. Down 8-1, Oklahoma mounted a furious rally in the bottom of the seventh, led off by Destinee Martinez's triple. She scored on Lauren Chamberlain's single. After pitcher Ricketts singled, catcher Jessica Shults blasted the first pitch over the right field fence for a three-run home run, which cut the deficit to 8-5. The Sooners added another run on Erica Sampson's run-scoring groundout. But the rally fell short when winning pitcher Traina struck out Javen Henson, forcing a third and deciding game. Traina allowed six runs on nine hits while striking out eight batters in the 8-6 Alabama win. Ricketts was knocked out in the fourth inning after giving up six runs on three hits. She hit five Alabama players for a women's series record. Michelle Gascoigne relieved Ricketts and finished the game, allowing one hit and two runs. "That was one of the proudest moments I've had with this team in not quitting," Sooner coach Patty Gasso said in the locker room afterward.

The third and final game to decide the 2012 national champion was delayed nearly three hours by rain with no play until nearly 10 p.m. Oklahoma took the lead in the second when Ricketts curled a leadoff home run just inside the right-field foul pole. Lauren Chamberlain followed in the third with a two-out, two-run shot over left field to give the Sooners a 3-0 lead. With intermittent rainfall, Alabama took advantage of Ricketts's wildness to score four runs in the fourth. The Tide's Kaila Hunt opened the fourth by singling to left, then scored on three wild pitches. After the third errant toss, Oklahoma's Gasso complained to the umpires that Ricketts could not properly grip the ball. The game was delayed for thirteen minutes—over Alabama coach Pat Murphy's protests. When the game resumed, Amanda Locke delivered a two-out RBI single, and Courtney Conley followed with a double to center field to tie the game. A throwing error by Oklahoma shortstop Jessica Vest allowed Jazlyn Lunceford to reach base and Conley to score, putting the Crimson Tide up 4-3. Ricketts had four wild pitches in the fourth inning.

In the top of the fifth with two outs, Traina walked Chamberlain and hit Ricketts. But right fielder Jazlyn Lunceford caught Jessica Shults's fly ball at the wall to retire the Sooners. Alabama added an insurance run in the bottom of the fifth when Jennifer Fenton reached on a leadoff bunt single and scored on an RBI single by Traina. With the Sooners trailing 5-3 in the seventh, Chamberlain's home run made it close, but Traina fanned Ricketts to end the game. Alabama (60-8) and the SEC had its first national softball championship. "For us, I don't think it's sunk in yet," Alabama coach Pat Murphy said after the game. "It's been a long time coming. It's just been an incredible nine or ten days here in Oklahoma City and each game just got better and better." Traina hurled a five-hitter to get the tense 5-4 win. Ricketts gave up seven hits.

Traina was named the tournament's most outstanding player and was joined

## 2012 Women's College World Series Bracket
### Oklahoma City • May 31-June 6

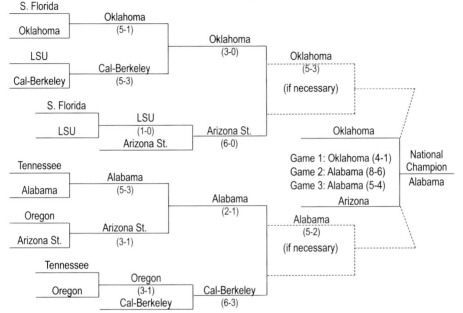

## 2012 Final Standings

| | |
|---|---|
| University of Alabama (Tuscaloosa) | 5-1 |
| University of Oklahoma (Norman) | 4-2 |
| Arizona State University (Tempe) | 2-2 |
| University of California (Berkeley) | 2-2 |
| University of Oregon (Eugene) | 1-2 |
| Louisiana State University (Baton Rouge) | 1-2 |
| University of Tennessee (Knoxville) | 0-2 |
| University of South Florida (Tampa) | 0-2 |

on the all-tournament team by Tide teammates Kayla Braud (LF), Jennifer Fenton (CF) and Amanda Locke (DH); Oklahoma's Lauren Chamberlain (1B), Keilani Ricketts (P), Jessica Shults (C), Destinee Martinez (CF) and Brianna Turang (LF); Arizona State's Amber Freeman (C); and Oregon's Samantha Pappas (RF) and Alexa Peterson (C). Arizona State's Annie Lockwood led all hitters with a .563 average.

Total attendance for the 2012 women's series tallied a record 75,960, breaking the former mark of 67,531. The tournament featured five of the top-ten, single-session attendance figures in event history, including the top three: 9,209 Friday night; 9,310 Saturday night; and 9,167 Sunday afternoon.

# Epilogue

A S THE 2013 WOMEN'S COLLEGE WORLD SERIES began play at the release of this book, the national championship's home in Oklahoma City appeared secure for some time to come. The City of Oklahoma City and event sponsor Oklahoma City All Sports Association were beginning ambitious additions and improvements to ASA Hall of Fame Stadium. Some of this work had been completed by the tournament's start in 2013, including a new interview room for use by the media and a parking pad for ESPN television network's vehicles and broadcast equipment.

ESPN's live coverage of the tournament had greatly added to the event's popularity nationwide, and organizers intended to support the television network whenever possible. "ESPN has been integral to the growth of this event and will be in the future," All Sports Association executive director Tim Brassfield said just before the 2013 championship event.

Several phases of development were planned for the stadium between 2013 and 2018. The most significant of these improvements included the addition of some 4,200 permanent seats. These seats will be added with the construction of an upper deck to the existing stadium and will bring seating capacity to approximately 12,500 upon completion. The addition of the upper deck is just part of a major overhaul to the existing facility. "These improvements will basically change the entire structure of the stadium," Brassfield said.

The cost of these stadium enhancements was estimated at $20 million and will be provided from a mix of public and private funds. Officials at All Sports Association believed that these stadium investments could lead to the NCAA's commitment to a longer-term contract than the two-year agreement in 2013.

# Appendix

## Teams in Women's Series and Year(s) of Participation

Adelphi: 1984–85, 1988

Alabama: 2000, 2003, 2005–06,
2008–09, 2011–12

Arizona: 1974, 1975, 1977, 1979,
1988–2003, 2005–10

Arizona State: 1971–1973, 1976–79,
1982, 1987, 1999, 2002, 2006–09,
2011–12

Ball State: 1973, 1975

Baylor: 2007, 2011

Black Hills State College: 1969

Buena Vista College: 1971

California (Berkeley): 1980–82, 1986,
1992, 1996, 1999, 2000–05, 2011–12

California (Los Angeles): 1978–79,
1981–85, 1987–97, 1999–2006,
2008, 2010

California Polytechnic Pomona:
1978–80, 1984–85, 1988–89

California State (Fresno): 1982, 1984,
1987–92, 1994, 1997–99

California State (Fullerton): 1980–83,
1985–1987, 1995

California State (Long Beach): 1986,
1990–93

California State (Northridge): 1993–94

California State (Sacramento): 1976–77

Central Michigan: 1982, 1987

Central Missouri State College: 1971–72

Chapman College: 1979

Colorado State College: 1969

Concordia Teachers College: 1970–71

Connecticut: 1993

Creighton: 1969, 1980–82, 1986

DePaul: 1999, 2000, 2005, 2007

East Stroudsburg State College: 1975–76

Eastern Illinois: 1971, 1974

Emporia State University: 1979

Florida: 2008–11

Florida State: 1987, 1990–93, 2002, 2004

Georgia: 2009–10

Golden West College: 1974

Hawaii: 2010

Illinois (Chicago): 1994

Illinois State: 1969–73, 1976, 1978, 1981

Indiana: 1979–80, 1983, 1986

Indiana State: 1974, 1976,

Iowa: 1995–97, 2001

Iowa State: 1971, 1973

John F. Kennedy College: 1969–71

Kansas: 1973–77, 1979, 1992

Kansas State Teachers College
(Emporia): 1971–72

Kearney State College: 1969–71

Keene State College: 1972

Kent State University: 1990

Louisiana (Lafayette)[1]: 1993, 1995–96,
2003, 2008

Louisiana State: 2001, 2004, 2012

Louisiana Tech: 1983, 1985–86

Luther College: 1970–72, 1974

Mankato State: 1975

[1]Officially Southwestern Louisiana University before 1997.

Massachusetts: 1974, 1978, 1980, 1992, 1997, 1998
Mayville State College: 1976
Michigan: 1982, 1995–98, 2001–02, 2004–05, 2009
Michigan State: 1973–77, 1981
Midland Lutheran College: 1970-71
Midwestern College: 1970
Minnesota (Duluth): 1970–71
Minnesota (Minneapolis): 1976, 1978
Minot State College: 1970–72
Missouri: 1981, 1983, 1991, 1994, 2009–11
Nassau Community College: 1974
Nebraska (Lincoln): 1970–71, 1982, 1984–85, 1987–88, 1998, 2002
Nebraska (Omaha): 1969–73, 1975–79
Nevada-Las Vegas: 1990–91, 1995
New Mexico: 1980–81
New Mexico State: 1981
North Dakota State: 1973–75
Northern Colorado: 1970–79
Northern Illinois University: 1988
Northern Iowa: 1973, 1975–77
Northern State College (Aberdeen, S.D.): 1975–76
Northwestern: 1984–86, 2006–07
Northwest Missouri State: 1975
Northwestern Oklahoma State: 1976
Ohio State: 1982
Ohio University: 1975
Oklahoma: 1975, 1980–82, 2000–04, 2011–12
Oklahoma State: 1977, 1980–82,[2] 1989–90, 1993–94, 1998, 2011
Oregon: 1976, 1980, 1989, 2012
Oregon College of Education: 1975
Oregon State: 1977–79, 2006
Pacific: 1983
Parsons College: 1971
Portland State: 1978
Princeton: 1995–96
Purdue: 1972

Rhode Island: 1982
Rutgers: 1979, 1981
Simpson College: 1971
South Carolina: 1972–74, 1976, 1978–79, 1980–81, 1983, 1989, 1997
South Dakota: 1971
South Dakota State: 1971–74
South Florida: 2012
Southern Illinois: 1970–71, 1977–78
Southern Mississippi: 1999–2000
Southwest Baptist College: 1971
Southwest Missouri State: 1969–74, 1977–78, 1980, 1982
Springfield College: 1977
St. Petersburg Junior College: 1969
Stanford: 2001, 2004
Stephen F. Austin: 1978
Tarkio College: 1976
Tennessee: 2005–07, 2010, 2012
Texas: 1998, 2003, 2005–06
Texas (Arlington): 1976–77
Texas A&M: 1979–84, 1986–88, 2007–08
Texas Woman's University: 1975, 1978–79
Tokyo-Nihon: 1972
Toledo: 1989
U.S. International University: 1982
Upper Iowa: 1970–71
Utah: 1976, 1982, 1985, 1991, 1994
Utah State: 1978, 1980–81, 1984
Virginia Polytechnic Institute: 2008
Wartburg College: 1971
Washington: 1996–2000, 2003–04, 2007, 2009–10
Wayne State College: 1970–74
Weber State College: 1973–75
West Chester State College: 1977
West Georgia College: 1974
Western Illinois: 1970, 1972–73, 1975, 1977, 1979–80, 1982
Western Michigan: 1980–82
Winona State College: 1974
Wisconsin State (Eau Claire): 1971

[2] Oklahoma State played in AIAW and NCAA national championships in 1982.

# Women's Series Championship Results (1969-2012)

| Year | National Champion | Head Coach | Runner-Up | Host City |
|------|-------------------|------------|-----------|-----------|
| 1969 | J. F. Kennedy College | Don Joe | Illinois State | Omaha, Neb. |
| 1970 | J. F. Kennedy College | Ken Christensen | S.W. Missouri | (ditto) |
| 1971 | J. F. Kennedy College | Ken Christensen | Iowa State | (ditto) |
| 1972 | Arizona State | Mary Littlewood | Univ. of Tokyo | (ditto) |
| 1973 | Arizona State | Mary Littlewood | Illinois State | (ditto) |
| 1974 | Southwest Missouri St. | Mary Kay Hunter | N. Colorado | (ditto) |
| 1975 | Nebraska (Omaha) | Connie Claussen | N. Iowa | (ditto) |
| 1976 | Michigan State | Diane Ulibarri | N. Colorado | (ditto) |
| 1977 | Northern Iowa | Jane Mertesdorf | Arizona | (ditto) |
| 1978 | UCLA | Sharron Backus | N. Colorado | (ditto) |
| 1979 | Texas Woman's Univ. | Donna Terry | UCLA | (ditto) |
| 1980 | Utah State | Kelly Phipps | Indiana | Norman, Okla. |
| 1981 | Utah State | Lloydene Searle | Cal-Fullerton | (ditto) |
| 1982 [1] | Texas A&M | Bob Brock | Oklahoma St. | (ditto) |
| 1982 [2] | UCLA | Sharron Backus | Fresno St. | Omaha, Neb. |
| 1983 | Texas A&M | Bob Brock | Cal-Fullerton | (ditto) |
| 1984 | UCLA | Sharron Backus | Texas A&M | (ditto) |
| 1985 | UCLA | Sharron Backus | Nebraska [3] | (ditto) |
| 1986 | Cal-State Fullerton | Judi Garman | Texas A&M | (ditto) |
| 1987 | Texas A&M | Bob Brock | UCLA | (ditto) |
| 1988 | UCLA | Sharron Backus | Fresno State | Sunnyvale, Calif. |
| 1989 | UCLA | Sharron Backus | Fresno State | (ditto) |
| 1990 | UCLA | Sharron Backus | Fresno State | Oklahoma City |
| 1991 | Arizona | Mike Candrea | UCLA | (ditto) |
| 1992 | UCLA | Sharron Backus | Arizona | (ditto) |
| 1993 | Arizona | Mike Candrea | UCLA | (ditto) |
| 1994 | Arizona | Mike Candrea | Cal-Northridge | (ditto) |
| 1995 | UCLA [4] | Sharron Backus | Arizona | (ditto) |
| 1996 | Arizona | Mike Candrea | Washington | Columbus, Ga. |
| 1997 | Arizona | Mike Candrea | UCLA | Oklahoma City |
| 1998 | Fresno State | Margie Wright | Arizona | (ditto) |
| 1999 | UCLA | Sue Enquist | Washington | (ditto) |
| 2000 | Oklahoma | Patty Gasso | UCLA | (ditto) |
| 2001 | Arizona | Mike Candrea | UCLA | (ditto) |
| 2002 | Cal-Berkeley | Diane Ninemire | Arizona | (ditto) |
| 2003 | UCLA | Sue Enquist | Cal-Berkeley | (ditto) |
| 2004 | UCLA | Sue Enquist | Cal-Berkeley | (ditto) |
| 2005 | Michigan | Carol Hutchins | UCLA | (ditto) |
| 2006 | Arizona | Mike Candrea | Northwestern | (ditto) |
| 2007 | Arizona | Mike Candrea | Tennessee | (ditto) |
| 2008 | Arizona State | Clint Myers | Texas A&M | (ditto) |
| 2009 | Washington | Heather Tarr | Florida | (ditto) |
| 2010 | UCLA | Kelly Inouye-Perez | Arizona | (ditto) |
| 2011 | Arizona State | Clint Myers | Florida | (ditto) |
| 2012 | Alabama | Patrick Murphy | Oklahoma | (ditto) |

[1] Final AIAW national softball championship (May 1982).
[2] First NCAA national softball championship (May 1982).
[3] Nebraska's second-place finish vacated because of ineligible student-athletes.
[4] UCLA's first-place finish vacated because of scholarship violations.

# Notes

**CHAPTER 1**
**Introduction:**
Mary Littlewood interview, Dec. 2012.
Connie Claussen interview, Dec. 2012.
*Balls & Strikes*: February 1969, June 1969, March 1974.
Connie Claussen personal files.
O.W. (Bill) Smith personal files.

**1969:** Cathy Buell quote: interview by authors, Dec. 2012.
Unidentified player quote: *Guide Tribune* (Fremont, Neb.), May 14, 1969.
Connie Claussen interview by authors, Dec. 2012.
Connie Claussen personal files.
*Omaha World-Herald*, 1969. [Hereafter *OW-H*]
*Guide Tribune*, 1969.
*Balls & Strikes*, June 1970.

**1970:** Reba Sims quotes: interview by authors, Dec. 2012.
Beth Richards quote: interview by authors, Dec. 2012.
*OW-H*, 1970.
*Balls & Strikes*, May 1970.
Connie Claussen personal files.

**1971:** Cathy Buell quote: interview by authors, Dec. 2012.
Pat Noe quote: *OW-H*, May 16, 1971.
Mary Littlewood quotes: Littlewood, Mary. *The Path to the Gold: An Historical Look at Women's Fastpitch in the United States* (Columbia, Missouri: National Fastpitch Coaches Association), 1998.
Connie Claussen personal files.
*Balls & Strikes*, May 1971.
*OW-H*, May 1971.
**1972:** Carl Kelley quotes: *OW-H*, April 28, 1972.
Connie Claussen quotes: *OW-H*, April 28.
Ken Christensen quotes: *Fremont Tribune*, April 2, 1982.
Sandy Fischer quotes: interview by authors, Dec. 2012.
Paula Miller quotes: *OW-H*, May 19, 1972.
Connie Claussen personal files.
*Balls & Strikes*, June 1972.
*OW-H* 1972.
Fresno State University website, 2013.

Arizona Softball Foundation website, 2013.

**CHAPTER 2**
**Introduction:** Connie Claussen personal files.
Christine Grant quotes and other information: Pamela Grundy and Susan Shackleford. *Shattering the Glass* (New York: The New Press), 2005.
Judi Garman quote and other information: Gogol, Sara. *Hard Fought Victories: Women Coaches Making a Difference* (Terre Haute, Ind.: Wish Publishing), 2002.
Blumenthal, Karen. *Let Me Play: The Story of Title IX* (New York: Atheneum Books for Young Readers), 2005.
Carpenter, L. J. and Acosta, R. V. *Title IX* (Champaign, Ill.: Human Kinetics), 2005.

**1973:** Ann Fulkerson quote: *OW-H*, May 17, 1973.
G. I. Willoughby quote: *OW-H*, May 17, 1973.
Margie Wright quote: Plummer, Bill and Clarfield, Steven. *Women's Fastpitch Softball: Best of the Best* (Manalapan, N.J.: Clear Vision Publishing), 2012.
Margie Wright quote: interview by authors, Feb. 2013.
Sandy Fischer quote: interview by authors, Dec. 2012.
Connie Claussen personal files.
*Balls & Strikes*, June 1973.
*OW-H*, 1973.
Fresno State University website, Jan. 2013.

**1974:** Cindy Henderson quote: *OW-H*, May 20, 1974.
Mary Kay Hunter quote: *OW-H*, May 20, 1974.
*OW-H*, 1974.
*Balls & Strikes*, May 1974.
Connie Claussen personal files.

**1975:** Carl Kelley quote: *OW-H*, May 15, 1975.
Amy Dahl quote: *OW-H*, May 16, 1975.
Connie Claussen quotes: *OW-H*, May 19, 1975.
*OW-H*, May 1975.
Connie Claussen personal files.
*OW-H*, May 1975.

**1976:** Ralph Raymond quote: *OW-H*, May 15, 1976.
Connie Claussen quotes: *OW-H*, May 12 & 17, 1976.

Diane Spoelstra quote: Michigan State
   University Spartans website, Jan. 2012.
Connie Claussen personal files.
*OW-H*, 1976.
*Balls & Strikes*, 1976.
*Fastpitch Softball News*, 1976.

**1977**: Connie Claussen quote: *OW-H*, May 24,
   1977.
Butch McBroom quote: *OW-H*, May 27, 1977.
Tonja Adreon quote: *OW-H*, May 29, 1977.
Ginny Parrish quote: *OW-H*, May 30, 1977.
Pat Stockman quotes: *OW-H*, May 29, 1977.
Tonja Adreon quotes: *Tucson Weekly* newspaper
   website, Dec. 2012.
Connie Claussen quote: *OW-H*, June 13, 1977.
*Balls & Strikes*, 1977.
*OW-H*, 1977.
Connie Claussen personal files.
University of Northern Iowa website, Dec. 2012.

**1978**: Kathy Arendsen quote: *OW-H*, May 27,
   1978.
Sharron Backus quotes: *OW-H*, May 30, 1978.
Connie Claussen personal files.
*Balls & Strikes*, 1978.
*OW-H*, 1978.
*Sports Illustrated*, 1978.

**1979**: Gail Lehrmann quote: *OW-H*, May 20, 1979.
Jane Jensen quote: *OW-H*, May 26, 1979.
Sharron Backus quotes: *OW-H*, May 27, 1979.
Kathy Arendsen quote: *OW-H*, May 27, 1979.
Kathy Arendsen quote: *OW-H*, May 28, 1979.
Connie Claussen personal files.
*Balls & Strikes*, 1979.
*Omaha World-Herald*, 1979.
Texas Woman's University Athletics website,
   Jan. 2013.

**CHAPTER 3**
**Introduction:** Connie Claussen quote: UNO
   *Alumni News*, summer 1978.
Connie Claussen quote: *OW-H*, May 24, 1979.
Judith Holland quote: *OW-H*, May 28, 1978.
Donna Lopiano quote: *OW-H*, May 24, 1979.
University of Oklahoma Athletic Dept. files.
*The (Norman, Okla.) Transcript Press*, 1980.
*Fastpitch Delivery*, Dec. 2008.

**1980**: Judi Garman quote: *The Daily Oklahoman*,
   May 22, 1980. [Hereafter *Oklahoman*]
Bill Galloway quote: *Oklahoman*, May 18, 1980.
Kelly Phipps quote: *Oklahoman*, May 26, 1980.
Kelly Phipps quote: *The Herald Journal*
   (Bridgerland, Utah) website, Sept. 8, 2011.
*Oklahoman*, May 1980.
*The (Norman, Okla.) Transcript Press,* May 1980.
University of Oklahoma Athletic Dept. files.
Connie Claussen personal files.
Western Michigan University website, Jan. 2013.

Utah State University website, Jan. 2013.

**1981:** Kirk Hendrix quote: *The Norman Transcript*,
   May 21, 1981.
Bill Galloway quote: *Oklahoman*, May 22, 1981.
Lloydene Searle quotes: *Oklahoman*, May 24,
   1981.
Judi Garman quote: *The (Norman, Okla.) Transcript
   Press*, May 25, 1981.
Lloydene Searle quotes: *The Herald Journal*
   (Bridgerland, Utah) website, Jan. 2013.
*Oklahoman*, May 1981.
University of Oklahoma Athletic Dept. files.
Utah State University website, Jan. 2013.
Cal State-Fullerton website, Jan. 2013.

**1982: (Norman, Okla., tournament)**: Bob Brock
   interview with authors, Jan. 2013.
Bonnie Johnson quote: *Oklahoman*, May 20, 1982.
Sandy Fischer quote: *Oklahoman*, May 20, 1982.
Sandy Fischer quote: *Oklahoman*, May 25, 1982.
Nancy Teehee quote: Nancy Teehee interview with
   the authors, Jan. 2013.
*Oklahoman*, May 1982.
*The (Norman, Okla.) Transcript Press*, May 1982.
University of Okla. Athletic Department files.

**CHAPTER 4**
**Introduction:** Carole Mushier quote: Jan. 1980
   speech to the AIAW delegate assembly.
Mary Higgins quote: *OW-H*, May 13, 1981.
Connie Claussen quote: *OW-H*, May 13, 1981.
Donna Lopiano quote: Jan. 1982 speech to the
   AIAW delegate assembly.
*OW-H*, 1981 and 1982.
*Sports Illustrated*, May 1982.
Festle, Mary Jo. *Playing Nice.*

**1982: (Omaha tournament)**: Sandy Fischer
   quotes: interview with authors, Jan. 2013.
Cindy Smith quote: *OW-H*, May 28, 1982.
Kathy Van Wyk quote: *OW-H*, May 28, 1982.
Sharron Backus quote: *OW-H*, May 31, 1982.
Judi Garman quote: *OW-H*, May 31, 1982.
Donna Pickel quote: *OW-H*, June 1, 1982.
Debbie Doom quotes: *OW-H*, June 1, 1982.
Sharron Backus quote: *OW-H*, June 1, 1982.
*Balls & Strikes*, June 1982.
*The Transcript Press*, May 1982.
*OW-H*, May 1982.
*Oklahoman*, May 1982.
NCAA Championship Archives (1982) online.
*Women's College World Series Record Book*
   (NCAA), 2012. [Hereafter *NCAA WCWS
   Record Book*]

**1983**: Sharron Backus quote: *OW-H*, May 28, 1983.
Judi Garman quote: *OW-H*, May 26, 1983.
Lou Piel quote: *OW-H*, May 26, 1983.
Tracy Compton quote: *OW-H*, May 27, 1983.
Joyce Compton quote: *OW-H*, May 27, 1983.

Dottie Richardson quotes: Richardson, D. and Yaeger, D. *Living the Dream* (New York: Kensington Books), 1997.
Bob Brock quotes: Jan. 2013 interview with the authors.
*Balls & Strikes*, 1983.
*OW-H*, 1983.
NCAA News, 1983.
NCAA Championship Archives (1983) online.
*NCAA WCWS Record Book.*

**1984:** Mary Higgins quotes: *OW-H*, May 23, 1984.
Jennifer Simm quote: *OW-H*, May 24, 1984.
Lisa Ishikawa quote: *OW-H*, May 24, 1984.
Shawn Andaya quotes: Plummer and Clarfield, *Best of the Best*, 92.
Julie Bolduc quote: *OW-H*, May 26, 1984.
Wayne Daigle quote: *OW-H*, May 27, 1984.
Sharron Backus quote: *OW-H*, May 29, 1984.
*OW-H*, 1984.
NCAA Championship Archives (1984) online.
*NCAA WCWS Record Book.*

**1985:** Mary Higgins quote: *OW-H*, May 21, 1985.
Carol Spanks quote: *OW-H*, May 21, 1985.
Sharon Drysdale quote: *OW-H*, May 25, 1985.
Kathryn Raub quote: *OW-H*, May 26, 1985.
Janet Pinneau quote: *OW-H*, May 27, 1985.
Debbie Doom quote: *OW-H*, May 1985.
*OW-H*, 1985.
NCAA News, 1985.
*Balls & Strikes*, June 1985.
NCAA Championship Archives (1985) online.
*NCAA WCWS Record Book.*

**1986:** Bob Brock quote: *OW-H*, May 21, 1986.
Bill Galloway quote: *OW-H*, May 21, 1986.
Bob Brock quote: *OW-H*, May 22, 1986.
Judi Garman quote: *OW-H*, May 23, 1986.
Mary Higgins quote: *OW-H*, May 24, 1986.
Gale Blevins quote: *OW-H*, May 24, 1986.
Connie Clark quote: *OW-H*, May 24, 1986.
JoAnn Ferrieri's quote: *OW-H*, May 26, 1986.
Judi Garman quote: *OW-H* May 26, 1986.
NCAA Championship Archives (1986) online.
*NCAA WCWS Record Book.*

**1987:** Margie Wright quote: *OW-H*, May 19, 1987.
Ron Wolforth quote: *OW-H*, May 23, 1987.
Bob Brock quote: *OW-H*, May 23, 1987.
Judi Garman quote: *OW-H*, May 24, 1987.
Sharron Backus quotes: *OW-H*, May 24, 1987.
Shawn Andaya quote: *OW-H*, May 24, 1987.
Bob Brock quotes: *OW-H*, May 25, 1987.
*The Eagle* (Bryan-College Station, Texas), 1987.
*OW-H*, 1987.
NCAA Championship Archives (1987) online.
*NCAA WCWS Record Book.*

**CHAPTER 5**
**Introduction**: Mary Higgins quotes: *OW-H*, Feb. 18, 1987.

Marie Tuite interview by authors, March 8, 2013.
*OW-H*, Feb. 18, 1987.
*San Jose Mercury News*, May 18, 1988. [Hereafter *Mercury News*]
*Oklahoman*, May 20, 1990.

**1988:** Bob Brock quote: *Mercury News*, May 26, 1988.
Mike Candrea quote: *Mercury News*, May 27, 1988.
Carol Spanks quote: *Mercury News*, May 27, 1988.
Kathy Mayer quote: *Mercury News*, May 29, 1988.
Mike Candrea quote: *Mercury News*, May 29, 1988.
Margie Wright quote: *Mercury News*, May 30, 1988.
Sharron Backus quote: *Mercury News*, May 30, 1988.
*Mercury News*, 1988
NCAA Championship Archives (1988) online.
*NCAA WCWS Record Book.*

**1989:** Kerry Dienelt quote: NCAA Championship Archives (1989) online.
Tiffany Boyd quote: *Mercury News*, May 25, 1989.
Holly DeLuca quote: NCAA Championship Archives online, 1989.
Mike Candrea quote: NCAA Championship Archives (1989) online.
Kelly Inouye quote: *Mercury News*, May 28, 1989.
Sandy Fischer quote: Sandy Fischer interview with authors, Feb. 2013.
Kerri Donis quote: *Mercury News*, May 29, 1989.
Tiffany Boyd quote: *Mercury News*, May 29, 1989.
*Oklahoman*, 1989.
*Mercury News*, 1989.
NCAA Championship Archives (1989) online.
*NCAA WCWS Record Book.*

**CHAPTER 6**
**Introduction**: Marita Hynes quote: *Oklahoman*, May 20, 1990.
Marita Hynes quote: *Oklahoman*, May 21, 2003.
Pete White interview with authors, March 8, 2013.
Glenn Boyer interview with authors, March 11, 2013.
*Oklahoman*, Sept. 8, 1993.

**1990:** Sue Lilley quote: *Oklahoman*, May 24, 1990.
Mike Candrea quote: *Oklahoman*, May 26, 1990.
JoAnne Graf quote: *Oklahoman*, May 26, 1990.
Margie Wright quote: *Oklahoman*, May 27, 1990.
Leslie Barton quote: *Oklahoman*, May 27, 1990.
Sandy Fischer quote: *Oklahoman*, May 28, 1990.
Carie Dever quote: *Oklahoman*, May 29, 1990.
Margie Wright quote: NCAA Championship Archives (1990) online.
*Oklahoman*, 1990.
Lisa Longaker interview with authors, April 2013.
University of La Verne website, 2013.
NCAA Championship Archives (1990) online.
*NCAA WCWS Record Book.*

**1991:** Sharron Backus quote: *Oklahoman*, May 22, 1991.
Mike Candrea quotes: NCAA Championship Archives (1991) online.
Terry Carpenter quote: *Oklahoman*, May 25, 1991.
Mike Candrea quote: *Oklahoman*, May 25, 1991.
Margie Wright quote: NCAA Championship Archives (1991) online.
Mike Andrea quote: NCAA Championship Archives (1991) online.
*Oklahoman*, 1991.
Purdue University website, 2013.
Amateur Softball Association website, 2013.
NCAA Championship Archives (1991) online.
*NCAA WCWS Record Book.*

**1992:** Michele Bento quote: *Oklahoman*, May 23, 1992.
Pete Manarino quote: NCAA Championship Archives (1992) online.
Rachel Lawson quote: *Oklahoman*, May 23, 1992.
Sharron Backus quote: *Oklahoman*, May 24, 1992.
Angyla Brumm quote: *Oklahoman*, May 25, 1992.
Margie Wright quote: *Oklahoman*, May 25, 1992.
Mike Candrea quote: *Oklahoman*, May 25, 1992.
Jennifer Brewster quote: *Oklahoman*, May 26, 1992.
Sharron Backus quote: *Oklahoman*, May 26, 1992.
*Oklahoman*, 1992.
UCLA website, 2013.
University of Arizona website, 2013.
NCAA Championship Archives (1992) online.
*NCAA WCWS Record Book.*

**1993:** Gary Torgeson quote: *Oklahoman*, May 29, 1993.
Susie Parra quote: *Oklahoman*, May 29, 1993.
Sharron Backus quote: *Oklahoman*, May 30, 1993.
Sandy Fischer quote: *Oklahoman*, May 30, 1993.
Mike Candrea quote: *Oklahoman*, May 31, 1993.
Sandy Fischer quote: *Oklahoman*, May 31, 1993.
Yvette Girouard quote: *Oklahoman*, June 1, 1993.
Lisa Fernandez quote: *Oklahoman*, June 1, 1993.
Mike Candrea quote: *Oklahoman*, June 1, 1993.
*Oklahoman*, 1993.
University of Arizona website, 2013.
NCAA Championship Archives (1993) online.
*NCAA WCWS Record Book.*

**1994:** Sharron Backus quote: *Oklahoman*, May 26, 1994.
Maureen Brady quote: NCAA Championship Archives (1994) online
Mike Candrea quote: *Oklahoman*, May 28, 1994.
Karie Langelier quote: *Oklahoman*, May 29, 1994.
Mike Candrea quote: *Oklahoman*, May 30, 1994.
Sandy Fisher quote: *Oklahoman*, May 30, 1994.
Mike Candrea quote: *Oklahoman*, May 31, 1994.
*Oklahoman*, 1994.
NCAA Championship Archives (1994) online.
*NCAA WCWS Record Book.*

**1995:** Mike Candrea quote: *Oklahoman*, May 26, 1995.
Julie Williams quote: *Oklahoman*, May 26, 1995.
Cheryl Longeway quote: NCAA Championship Archives (1995) online.
Sue Enquist quote: *Oklahoman*, May 27, 1995.
Mike Candrea quote: *Oklahoman*, May 27, 1995.
Yvette Girouard quote: NCAA Championship Archives (1995) online.
Shan McDonald quote: *Oklahoman*, May 28, 1995.
Gayle Blevins quote: *Oklahoman*, May 28, 1995.
Kari Knopf quote: NCAA Championship Archives (1995) online.
Mike Candrea quote: *Oklahoman*, May 30, 1995.
Sue Enquist quote: *Oklahoman*, May 30, 1995.
*Oklahoman*, 1995.
NCAA Championship Archives (1995) online.
*NCAA WCWS Record Book.*

**CHAPTER 7**
**Introduction**: Cindy Cohen quote: *Oklahoman*, May 26, 1995.
Mike Candrea quote: *Oklahoman*, May 26, 1995.
Blumenthal, Karen. *Let Me Play.*
Littlewood, Mary L. *Women's Fastpitch Softball.*

**1996:** Yvette Girouard, Mindy Williams, B'Ann Burns, Mike Candrea, Jenny Dalton quotes: NCAA Championship Archives (1996) online.
*NCAA WCWS Record Book.*

**1997:** Leah O'Brien quote: *Oklahoman*, May, 1997.
Stanley Draper quote: *Oklahoman*, May 20, 1997.
Margie Wright quote: NCAA Championship Archives (1997) online.
Melissa Gentile quote: NCAA Championship Archives (1997) online.
Joyce Compton quote: *Oklahoman*, May 23, 1997.
Teresa Wilson quote: NCAA Championship Archives (1997) online.
Carol Hutchins quote: *Oklahoman*, May 25, 1997.
Jamie Graves quote: *Oklahoman*, May 26, 1997.
Mike Candrea quote: *Oklahoman*, May 27, 1997.
*Oklahoman*, 1997
DePaul University website, March 2013.
University of Texas website, March 2013.
NCAA Championship Archives (1997) online.
*NCAA WCWS Record Book.*

**1998:** Teresa Wilson quote: *Oklahoman*, May 21, 1998.
Margaret Rebenar quote: *Oklahoman*, May 22, 1998.
Teresa Wilson quote: NCAA Championship Archives (1998) online.
Teresa Wilson quote: *Oklahoman*, May 23, 1998.
Danielle Henderson quote: *Oklahoman*, May 25, 1998.
Jamie Fuente quote: NCAA Championship (1998) Archives online.
Margie Wright quote: *Oklahoman*, May 25, 1998.

Nina Lindenberg quote: NCAA Championship (1998) Archives online.
Margie Wright quote: *Oklahoman*, May 26, 1998.
*Oklahoman*, 1998.
NCAA Championship Archives (1998) online.
*NCAA WCWS Record Book*.

**1999:** Eugene Lenti quote: *Oklahoman*, May 28, 1999.
Courtney Blades quote: *Oklahoman*, May 30, 1999.
Kirsten Drake quote: *Oklahoman*, May 30, 1999.
Eugene Lenti quote: *Oklahoman*, May 31, 1999.
Sue Enquist quotes: *Oklahoman*, June 1, 1999.
*Oklahoman*, 1999.
NCAA Championship Archives (1999) online.
*NCAA WCWS Record Book*.

**2000:** Eugene Lenti quote: *Oklahoman*, May 26, 2000.
Pat Murphy quote: *Oklahoman*, May 26, 2000.
Patty Gasso quote: *Oklahoman*, May 26, 2000.
Teresa Wilson quote: *Oklahoman*, May 27, 2000.
Diane Ninemire quote: *Oklahoman*, May 28, 2000.
Lisa Carey quote: *Oklahoman*, May 29, 2000.
Becky Lemke quote: *Oklahoman*, May 29, 2000.
Patty Gasso quote: *Oklahoman*, May 31, 2000.
*Oklahoman*, 2000.
University of Oklahoma website, 2013.
NCAA Championship Archives (2000) online.
*NCAA WCWS Record Book*.

**2001:** Mike Candrea quote: *Oklahoman*, May 25, 2001.
Erin Doud quote: *Oklahoman*, May 27, 2001.
Mike Candrea quote: *Oklahoman*, May 28, 2001.
Jennie Finch quote: *Oklahoman*, May 29, 2001.
*Oklahoman*, 2001.
Louisiana State University website, 2013.
University of Oklahoma website, 2013.
University of Arizona website, 2013.
NCAA Championship Archives (2001) online.
*NCAA WCWS Record Book*.

**2002:** Carol Hutchins quote: NCAA Championship Archives (2002) online.
Mike Candrea quote: NCAA Championship Archives (2002) online.
Leslie Malerich quote: NCAA Championship Archives (2002) online.
Jennie Finch quote: The NCAA Championship Archives (2002) online
Diane Ninemire quote: *Oklahoman*, May 28, 2002.
University of California (Berkeley) website, 2013.
University of Arizona website, 2013.
University of Oklahoma website, 2013.
Florida State University website, 2013.
*Oklahoman*, 2002.
NCAA Championship Archives (2002) online.
*NCAA WCWS Record Book*.

**2003:** Lisa Vad Thorner quote: *Oklahoman*, May 21, 2003.
Alicia Hollowell quote: NCAA Championship. Archives (2003) online.
Patrick Murphy quote: University of Alabama website, 2013.
Cat Osterman quote: NCAA Championship Archives (2003) online.
Connie Clark quote: *Oklahoman*, May 24, 2003.
Sue Enquist quote: *Oklahoman*, May 27, 2003.
*Oklahoman*, 2003.
UCLA website, 2013.
University of Arizona website, 2013.
University of California (Berkeley) website, 2013.
NCAA Championship Archives (2003) online.
*NCAA WCWS Record Book*.

**2004:** Sharon Cessna quote: *Oklahoman*, May 26, 2004.
Carol Hutchins quote: *Oklahoman*, May 27, 2004.
Patty Gasso quote: *Oklahoman*, May 29, 2004.
Jessica van der Linden quote: *Oklahoman*, May 30, 2004.
Sue Enquist quote: *Oklahoman*, May 31, 2004.
Sue Enquist quote: *Oklahoman*, June 1, 2004.
*Oklahoman*, 2004.
LSU Website, 2013.
University of California (Berkeley) website, 2013.
UCLA website, 2013.
University of Oklahoma website, 2013.
NCAA Championship Archives (2004) online.
*NCAA WCWS Record Book*.

## CHAPTER 8

**Introduction:** Caitlin Lowe quote: *Oklahoman*, May 31, 2007.
Marita Hynes quote: *Oklahoman*, June 4, 2006.
Tim Brassfield quote: *Oklahoman*, June 3, 2009.
Myles Brand quote: *Oklahoman*, June 2, 2007.
Tramel, Berry. "Ode to Joy," *Oklahoman*, June 2, 2007.

**2005:** Carol Stiff quote: *Oklahoman*, June 1, 2005.
Ashley Cline quote: *Oklahoman*, June 3, 2005.
Sue Enquist quote: *Oklahoman*, June 3, 2005.
Cat Osterman quote: University of Texas website, March 2013.
Monica Abbott quote: *Oklahoman*, June 4, 2005.
Carol Hutchins quote: University of Michigan website, March 2013.
Connie Clark quote: University of Texas website, March 2013.
Sue Enquist quote: UCLA website, 2013.
Carol Hutchins quote: University of Michigan website, 2013.
*Oklahoman*, 2005.
University of California (Berkeley) website, 2013.
University of Michigan website, 2013.
UCLA website, 2013.
NCAA Championship Archives (2005) online.
*NCAA WCWS Record Book*.

**2006:** Carol Stiff quote: *Oklahoman*, June 2, 2006.
Marita Hynes quote: *Oklahoman*, June 4, 2006.
Cat Osterman quote: University of Texas website, 2013.
Pat Murphy quote: University of Alabama website, 2013.
Ralph Weekly quote: *Oklahoman*, June 3, 2006.
Jennifer Griffin quote: *Oklahoman*, June 4, 2006.
Alicia Hollowell quote: *Oklahoman*, June 5, 2006.
Mike Candrea quote: *Oklahoman*, June 7, 2006.
*Oklahoman*, 2006.
UCLA website, 2013.
Arizona State University website, 2013.
Northwestern University website, 2013.
University of Tennessee website, 2013.
*NCAA WCWS Record Book*.
NCAA Women's College World Series files.

**2007:** Danielle Lawrie quote: *Oklahoman*, June 1, 2007.
India Chiles quote: *Oklahoman*, June 1, 2007.
Karen Weekly quote: University of Tennessee website, 2013.
Shannon Doepking quote: *Oklahoman*, June 6, 2007.
Mike Candrea quote: *Oklahoman*, June 7, 2007.
*Oklahoman*, 2007.
Arizona State website, 2013.
Northwestern University website, 2013.
Arizona website, 2013.
Baylor University website, 2013.
*NCAA WCWS Record Book*.
NCAA Women's College World Series files.

**2008:** Holly Tankersley quote: *Oklahoman*, May 30, 2008.
Jo Evans quote: Texas A&M website, 2013.
Rhiannon Kliesing, *Oklahoman*, May 31, 2008.
Pat Murphy quote: *Oklahoman*, June 1, 2008.
Tim Walton quote: *Oklahoman*, June 1, 2008.
Clint Myers quote: *Oklahoman*, June 4, 2008.
*Oklahoman*, 2008.
Arizona State University website, 2013.
Texas A&M website, 2013.
University of Alabama website, 2013.
*NCAA WCWS Record Book*.
NCAA Women's College World Series files.

**2009:** Pat Murphy quote: *Oklahoman*, May 28, 2009.
Carol Hutchins quote: *Oklahoman*, May 29, 2009.
Heather Tarr quote: *Oklahoman*, May 30, 2009.
Mike Candrea quote: *Oklahoman*, May 31, 2009.
Pat Murphy quote: University of Alabama website, 2013.
Heather Tarr quote: *Oklahoman*, June 3, 2009.
*Oklahoman*, 2009.
University of Florida website, 2013.
University of Arizona website, 2013.

University of Washington website, 2013.
*NCAA WCWS Record Book*.
NCAA Women's College World Series files.

**2010:** Ehren Earleywine quote: *Oklahoman*, June 4, 2010.
Kelly Inouye-Perez quote: *Oklahoman*, June 5, 2010.
Heather Tarr quote: *Oklahoman*, June 6, 2010.
Mike Candrea quote: *Oklahoman*, June 7, 2010.
Kelly Inouye-Perez quote: *Oklahoman*, June 8, 2010.
*Oklahoman*, 2010.
University of Washington website, 2013.
University of Arizona website, 2013.
University of Florida website, 2013.
*NCAA WCWS Record Book*.
NCAA Women's College World Series files.

**2011:** Pat Murphy quote: *Oklahoman*, June 3, 2011.
Pat Murphy quote: *Oklahoman*, June 4, 2011.
Glenn Moore quote: Baylor University website, 2013.
Kelsey Bruder quote: *Oklahoman*, June 6, 2011.
Clint Myers quote: *Oklahoman*, June 8, 2011.
ASU website, 2013.
Baylor University website, 2013.
University of Alabama website, 2013.
*Oklahoman*, 2011.
*NCAA WCWS Record Book*.
NCAA Women's College World Series files.

**2012:** Clint Myers quote: *Oklahoman*, May 31, 2012.
Jace Williams quote: *Oklahoman*, June 2, 2012.
Beth Torina quote: LSU website, 2013.
Patty Gasso quote: *Oklahoman*, June 6, 2012.
Pat Murphy quote: University of Alabama website, 2013.
*Oklahoman*, 2012.
Arizona State University website, 2013.
Louisiana State University website, 2013.
University of Oklahoma website, 2013.
NCAA Women's College World Series files.

**Epilogue:** Tim Brassfield interview with the authors, April 2013.

# Index of Names

# Index of Teams
(Final Standings by Tournament)

✏✏✏✏

# About the Authors
&#x204c;&#x2040;&#x204c;&#x2040;

This is the fourteenth softball book Bill Plummer III has been involved with during his sports journalism career. A journalism graduate from Indiana University, he has written one book, co-authored two others and contributed to eleven more. A native of Syracuse, N.Y., he has lived in Oklahoma City since 1979. For more than thirty years he worked as the communications coordinator/National Softball Hall of Fame services manager at the national office of the Amateur Softball Association, the national governing body of softball in the United States. A member of five softball halls of fame, Plummer retired from the Amateur Softball Association in 2009 and has since devoted much of his time writing about softball for several online sports magazines. He also serves on the selection committee for the Lowe's Softball CLASS winner and writes a column on the winner each year.

Larry C. Floyd has been a business and sports journalist in Oklahoma City for many years. He photographed the first two women's series in Oklahoma City (1990-91) for the Amateur Softball Association, where he worked in the communications department in the early 1990s. He is a co-author of *Oklahoma Hiking Trails* (University of Oklahoma Press, 2010) and teaches U.S. history at Oklahoma State University (Oklahoma City).